Lecture Notes in Computer S

Commenced Publication in 1973
Founding and Former Series Editors:
Gerhard Goos, Juris Hartmanis, and Jan van Leeuwen

Manuel Núñez   Zakaria Maamar
Fernando L. Pelayo   Key Pousttchi
Fernando Rubio (Eds.)

Applying Formal Methods: Testing, Performance, and M/E-Commerce

FORTE 2004 Workshops The FormEMC, EPEW, ITM
Toledo, Spain, October 1-2, 2004
Proceedings

 Springer

Volume Editors

Manuel Núñez
Universidad Complutense de Madrid
Departamento de Sistemas Informática y Programacion
E-mail: mn@sip.ucm.es

Zakaria Maamar
Zayed University
College of Information Systems
E-mail: zakaria.maamar@zu.ac.ae

Fernando L. Pelayo
Universidad de Castilla-La Mancha
Departamento de Informatica
E-mail: fpelayo@info-ab.uclm.es

Key Pousttchi
University of Augsburg
Business Informatics and Systems Engineering
E-mail: key.pousttchi@wiwi.uni-augsburg.de

Fernando Rubio
Universidad Complutense de Madrid
Dept. Sistemas Informáticos y Programación
E-mail: fernando@sip.ucm.es

Library of Congress Control Number: 200112846

CR Subject Classification (1998): D.2, C.2.4, F.3, D.4, C.4, K.4.4, C.2

ISSN 0302-9743
ISBN 3-540-23169-2 Springer Berlin Heidelberg New York

Springer is a part of Springer Science+Business Media

springeronline.com

© Springer-Verlag Berlin Heidelberg 2004
Printed in Germany

Typesetting: Camera-ready by author, data conversion by DA-TeX Gerd Blumenstein
Printed on acid-free paper   SPIN: 11324263   06/3142   5 4 3 2 1 0

Preface

This volume contains the refereed proceedings of the first edition of three workshops colocated with the International Conference on Formal Techniques for Networked and Distributed Systems (FORTE). The workshops took place in Toledo (Spain) on the 1st and 2nd of October of 2004, and they dealt with different topics related to the application of formal methods. The names of the workshops were the following:

- TheFormEMC: 1st International Workshop on Theory Building and Formal Methods in Electronic/Mobile Commerce
- EPEW: 1st European Performance Engineering Workshop
- ITM: 1st International Workshop on Integration of Testing Methodologies

In total, the calls for papers of the workshops attracted 62 high-quality submissions. The program committees of the workshops selected 27 papers after a rigorous review process in which every paper was reviewed by at least three reviewers. In these proceedings, the papers are grouped according to the workshop they belong to. In addition to the selected papers, there was a keynote speech by Prof. Rob Pooley, from the Heriot-Watt University, UK.

We want to express our gratitude for their financial support both to the Universidad de Castilla-La Mancha and to the Junta de Comunidades de Castilla-La Mancha. Besides, we are in debt to all the authors who submitted high-quality papers to the workshops: Without their effort and interest, it would have been impossible to organize the workshops. We would also like to thank the program committee members of the three workshops for their collaboration during the reviewing process. Last, but not least, we would like to thank the organizers of each of the workshops for their fine work.

In the next pages of this preface, the main characteristics of each of the workshops are described. We hope that these proceedings will be interesting not only for the workshop attendants, but also for a wider community of researchers working on the application of formal methods.

October 2004

Manuel Núñez
Zakaria Maamar
Fernando L. Pelayo
Key Pousttchi
Fernando Rubio

TheFormEMC

Electronic commerce (e-commerce) places new demands not only on support and delivery information technology, but also on the way business processes have to be designed, implemented, monitored, and maintained. Reliability, efficiency, scalability, and fault-tolerance are among the features that have to be embedded into e-commerce processes. Initially, research focused on how to deal with the technical issues. However, the increasing challenges of deploying reliable, efficient, secure, and fault-tolerant applications have highlighted the added value of having theoretical foundations and rigorous formal methods for specifying and validating the design of such applications. In addition, new possibilities extend *static* systems with mobility capabilities. In this sense, the TheFormEMC workshop tried to get together researchers working on theoretical aspects that can be applied to e-commerce and m-commerce systems.

The TheFormEMC workshop attracted 16 high-quality submissions from 9 different countries. The multidisciplinary nature of e-commerce and m-commerce technologies presents challenges for evaluating technical papers. The program committee comprised of experts from several disciplines selected 8 papers after a rigorous double-blind review process in which every paper was reviewed by at least three reviewers.

Program Committee Chairs

Key Pousttchi	University of Augsburg, Germany
Zakaria Maamar	Zayed University, UAE
Manuel Núñez	Universidad Complutense de Madrid, Spain

Organizing Committee Chair

Bettina Bazijanec	University of Augsburg, Germany

Program Committee

Djamel Benslimane	Université Claude Bernard Lyon 1, France
Mario Bravetti	University of Bologna, Italy
Sviatoslav Braynov	State University of New York at Buffalo, USA
Milena M. Head	McMaster eBusiness Research Centre, Canada
Lyes Khelladi	CERIST, Algeria
Birgitta Koenig-Ries	Technical University of Munich, Germany
Winfried Lamersdorf	University of Hamburg, Germany
Franz Lehner	University of Regensburg, Germany
Natalia López	Universidad Complutense de Madrid, Spain
Wathiq Mansoor	Zayed University, UAE
Ismael Rodríguez	Universidad Complutense de Madrid, Spain
Klaus Turowski	University of Augsburg, Germany
Pallapa Venkataram	Indian Institute of Science Bangalore, India
Peter Wurman	North Carolina State University, USA

EPEW

EPEW is a new European forum for the presentation of all aspects of performance modelling and analysis of computer and telecommunication systems. The EPEW workshop attracted 36 high-quality submissions from 15 different countries. The program committee comprised of experts from several disciplines selected 14 papers after a rigorous review process in which every paper was reviewed by at least three reviewers. The 14 accepted papers cover a broad range of topics including performance modelling and analysis of computer systems and networks, performance engineering tools, formal modelling paradigms and methods for performance prediction.

Program Committee Chair

Fernando López Pelayo (Universidad Castilla-La Mancha, Spain)

Program Committee

J. Bradley (Imperial College, UK)   D.D. Kouvatsos (U. Bradford, UK)
M. Bravetti (U. Bologna, Italy)   K.G. Larsen (U. Aalborg, Denmark)
J. Campos (U. Zaragoza, Spain)   M. Núñez (UCM, Spain)
F. Cuartero (UCLM, Spain)   L. Orozco (UCLM, Spain)
K. Djemame (U. Leeds, UK)   R.J. Pooley (U. Heriot-Watt, UK)
D. de Frutos (UCM, Spain)   R. Puigjaner (U. Illes Balears, Spain)
N. Georganas (U. Ottawa, Canada)   M. Silva (U. Zaragoza, Spain)
S. Gilmore (U. Edinburgh, UK)   N. Thomas (U. Durham, UK)
H. Hermanns (U. Saarland, Germany)   V. Valero (UCLM, Spain)

Additional Reviewers

A. Argent-Katwala   C. Guidi   N. López   I. Rodríguez
S. Bernardi   P. Harrison   R. Lucchi   F. Rubio
D. Cazorla   L. Kloul   C. Pérez Jiménez   F. Tricas
S. Galmes   L. Llana   M. Ribaudo

Organizing Committee Chair

Fernando Cuartero Gómez (Universidad Castilla-La Mancha, Spain)

Organizing Committee

Enrique Arias   Gregorio Díaz   Juan José Pardo
Antonio Bueno   Natalia López   María L. Pelayo
Emilia Cambronero   Hermenegilda Macià   Fernando Rubio
Diego Cazorla   Encarnación Moyano   Mª Carmen Ruiz

ITM

Even though testing activities are considered to be rather important, we have to overcome the problem that different testing communities use different methods. We may roughly identify two testing communities: testing of software, and testing of communicating systems. Until very recently, research had been carried out with almost no interactions between these two communities, even though they have complementary know-how. The ITM workshop has born to help find a synthesis between the different techniques developed by each community.

The ITM workshop attracted 10 high-quality submissions from 7 different countries. The program committee selected 5 papers after a rigorous review process in which every paper was reviewed by at least three reviewers. The papers present a well-balanced view of testing technologies, combining both theoretical and practical issues.

Program Committee Chair

Manuel Núñez (Universidad Complutense de Madrid, Spain)

Program Committee

A. Bertolino (ISTI-CNR, Italy)   M. Núñez (UCM, Spain)
R. Castanet (LABRI, France)   F. Ouabdesselam (IMAG, France)
A. Cavalli (GET-INT, France)   M. Pezzè (Milano Bicocca, Italy)
F. Cuartero (UCLM, Spain)   J. Tretmans (Nijmegen, Netherlands)
R. Dssouli (Concordia U., Canada)   F. Rubio (UCM, Spain)
J. Grabowski (Göttingen, Germany)   I. Schieferdecker (FOKUS, Germany)
R. Hierons (Brunel U., UK)   H. Ural (Ottawa, Canada)
T. Higashino (Osaka, Japan)   U. Uyar (CUNY, USA)
D. Hogrefe (Göttingen, Germany)   J. Wegener (DaimlerChrysler, Germany)
P. Le Gall (Evry, France)   N. Yevtushenko (Tomsk State U., Russia)
D. Lee (Bell Laboratories, USA)

Additional Reviewers

D. Chen   L. Frantzen   N. López   I. Rodríguez   T. Willemse
A. En-Nouaary X. Fu   S. Papagiannaki   Z. Wang

Organizing Committee Chair

Fernando Rubio (Universidad Complutense de Madrid, Spain)

Organizing Committee

Alberto de la Encina   Olga Marroquín   Fernando Rubio
Mercedes Hidalgo   Juan José Pardo   María del Carmen Ruiz
Natalia López   Ismael Rodríguez

Table of Contents

III   ITM

Formal Analysis
of the Internet Open Trading Protocol

Chun Ouyang and Jonathan Billington

Computer Systems Engineering Centre
School of Electrical and Information Engineering
University of South Australia, SA 5095, AUSTRALIA
{Chun.Ouyang,Jonathan.Billington}@unisa.edu.au

Abstract. The Internet Open Trading Protocol (IOTP) is an electronic commerce (e-commerce) protocol developed by the Internet Engineering Task Force (IETF) to support online trading activities. The core of IOTP is a set of financial transactions and therefore it is vitally important that the protocol operates correctly. An informal specification of IOTP is published as Request For Comments (RFC) 2801. We have applied the formal method of Coloured Petri Nets (CPNs) to obtain a formal specification of IOTP. Based on the IOTP CPN specification, this paper presents a detailed investigation of a set of behavioural properties of IOTP using state space techniques. The analysis reveals deficiencies in the termination of IOTP transactions, demonstrating the benefit of applying formal methods to the specification and verification of e-commerce protocols.

1 Introduction

Electronic commerce (e-commerce) applications are susceptible to failures if the underlying protocols are not properly designed and analysed. These failures could result in financial loss to any participant, e.g., commercial traders, financial institutions or consumers. However, ensuring the correctness of complex e-commerce protocols is a difficult task and informal methods are inadequate. Formal methods [6] are necessary for the construction of unambiguous and precise models that can be analysed to identify errors and verify correctness before implementation. Application of formal methods will lead to more reliable and trustworthy e-commerce protocols [16].

An important example of an e-commerce protocol is the Internet Open Trading Protocol (IOTP) [5] developed by the Internet Engineering Task Force (IETF) to support trading activities over the Internet. It is also referred to as a shopping protocol [3, 10] which encapsulates different payment systems such as Secure Electronic Transaction (SET) [18] and Mondex [11]. The specification of IOTP, Request For Comments (RFC) 2801 [4], is the largest RFC developed by IETF spanning 290 pages. The RFC contains an informal narrative description of IOTP, and so far no complete implementation of IOTP exists [17, 7]. The development of IOTP is still in an early stage and can therefore benefit from the use of formal methods to verify its functional correctness.

M. Núñez et al. (Eds.): FORTE 2004 Workshops, LNCS 3236, pp. 1–15, 2004.

We apply Coloured Petri Nets (CPNs) [8] to model and analyse IOTP. CPNs are a formal modelling technique that combines the graphical notation of Petri nets with the power of abstract data types allowing data and control flow to be visualised. CPNs have been used successfully for protocol modelling and analysis for 2 decades [2]. Babich and Deotto [1] provide a recent survey comparing this approach with the other main approaches. CPN models are executable and can be analysed using state spaces to detect errors such as deadlocks. We use a tool called Design/CPN [12] for constructing and analysing our CPN models.

In previous work [14], we developed a hierarchical formal specification of IOTP and briefly mentioned some initial analysis results. In contrast, this paper describes our analysis approach in detail. With the state space generated from the CPN model, we investigate and formally reason about a set of desired properties of IOTP (e.g., correct termination). The analysis reveals errors in the current design.

The paper is organised as follows. Section 2 gives an introduction to IOTP's basic concepts and procedures. Section 3 describes the IOTP CPN specification, with focus on its hierarchical structure. Section 4 presents a detailed investigation of several desired properties of IOTP. Finally, we conclude this paper and discuss future work in Sect. 5.

2   The Internet Open Trading Protocol

IOTP [4] focuses on consumer-to-business e-commerce applications. It defines five *trading roles* to identify the different roles that organisations can assume while trading. These are *Consumer*, *Merchant*, *Payment Handler* (a bank), *Delivery Handler* (a courier firm) and *Merchant Customer Care Provider*. The core of IOTP is an *Authentication* transaction and five payment-related transactions named *Purchase*, *Deposit*, *Withdrawal*, *Refund* and *Value Exchange*. Each transaction comprises a sequence of message exchanges between trading roles.

Document Exchanges and Transactions. IOTP defines a set of document exchanges as building blocks for implementation of transactions. These are: *Authentication*, *Brand Dependent Offer*, *Brand Independent Offer*, *Payment*, *Delivery*, and *Payment-and-Delivery*. An Authentication transaction consists of just an Authentication (document) exchange. A Purchase transaction comprises an optional Authentication, an Offer (either a Brand Dependent Offer or a Brand Independent Offer), and then, a Payment exchange, a Payment followed by a Delivery exchange, or a Payment-and-Delivery exchange. A Deposit, Withdrawal, or Refund transaction starts with an optional Authentication, an Offer, and a Payment exchange. Finally, a Value Exchange transaction begins with an optional Authentication followed by an Offer and two Payment exchanges in sequence.

Below, we consider an example of a Purchase transaction which comprises an Authentication, a Brand Dependent Offer, and a Payment followed by a Delivery exchange. Figure 1 shows a possible sequence of messages exchanged between the four trading roles involved in the transaction.

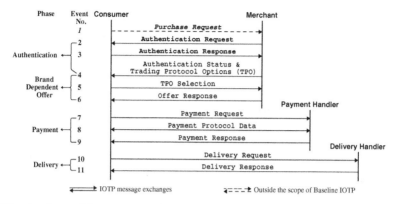

Fig. 1. A possible sequence of message exchanges in a Purchase transaction

In the beginning, the Consumer decides to buy goods, and sends a Purchase Request (event 1) to the Merchant. This event initiates a Purchase transaction, however it is not part of Baseline IOTP.

Upon receiving the Purchase Request, the Merchant starts an Authentication document exchange (events 2-4) to verify the *bona fides* of the Consumer. In IOTP's terminology, the Merchant acts as the *Authenticator* and the Consumer the *Authenticatee*. At first, an Authentication Request is issued by the Merchant (event 2), specifying the authentication algorithm to be used. As a result, the Consumer replies with an Authentication Response containing the authentication data obtained using the above algorithm (event 3). After verifying the Consumer's response, the Merchant generates an Authentication Status indicating that the authentication is successful (see event 4).

Once the authentication completes, the Merchant continues to a Brand Dependent Offer document exchange (events 4-6) by providing the Consumer a list of Trading Protocol Options (TPO). This includes the available payment methods and associated payment protocols. The message combining the TPO and the above Authentication Status is then sent to the Consumer (event 4). The Consumer chooses one of the options, and sends it back as a TPO Selection (event 5). The Merchant uses the selection to create and send back an Offer Response (event 6), which contains details of the goods to be purchased together with payment and delivery instructions.

Next, a Payment document exchange starts between the Consumer and the Payment Handler (events 7-9). After checking the Offer Response for purchase details, the Consumer sends the Payment Handler a Payment Request (event 7). The Payment Handler checks the Payment Request, and if valid, the payment is conducted using Payment Protocol Data exchanges (events 8) as determined by the encapsulated payment protocol (e.g., SET). After the payment protocol data exchange has finished, the Payment Handler sends a Payment Response (event 9) containing the payment result (e.g., receipt).

Finally, a Delivery document exchange is carried out between the Consumer and the Delivery Handler (events 10-11). After checking the Payment Response, the Consumer sends the Delivery Handler a Delivery Request (event 10). The Delivery Handler schedules the delivery and sends the Consumer a Delivery Response (event 11) containing details of the delivery, and possibly the actual delivery if the goods are electronic (e.g., an e-journal).

Also, it should be mentioned that event 5 in the above scenario may or may not take place in an Offer exchange, which results in the distinction between a Brand Dependent Offer and a Brand Independent Offer. The Brand Dependent Offer occurs when the Merchant offers some additional benefit (e.g., price discount) in the Offer Response *depending* on the specific *payment brand* (e.g., VISA or MasterCard) chosen in the Consumer's TPO Selection. In the Brand Independent Offer, the Offer Response is *independent* of the *payment brand* selected by the Consumer. In this case, the Merchant does not require the Consumer's TPO Selection before the Offer Response can be generated. IOTP defines a combined TPO and Offer Response message to be used in the Brand Independent Offer.

Transaction Cancellation and Error Handling. These are two important procedures related to IOTP transactions. A transaction may be cancelled by any trading role engaged in that transaction. For example, in the Purchase transaction shown in Fig. 1, the Merchant would cancel the transaction if the Consumer's Authentication Response has failed. Error handling is concerned with how trading roles handle technical errors and exceptions that occur during a transaction. For example, in Fig. 1, the Merchant may re-send the TPO upon a time-out when expecting the Consumer's TPO Selection. A Cancel message is used for transaction cancellation and an Error message for reporting errors.

3   A Formal Specification of IOTP

RFC 2801 [4] contains an informal narrative description of IOTP and suffers from ambiguities and incompleteness. We have created a CPN model of IOTP to obtain a formal specification of IOTP that truly reflects the intent of its RFC specification. When ambiguities and gaps are detected, assumptions are made to clarify the ambiguities and fill in the gaps. A detailed description of this formal specification of IOTP is presented in [14]. Figure 2 shows the *hierarchy page* for the IOTP CPN model. It provides an overview of the *pages* (modules) constituting the model. There are 31 pages organised into four hierarchical levels. An arc between two pages indicates that the destination page is a *subpage* (submodule) of the source page. The four-level hierarchy of the IOTP CPN model provides a logical structure that can be validated against RFC 2801.

The first (top) level presents an abstract view of IOTP on one page, namely IOTP_TopLevel. It has four subpages: Consumer, Merchant, PHandler and DHan-

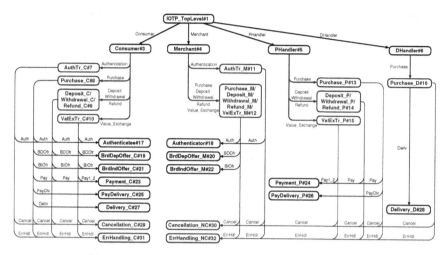

Fig. 2. The hierarchy page of the IOTP CPN model

dler, corresponding to four trading roles[1]. We refer to these pages as *trading role pages*, which comprise the second level of the IOTP CPN model.

Each trading role page has a set of subpages specifying the possible Authentication and Payment-related transactions for that trading role. All these subpages, which we call *transaction pages*, constitute the third level of the model. For example, the page Consumer has four subpages modelling six transactions for the Consumer. The three transactions Deposit, Withdrawal and Refund use the same procedure and therefore are modelled on one page named Deposit_C/Withdrawal_C/Refund_C. The initial letter of each trading role name is used as a suffix of the name of transaction pages modelled for that trading role. For example, the subpages AuthTr_C and AuthTr_M represent an Authentication transaction between the Consumer and Merchant. It can be seen that both the Consumer and the Merchant are involved in all six transactions, the Payment Handler is engaged in all transactions except Authentication and the Delivery Handler is only involved in Purchase transactions.

Each transaction page is further decomposed into a set of subpages modelling the document exchanges that are used to construct that transaction as well as the error handling and cancellation procedures. All these subpages, which we call *exchange level pages*, constitute the fourth level of the model. For example, the page Purchase_C has six subpages modelling the six document exchanges used to implement a Purchase transaction for the Consumer and two others modelling how the Consumer handles technical errors and cancels an ongoing transaction. Since a document exchange always involves two trading roles, we have modelled each exchange as a pair of pages - one for each trading role. For example, the pages Authenticatee and Authenticator represent an Authentication

---

[1] The Merchant Customer Care Provider, currently not used in any transactions, is not modelled.

document exchange where the Consumer is authenticated by the Merchant. In a similar way to the transaction pages, most of the exchange level pages have a name which is suffixed by the initial letter of the corresponding trading role. For example, the pages Delivery_C and Delivery_D represent a Delivery document exchange between the Consumer and the Delivery Handler. In addition, the procedures of error handling and transaction cancellation are different between Consumer and non-Consumer entities. We have also modelled each of these two procedures using only a pair of pages - one (whose name ends with the letter C) for the Consumer, the other (whose name ends with the two letters NC) for any non-Consumer entity (Merchant, Payment Handler or Delivery Handler). Each pair of ErrHandling or Cancellation pages are used by all transaction pages.

4   Formal Analysis of IOTP Properties

We use state space analysis to investigate the functional behaviour of IOTP. In state space analysis we generate all system execution paths and store them as a directed graph (called a state space). Nodes in the state space represent states, and arcs represent state changes. The state of a CPN is called a *marking*, and the state changes are represented by *occurrences of transitions* where a transition in CPNs represents an event. The state space of the IOTP CPN model can be generated, allowing several properties of IOTP to be verified.

4.1   Analysis Approach

Our analysis of IOTP focuses on the six Authentication and Payment-related transactions. The IOTP CPN model specifies these six transactions in a modular fashion. All six transactions are independent of each other and it is therefore valid to analyse one transaction at a time. For the analysis of a particular transaction, the IOTP CPN model needs to be initialized for the execution of that transaction *only*. This is given by the *Transaction* parameter used in the model. For example, if *Transaction* has a value Purchase, the IOTP CPN model can be executed to capture all possible executions of a Purchase transaction and to generate the state space for the transaction. For each transaction, there are also different cases we can analyse by changing the maximum value of the message retransmission counters (denoted by $RCmax$) for each of the four trading roles. Once the number of retransmissions reaches $RCmax$, the transaction will be cancelled. Accordingly, the analysis of transactions involves selecting appropriate values for both the *Transaction* and $RCmax$ parameters, and thereby defining the configurations of IOTP.

IOTP is designed to be payment system-independent. A Payment document exchange may involve payment data exchanges that can occur any finite number of times (see event 8 in Fig. 1), catering for various payment systems to be encapsulated by IOTP. In the IOTP CPN model, the message identifier is used for checking duplicates, and is incremented with each payment data exchange.

As a result, we obtain infinite state space if the number of payment data exchanges is unbounded. However, in the current design of IOTP [4], a payment data exchange is only used to encapsulate payment system-specific messages (e.g., a SET message) and its occurrence in a (Payment-related) transaction is optional. This allows us to hide any payment data exchange from the analysis of the core behaviour of each Payment-related transaction.

4.2   Desired Properties of IOTP Transactions

We define three properties that IOTP transactions should satisfy: proper termination in terms of absence of undesired terminal states; absence of undesired cycles; and absence of procedures that are specified but never executed.

Property 1 (Valid Transaction Termination). The dead markings in each transaction state space represent all valid terminal states of that transaction.

A *dead marking* of a CPN model is a marking in which no transitions can occur. The set of dead markings in the state space of a transaction therefore defines the terminal states of the transaction. If a transaction terminates properly, each of the trading roles that have started the transaction must enter a valid terminal state. In the IOTP CPN model, there are two valid terminal states for a trading role: COMPLETED indicating that a transaction terminates successfully, and CANCELLED indicating the transaction is cancelled. It follows from Property 1 that any dead marking that does not represent the valid transaction termination is undesirable, i.e., a deadlock. So, if Property 1 is true, we can prove that the transaction is deadlock free.

Property 2 (Absence of Livelocks). There must be no livelocks in each transaction state space.

If a state space contains a cycle that leads to no markings outside the cycle, then once the cycle is entered it will repeat for ever. This is called a *livelock*. A transaction, which provides meaningful operations and terminates properly, should be free from livelocks. A *strongly connected component* (SCC) of the state space is a maximal sub-graph whose nodes are mutually reachable from each other [9]. If the state space is isomorphic to the SCC graph, and contains no self-loops, then the state space has no livelocks. If Property 2 is true, we can prove that it is always possible for a transaction to terminate in one of the terminal states represented by dead markings.

Property 3 (Absence of Unexpected Dead Transitions). There must be no unexpected dead transitions in each transaction state space, unless those transitions model events that are not activated under certain configurations of IOTP.

If a transition is not able to occur in any reachable marking then this transition is a *dead transition*. A dead transition in a transaction state space of IOTP indicates the protocol operation modelled by that transition never occurs. We expect transitions which model protocol operations that are not activated under certain configurations of IOTP to be dead. An unexpected dead transition means a protocol operation is redundant or that unexpected behaviour has occurred, resulting in that operation not being utilized.

Table 1. State space size and number of dead markings for Configuration Set 1

Configuration	Nodes	Arcs	Dead markings	Time(sec)
(Authentication, 1)	276	759	4	1
(Purchase, 1)	3695	10021	37	28
(Deposit, 1)/ (Withdrawal, 1)/ (Refund, 1)	2465	7021	19	16
(ValueExchange, 1)	2919	8148	25	20

4.3 State Spaces for Selected Configurations of IOTP

Six configurations of IOTP are used for our analysis. They represent each of the six Authentication and Payment-related transactions and have the *RCmax* parameter set to 1, allowing a single retransmission of an IOTP message at each trading role. A configuration is denoted by a pair of values - one assigned to the *Transaction* parameter, the other to *RCmax*. For example, (Purchase, 1) denotes the configuration of a Purchase transaction in which all the trading roles cannot re-send a message more than once. Also, we refer to the set of configurations with $RCmax = 1$ as Configuration Set 1.

The state spaces are generated for the IOTP CPN model with configurations in Configuration Set 1, using Design/CPN. Table 1 summarises the statistics of the state space size, the number of dead markings and the generation time (on a 700MHz Intel Pentium computer with 512MB RAM), for each configuration.

4.4 Analysis of Transaction Termination Property

By examining the dead markings in the state space of a transaction, we can determine whether the transaction terminates properly. Below, we illustrate our approach to the inspection of all terminal states of an IOTP transaction, using Purchase as a representative example. The Purchase transaction involves four trading roles and six document exchanges, and is thus the most complicated among all IOTP transactions.

Table 2 lists 37 dead markings in the state space of the transaction with configuration (Purchase, 1). The corresponding states of each trading role are: CMP for COMPLETED and CNL for CANCELLED. The subscript of a state specifies the document exchange in question, i.e., Auth for Authentication, BDOfr for Brand Dependent Offer and BIOfr for Brand Independent Offer, Pay for Payment and PayDlv for Payment-and-Delivery. The subscript NoExch is used when it is not clear which document exchange to start. A trading role without the above information (represented by "-") is not involved, or has not yet started, in the transaction. We divide the above dead markings into seven groups with their group numbers given in the first column of Table 2. In the following, the transaction with configuration (Purchase, 1) is referred to as transaction *(Purchase, 1)*, and marking n is written as M_n.

Table 2. Dead markings of the transaction with configuration (Purchase, 1)

Group No.	Dead markings	Consumer	Merchant	PHandler	DHandler
			Trading role state		
1	1145, 555	CMP_{Pay}	$CMP_{BDO\ fr,\ B\ D\ fr}$	CMP_{Pay}	–
	2144, 1423	$CMP_{PayD\ lv}$	$CMP_{BDO\ fr,\ B\ D\ fr}$	$CMP_{PayD\ lv}$	–
	2376, 1655	CMP_{Deliv}	$CMP_{BDO\ fr,\ B\ D\ fr}$	CMP_{Pay}	CMP_{Deliv}
2	36, 47, 42	CNL_{NoExch}	$CNL_{Auth,\ BDO\ fr,\ B\ D\ fr}$	–	–
	65	CNL_{Auth}	CNL_{Auth}	–	–
	80	$CNL_{BDO\ fr}$	$CNL_{BDO\ fr}$	–	–
	152	$CNL_{B\ D\ fr}$	$CNL_{B\ D\ fr}$	–	–
	472, 453	CNL_{Auth}	$CNL_{BDO\ fr,\ B\ D\ fr}$	–	–
3	1626, 954	CNL_{Pay}	$CNL_{BDO\ fr,\ B\ D\ fr}$	CMP_{Pay}	–
4	929, 393	CNL_{Pay}	$CMP_{BDO\ fr,\ B\ D\ fr}$	CNL_{NoExch}	–
	1156, 566	$CNL_{PayD\ lv}$	$CMP_{BDO\ fr,\ B\ D\ fr}$	CNL_{NoExch}	–
	1142, 552	CNL_{Pay}	$CMP_{BDO\ fr,\ B\ D\ fr}$	CNL_{Pay}	–
	1638, 966	$CNL_{PayD\ lv}$	$CMP_{BDO\ fr,\ B\ D\ fr}$	$CNL_{PayD\ lv}$	–
5	2121, 1400	CNL_{Deliv}	$CMP_{BDO\ fr,\ B\ D\ fr}$	CMP_{Pay}	CNL_{NoExch}
	2374, 1653	CNL_{Deliv}	$CMP_{BDO\ fr,\ B\ D\ fr}$	CMP_{Pay}	CNL_{Deliv}
6	47, 619	$CNL_{NoExch,\ Auth}$	$CMP_{B\ D\ fr}$	–	–
	382	$CNL_{BDO\ fr}$	$CMP_{BDO\ fr}$	–	–
7	1378, 748	CNL_{Pay}	$CMP_{BDO\ fr,\ B\ D\ fr}$	CMP_{Pay}	–
	2146, 1425	$CNL_{PayD\ lv}$	$CMP_{BDO\ fr,\ B\ D\ fr}$	$CMP_{PayD\ lv}$	–
	2608, 1916	CNL_{Deliv}	$CMP_{BDO\ fr,\ B\ D\ fr}$	CMP_{Pay}	CMP_{Deliv}

Successful Transaction Termination. The dead markings in Group 1 represent all successful terminations of a Purchase transaction. The transaction may be completed with 1) the Payment exchange in M_{1145} or M_{555}; 2) the Payment-and-Delivery exchange in M_{2144} or M_{1423}; or 3) the Delivery exchange in M_{2376} or M_{1655}. Figure 3 shows a path leading to M_{2376} in the state space of transaction (Purchase, 1). A node represents a marking, e.g., the node number 2376 (on bottom right of Fig. 3) represents M_{2376}. An arc represents a transition occurrence, and the dashed box attached to the arc lists the occurring transition. For example, the arc number 1 leading from node 1 to node 2 (written as 1:1→2 in the dashed box) represents the occurrence of transition InitiateTr_M on page Merchant (written as Merchant'InitiateTr_M in the dashed box), upon which the state of the transaction changes from M_1 to M_2. The sequence of transition occurrences defined by the path shown in Fig. 3, captures the Purchase transaction scenario shown in Fig. 1. For example, the sequence of transition occurrences represented by the arc list (3,8,18) in Fig. 3 corresponds to event 2 in Fig. 1.

Cancelled Transaction between Consumer and Merchant. The dead markings in Group 2 represent the transaction being cancelled between the Consumer and Merchant, after the Merchant has initiated an Authentication or Offer exchange but before the Consumer starts a Payment exchange. In M_{36}, M_{47} and M_{42}, the transaction is cancelled before the Consumer initiates an Au-

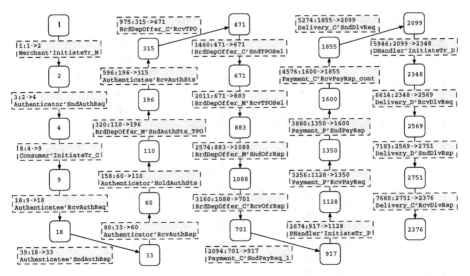

Fig. 3. A path leading to M_{2376} in the state space of transaction (Purchase, 1) and capturing the Purchase transaction scenario shown in Fig. 1

thentication or Offer exchange at the beginning of the transaction. In M_{65}, the transaction is cancelled during an Authentication exchange. In M_{80} and M_{152}, the transaction is cancelled during an Offer exchange. In M_{472} and M_{453}, the transaction is cancelled within an Authentication exchange at the Consumer, while it is cancelled within an Offer exchange at the Merchant. These two markings are expected because of combining the Authentication Status with the first message in the Offer exchange. Figure 4 shows a path leading to M_{472} in the state space of transaction (Purchase, 1) (Fig. 4 (a)) and the transaction scenario captured by the corresponding sequence of transition occurrences (Fig. 4 (b)). In this scenario, the Consumer cancels the transaction (Cancellation_C'SndCnl, M_{196} to M_{313} in Fig. 4 (a)) before receiving the Authentication Status & TPO message from the Merchant, and is therefore still in the Authentication exchange when the transaction is cancelled. Also, the Consumer discards any message received after the transaction has been cancelled (ErrHandling_C'Discard, M_{464} to M_{472} in Fig. 4 (a)), e.g., the Authentication Status & TPO message in the above scenario.

The dead markings in Group 3 represent the transaction being cancelled between the Consumer and Merchant, after the Payment exchange has completed but before the Delivery exchange starts. As defined in IOTP, the Consumer generates and sends a Cancel message to the Merchant but not the Payment Handler. As a result, the Merchant enters the CANCELLED state and the Payment Handler remains in COMPLETED. Since the Merchant is aware of the cancellation, the Consumer would be able to receive a refund by initiating a Refund transaction.

Merchant not Informed of Transaction Cancellation between Other Trading Roles. The dead markings in Groups 4 and 5 represent the transaction being cancelled between the Consumer and the Payment Handler or Delivery

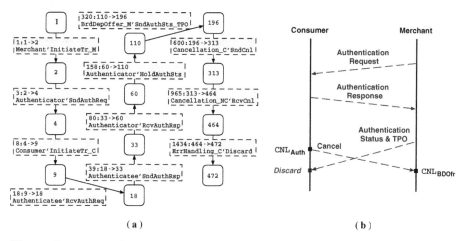

Fig. 4. Inspection of M_{472} in the state space of transaction (Purchase, 1): (a) a path leading to M_{472} in the state space and (b) the corresponding transaction scenario

Handler. According to IOTP, the Merchant is not informed of such transaction cancellation and therefore remains in the COMPLETED state when the transaction is cancelled. Closer inspection reveals deficiencies related to the corresponding transaction terminations.

In Group 4, the Merchant may have received the goods from the manufacturer but *unexpectedly* the Consumer does not purchase the goods. Since the Merchant is not aware of the transaction cancellation between the Consumer and Payment Handler, the Merchant still expects the purchase to proceed. This may result in an *inventory problem*, i.e, goods building up in the Merchant's warehouse.

In Group 5, neither the Merchant nor the Payment Handler is notified of the cancellation between the Consumer and Delivery Handler. In this case, the Consumer will not receive the goods that was paid for, the Merchant will expect the goods to be delivered, and the Payment Handler will believe that the payment is completed. This situation may be recovered by the Consumer invoking a Refund transaction where evidence of the payment (e.g., the payment receipt) is provided to the Merchant. However, the Merchant will need to check (somehow) that the goods were not delivered to that Consumer. If the Consumer does not request a refund, then the inventory problem remains.

Transaction Cancelled at Consumer but Completed at Other Trading Roles. The dead markings in Groups 6 and 7 represent a Purchase transaction being cancelled at the Consumer side *only*.

In Group 6, the cancelled transaction involves just two trading roles, the Consumer and the Merchant. This does no harm to the Consumer since no payment has yet been made, but it may still result in the inventory problem.

In Group 7, the transaction is cancelled after the Payment Handler has completed the Payment exchange, and the cancellation is evident at the Consumer only. Since all the other trading roles involved in the transaction believe that

12   Chun Ouyang and Jonathan Billington

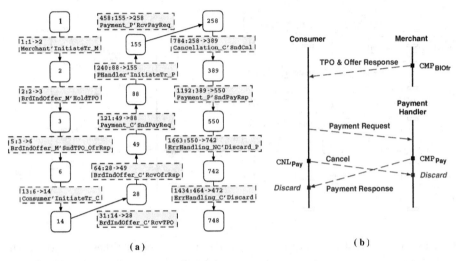

Fig. 5. Inspection of M_{748} in the state space of transaction (Purchase, 1): (a) a path leading to M_{748} in the state space and (b) the corresponding transaction scenario

the transaction has successfully terminated, it may result in a *non-refundable payment problem*, i.e., the Consumer not being able to obtain a refund. For example, Fig. 5 shows a path leading to M_{748} in the state space of transaction (Purchase, 1) (Fig. 5 (a)) and the transaction scenario captured by the corresponding sequence of transition occurrences (Fig. 5 (b)). In this scenario, the Consumer cancels the transaction (Cancellation_C'SndCnl, M_{258} to M_{389} in Fig. 5 (a)) before receiving the Payment Response. However, the Payment Handler has already sent the Payment Response and entered the COMPLETED state (Payment_P'SndCnl, M_{389} to M_{550} in Fig. 5 (a)) and therefore discards the Cancel message from the Consumer (ErrHandling_NC'Discard_P, M_{550} to M_{742} in Fig. 5 (a)). The Merchant is not notified of the cancellation and therefore remains in COMPLETED.

From the above, the dead markings in Groups 4 to 7 represent undesired terminations of a Purchase transaction, where an inventory problem may occur at the Merchant (Groups 4 to 6) or a non-refundable payment problem may occur to the Consumer (Group 7).

Analysis of the transaction termination properties of other transactions (in Configuration Set 1) is performed in a similar way to the analysis of a Purchase. The results show that all dead markings of an Authentication transaction represent desired terminal states of the Authentication. Since a Deposit, Withdrawal and Refund use the same transaction procedure as a Purchase without delivery, the dead markings of each of them are a subset of those of a Purchase. This subset of dead markings does not have any trading role state information in the Delivery and the Payment-and-Delivery exchanges. A Value Exchange transaction involves two Payment exchanges and therefore has new dead markings concern-

Table 3. Statistics of SCC graphs for transactions in Configuration Set 1

Configuration	SCC Nodes	SCC Arcs	Terminal SCCs	Time(sec)
(Authentication, 1)	276	759	4	1
(Purchase, 1)	3695	10021	37	28
(Deposit, 1)/ (Withdrawal, 1)/ (Refund, 1)	2465	7021	19	16
(ValueExchange, 1)	2919	8148	25	20

ing transaction terminations in the second Payment exchange. Inspection of the dead markings for each of the above four Payment-related transactions shows that, there will not be any inventory problem for the Merchant, however, the non-refundable payment problem may still occur to the Consumer.

Hence, we prove that Property 1 holds for an Authentication transaction, but does not hold for all Payment-related transactions.

4.5   Absence of Livelocks

To check whether IOTP transactions involve livelocks, the SCC graphs are generated for the transactions with configurations in Configuration Set 1. A SCC graph has a node for each SCC and arcs which connect two different SCCs. The terminal SCC is a SCC without outgoing arcs. Table 3 lists the statistical information of the SCC graphs for transactions in Configuration Set 1.

The comparison between Tables 1 and 3 shows that each transaction state space has the same number of nodes and arcs as its SCC graph. Therefore, each transaction state space is isomorphic to its SCC graph and contains no self-loops. This proves Property 2 for all configurations in Configuration Set 1.

4.6   Absence of Unexpected Dead Transitions

When the IOTP CPN model is executed, we expect transitions which model protocol operations that are not activated under certain configurations of IOTP to be dead. For example, each transaction page in the model is specific to the transaction indicated by its page name (see the Hierarchy page of the model in Fig. 2). Suppose that the model is executed for an Authentication transaction. Only two transaction pages, AuthTr_C and AuthTr_M, and their subpages, the six exchange level pages, Authenticatee, Authenticator, Cancellation_C, Cancellation_NC, ErrHandling_C and ErrHandling_NC will be executed. The remaining transaction pages and exchange level pages will not be activated, and therefore all the transitions on these pages are expected to be dead. In a similar way, we can see which transaction pages and exchange level pages are activated for each of the other five transactions. From the transaction state space the dead transitions for each configuration in Configuration Set 1 are those expected, proving Property 3 for all configurations analysed.

5   Conclusions

Based on the IOTP CPN specification in [14], we have analysed three desired properties of IOTP: 1) valid transaction termination; 2) absence of livelocks; and 3) absence of non-executable protocol operations (indicated by unexpected dead transitions). Inspection of the transaction termination property has revealed deficiencies in the current design of IOTP, where the Payment-related transaction fails to terminate correctly. The problems are: 1) the Merchant not being informed of transaction cancellation between Consumer and Payment Handler or Delivery Handler, which may cause an inventory problem for the Merchant (in a Purchase transaction); and 2) a transaction cancelled at the Consumer side only, which may introduce a non-refundable payment problem to the Consumer (in all Payment-related transactions).

Future work will involve proposing solutions for the above problems, changing the CPN model accordingly, and re-analysing it to verify that the solutions work correctly. Also we would like to continue our work in [13] on proving that IOTP conforms to its intended service defined in [15].

Acknowledgements

This work was carried out with financial support from a University of South Australia and Divisional Small Grant. We acknowledge Dr Lars Michael Kristensen for his comments on this work.

References

[1] F. Babich and L. Deotto. Formal methods for the specification and analysis of communication protocols. *IEEE Communication Surveys*, 4(1):2–20, Third Quarter 2002. 2

[2] J. Billington, G. E. Gallasch, and B. Han. A Coloured Petri Net approach to protocol verification. In *Lectures on Concurrency and Petri Nets*, volume 3098 of *Lecture Notes in Computer Science*. 80 pages. Springer-Verlag, 2004 (in press). 2

[3] D. Birch. Shopping Protocols - Buying online is more than just paying. *Journal of Internet Banking and Commerce*, 3(1), January 1998. Available via: http://www.arraydev.com/commerce/JIBC/9801-9.htm. 1

[4] D. Burdett. *Internet Open Trading Protocol - IOTP Version 1.0*. IETF RFC 2801, April 2000. Available via: http://www.ietf.org/rfc/rfc2801. 1, 2, 4, 7

[5] D. Burdett, D. E. Eastlake, and M. Goncalves. *Internet Open Trading Protocol*. McGraw-Hill, 2000. 1

[6] E. M. Clarke and J. M. Wing. Formal methods: state of the art and future directions. *ACM Computing Surveys*, 28(4):626–643, December 1996. 1

[7] InterPay I-OTP. URL: http://www.ietf.org/proceedings/01aug/slides/trade-1/index.html, August 2001. 1

[8] K. Jensen. *Coloured Petri Nets. Basic Concepts, Analysis Methods and Practical Use. Volume 1, Basic Concepts*. Monographs in Theoretical Computer Science. Springer-Verlag, Berlin, second edition, 1997. 2

[9] K. Jensen. *Coloured Petri Nets. Basic Concepts, Analysis Methods and Practical Use. Volume 2, Analysis Methods.* Monographs in Theoretical Computer Science. Springer-Verlag, Berlin, second edition, 1997. 7

[10] G. C. Kessler and N. T. Pritsky. Payment protocols: Cache on demand. *Information Security Magazine*, October 2000. Available via: http://www.infosecuritymag.com/articles/october00/features2.shtml. 1

[11] Mondex. URL: http://www.mondexusa.com. 1

[12] Design/CPN Online. URL: http://www.daimi.au.dk/designCPN. 2

[13] C. Ouyang and J. Billington. On verifying the Internet Open Trading Protocol. In *Proceedings of 4th International Conference on Electronic Commerce and Web Technologies (EC-Web2003)*, volume 2738 of *Lecture Notes in Computer Science*, pages 292–302, Prague, Czech Republic, 1-5 September 2003. Springer-Verlag. 14

[14] C. Ouyang and J. Billington. An improved formal specification of the Internet Open Trading Protocol. In *Proceedings of the 2004 ACM Symposium on Applied Computing (SAC2004)*, pages 779–783, Nicosia, Cyprus, 14-17 March 2004. ACM Press. 2, 4, 14

[15] C. Ouyang, L. M. Kristensen, and J. Billington. A formal service specification of the Internet Open Trading Protocol. In *Proceedings of 23rd International Conference on Application and Theory of Petri Nets (ICATPN2002)*, volume 2360 of *Lecture Notes in Computer Science*, pages 352–373, Adelaide, Australia, 24-30 June 2002. Springer-Verlag. 14

[16] M. Papa, O. Bremer, J. Hale, and S. Shenoi. Formal analysis of e-commerce protocols. *IEICE Transactions on Information and Systems*, E84-D(10):1313–1323, 2001. 1

[17] Standard SMart Card Integrated SettLEment System Project SMILE Project. URL: http://www.ietf.org/proceedings/99mar/slides/trade-smile-99mar, April 1999. 1

[18] Visa and MasterCard. *SET Secure Electronic Transaction Specification. Vol 1-3*, May 1997. Available via: http://www.setco.org/set_specifications.html. 1

Life-Cycle E-commerce Testing
with OO-TTCN-3*

Robert L. Probert[1], Pulei Xiong[1], and Bernard Stepien[2]

[1] School of Information and Technology Engineering, University of Ottawa
800 King Edward Avenue, Ottawa, Ontario, K1N 6N5 Canada
bob,xiong@site.uottawa.ca
[2] Bernard Stepien International Inc.
bernard.stepien@sympatico.ca

Abstract. E-Commerce systems have become ubiquitous. However, it
is a challenge to create high quality e-commerce systems respecting time
and budgetary constraints. In this paper, we present a life-cycle testing
process for e-commerce systems by adapting OO-TTCN-3, an object-
oriented extension of a formal test language TTCN-3, to enable the efficient specification of tests in object-oriented, e-commerce development
environments. This extension is meant to ease life-cycle testing, facilitate test case reuse between different test phases, and provide a unified
Abstract Test Suite (ATS) interface to test tools. A case study shows
how to apply the approach to a typical e-commerce system based on
a high-yield, risk-directed strategy.

1 Introduction

Web techniques have grown very fast in recent years. *Electronic Commerce* (E-
Commerce) systems, which facilitate the conduct of business over the Internet
with the assistance of Web techniques, have been adopted by more and more
companies as the architecture of their enterprise information systems. It is a challenge to build a quality e-commerce system under the constraints of time and
budget. Software testing is an essential and effective means of creating quality
e-commerce systems.

Software testing is a *life-cycle* process which parallels the software development process [8, 1]. Generally, a complete software testing life cycle includes
the following phases: test planning, verification and validation (V&V) of system
analysis and design (AD) models, unit testing, integration testing, functional
testing, and non-functional system testing. In these testing phases, we need to
build and test various AD models, as well as the implementation, by applying
multiple testing methods and utilizing multiple testing tools.

---

* This work was partially supported by Communications and Information Technology
Ontario (CITO) in a collaborative project with IBM, and by Testing Technologies
IST GmbH. The authors are grateful for the comments of the anonymous refer-
ees,which improved the paper considerably.

M. Núñez et al. (Eds.): FORTE 2004 Workshops, LNCS 3236, pp. 16–29, 2004.
© Springer-Verlag Berlin Heidelberg 2004

Life-cycle testing, however, does not guarantee testing software thoroughly. In the real world of software projects, software should be tested in a cost-effective way: executing a limited number of test cases, but still providing enough confidence. A *high-yield, risk-directed* test strategy introduced in [12] is a cost-effective approach of test case design: test cases that are high-yield (that have the highest probability of detecting the most errors) and high-risk-directed (that have the most serious consequences if they fail) are developed and executed with high priorities.

In this paper, we propose a life-cycle e-commerce testing approach based on a high-yield, risk-directed strategy by specifying test cases at an abstract level in *OO-TTCN-3*. The paper is organized as follows. In section 2 we discuss briefly the nature and architecture of web applications, and discuss related work on web application modeling and testing. In section 3 we introduce a life-cycle testing approach, and propose a useful object-oriented extension to TTCN-3. In section 4 we present a case study in which we apply the proposed testing approach. In section 5 we present a summary and discuss possible future work.

Web application, a term similar to *e-commerce system*, is also used in this paper. There is no essential difference between these two terms. Informally, we consider that *e-commerce system* is a term with broader scope than *web application*: an e-commerce system may consist of several relatively independent web applications.

2   Testing E-commerce Systems: Background and Related Work

2.1   The Nature and Architecture of Web Applications

Generally, web applications are a kind of thin-client Client/Server (C/S) system. However, compared to traditional C/S software systems, web applications have natures which make them more complex to design and test: (1) server-based application architecture such that no special software or configuration are required on client side (2) navigation-based interaction structure (3) n-tiered system architecture such that the components of each tier may be distributed and run on heterogeneous hardware and software environments (4) independent of types, brands, and versions of web servers and browsers (5) the web server may concurrently process tens of thousands of requests from client applications (6) code contains a blend of object-oriented and procedure-oriented programming.

Today, most e-commerce systems are running on the 4-tiered architecture, that is, client tier, web tier, business tier, and Enterprise Information System (EIS) tier. Each tier is built on component-based techniques.

2.2   Web Application Modeling and Testing

There has been much research into web application modeling and testing.

UML (Unified Modeling Language) is suited to modeling web applications, but needs some extensions to describe web-specific elements. Some extensions to

UML were proposed in [7] to represent web-specific components, such as client pages, server pages, forms, hyperlinks, and Java Applets. The authors of [9] discussed how to apply extended UML to build a business model, navigation model and implementation model.

Several approaches have been proposed to support web application testing. In [18], an object-oriented architecture for web application testing was proposed which contains several analysis tools that facilitate the testing of web-specific components. In [3], the authors presented a testing methodology for web applications based on an object-oriented web test model, which captures test artifacts from three different aspects: the object aspect, the behavior aspect, and the structure aspect. In [10], the authors proposed a definition of unit and integration testing in the context of web applications. The testing approaches discussed above focus on testing web applications after they have been built. Alternatively, in [13], the authors presented a formal method which integrates testing into the development process as early as the system analysis and design phases. The paper demonstrated how to use the Specification and Description Language (SDL), Message Sequence Charts (MSCs), the Tree and Tabular Combined Notation (TTCN), and industrial-strength system design tools such as Telelogic TAU to develop and test a CORBA-based e-commerce system.

These testing approaches contributed to the improvement of web application quality. However, they only applied to part of development life-cycle: either in the analysis and design phases or the implementation phase. In addition, the test cases developed in a testing approach are written in a specific script language and depend on proprietary or specific industrial tools. These test scripts can not be reused by other testing approaches. In this paper, we intend to propose a life-cycle testing approach which leverages multiple testing methods in a life-cycle testing process. Furthermore, we integrate all the testing phases by specifying test cases on the abstract level with Object-Oriented TTCN-3. These abstract test cases can be easily reused in the whole testing process, and are independent of specific testing tools.

3   A Life-Cycle Testing Approach with OO-TTCN-3

3.1   A Life-Cycle Testing Process

Life-cycle e-commerce testing is a process of applying multiple testing methods to AD models and implementations in different testing phases, with assistance of various test tools, as shown in Figure 1. In this process, we specify all test cases in OO-TTCN-3. The dashed lines in Figure 1 indicate the possible ATS reuse. The ATS expressed in OO-TTCN-3 provides a unified interface. This makes test scripts independent from specific test tools. This also facilitates ATS reuse between different test phases: e.g., test scripts for unit testing can possibly be reused by integration testing without any modification, and different test tools may be used for the unit testing and integration testing.

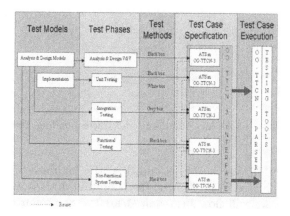

Fig. 1. Life-cycle Testing Process Model with OO-TTCN-3 for E-Commerce Systems

3.2   Introduction to TTCN-3

TTCN-3 has been developed and standardized by ITU and ETSI (European Telecommunication Standards Institute) for general testing purposes. An ATS specified in TTCN-3 is independent of languages, platforms, and testing tools. TTCN-3 is built from a textual core notation on which several optional presentation formats are defined, such as the tree and tabular format (TFT) and the Graphical Presentation Format (GFT) [4, 5]. Complex distributed test behavior can be specified at an abstract level in TTCN-3 flexibly and easily in terms of sequences, alternatives, loops and parallel stimuli and responses. Practical applications of TTCN-3 were introduced in [14, 2, 15, 16]. In addition, an extension for TTCN-3 were proposed in [2] to handle specific issues in testing real-time systems.

3.3   Object-Oriented TTCN-3

In this paper, we do not intend to make TTCN-3 fully object-oriented. Instead, our extension only focuses on specifying inheritance hierarchies and aggregation relationships between test modules.

Inheritance When we test an object-oriented system, if an inheritance relationship in the system is introduced during design in accordance with the Substitution Principle, an inheritance relation also will hold for the test cases for this inheritance hierarchy [11]. As shown in Figure 2, class B is derived from class A in accordance with the Substitution Principle, and TM_A and TM_B are test modules for class A and B, respectively. There exists an inheritance relationship between TM_B and TM_A. The allowed ways of introducing inheritance as required by the Substitution Principle, and corresponding test case design considerations are as follows [11].

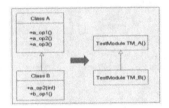

Fig. 2. Class Inheritance Hierarchy and Corresponding Test modules

- A new operation, say b_op1, is added to the interface of B and possibly a method is created to implement the operation. In this way, specification-based test cases will now be required for the operation in TM_B. If the operation has an implementation, implementation-based test cases need to be added to comply with coverage criteria.
- If an operation in B, say a_op1 which is inherited from A, has not changed in any way, either in specification or in implementation, the test cases for this operation in TM_A still apply to TM_B, which means the test cases do not need to be rerun in TM_B if they have passed in the execution of TM_A.
- The specification of an operation in B, say a_op2 which is inherited from A, has changed. In this case, new specification-based test cases are required for the operation in TM_B, which will satisfy any weakened preconditions and check outputs for the new expected results from any strengthened postconditions. The test cases for this operation in TM_A must be re-run. If the expected results need to be revised according to the strengthened postcondition, the test cases in TM_B need to be overridden.
- An operation in B, say a_op3 which is inherited from A, has been overridden. In this case, all the specification-based test cases for the operation in TM_A still apply in TM_B. The implementation-based test cases need to be reviewed. Some test cases need to be overridden, and new test cases need to be added to meet the test criteria for coverage.

In short, test cases in TM_A can be reused in TM_B. TTCN-3 provides a way to reuse definitions in different modules by using the import statement. However, as a procedure-oriented language, TTCN-3 is incapable of specifying the inheritance relationship between TM_A and TM_B.

Therefore, we extend TTCN-3 with a fundamental object-oriented mechanism, namely inheritance (extend and override), to make it capable of specifying derived test modules. The extension helps to specify the inheritance hierarchies in test modules clearly, and it eases the reuse of test case definitions in unit testing at the class level. For example, for a simple inheritance hierarchy shown in Figure 3, we can develop test cases based on the specification and implementation (if any) of an abstract class Account, and specify them in OO-TTCN-3 in test module AccountTest, even before the creation of two subclasses: EXAccount and BankAccount. After the two subclasses have been designed and implemented, the test cases in AccountTest are ready to be reused for test module EXAccountTest

Fig. 3. Partial Class Diagram for Account, EXAccount and BankAccount

and BankAccountTest which are inherited from AccountTest. In addition, if any subclass is derived from the class Account in the next development iteration, the test module for the new subclass can also benefit from the existing testing module hierarchy.

In section 4.3.3, we show how to use OO-TTCN-3 to specify a derived test module.

Extending TTCN-3 with an Inheritance Mechanism To extend TTCN-3 for specifying inheritance relationships between test modules, we investigate which elements in a test module are likely to be reused, and which elements can be extended or overridden in its derived test module. The result is shown in Table 1. From the table, we see that almost all of the elements can be reused directly, and some elements can be reused by means of an extend or override mechanism.

Table 1. Element reuse in a test module in TTCN-3

Elements			Reuse	Extend	Override
Definition	Type Definition	Built-in	N	N	N
		User-defined	Y	N	N
		RP Signature	Y	N	Y
	Test Data	Constant	Y	N	N
		Data Template	Y	N	N
		Signature Template	Y	N	Y
	Test Configuration	Communication Port	Y	Y	N
		Component	Y	Y	N
	Behavior	Function	Y	N	Y
		Named Alternatives	Y	N	Y
		Test Case	Y	N	Y
Control			N	N	N

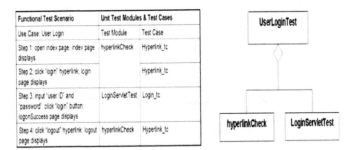

Fig. 4. Aggregation Relationship between Test Modules

We extend TTCN-3 by adding two key words: *private* and *public*, to indicate if an element is ready to be reused in a derived test module, and we assume that if an element is not specified explicitly with the key word private, the element is defined to be public by default. We also propose to add a key word *extends*, which is used to specify that a test module is inherited from another test module. The modified TTCN-3 syntax in BNF form is as follows (the sequence numbers correspond to those defined in Annex A in [4]):

```
1. TTCN3Module::=TTCN3ModuleKeyword TTCN3ModuleId[extends TTCN3ModuleId]
   BeginChar
   [ModuleDefinitionsPart] [ModuleControlPart]
   EndChar
   [WithStatement] [SemiColon]
52. PortDefBody::=PortTypeIdentifier[extends PortTypeIdentifier] PortDefAttribs
73. ComponentDef::=ComponentKeyword ComponentTypeIdentifier
   [extends ComponentTypeIdentifier]
   BeginChar [ComponentDefList] EndChar
```

Aggregation There may also exist an aggregation relationship between test modules, e.g. between test modules for functional testing and those for unit testing. In Figure 4, a functional test scenario derived from the User Login use case consists of four steps. Each step corresponds to one test case defined in the test module for unit testing. The functional test scenario can be realized by executing these test cases. This relationship can be expressed as an aggregation relationship in UML. In section 4.5, we show how to specify a test module for a functional test scenario by reusing test cases defined in unit testing.

4   Case Study

In this section we present part of a case study in which we apply our life-cycle testing approach with OO-TTCN-3 to a typical e-commerce system based on a high-yield, risk-directed strategy. The complete case study can be found in [17].

4.1   Overview of EX System

The EX system is an on-line currency exchange system which acts as a broker to provide customers the best exchange rate between Canadian Dollars (CND) and

Test Scenario	Yield	Risk	Priority

[TS001]
Pre-conditions:
  1. Login page is displayed
  2. User account is not locked
Action:
  Enter valid *User ID* and *Password*, click *Login* button
Post-conditions:
  Web page with account information is displayed, and a
  session is created
	Low	Medium	Low

[TS007]
Pre-conditions:
  1. Login page is displayed
  2. User account is **locked**
Action:
  Enter valid *User ID* and *Password*, click *Login* button
Post-conditions:
  1. Web page with account locked message is displayed
  2. User account is locked
	High	High	High

Fig. 5. Test scenarios for the User Login use case

U.S. Dollars (USD) among its linked banks at remote sites. The entire EX system can be divided into three subsystems: EX web application subsystem (EAS), bank subsystem (BS), and post office subsystem (PS). EAS obtains quotes from banks and presents the best one to web clients (WC).

4.2 Verify and Validate the System Analysis and Design Models

During the system AD phases, the AD models, e.g., UML use cases, need to be verified and validated. For example, guided inspection can be used to verify the use case model for correctness, completeness and consistency [22]. Then, test scenarios can be developed from the verified use cases: one is the normal scenario which is considered low-yield and low-risk/medium-risk; one or more are for alternative and exceptional scenarios which are considered high-yield and high-risk/medium-risk. Figure 5 lists part of the test scenarios derived from the User Login use case. Some design models, e.g., activity diagrams, can be used to analyze and improve the coverage of the test scenarios [17].

The test scenarios above can be specified in GFT, as shown in Figure 6. These GFTs can be used to validate whether the design models conform to the requirements, e.g. comparing them with the MSCs created in the development process.

After the GUI design has been done, test cases can be developed from test scenarios and the GUI design. The development of high-yield test cases consists of three basic steps: (1) Partition input conditions into equivalence classes. (2) Create test data based on boundary-value analysis. (3) Design test cases to cover all test scenarios [17]. These test cases then are ready for functional testing.

4.3 Unit Testing

The unit testing level corresponds to the n-tier architecture of web applications: client tier testing, web tier testing, business tier testing, and EIS tier testing

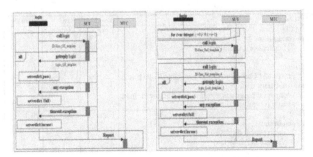

Fig. 6. Test Scenario 1 & 7 in GFT

(which we will not discuss in this paper). This is because each tier is a relatively independent set of components. The techniques used with these components are similar in the same tier, but may be different in different tiers. Also, each tier has different responsibilities.

Client Tier Typical components in the client tier are html files, scripts embedded in an html file, and Java Applets. They run on the client side, usually within the content of a browser. From a functional perspective, common testing activities in the client tier include validating that every hyperlink in an html file is valid and that scripts and applets act as expected. Testing models based on the analysis of data flow and control flow of source code can be used to derive test cases [3]. The following TTCN-3 script demonstrates how to check the validity of a hyperlink.

```
module hyperlinkCheck{
modulepar {charstring testtype};
type record url {charstring protocol, charstring host, charstring portNum,
 charstring path}
template url hyperlink_index := {protocol:=https://,host:=www.site.uottawa.ca,
 portNum:=:1180, path:=ex/index.html}
template charstring status_ok := 200;
template charstring status_timeout := 408;
type port hyperlinkPortType message {out url; in charstring}
type port mCPType message {in    verdicttype}
type port pCPType message {out verdicttype}
type component hyperlinkComponent {port hyperlinkPortType hyperlinkPort;
 port pCPType CP}
type component mtcComponent {port mCPType CP;
 port hyperlinkPortType hyperlinkPort;
 var integer activePTCs := 0;}
type component TSI {port hyperlinkPortType hyperlinkTSI}
function hyperlink_check (in url hyperlink, mtcComponent theSystem)
 runs on hyperlinkComponent {
  map(self:hyperlinkPort, theSystem:hyperlinkPort);
  hyperlinkPort.send(hyperlink);
  alt {
    [] hyperlinkPort.receive(status_ok) {setverdict(pass)}
    [] hyperlinkPort.receive(status_timeout) {setverdict(inconc)}
    [] hyperlinkPort.receive() {setverdict(fail)} }
  CP.send(getverdict); }
testcase hyperlink_tc(in url hyperlink, integer loops, out integer passedTCs,
 integer failedTCs,integer inconcTCs)runs on mtcComponent system mtcComponent{
```

```
var verdicttype theVerdict;
var hyperlinkComponent theNewPTC[loops];
for (i:=1;i<=loops;i:=i+1) {
 theNewPTC[i]:= hyperlinkComponent.create;
 activePTCs  := activePTCs + 1;
 connect(mtc:CP, theNewPTC[i]:CP);
 theNewPTC[i].start(hyperlink_check(hyperlink, system)); }
while (activePTCs > 0) {
  CP.receive(verdicttype:?)-> value theVerdict;
  activePTC := activePTC - 1;
  setverdict(theVerdict);
  if (theVerdict == pass)   { passedTCs := passedTCs + 1; }
  else if (theVerdict == fail)  { failedTCs := failedTCs + 1; }
  else if (theVerdict == inconc) { inconcTCs := inconcTCs + 1; } }
 all component.done; }
function basicFunctionality() return verdicttype {
 var verdicttype localVerdict;
 var integer nrP := 0, nrF := 0, nrI := 0;
 localVerdict := execute(hyperlink_tc(hyperlink_index,1,nrP,nrF,nrI));
 return localVerdict; }
control {
 var verdicttype overallVerdict;
 if (testtype == basicFunctionality) {
   overallVerdict := basicFunctionality(); } } }
```

Web Tier Components running in the web tier are JSP files, Java Servlets, and CGI programs etc. Web components are also identified by URLs, in the same way as html files, but run on the server side. In addition, servlet and CGI programs may utilize parameters wrapped in an HTTP request. These components are usually referred to as server pages, while html files are referred as client pages. Test modules in TTCN-3 for server pages are similar to those for client pages, but with a significant difference: using procedure-based ports which are based on a synchronous communication mechanism to specify procedure calls in remote entities, instead of message-based ports which are based on asynchronous message exchange. The following code segment shows how to specify a test module for testing Login Servlet by using a procedure-based port:

```
signature loginServlet(in url url_loginServlet, charstring ID,
 charstring password) return boolean exception (reasonType);
template loginServlet validLogin := {url_loginServlet := url_login_template,
 ID := C001, password := C001}
type port loginPortType procedure {out loginServlet}
```

Business Tier The objects in the business tier are used to implement the business logic of web applications. The objects can be represented by class diagrams, possibly with constraints written in Object Constraint Language (OCL). Test cases can be derived from the class diagrams and constraints. Often, there exists an inheritance relationship between these test cases, as we have discussed in section 3.3.1. Test modules for specifying these test cases can be specified in OO-TTCN-3, which can specify the inheritance relationship between test modules appropriately.

In the EX system, Account is an abstract class (see Figure 3). It contains two attributes: accNum and user. One of the methods defined and implemented in the class Account is getAccountNo(), which returns the account number of

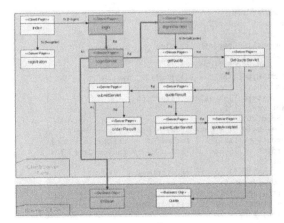

Fig. 7. Partial Object Relation Diagram for EX system

the current user. Two subclasses, BankAccount and EXAccount, are derived from Account. BankAccount is used to describe the attributes and behaviors of bank accounts. EXAccount is used to describe the accounts in the EX system. The signatures and implementations of getAccountNo() do not change in the two derived classes. Therefore, test cases developed for getAccountNo() can be reused by the test modules for BankAccount and ExAccount. In addition, we only need to run the test suites once, either in the test module for BankAccount or in the module for EXAccount, to validate the method in the three classes. This also avoids testing the abstract class Account, which cannot be instantiated and is difficult to test directly. The following is a code segment which shows how to specify the test modules in OO-TTCN-3:

```
module AccountTest {
signature Acc_constr(in charstring AccNum,charstring user)exception(charstring);
signature getAccountNo () return charstring exception (charstring);
testcase getAccountNo_tc() runs on mtcType system mtcType{...} }
module BankAccountTest() extends AccountTest {
control {execute(getAccountNo_tc());} }
```

4.4   Integration Testing

The purpose of integration testing is to make sure all components of a software system work together properly. ATS defined for unit testing can be reused directly for integration testing. Figure 7 is the partial ORD (Object Relation Diagram) for the EX system. The test module LoginServletTest defined for web tier testing is ready for integration testing, which includes the components login server page, LoginServlet servlet, logonSuccess server page, and EXBean, and interactions between these components.

4.5   Functional Testing

The purpose of functional testing is to ensure the behaviors of a software system meet its functional requirements. Test scenarios in GFT developed at the system analysis and design phases can be used to generate test cases for functional testing. Actually, a bidirectional mapping between the core language and GFT is defined in [5], which makes it is possible to generate test scripts in core language from the scenarios in GFT automatically, or vice-versa, given specific tool support. On the other hand, test modules in TTCN-3 can be built manually. We can specify test cases developed in the system AD phases in TTCN-3. In addition, test scripts produced in unit testing can be reused in functional testing. The following is a code segment to test User Login functionality, which utilizes part of the definitions from test modules hyperlinkCheck and LoginServlettest.

```
function validLogin() return verdicttype {
  localVerdict:=execute(hyperlinkCheck.hyperlink_tc(hyperlink_index,1,0,0,0));
  if (localVerdict != pass) {return localVerdict;}
localVerdict := execute(hyperlinkCheck.hyperlink_tc(hyperlink_login,1,0,0,0));
  if (localVerdict != pass) {return localVerdict;}
  localVerdict := execute(LoginServletTest.validLogin_tc());
  if (localVerdict != pass) {return localVerdict;}
  localVerdict:=execute(hyperlinkCheck.hyperlink_tc(hyperlink_logout,1,0,0,0));}
```

4.6   Non-functional System Testing

Non-functional system testing is the process of testing an integrated software system to verify that the system meets its specified non-functional requirements. Test cases for non-functional system test cases, such as performance tests, can be specified in TTCN-3. Test scripts developed in the previous testing stages, such as functional testing, may be reused for non-functional testing. The following is an example of performance testing: adding a function in the hyperlinkCheck test module to simulate 1000 times of clicking on index.html, and then observing how many requests timeout or fail:

```
function performanceTesting() return verdicttype {
  localVerdict   := execute(hyperlink_tc(hyperlink_index,1000,nrP,nrF,nrI)); }
```

4.7   Concrete Requirements and Results

The above abstract test suite can be executed after transforming it into executable code in an implementation language such as Java. This has been achieved by using one of the many commercially available TTCN-3 tools, like in our case, TTthree [6]. After that the actual execution of this code can be performed using a runtime environment like TTman [6] that allows a user to select a given test case to be executed. However, the abstract test suite can be executed only after organizing some adapter and coding/decoding code to transfer data from an internal representation to the real world representation. This can be achieved by using ETSI standard tri and tci classes interfaces and a set of APIs. Sample code can be viewed at www.site.uottawa.ca/ bob/ECTesting. Once the adapter and codec code compiled, they can be fed to the muTTman test case manager that shows a list of test cases and upon execution a test case execution trace as shown in Figure 8.

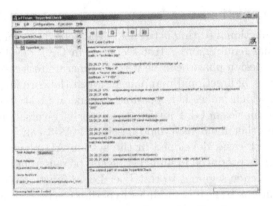

Fig. 8. Test Case Execution Result

5   Summary and Future Work

In this paper, we proposed an approach which realizes a life-cycle test process
for e-commerce systems by specifying the ATS in OO-TTCN-3. The approach
facilitates the reuse of test scripts. It also provides a unified and standard ATS
interface to test tool vendors. This has significant potential to attract more
support from the IT industry.

Making a complete object-oriented extension to TTCN-3 would be quite
complex. In this paper we present a preliminary such extension. A formal description of this extension and a prototype tool that supports OO-TTC-3 will
be considered in future work.

References

[1] Imran Bashir and Amrit L. Goel. *Testing Object-Oriented Software: Life-Cycle
    Solutions.* Springer-Verlag, 1999. 16
[2] Z. R. Dai, J. Grabowski, and H. Neukirchen. Timed TTCN-3 A Real-Time Ex-
    tension for TTCN-3. *Testing of Communicating Systems*, 14, March 2002. 19
[3] Kung D. C., Chien-Hung Liu, and Pei Hsia. An Object-Oriented Web Test Model
    for Testing Web Applications. In *Proc. of First Asia-Pacific Conf. on Quality
    Software*, pages 111–120, 2000. 18, 24
[4] ETSI. *The Testing and Test Control Notation version 3, Part1: TTCN-3 Core
    Language, V2.2.1.* European Institute Standards Telecommunication, 2003. 19,
    22
[5] ETSI. *The Testing and Test Control Notation version 3, Part3: TTCN-3 Graphi-
    cal Presentation Format (GFT), V2.2.1.* European Institute Standards Telecom-
    munication, 2003. 19, 27
[6] Testing Technologies IST GmbH. The Ttthree and Ttman TTCN-3 Tool Chain,
    2004. http://www.testingtech.de. 27
[7] Conallen Jim. Modeling Web Application Architectures with UML. *Communi-
    cations of the ACM*, 42(10):63–77, October 2003. 18

[8] Edward Kit. *Software Testing in the Real World*. Addison-Wesley, 1995. 16

[9] Jingfeng Li, Jian Chen, and Ping Chen. Modeling Web Application Architecture with UML. In *Proc. of 36th Intel. Conf. on Technology of Object-Oriented Languages and Systems*, pages 265–274, 2000. 18

[10] G. A. Di Lucca, A. R. Fasolino, F. Faralli, and U. De Carlini. Testing Web Applications. In *Proc. of Intel. Conf. on Software Maintenance*, pages 310–319, 2002. 18

[11] John D. McGregor and David A. Sykes. *A Practical Guide to Testing Object-Oriented Software*. Addison-Wesley, 2001. 19

[12] R. L. Probert, D. P. Sims, B. Ghazizadeh, and W. Li. A Risk-Directed E-Commerce Test Strategy. In *Proc. of Quality Week Europe 2000 Conf. (QWE)*, pages 388–401, November 2000. 17

[13] Robert L. Probert, Yanping Chen, Behrad Ghazizadeh, D. Paul Sims, and Maurus Cappa. Formal Verification and Validation for E-Commerce: Theory and Best Practices. *Information and Software Technology*, 45:763–777, 2003. 18

[14] I. Schieferdecker, S. Pietsch, and T. Vassiliou-Gioles. Systematic Testing of Internet Protocols - First Experiences in Using TTCN-3 for SIP. In *Proc. of 5th IFIP Africom Conf. on Communication Systems*, 2001. 19

[15] I. Schieferdecker and B. Stepien. Automated Testing of XML/SOAP Based Web Services. In *Proc. of 13th Fachkonferenz der Gesellschaft fur Informatik (GI) Fachgruppe Kommunikation in verteilten Systemen*, 2003. 19

[16] Ina Schieferdecker and Theofanis Vassiliou-Gioles. Tool Supported Test Frameworks in TTCN-3. *Electronic Notes in Theoretical Computer Science*, 80, 2003. 19

[17] Pulei Xiong. Life-Cycle E-Commerce Testing with Object-Oriented TTCN-3. Master's thesis, University of Ottawa, 2004. 22, 23

[18] Ji-Tzay Yang, Jiun-Long Huang, Feng-Jian Wang, and W. C. Chu. An Object-Oriented Architecture Supporting Web Application Testing. In *Proc. of 23rd Annual Intel. Computer Software and Applications Conf.*, pages 122–127, 1999. 18

Specification of Autonomous Agents
in E-commerce Systems*

Ismael Rodríguez, Manuel Núñez, and Fernando Rubio

Dept. Sistemas Informáticos y Programación
Universidad Complutense de Madrid, E-28040 Madrid. Spain
e-mail: {isrodrig,mn,fernando}@sip.ucm.es

Abstract. We present a generic formal framework to specify e-commerce systems. Specifically, we introduce a formalism to represent the behavior of the agents involved in the system. We will concentrate only on the *high level* behavior, that is, the one related to the economic performance of the agents. Finally, we apply our framework to the specification of the e-commerce system Kasbah.

1 Introduction

Among those areas where computers are yielding a higher impact during the last years we may remark electronic commerce. In fact, commerce activities under electronic, computer, and telecommunication support have several advantages with respect to traditional commerce. Nevertheless, e-commerce applications are usually very complex. Thus, it is hard to ensure reliability and correctness. Actually, e-commerce applications use to be distributed environments consisting of a big amount of heterogeneous components, being each of these components eventually depending on a different party. Besides, e-commerce applications usually have repercussions on the private patrimony of the users, either by conducting the user decisions through recommendations or by performing transactions in his name. Therefore, the success of an e-commerce platform dramatically depends on the confidence the users have on it. So, a key issue in the current and future development of e-commerce systems is the introduction of techniques to validate their behavior so that all users can trust the platform.

An aspect that has attracted a lot of attention is the *communication validation* of e-commerce protocols. Transactions in e-commerce environments involve a lot of communications, being critical in the sense that any transmitted message must conform to the meaning the emitter initially gave to it. Only in this case, the actions of a user will depend on his own responsibility, which is a requirement in any economic environment. Thus, typical problems to be issued are authentication, privacy, integrity of data, and (no) repudiation (see e.g. [1, 2]). In this line, some formal approaches have been proposed to check the behavior of some

---

* This research has been supported by the Spanish MCyT project *MASTER* (TIC2003-07848-C02-01), the Junta de Castilla-La Mancha project *DISMEF* (PAC-03-001) and the Marie Curie RTN *TAROT* (MCRTN 505121).

M. Núñez et al. (Eds.): FORTE 2004 Workshops, LNCS 3236, pp. 30–44, 2004.

e-commerce environments. These solutions focus on formalizing and studying the communication protocols used in the corresponding e-commerce application. In fact, they are not specific of e-commerce domains, as they are used in the same way when any other communication protocol is validated, that is, they deal with a *part* of the *low-level* behavior of an e-commerce application. Thus, they cannot be considered as *specific* e-commerce validation formal techniques. We think that the e-commerce field contains enough specific aspects to deserve its own validation techniques and tools to efficiently deal with its intrinsic features.

The aim of this paper is to develop a specific framework to specify and check the correctness of the *high-level* part of e-commerce applications. To become more definite, we introduce a formalism to specify the behavior of *autonomous commerce agents*. In fact, autonomous commerce agents are one of the most interesting and challenging technologies in e-commerce (see e.g. [6, 14, 11, 8]). They are autonomous entities that perform transactions in the name of their respective users. Their high-level specification can be defined as *"get what the user said he wants and when he wants it"*. We will consider that the specific preferences of the users will conform a *specification*.[1] Therefore, we will need a proper formalism to represent this kind of specifications, that we will call *utility state machines* and were introduced in a slightly different form in [13].

In terms of related work there are innumerable papers on e-commerce in general or on topics as e-commerce systems/arquitectures and agent-mediated e-commerce. This number strongly decreases when considering formal approaches to e-commerce. In this case we may mention [9, 10] where, taking as basis the language PAMR [12], process algebras to specify e-barter systems (that is, a restricted notion of e-commerce) were introduced.

The rest of the paper is structured as follows. In Section 2 we present the formalism that allows us to specify autonomous commerce agents. In Section 3, we define how agents can be combined to build systems of agents. In Section 4 we apply our formal framework to the Kasbah system. Finally, in Section 5 we present our conclusions and some lines for future work.

2   Utility State Machines

In this section we present the formalism we will use to specify our autonomous exchange agents. As we said in the introduction, our validation methodology will focus on determining whether an implementation fulfills the desires of the users in terms of gained utility. Nevertheless, we will not be interested in *how* the utility is gained. So, the formalism will not include details about how private data are encrypted, how to find potential customers, how to estimate the confidence level on a given vendor, or what is the specific strategy to compete with other agents. Instead, we will check whether the transactions are performed according to the preferences of the users. Obviously, the performance of agents will be influenced

---

[1] In this paper we do not deal with how agents *infer* the exact desires of the users since this goes beyond the scope of the paper (see e.g. [4, 5, 7]).

by low-level details, but this influence will be considered only on the basis of its consequences, that is, on the basis of the high-level behavior.

The objectives of the users may be different according to the situation. In an e-commerce environment the objectives are measured in terms of the obtained *resources*. Users will have different preferences and the first step to construct the specification of the corresponding agent consists in expressing these preferences. The preferences of the user in a given moment will be given by its *utility function*. Utility functions associate a value (a utility measure) with each possible combination of resources a user could own.

Definition 1. We consider $\mathbb{R}_+ = \{x \in \mathbb{R} | x \geq 0\}$. We will usually denote *vectors* in $\mathbb{R}^n$ (for $n \geq 2$) by $\bar{x}, \bar{y}, \ldots$ We consider that $\bar{0}$ denotes the tuple having all the components equal to zero. Given $\bar{x} \in \mathbb{R}^n$, x_i denotes its *i-th* component. We extend some usual arithmetic operations to vectors. Let $\bar{x}, \bar{y} \in \mathbb{R}^m$. We define $\bar{x} + \bar{y} = (x_1 + y_1, \ldots, x_n + y_n)$ and $\bar{x} \cdot \bar{y} = (x_1 \cdot y_1, \ldots, x_n \cdot y_n)$. We write $\bar{x} \leq \bar{y}$ if for any $1 \leq i \leq n$ we have $x_i \leq y_i$.

Let us suppose that there exist n different kinds of resources. A *utility function* is any function $f : \mathbb{R}_+^n \longrightarrow \mathbb{R}_+$.   □

Intuitively, if f is a utility function then $f(\bar{x}) > f(\bar{y})$ means that $\bar{x}$ is preferred to $\bar{y}$. For instance, if the resource x_1 denotes the amount of apples and x_2 denotes the amount of oranges, then $f(x_1, x_2) = 3 \cdot x_1 + 2 \cdot x_2$ means that, for example, the user is equally happy owing 2 apples or 3 oranges. Let us consider another user whose utility function is $f(x_1, x_2) = x_1 + 2 \cdot x_2$. Then, both users can make a deal if the first user gives 3 oranges in exchange of 4 apples: After the exchange both users are happier. Let us suppose now that x_2 represents the amount of money (in euros). In this situation, the first user would be the customer while the second one might represent the vendor. Let us remark that utility functions allow a great expressivity in preferences. For instance, $f(x_1, x_2) = x_1 \cdot x_2$ represents a utility function denoting that variety is preferred. A usual assumption is that no resource is a *bad*, that is, $\frac{\Delta f(x_1, \ldots, x_n)}{\Delta x_i} \geq 0$ for any $x_1, \ldots, x_n \in \mathbb{R}$ and $1 \leq i \leq n$. This requirement does not constrain the expressive power of utility functions, as the existence of any undesirable resource can be always expressed just by considering another resource representing the *absence* of it.

In order to formally specify autonomous commerce agents we have to represent the different objectives of the corresponding user along time. Thus, our formalism will provide the capability of expressing different utility functions depending on the situation, represented by the current *state*. Besides, *objectives*, represented by utility functions, will change depending on the availability of resources. These events will govern the transitions between states. Our formalism, that we call *utility state machines*, is indeed an adaption and extension to our purposes of the classical notion of *extended finite state machines* (EFSM). We will be able to deal with *time* as a factor that influences the preferences of users, either by affecting the value returned by a given utility function (e.g. the interest in a given item could decay as time passes) or by defining when the utility function must change (e.g. an old technology is considered obsolete and it is no longer interesting). Besides, time will affect agents in the sense that any negative transaction will imply a deadline for the agent to retrieve the benefits of it. In fact, gaining profit in the long run may sometimes require to perform actions that, considered in the short term, are detrimental. Thus, time will be used to check whether the transaction was beneficial in the long term. In addition, time will appear as part of the freedom that specifications give to implementations: It does not matter whether an agent immediately performs a transaction as long as its decision is useful to improve the utility in the long term.

Definition 2. We say that the tuple $M = (S, s_{in}, V, U, at, mi, T)$ is a *utility state machine*, in short USM, where we consider that

- S is a *set of states*.
- $s_{in} \in S$ is the *initial state* of M.
- $V = (t, x_1, \ldots, x_n)$ is a *tuple of variables*, where t represents the *time* elapsed since the machine entered the current state and $x_1, \ldots, x_n$ represent the resources that are available to be traded in the e-commerce environment.
- $U : S \longrightarrow (\mathbb{R}_+^{n+1} \longrightarrow \mathbb{R}_+)$ is a function associating a utility function with each state in M.
- at is the *amortization time*. It denotes the maximal time M may stay without retrieving the profit of the negative transactions that were performed in the past.
- mi is the *maximal investment*. It denotes the maximal amount of negative profit the machine should afford.
- T is the set of *transitions*. Each transition is a tuple (s, Q, Z, s'), where $s, s' \in S$ are the initial and final state of the transition, $Q : \mathbb{R}_+^{n+1} \longrightarrow$ Bool is a predicate on the set of variables, and $Z : \mathbb{R}_+^n \longrightarrow \mathbb{R}_+^n$ is a transformation over the current variables. We require that for any state s there do not exist two different transitions $t_1, t_2 \in T$, with $t_1 = (s, Q_1, Z_1, s_1')$ and $t_2 = (s, Q_2, Z_2, s_2')$, and a tuple $\bar{r}$ such that both $Q_1(\bar{r})$ and $Q_2(\bar{r})$ hold.

$\square$

We can consider environments where the resources increase/decrease as a result of the agent activities. These modifications represent the decision of the user to introduce new resources in the market or to take away some of them. Both activities are accounted for by the Z functions appearing in transitions. Besides, let us remark that available resources and time influence the conditions required to change the state of the machine. This is taken into account by the Q functions appearing in transitions. Let us also note that in these constraints we may also consider the time previously consumed. In fact, we could use an additional *abstract* resource to accumulate the time consumed in previous states.

It is worth to point out that the set of transitions T does not include the complete set of transitions the specification will allow real agents to perform. Some additional transitions must be considered: *transactions* and *passing of time*. The former will be used to denote the transactions agents will be allowed to perform. These transactions will include some simple constraints that allow us to avoid that an agent gives more resources than those actually owned, or to avoid giving resources if the amount of value lost in previous negative transactions, and not retrieved yet, is too high. Passing of time denotes the free decision of agents to idle. We consider two constraints on passing of time. First, an agent should not let the time pass so that previous negative transactions are not retrieved before their deadlines. Second, time conditions may trigger the modification of the state of an agent. Thus, in the exact time it happens, and before the passing of time *action* continues, the transition between states will be performed. Given a USM M, both transaction and time consumption transitions may be *implicitly* inferred from the definition of M. We will give the formal representation in the forthcoming Definition 5. Next we introduce the notion of *configuration*, that is, the data denoting the current situation of a USM. A configuration consists of the current state, the current values of the variables, and the *pending accounting* of the machine.

Definition 3. Let $M = (S, s_{in}, V, U, at, mi, T)$ be a USM. A *configuration* of M is a tuple $(s, \overline{r}, l)$ where

- $s \in S$ is the *current state* in M,
- $\overline{r} = (u, r_1, \ldots, r_n) \in \mathbb{R}_+^{n+1}$ is the current value of V, and
- $l = [(p_1, e_1), \ldots, (p_m, e_m)]$ is a list of pairs (profit,time) representing the list of *pending accounts*.

$\square$

For each pair $(p, e) \in l$ we have that p represents a (positive or negative) *profit* and e represents the *expiration date* of p, that is, the time in which a profit greater than or equal to $-p$ must be retrieved, in the case that p is negative, or the time in which p will be considered a *clear* profit if no negative profit is registered before. In order to explain the main characteristics of our framework, we will consider a simple (but illustrative) running example where some kids engage in the complicated world of becoming *entrepreneurs*.

Example 1. Let us suppose that little Jimmy wants to sell lemonade in the market of his town. We will construct a USM $J = (S, s_{in}, V, U, at, mi, T)$ to represent the economic behavior of Jimmy. The tuple of variables $V = (t, l, d, s, m)$ contains a value denoting time (t) and the amount of each resource: lemons (l), lemonades (d), selling licenses (s), and money (m).

This USM is depicted in Figure 1. The initial state s_1 represents a situation where Jimmy has no license to sell lemonade in the market. Unfortunately, all stands in the market are occupied. So, Jimmy has to buy it from another vendor. The utility function in s_1 is given by $U(s_1)(\overline{r}) = 10 \cdot s + m$, that is, Jimmy would pay up to \$10 for a selling licence. Besides, lemons and lemonades are irrelevant at this preliminary stage. There are two possibilities for leaving the state s_1. On the one hand, if a week passes and Jimmy has not bought the selling license yet, then he will raise his effort to get the license. The transition $tran_1 = (s_1, Q_2, Z_2, s_2)$, where $Q_2(t, \overline{r}) = (t = 7)$ and $Z_2(\overline{r}) = \overline{r}$, leads Jimmy to

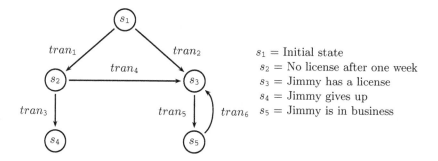

Fig. 1. Example of USM: Jimmy's business

the new state. In state s_2 we have $U(s_2)(\overline{r}) = 20 \cdot s + m$, which denotes that Jimmy would pay now up to \$20. On the other hand, if Jimmy gets the license then the transition $tran_2 = (s_1, Q_3, Z_3, s_3)$, where $Q_3(t, \overline{r}) = (s = 1)$ and $Z_3(\overline{r}) = (l, d, s-1, m)$, leads him to s_3. The function Z_3 represents that Jimmy will take away the license from his trading basket because he wants to keep it for himself. The utility function in s_3 is represented by $U(s_3)(\overline{r}) = 0.2 \cdot l + m$. This means that Jimmy wants to stock up with lemons to make lemonades. He will pay up to 20 cents for each lemon.

If Jimmy is in state s_2 then there are two possibilities as well. If another week elapses and Jimmy remains with no license then he gives up his project. This is denoted by the transition $tran_3 = (s_2, Q_4, Z_4, s_4)$, where $Q_4(t, \overline{r}) = (t = 7)$ and $Z_4(\overline{r}) = (0, 0, 0, 0)$. The function Z_4 denotes that all resources are taken away from the trading environment. Hence, $U(s_4)(\overline{r})$ is irrelevant. The second possibility happens if Jimmy finally gets his license. In this case, the transition $tran_4 = (s_2, Q_3', Z_3', s_3)$, where $Q_3' = Q_3$ and $Z_3' = Z_3$, leads him to s_3.

We suppose that Jimmy uses 3 lemons for each lemonade. Thus, when Jimmy is in the state s_3 and stocks up with 12 lemons then he makes 4 lemonades. This is represented by the transition $tran_5 = (s_3, Q_5, Z_5, s_5)$, where $Q_4(t, \overline{r}) = (l = 12)$ and $Z_4(\overline{r}) = (l - 12, d + 4, s, m)$. In the state s_5, Jimmy wants to sell his new handmade lemonades. The utility function $U(s_5)(\overline{r}) = 2 \cdot d + m$ means that he will sell lemonades for, at least, \$2. Finally, when lemonades run out, Jimmy thinks again about stocking up with lemons. So, the transition $tran_6 = (s_5, Q_6, Z_6, s_3)$, where $Q_6(t, \overline{r}) = (d = 0)$ and $Z_4(\overline{r}) = (\overline{r})$, moves Jimmy back to s_3.

A possible initial configuration of J is $(s_1, (0, 0, 0, 0, 50), [\ ])$, which means that Jimmy begins his adventure with \$50 and without pending accounts. $\square$

Next we present some auxiliary definitions. First, we define the maximal time a USM is allowed to idle. Intuitively, this limit will be given by the minimum between the minimal time in which the machine has to change its state and the

time in which the oldest pending account expires. If the minimum is given by
the second value then we will use two auxiliary predicates to denote two special
situations. The first predicate holds if an old positive profit expires at its amortization time. In this case, the profit will be considered *clear*, since it has not been
used to compensate any subsequent negative profit. The second one holds in the
opposite case, that is, an old negative profit expires without being compensated
before. This case denotes an *undesirable* situation in which the corresponding
agent does not not fulfill its economic objectives. Let us note that even though
this situation will be produced according to the behavior specified by a USM, it
will be convenient that the implementation does not show such a behavior, since
it is contrary to the economic objectives of the agent. Therefore, that information will have a special relevance to assess whether an implementation fulfills
the requirements imposed by a specification. After introducing these predicates,
we will present how the list of pending accounts must be updated when a new
transaction is performed. If the sign of the new transaction coincides with those
of the listed transactions (that is, either all of them are positive or all of them are
negative) then this transaction will be added to the list. Otherwise, the value of
the new transaction will *compensate* the listed transactions as much as its value
can, from the oldest transaction to the newest. Finally, we will define how to
add the profit accumulated in the list of pending accounts.

Definition 4. Let $M = (S, s_{in}, V, U, at, mi, T)$ be a USM and $c = (s, \bar{r}, l)$ be
a configuration of M, with $\bar{r} = (u, r_1, \ldots, r_n)$ and $l = [(p_1, e_1), \ldots, (p_m, e_m)]$. The
maximal waiting time for M in the configuration c, denoted by $\texttt{MaxWait}(M, c)$,
is defined as

$$\min\{e_1, \min\{u' \mid \exists (s, Q, Z, s'') \in T : u' \geq u \wedge Q(u', r_1, \ldots, r_n) = \texttt{True}\}\}$$

If e_1 is actually the minimal value and $p_1 > 0$ then we say that M performs a *clear profit*, which is indicated by setting true the auxiliary condition
$\texttt{ClearProfit}(M, c)$. On the contrary, if e_1 is the minimal value and $p_1 < 0$ then
we say that M *fails its economic objective*, which is indicated by setting *true* the
auxiliary condition $\texttt{TargetFailed}(M, c)$.

The *update* of the list of pending accounts l with the new profit a, denoted
by $\texttt{Update}(l, a)$, is defined as:

$$\texttt{Update}(l, a) = \begin{cases} [(a, at + u)] & \text{if } l = [\,] \\ l \mathbin{+\!\!+} [(a, at + u)] & \text{if } l = (p_1, e_1) : l' \wedge \frac{p_1}{a} \geq 0 \\ (p_1 + a, e_1) : l' & \text{if } l = (p_1, e_1) : l' \wedge \frac{p_1}{a} < 0 \wedge \frac{p_1 + a}{a} \geq 0 \\ \texttt{Update}(l', p_1 + a) & \text{if } l = (p_1, e_1) : l' \wedge \frac{p_1}{a} < 0 \wedge \frac{p_1 + a}{p_1} < 0 \end{cases}$$

Finally, the accumulated profit of a list of pending accounts l, denoted by
$\texttt{Accumulated}(l)$, is defined as

$$\texttt{Accumulated}(l) = \begin{cases} 0 & \text{if } l = [\,] \\ p + \texttt{Accumulated}(l') & \text{if } l = (p, e) : l' \end{cases}$$

□

Let us note that profits in any (non-empty) list of pending accounts are either all positive or all negative. In the definition of Update, conditions such as $\frac{n}{m} \geq 0$ denote that n and m have the same sign. As we said before, if a (i.e. the new profit) has the same sign as (all) the profits in the list (e.g. the sign of p_1) then the new transaction is added to the list. On the contrary, if both signs are opposite then a compensates the oldest profit p_1 as much as its value can. In this case, if $\frac{p_1+a}{p_1} \geq 0$ then the absolute value of a is lower than the absolute value of p_1. So, a does not completely compensates p_1. If $\frac{p_1+a}{p_1} < 0$ then we have the opposite situation, that is, p_1 is completely eliminated and the remainder of a is recursively applied to the rest of the list. We have used a functional programming notation to define lists: $[\,]$ denotes an empty list, $l ++ l'$ denotes the concatenation of the lists l and l', and $x : l$ denotes the inclusion, as first element, of x into the list l.

Example 2. Let us revisit Example 1. After a month, let us suppose that Jimmy is in configuration $(s_3, (31, 0, 4, 0, 8.50), [\,])$. Besides, let us suppose that Jimmy accepts payments for the lemonade in instalments. Today, Timmy consumes a lemonade at \$2 but pays \$1 as down payment. Besides, the next day Johnny consumes a lemonade at \$2 and pays only \$0.50 as deposit. Let us suppose that the amortization time of Jimmy is a week. Then, a possible configuration for Jimmy is $(s_3, (32, 0, 2, 0, 10), [(-1, 38), (-1.50, 39)])$. At this time, Mr. Brown buys a lemonade, paying cash, for \$3.50. Then, the new configuration for Jimmy is $(s_3, (32, 0, 1, 0, 13.50), [(-1, 39)])$. □

Given a USM M, an *evolution* of M represents a configuration that the USM can take from a previous configuration. Formally, evolutions are tuples $(c, c', tc)_K$ where c and c' are the previous and new configurations, respectively, tc is the time consumed by the evolution, and $K \in \{\alpha, \beta, \beta', \gamma\}$ is the type of evolution (*changing the state, passing of time, passing of time with failure,* and *performing a transaction*). The difference between β and β' transitions is that in the second case the agent fails its economic objectives since a past negative profit expires at its amortization time.

Definition 5. Let $M = (S, s_{in}, V, U, at, mi, T)$ be a USM and $c = (s, \bar{r}, l)$ be a configuration of M, with $\bar{r} = (u, r_1, \ldots, r_n)$ and $l = [(p_1, e_1), \ldots, (p_m, e_m)]$. An *evolution* of M from c is a tuple $(c, c', tc)_K$ where $c' = (s', \bar{r'}, l')$, $K \in \{\alpha, \beta, \beta', \gamma\}$ and $tc \in \mathbb{R}_+$ are defined according to the following options:

(1) (*Changing the state*) If there exists $(s, Q, Z, s'') \in T$ such that $Q(\bar{r})$ holds then $K = \alpha$, $tc = 0$, $s' = s''$, and $\bar{r'} = (0, r'_1, \ldots, r'_n)$, where $(r'_1, \ldots, r'_n) = Z(r_1, \ldots, r_n)$ and $l' = [(p_1, e_1 - u), \ldots, (p_m, e_m - u)]$.

(2) (*Passing of time*) If the condition of (1) does not hold then for any $tr \in \mathbb{R}_+$ such that $0 < tr \leq \mathtt{MaxWait}(M, c) - u$, we have $tc = tr$, $s' = s$, $\bar{r'} = (u + tr, r_1, \ldots, r_n)$, and l' is defined as follows:

$$l' = \begin{cases} [(p_2, e_2), \ldots, (p_m, e_m)] & \text{if } \mathtt{ClearProfit}(M, c) \lor \mathtt{TargetFailed}(M, c) \\ l & \text{otherwise} \end{cases}$$

In addition, $K = \beta'$ if $\mathtt{TargetFailed}(M, c)$ and $K = \beta$ otherwise.

(3) (*Transaction*) If the condition of (1) does not hold then for any $\overline{r''} = (u, r_1'', \ldots, r_n'') \geq \overline{0}$ such that $U(s)(\overline{r''}) - U(s)(\overline{r}) + \texttt{Accumulated}(l) > -mi$, we have $K = \gamma$, $tc = 0$, $s' = s$, $\overline{r'} = \overline{r''}$, and $l' = \texttt{Update}(l, U(s)(\overline{r'}) - U(s)(\overline{r}))$.

We denote by $\texttt{Evolutions}(M, c)$ the set of evolutions of M from c.

A *trace* of M from c is a list of evolutions l with either $l = [\,]$ or $l = e : l'$, where $e = (c, c', v)_K \in \texttt{Evolutions}(M, c)$ and l' is a trace of M from c'. We denote by $\texttt{Traces}(M, c)$ the set of traces of M from c. $\qquad\square$

Let us comment the previous definition. First, if one of the guards associated with a transition between states holds then the state changes. In addition, the time counter of the state is reset to 0 and the expiration dates of the pending accounts are shifted to fit the new counter. The second clause reflects the situation where the machine let the time pass by. In this case, the amount of time has to be less than or equal to the maximal waiting time. Besides, if the elapsed time is the one in which a positive or negative previous profit expires, then either this profit is considered *clear* or a *failure* is produced, respectively, being such profit eliminated from the list. In the second case, we label the transition by β' to denote an undesirable behavior of the agent associated to the corresponding USM. Finally, if a machine performs a transaction then we require that it does not give resources that it does not own and that the accumulated losses stay below the maximal threshold. When a transaction is executed then the pending accounts are updated to register the new transaction. Let us remark that the second and third types of transition can be performed only if the corresponding USM cannot change its state.

In the next definition we identify the traces that are free of failures.

Definition 6. Let M be a USM and c be a configuration of M. Let us suppose $c_1 = c$ and let $\sigma = [(c_1, c_2, t_1)_{K_1}, \ldots, (c_{n-1}, c_n, t_{n-1})_{K_{n-1}}] \in \texttt{Traces}(M, c)$ be a trace of M from c. We say that σ is a *valid trace* of M from c if there does not exist $1 \leq i \leq n-1$ such that $K_i = \beta'$. We define the set of valid traces of M from c by $\texttt{ValidTraces}(M, c)$. $\qquad\square$

3 Composing Single Agents to Create Systems

In the previous section we have defined the full set of valid transitions a USM can perform. Thus, the definition of the formal specification framework for a single agent is complete. At this point we have to extend the previous framework so that *systems*, made of USMs interacting among them, can be defined. This notion will allow us to represent e-commerce multi-agent environments. Intuitively, systems will be defined just as tuples of USMs, while the configuration of a system will be given by the tuple of configurations of each USM.

Definition 7. Let have $M_i = (S_i, s_{in\ i}, V, U_i, at_i, mi_i, T_i)$. We say that the tuple $S = (M_1, \ldots, M_m)$ is a *system* of USMs. For any $1 \leq i \leq m$, let c_i be the configuration of M_i. We say that $c = (c_1, \ldots, c_m)$ is the *configuration* of S. $\qquad\square$

The transitions of a system will not be the simple addition of the transitions of each USM within the system, as some of the actions a USM can perform will require *synchronization* with those performed by other USMs. This will be the case of passing of time and transactions. In the former case, the system will be able to idle an amount of time t provided that all of the USMs can idle t units of time. This does not constrain the capacity of agents to idle for longer periods since a long period of time could be denoted by several *time steps*. Let us note that passing of time will affect equally to all the USMs in the system. In other words, if a certain amount of time passes for one machine then it must also pass for any other machine of the system. Regarding synchronization of transactions, we will suppose that they are *conservative* in the sense that the total amount of resources existing in a system remains invariant after a transaction is performed. The only actions that do not require a synchronization are the ones associated with changing the state of a USM. In contrast with transactions and passing of time, changing the state is not a *voluntary* action. In other words, if the condition for a USM to change its state holds then that USM must change its state. In the meanwhile, transactions and passing of time transitions will be forbidden.

In the following definition we identify the set of evolutions a system can perform from a given configuration. Once again, a transition may be a changing of state, a passing of time, or a transaction. In order to make explicit the *failure* of any of the USMs in the system, we distinguish passing of time transitions producing a failure. In this case, we will explicitly indicate the set of USMs producing a failure. Hence, the label β_A denotes a passing of time transition in which the USMs included in A produced a failure. So, a failures-free passing of time transition is denoted by $\beta_\emptyset$.

Definition 8. Let $S = (M_1, \ldots, M_m)$ be a system and $c = (c_1, \ldots, c_m)$ be a configuration such that we have $M_i = (S_i, s_{in\ i}, V, U_i, at_i, mi_i, T_i)$ and $c_i = (s_i, \overline{r_i}, l_i)$ for any $1 \leq i \leq m$. An *evolution* of S from c is a tuple $(c, c', tc)_K$ where $c' = (c'_1, \ldots, c'_m)$, with $c'_i = (s'_i, \overline{r'_i}, l'_i)$, $K \in \{\alpha, \gamma\} \cup \{\beta_A \mid A \subseteq \{1, \ldots, m\}\}$, and $tc \in \mathbb{R}_+$ are defined according to the following options:

(1) (*Changing the state*) If there exists $(c_i, c''_i, 0)_\alpha \in \texttt{Evolutions}(M_i, c_i)$ then $K = \alpha$, $tc = 0$, and for any $1 \leq j \leq m$ we have $c'_j = c_j$ if $i \neq j$, while $c'_i = c''_i$.

(2) (*Passing of time*) If the condition of (1) does not hold and there exits tr such that for any $1 \leq i \leq m$ there exists $(c_i, c''_i, tr)_\delta \in \texttt{Evolutions}(M_i, c_i)$ with $\delta \in \{\beta, \beta'\}$, then $tc = tr$, $c'_i = c''_i$ for any $1 \leq i \leq m$, and $K = \beta_A$ where the set A is defined as $A = \{i \mid (c_i, c''_i, tr)_{\beta'} \in \texttt{Evolutions}(M_i, c_i)\}$.

(3) (*Transaction*) If the condition of (1) does not hold and there exist two indexes j and k, with $j \neq k$, such that for $l \in \{j, k\}$ we have $(c_l, c''_l, 0)_\gamma \in \texttt{Evolutions}(M_l, c_l)$ and $c''_l = (s''_i, \overline{r''_i}, l''_i)$, with $\overline{r_j} + \overline{r_k} = \overline{r''_j} + \overline{r''_k}$, then $K = \gamma$, $tc = 0$, $c'_j = c''_j$, $c'_k = c''_k$, and for any $1 \leq i \leq m$, with $i \neq j, k$, we have $c'_i = c_i$.

We denote by $\texttt{Evolutions}(S, c)$ the set of evolutions of S from c.

A *trace* of S from c is a list of evolutions l where either $l = [\,]$ or $l = e : l'$, being $e = (c, c', v)_K \in \texttt{Evolutions}(S, c)$ and l' a trace of S from c'. We denote by $\texttt{Traces}(S, c)$ the set of traces of S from c. □

Let us comment the previous definition. If a USM can change its state then the corresponding transition is performed while any other USM remains unmodified. If no USM can modify its state then passing of time and transaction transitions are enabled. In the first case, the system can let the time pass provided that all the USMs belonging to the system can. In the second case we require that trading USMs can (individually) perform the exchange and that goods are not created/destroyed as a result of the exchange. Let us note that only bilateral transactions are considered since any multilateral exchange can be expressed by means of the concatenation of some bilateral transactions.

Next we present a useful result in order to understand the behavior of transactions. We show that the utility of the agents that do not fail cannot decrease as long as they remain in the same state (that is, as long as they keep the same preferences), provided that the time has no influence on the utility in that state.

Lemma 1. Let $S = (M_1, \ldots, M_m)$ be a system where for any $1 \le j \le m$ we have $M_j = (S_j, s_{j\ in}, V_j, U_j, at_j, mi_j, T_j)$. Besides, let σ be a trace of S such that $\sigma = [(c_1, c_2, t_1)_{K_1}, \ldots, (c_{n-1}, c_n, t_{n-1})_{K_{n-1}}]$, where for any $1 \le j \le n$ we have $c_j = ((s_1^j, \overline{r_1^j}, l_1^j), \ldots, (s_m^j, \overline{r_m^j}, l_m^j))$. Let us suppose that for some $1 \le k \le m$ we have $l_k^n = [\,]$ and let $1 \le i \le n$ be such that $l_k^i = [\,]$ and for any $i \le j \le n$ it holds $s_k^j = s_k^i$ and $K_j \notin \{\beta_A \mid k \in A\}$. Let us also suppose that $\frac{\Delta U_k(s_k)(\overline{x})}{\Delta t} = 0$ holds. Under these conditions we have $U(s_k)(\overline{r_k^n}) \ge U(s_k)(\overline{r_k^i})$.

Proof. The agent M_k stays in the same state s_k^i from configuration c_i to configuration c_n. Thus, its utility function does not change during this period. In addition, since there does not exist K_j, with $i \le j \le n$, such that $K_j = \beta_A$, with $k \in A$, the agent M_k does not fail in the evolution from configuration c_i to configuration c_n. Let us suppose $U(s_k)(\overline{r_k^n}) < U(s_k)(\overline{r_k^i})$. Then, since the time does not affect the utility function of k because $\frac{\Delta U_k(s_k)(\overline{x})}{\Delta t} = 0$, the reduction of utility must be produced by a transaction. So, the set $Q \subseteq \{i, \ldots, n\}$ such that for any $j \in Q$ it holds $K_j = \gamma$ and $U(s_k)(\overline{r_k^j}) < U(s_k)(\overline{r_k^{j-1}})$ must be non-empty. Let us note that for each $j \in Q$ the effect of such negative transaction will be immediately included in its list of pending accounts l_k^j. However, since $l_k^n = [\,]$, such a profit disappears from the list before the nth transition is performed. So, there are two possibilities: Either the negative profit expired (which is impossible, since M_k did not fail) or it was compensated before achieving c_n. Nevertheless, if it was compensated then it cannot influence negatively the final utility of M_k. Thus, we conclude that $U(s_k)(\overline{r_k^n}) < U(s_k)(\overline{r_k^i})$ is not possible.

□

Similarly to the reasoning that we did for single agents, we can identify the valid traces of systems. In this case, we are interested in identifying the traces such that a specific USM belonging to the system produces no failure.

Definition 9. Let $S = (M_1, \ldots, M_m)$ be a system and c be a configuration of S. Let us suppose $c_1 = c$ and let $\sigma = [(c_1, c_2, t_1)_{K_1}, \ldots, (c_{n-1}, c_n, t_{n-1})_{K_{n-1}}] \in$ Traces(S, c) be a trace of S from c. We say that σ is a *valid trace* of S from c for the USM M_i if there does not exist $1 \leq j \leq n-1$ such that $K_j = \beta_A$ with $i \in A$. We denote the set of valid traces of S from c for M_i by ValidTraces(S, c, M_i).

$\square$

4 Case Study: Kasbah

In this section we apply our formalism to specify the system Kasbah [3]. Kasbah is one of the pioneer proposals in the field of e-commerce multi-agent systems. It consists of a market of autonomous commerce agents that behave on behalf of their corresponding users. The agents interact with each other in order to reach good deals. Basically, agents are either *sellers* or *buyers*. Each agent is intended to buy or sell one single specific item at the best possible price (lowest or highest respectively). Every time a user wishes to perform a selling/buying operation, he creates a new Kasbah agent. Let us suppose that he wants to buy an item (the case of selling is symmetric). The user chooses the item he wants to buy and configures the agent according to four requirements: The initial price it should offer to an agent selling that item (ip), the maximal price it should pay in exchange of the item (mp), the deadline when it should refuse to buy the item (d), and a function denoting the way the agent should increase the buying price as time passes. This last function can be linear, square, or cubic. It will work so that the price mp will be offered exactly when d comes. The function will be defined by its exponent ex. So, if it denotes the kind of item the buying agent is interested in, mo denotes the money, and t denotes the time elapsed, then the utility function of the buying agent is defined as

$$u(t, it, mo) = mo + (ip + \alpha \cdot t)^{ex} \cdot it$$

where $\alpha = \frac{mp^{\frac{1}{ex}} - ip}{d}$. The value α can be easily obtained by taking into account that the maximal price mp should be paid just when the deadline d expires.

Using a similar reasoning, the utility function for a seller agent is defined as

$$u(t, it, mo) = mo + (ip - \alpha \cdot t)^{ex} \cdot it$$

where $\alpha = \frac{ip - mp^{\frac{1}{ex}}}{d}$. Both buyer and seller agents will be specified by using a USM with two states. The first one, s_1, will denote that the agent is active, that is, it can make transactions with other agents. The second one, s_2, represents that the agent is inactive. As long as the agent stays in s_1, it can make a deal with another agent provided that the transaction is *good* according to its utility function. If the time runs out and the deadline comes before any transaction is performed then the agent state changes to s_2. In s_2 no transaction is accepted by the agent. This will be expressed, in the case of the buyer, by using a utility function that gives a full importance to money, so transactions will be no longer

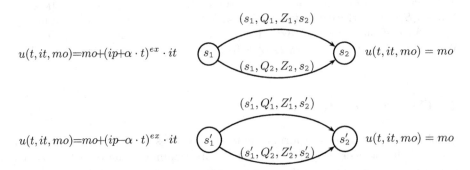

Fig. 2. USMs of the buyer and seller agents

possible. Besides, in the case that a transaction is performed before the deadline, the agent will immediately move to the state s_2. The corresponding transition will indicate that the item is deleted from the basket of resources of the agent, denoting that the agent sends the bought item to its user.

Definition 10. The USM M_b associated to a buyer agent is defined as the tuple $(S, s_{in}, V, U, at, mi, T)$, where $S = \{s_1, s_2\}$, $s_{in} = s_1$, $V = (t, it, mo)$, at and mi are set to any arbitrary values, U is defined as

$$U(s_1)(t, it, mo) = mo + (ip + \alpha \cdot t)^{ex} \cdot it \qquad \text{where } \alpha = \frac{mp^{\frac{1}{ex}} - ip}{d}$$
$$U(s_2)(t, it, mo) = mo$$

and the set of transitions T is defined as $T = \{(s_1, Q_1, Z_1, s_2), (s_1, Q_2, Z_2, s_2)\}$, where $Q_1(t, it, mo)$ holds iff $t \geq d$, $Z_1(it, mo) = (it, mo)$, $Q_2(t, it, mo)$ holds iff $it = 1$, and $Z_2(it, mo) = (it - 1, mo)$.   □

The definition of the USM M_s associated with sellers is quite similar. The only differences are the utility function in the first state s_1', which is defined as we said before, and the functions denoting the modification of resources in transitions. In this case, the roles of Z_1 and Z_2 must be swapped, as the item will be returned to the user in the case that it could not be sold. In Figure 2 we show graphical representations of the USMs corresponding to buyers and sellers. Once both buyer and seller agents are defined, a minimal system S can be trivially defined by composing both agents so that $S = (M_b, M_s)$. More complex systems can be defined containing several buyers and sellers that trade with different items.

5   Conclusions and Future Work

In this paper we have presented a framework to formally specify e-commerce systems where agents represent the interest of the users. We concentrated on the high level part of the behavior of agents. We have used a notion, called *utility state machines*, that allows us to specify the economic behavior of agents. Finally, we have applied our framework to the specification of the main entities appearing in Kasbah.

We contemplate two lines for future work. In the first one, with a major theoretical component, we plan to extend our notion of USM so that low level behavior is also taken into account. In the second one, with a more practical component, we would like to apply our framework to other agent-based e-commerce systems (as we have done with Kasbah).

References

[1] A. Bhimani. Securing the commercial Internet. *Communications of the ACM*, 39(6):29–35, 1996. 30

[2] S. Braynov. Tutorial on *agent-mediated electronic commerce* at AIMSA'02, 2002. 30

[3] A. Chavez and P. Maes. Kasbah: An agent marketplace for buying and selling goods. In *PAAM'96*, pages 75–90, 1996. 41

[4] M. Dastani, N. Jacobs, C. M. Jonker, and J. Treur. Modelling user preferences and mediating agents in electronic commerce. In *Agent Mediated Electronic Commerce, LNCS 1991*, pages 163–193. Springer, 2001. 31

[5] B. Geisler, V. Ha, and P. Haddawy. Modeling user preferences via theory refinement. In *Int. Conf. on Intelligent User Interfaces*, pages 87–90. ACM Press, 2001. 31

[6] R. Guttman, A. Moukas, and P. Maes. Agent-mediated electronic commerce: A survey. *The Knowledge Engineering Review*, 13(2):147–159, 1998. 31

[7] V. Ha and P. Haddawy. Similarity of personal preferences: Theoretical foundations and empirical analysis. *Artificial Intelligence*, 146(2):149–173, 2003. 31

[8] M. He, N. R. Jennings, and H. Leung. On agent-mediated electronic commerce. *IEEE Trans. on Knowledge and Data Engineering*, 15(4):985–1003, 2003. 31

[9] N. López, M. Núñez, I. Rodríguez, and F. Rubio. A formal framework for e-barter based on microeconomic theory and process algebras. In *Innovative Internet Computer Systems, LNCS 2346*, pages 217–228. Springer, 2002. 31

[10] N. López, M. Núñez, I. Rodríguez, and F. Rubio. A multi-agent system for e-barter including transaction and shipping costs. In *18th ACM Symposium on Applied Computing, SAC'03*, pages 587–594. ACM Press, 2003. 31

[11] M. Ma. Agents in e-commerce. *Communications of the ACM*, 42(3):79–80, 1999. 31

[12] M. Núñez and I. Rodríguez. PAMR: A process algebra for the management of resources in concurrent systems. In *FORTE 2001*, pages 169–185. Kluwer Academic Publishers, 2001. 31

[13] I. Rodríguez. Formal specification of autonomous commerce agents. In *19th ACM Symposium on Applied Computing, SAC'04*, pages 774–778. ACM Press, 2004. 31

[14] T. Sandholm. Agents in electronic commerce: Component technologies for auto-mated negotiation and coalition formation. In *CIA '98, LNCS 1435*, pages 113–134. Springer, 1998. 31

An Approach for Assessment of Electronic Offers

Bettina Bazijanec, Key Pousttchi, and Klaus Turowski

Business Informatics and Systems Engineering, University of Augsburg
Universitätsstraße 16, 86135 Augsburg, Germany
{bettina.bazijanec,key.pousttchi,klaus.turowski}@wiwi.uni-
augsburg.de

Abstract. Internet and mobile technology enable businesses to invent new business models by applying new forms of organization or offering new products and services. In order to assess these new business models there has to be a methodology that allows identifying advantages that are caused by electronic and mobile commerce. The proposed approach builds upon the theory of informational added values that provides a classification of gains produced by information work. This theory is extended by the definition of categories of technology inherent added values that result in informational added values. These informational added values can be perceived by users of information products and services and therefore be used to assess electronic offers. The relationship between technology inherent and informational added values will be clarified with examples of real business models. Furthermore, a classification of basic business model types will be provided.

1   Introduction

Applications that build upon Internet technology like E-mail and the World Wide Web made possible a completely new use of digitally available information. Starting from a simple text-based information exchange, the Internet has become a world-wide information system and application platform. In the end of the 1990's the Internet hype facilitated the foundation of many new companies that formed the so called New Economy. Even after the industry cooled down and many of the Dotcoms disappeared, companies are still in the position to make money on the Internet and Digital Transformation of organizations is going on. There has to be something inherent to this technology that causes positive effects on businesses and also on every day's life.

An analysis of the Internet's characteristics shows important properties that can help to explain this phenomenon: Global interconnectedness and instantaneous transport of information based on standardized protocols combined with a previously not possible presentation potential allowed to offer products and services based on new business models. In the recent years mobile communication techniques introduced new technical properties and expanded already present ones. They have become a basis for new business models. But again, the same happened with these business models as with the Internet-based ones: Many of them were presented and most of them already disappeared, e.g. in the field of mobile payment [6]. In order to assess existing and future business models based on modern information and communication

M. Núñez et al. (Eds.): FORTE 2004 Workshops, LNCS 3236, pp. 44-57, 2004.
© Springer-Verlag Berlin Heidelberg 2004

technologies there is a need for an evaluation methodology. Technological capabilities have to be identified as well as benefits that users and producers of electronic offers can achieve when using them.

The rest of this paper is organized as follows. Section 2 discusses related work in the field of assessment of business models and introduces the theory of informational added values. This theory allows describing advantages caused by information systems or goods and services that were produced with their help. These advantages are called informational added values and can be categorized depending on different aspects of utility. In section 3 Internet and mobile technology are analyzed in order to define characteristics of information and communication systems that are built upon them. These will be termed electronic added values and mobile added values. In section 4 it is explained how electronic and mobile added values can cause informational added values and how this can be used for an assessment of electronic offers. Furthermore, basic types of business models will be described and categorized that represent the building blocks for more complex ones. In section 5 an exemplary business model will be assessed with the help of the proposed methodology. Section 6 gives a summary and outlook.

2   Informational Added Values

Every business model has to prove that it is able to generate a benefit for the customers that will pay for it. This is especially true for businesses that offer their products or services on the Internet. Since the beginning of Internet business in the mid 1990s models have been developed that tried to explain advantages that arose from electronic offers. An extensive overview of approaches can be found in [11]. At first, models were rather a collection of at that time few business models that had already proven to be able to generate a revenue stream [3, 15, 18]. Later approaches extended these collections to a comprehensive taxonomy of business models observable on the web [13, 17]. Only [18] provided a first classification of eleven business models along two dimensions: innovation and functional integration. Due to many different aspects that have to be considered when comparing business models authors introduced taxonomies with different views on Internet business. This provides an overall picture of a firm doing Internet business [10], where the views are discussed separately [1, 2, 5, 14, 22]. Views are for example commerce strategy, organizational structure or business process. The two most important views that can be found in every approach are value proposition and revenue. A comparison of proposed views in different approaches can be found in [16]. While the view revenue describes the rather short-term monetary aspect of a business model the value proposition characterizes the type of business that is the basis of any revenue stream. To describe this value proposition authors decomposed business models into their atomic elements [9]. These elements represent offered services or products. Models that follow this approach are for example [1] and [22]. Another approach that already focuses on generated value can be found in [9]. There, four so called value streams are identified: virtual communities, reduction of transaction costs, gainful exploitation of information asymmetry, and a value added marketing process. Some approaches define an enterprise ontology to be able to describe actors and value exchanges in a given business model scenario [4, 17, 21]. However, no systematics is provided that links types of offered products and services to generated values for participating actors.

Since companies use Internet technology to improve their value production, it has to be determined what kinds of benefit can theoretically be realized for customers, vendors or even involved third parties. The *theory of informational added values* [8] provides an analysis of the impacts of information work in information markets. Utility that can be perceived by users of goods that result from information work is represented as a set of *informational added values (IAV)*. As there are different aspects of utility, informational added values can be classified into eight main categories. There are efficiency, effectiveness, aesthetic-emotional, flexible, innovative, organizational, strategic, and macroeconomic added values.

- *Efficiency added values* can be realized when the speed or the cost-effectiveness of an operation increases. For example, customers of online services like online banking or brokerage can initiate transactions at home instead of going to a certain location during business hours and therefore save time. Not only is this beneficial for customers but also for service providers because the task of collecting data and filling out forms is already performed by the customer. In this way a better cost-effectiveness can be achieved.

- *Effectiveness added values* cover an augmentation in output quality. This can be either a better achievement of a given goal or that something is made possible that previously did not work. An example would be a search engine that is able to find the location of books in a library based on the title. If books were also available as electronic editions, then this would allow downloading the document. This would further increase the achievement of the given goal, namely to find and read a book.

- *Aesthetic-emotional added values* address subjective factors such as well-being, job-satisfaction or acceptance of performance. This added value can be found for example in above mentioned online brokerage example. The user can access stock exchange information through an online-portal where multiple charts with information about the current trading situation are presented. The customer is now able to see a lot of information at once, without having to search for it.

- *Flexible added values* allow a higher level of flexibility in the production of goods and services that consist of information. This can for example be found in the production of personalized music CDs where tracks can be arranged according to the individual wish of a customer. Therefore the variability of goods increases, i.e. there is a greater range of offered products. This variability can also be achieved for classical goods and services with the help of modern information and communication techniques, e.g. with production planning systems. It is suitable to extend the definition of flexible added values to the production of classical goods.

- *Innovative added values* cover the creation of entirely new products or services (or a combination of both) through the usage of new means of communication. Online services that provide driving directions would not be possible without the use of the Internet. Another example is the customer-individual production of bulk articles through mass customization strategies. The innovative aspect here is that these personalized articles are sold with only a slightly higher price. But from an organization's perspective, innovative added values will disappear, when other companies offer the same product or service.

- *Organizational added values* cover the opportunity to build new forms of organization through the use of information and communication systems. This can affect companies' organization structures as well as the reorganization of their business processes. Focus here is on administrative and dispositional activities. Examples for the creation of organizational added values through information and communication technology are virtual companies as temporary, mission-bound networks or mobile access to enterprise resource planning systems.

- *Strategic added values* qualify advantages that go beyond the operational and tactical level by influencing a company's position in a market segment. If a significant competitive edge can be achieved or disadvantages regarding the market share can be avoided strategic added values are present. A strategic advantage is always based on one or more other added values, e.g. on the opportunity of worldwide customer acquisition for a small specialized company that has an added value with effectiveness impact on customer reach.

- *Macroeconomic added values* describe advantages that go beyond the level of single companies and result in impacts on economy or society as a whole. These added values also emerge from one or more of the other added values and denote improvements in the achievement potential of a society. For instance the effect of office automation to the occupational image of a secretary. Nowadays, the role of a secretary is more an executive assistant than a copy typist.

The different aspects of utility that are provided by these eight categories have also different user perspectives. Macroeconomic added values aim at improvements of a whole society. Strategic, organizational, innovative, and flexible added values can only be realized in organizations that offer goods or services. Efficiency, effectiveness, and aesthetic-emotional added values can even be realized by a single person. This can be a private user or employees of the above mentioned organizations. But organization-centric added values can also affect private users because improvements within companies can be handed on to customers for example by reducing prices or offering new or more products. It can also be noticed that often informational added values cannot be seen separately from each other. For example, there are interrelations between effectiveness and efficiency added values. In the library example, the goal achievement can be measured in increased speed of search and is therefore more efficient. Another example is increased customer satisfaction for a parcel service through enhanced skills in shipment tracking. An online tracking system produces aesthetic-emotional and effectiveness added values that can as well be accompanied with an efficiency added value, if this solution decreases the number of call center operators at the same time. Since strategic and macroeconomic added values can not appear individually, their existence can only be explained with the dependence on other added values. Therefore it can be stated that the determination of informational added values in electronic offers always depends on the particular point of view and the aspect one wants to examine. Also, it is not excluded that one added value causes another, e.g. organizational improvements can lead to cost savings or to higher job-satisfaction.

3   Electronic and Mobile Added Values

3.1   Concept

Informational added values as described in section 2 are impacts of information work that is performed in order to produce or use goods and services. This is based on technologies that provide new possibilities of handling and transport of information. Modern information and communication systems have advantageous properties that represent technology-specific added values. Such system technology-specific added values are not informational added values but they can cause them. IAV result from the use of information systems (or from goods and services that have been produced with their help) if users accept to pay for their anticipated benefit or if they appreciate them in another than monetary way [8]. To understand and discern conditions and results, technology-specific added values have to be identified. Technologies relevant to this question are the Internet and mobile communication techniques. Mobile communication builds upon techniques that are already used in Internetworking and adds some more properties to it. Therefore these two technologies will be analyzed separately to show, which characteristics dominate and which technology-specific added values exist in each case.

3.2   Electronic Added Values

In order to define general added values of Internet technology, its properties have to be analyzed. Networked computers are able to exchange digital data without any reasonable delay, i.e. *instantaneous transport* of information is possible. *Standardized* communication protocols like the TCP and IP as well as emerging standards for data exchange and media representation allow interconnection of computers based on different operating systems and application systems. These standards have led to a *global interconnectedness* of networks and computers. Every computer that is connected to the Internet is able to exchange data with every other in this global network even if they are separated by thousands of miles. Due to its non-proprietary character there are *no access restrictions* to the Internet. Another property is the enhanced *presentation potential* that was added to the Internet. Today, browsers are able to present not only text annotated with HTML-tags but also images, audio and even real-time video streams. Based on these properties four added values can be defined for Internet-based technology. These are called *electronic added values (EAV)*:

- *Reduction of temporal and certain spatial limitations*
  This added value is based on the properties instantaneous transport and interconnectedness. Online offers can therefore be accessed at any time and from almost everywhere without any noticeable time delay. Only a computer connected to the Internet is needed. Data exchange is not reduced to textual information so that digital products and services, e.g. music can also be transmitted. Even a combination with classical goods is possible where a product is ordered online and delivered by a logistics provider. This EAV mainly causes efficiency and organizational added values. It can be used for many business models because time and location independent access can be realized without much additional

effort. But to offer a 24/7 service a suitable server infrastructure has to be maintained.

- *Reduction of technical limitations*
  This EAV can be explained with the existence of communication and presentation standards. This facilitates the elimination of heterogeneity problems. A wide range of applications, especially business applications, benefit from this added value. Data and process integration can be achieved and inconsistencies caused by handoffs will be reduced. This added value leads in particular to organizational, efficiency and effectiveness added values.

- *Unrestricted access*
  The concept of the Internet is based on free access through standardized protocols. Everybody is able to connect to the network without having to buy expensive technology, and the number of participants is not restricted. For example, a Web site of a small company has the same preconditions as the one of a global player. Everyone can offer and use information or services on the Internet so that transparency of the market increases. To benefit from this transparency search engines and directories are needed in order to find certain offers. This EAV mainly causes strategic added values that are based on efficiency, effectiveness, and aesthetic-emotional added values.

- *Multi-mediality and interaction*
  Multi-mediality describes the enhanced presentation potential of the Internet that can be used to stimulate users. This is extended with interaction capabilities that make use of the instantaneous transport of data. Thus, direct and personalized interaction is possible, e.g. for product configuration. This EAV often leads to effectiveness and aesthetic-emotional added values and can also cause innovative added values.

3.3   Mobile Added Values

Mobile communication techniques extend Internet technologies and add some more characteristics that can be considered as additional benefits. Therefore an own class of technology-specific added values is defined and named *mobile added values (MAV)*. These added values based on mobility of portable devices are:

- *Ubiquity*
  This MAV describes the possibility to send and receive data anytime and anywhere. It is originated in the typical usage of mobile devices which accompany their user nearly anytime and anywhere. It permits the reception of time-critical and private information. Additionally, persistent attendance leads to an increased reachability. For example it allows getting warnings about stock exchange loss even if the recipient is not reachable by other forms of communication. This MAV can cause all of the mentioned IAV, especially efficiency, effectiveness, and aesthetic-emotional added values.

- *Context-sensitivity*
  Mobile devices can be used for delivery of customized products or services fitting the particular needs of the user in his current situation. This can be achieved in

several ways. The current location of the user can be determined and, if necessary, correlations with the location of other users can be analyzed. Sensors that are built into mobile devices can send information about an user's vital functions over the mobile network. Two other possibilities are already known from electronic business. Personalized preference profiles and direct interaction can also be applied in a mobile scenario where they get a higher importance. Typical applications based on the MAV of context-sensitivity are location based services. Context-sensitivity also leads to all IAV, and in particular, innovative added values are possible.

- *Identifying functions*
  The possibility to authenticate the owner of any mobile device through his subscriber identification is immanent to a cellular phone network. The typical 1:1-attribution of a mobile device to its user (which is perhaps not true for any other technical device except a wristwatch) and the possibility to use further means of authentication on the device result in *identifying functions* of mobile devices. This MAV can be used for applications with security restrictions like mobile payment or for applications that utilize user profiles based on the behavior of the customer, enabling 1:1 marketing concepts. Mainly, effectiveness added values can be realized with identifying functions.

- *Command and control functions*
  Mobile devices can be used as remote control for other devices using personal, local, or wide area networks. Mobile technology extends previous Internet-based solutions, where remote control was only possible for stationary devices. Now, the combination with ubiquity allows that the target device may be mobile, too. This could be the mobile phone of other users or a device with ubiquitous computing technology so that rule based automation and device-to-device (D2D)-communication is possible. Command and control functions primarily cause effectiveness added values.

4   Assessment of Electronic Offers

4.1   Methodology of the Added Value Concept

After having presented informational as well as electronic and mobile added values, it is possible to analyze dependencies between them. Benefits of an electronic offer are assessed by comparing it with a non-electronic offer [12]. Since it is not sufficient to simply make a conventional (non-electronic) offer available through a web site or mobile device, e.g. digital photographs of a newspaper, informational added values are necessary to give users a reason for accessing it. In order to determine how and which informational added values can be derived from electronic and mobile offers, a methodology will be introduced next.

When comparing an offline solution to an according electronic offer, e.g. a newspaper with its online edition, then informational added values have to be created for at least one participating group of actors, in this case users or publisher. These IAV can only be derived from electronic added values that were used to create this offer. Figure 1 shows the systematics of application.

If EAV are applicable, this results in IAV that have not been existent in the offline solution. If a mobile offer is examined, then MAV have to be identified that are applicable to this solution. These MAV result in additional IAV compared with the electronic offer. In our example, the online edition of a newspaper results, among other, in efficiency added values, because news can be presented immediately instead of the next day. A mobile solution, where news can be pushed on the device, results in additional efficiency added values, because it allows reaching the user faster. Considerations like that have to be done for every EAV-IAV-combination in an electronic offer and for mobile offers respectively.

The diagram shown in figure 2 allows a structured analysis of the dependencies between EAV and IAV. EAV can be found in the rows of the matrix and IAV in the columns. For a particular business model it is analyzed if an EAV is applicable at all. If yes, then for all possible IAV an estimation of influence is given. In this model *strong influence*, *influence*, or *no influence* is possible. The estimation is dependent on the person who analyzes. A customer would probably have another estimation as the service offerer. Ideally, an independent person should assess the business model and consider all points of view.

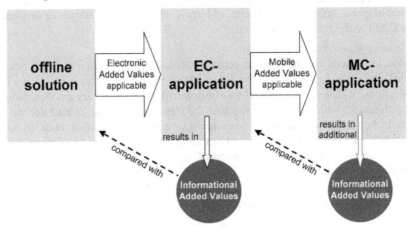

Fig. 1. Derivation of informational added values

There is only an ordinal scale provided, what can cause inconsistent assessments when more than one person separately analyze one offer. However, the possibility that dependencies between certain EAV and IAV are equally assessed is high, if for every IAV all necessary criteria are defined, e.g. efficiency added values describe the improvement of two criteria, namely time and cost.

4.2 Typology of Business Models

The evaluation of real business models showed that some few business model types recur. These basic business model types have been used for building up more complex business models. They can be classified according to the type of offered product or service. A categorization based on this criteria is highly extensible and thus very generic [19]. Unlike other classifications of electronic offers (see section 4.1) this approach can also be applied to mobile business models that e.g. use location based services to provide a user context. Even future business models can be integrated that are not yet known.

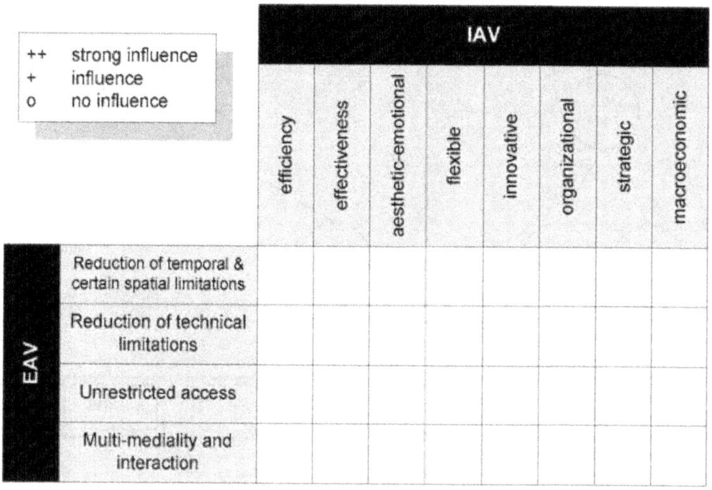

Fig. 2. Diagram for a structured analysis of dependencies

Figure 3 shows the categorization of business model types based on offered service. First, it has to be distinguished whether goods and services can be produced and exchanged exclusively in a digital way. If there is a part of production that cannot be done only by data exchange, i.e. there is a physical product involved. *Not digital* goods and services can be tangible or intangible. While physical products themselves are tangible services that only need physical objects to be performed are intangible. Hence two basic types can be derived: *classical goods* and *classical service*. Digital goods and services can be divided into *action* and *information*.

The category *information* represents the offering of data, e.g. multi-media content for entertainment purposes or daily news. Basic types are *context* and *content*. An offer has the basic type *context* if it describes, uses, or provides information about someone's situation, e.g. position, environment or needs. This can be achieved either by user profiling or more effectively by suitable mobile technology. The category *content* describes offers that provide news and information about politics, economics, entertainment, arts and so on. Online and mobile games are also included. Activities that process, manipulate, transform, select, or systematize data are contained in the category *action*. This category consists of three basic types: *Service*, *intermediation*, and *integration*. *Service* contains offers where activities using digitally encoded data are provided e.g. an online translation service. Activities that classify, search, select or mediate belong to the basic type *intermediation*, e.g. search engines. Finally, the category *integration* comprises offers that combine several other offers to one, probably with the use of personalization. This can even lead to user individual offers where the user does not even know about the combination of different offers. For example, an offer could be an insurance bundle specifically adjusted to a customer's needs. The individual products may come from different insurance companies.

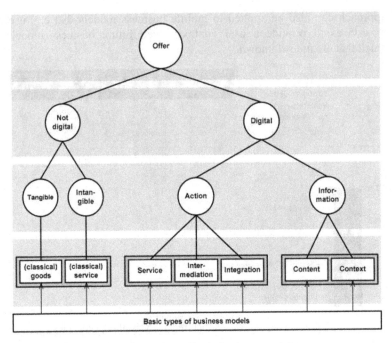

Fig. 3. Categorization of basic business model types

The goal of the proposed approach is to be able to assess business models and also non-commercial offers that are based on modern information and communication techniques. Therefore, an empirical analysis of real business models has to show, whether informational added values and the methodology to identify them is suitable. In a study, the methodology was successfully applied to 153 real business models of electronic and mobile commerce. In order to show how the approach was used, one example of an assessment will be presented next.

5   Example: The Business Model of TVinfo

TVinfo [20] provides television program information on the Internet. There is no printed edition. Unregistered users can browse the program and read news related to entertainment. Registration is free of charge and allows using more services. Registered users can customize their view, i.e. they can choose what channels will be displayed and also how information is presented. There is a service that allows putting a television program overview on private homepages. A personal agent can be used to find certain television programs based on title, director and actors. The agent searches the future television program based on these criteria. There is also the possibility to buy a program subscription which allows selecting movies online, and automatically program a digital video recorder based on special software provided by partner companies. This software can be ordered online as well as the subscription itself. Programs can be added to a reminder. Entries can be viewed online or sent to a mobile phone by a SMS-service. A second mobile offer is the possibility to download the customized television program to a PDA using the AvantGo software [7]. These two mobile offers will not be considered below.

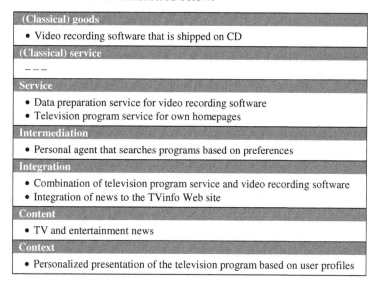

(Classical) goods
- Video recording software that is shipped on CD

(Classical) service
- – –

Service
- Data preparation service for video recording software
- Television program service for own homepages

Intermediation
- Personal agent that searches programs based on preferences

Integration
- Combination of television program service and video recording software
- Integration of news to the TVinfo Web site

Content
- TV and entertainment news

Context
- Personalized presentation of the television program based on user profiles

Fig. 4. Classification of the TVinfo's business model

Four participating groups of actors can be identified: Viewers, TV channels, TVinfo, and software vendors. For these groups all IAV have to be determined. Before this is done the business model of TVinfo will be classified according to the proposed categorization. For this purpose, a list is compiled where all seven basic business model types appear. For each basic business model type occurrences are documented. Fig. 4. shows the classification of TVinfo's business model. For each identified basic business model type the dependencies between EAV and IAV can now be analyzed. One can thereby revert to general relations between specific EAV and IAV that are reflected in specific business model types. For example, the business model type integration uses two EAV, namely reduction of technical limitations and multi-mediality and interaction. These result mainly in effectiveness added values so that this IAV is likely to appear when using this basic business model type. In the following these considerations have been made and aggregated so that for each EAV the resulting IAV can be listed.

Reduction of temporal and certain spatial limitations has a strong influence on efficiency. Users save time because there is no need to buy a television program magazine at a store. Cost can also be saved but only if the user has not to be online very long in order to get the desired information. Greater effectiveness can be perceived by the online publisher, software vendors, and the TV channels. Combined with the unrestricted access much more potential viewers can be informed about the television program. *Reduction of technical limitations* allows users to automate video recording by using TVinfo's program data with the recording software. This results primarily in increased effectiveness and also leads to efficiency and aesthetic-emotional added values, because the user can save the time of manually programming the video recorder. The software vendors that cooperate with TVinfo will be able to sell more of their recording software due to this effective advertising. From TVinfo's perspective more variants of its product can be offered and thus flexibility added values can be realized. Since such an automation of video recording has not been possible before this also causes innovative added values. *Unrestricted access* results in IAV for TV channels and viewers. TVinfo offers program information without having to register or pay. TV channels can reach more potential viewers with their television program and therefore realize effectiveness added values. Unregistered users of TVinfo are able to access full information what increases their contentedness. *Multi-mediality* and interaction allows personalization of the television program based on user input. Users are able to find information more quickly if their view is customized to their needs. This is more effective and also more efficient. Besides that personalization results in higher variability of the television program service and thus in flexible added values. Innovative added values are caused by the search agent that interacts with the user. As soon as an appropriate program is found it puts the information to a list so that the user is able to read it.

Since TVinfo has no printed edition the identified IAV have to form a strategic added value so that it can still exist on the market. Reachability is given by reduction of temporal and certain spatial limitation in combination with unrestricted access. The offer is highly customizable through the reduction of technical limitation and multi-mediality and interaction. Resulting from that the offer is primarily more effective compared to the offline solution. From the user's perspective also efficiency and aesthetic-emotional added values play an important role. TVinfo has increased flexibility in the production of its service and can also offer an innovative product in cooperation with its software partners. Figure 5 shows the matrix after assessment of the business model:

		IAV							
++ strong influence + influence o no influence		efficiency	effectiveness	aesthetic-emotional	flexible	innovative	organizational	strategic	macroeconomic
EAV	Reduction of temporal & certain spatial limitations	++	+	+	o	o	o	+	o
	Reduction of technical limitations	+	++	+	+	+	o	+	o
	Unrestricted access	o	+	+	o	o	o	+	o
	Multi-mediality and interaction	+	++	+	++	+	o	+	o

Fig. 5. Assessment of TVinfo's business model

6   Conclusion and Future Work

This paper presents an approach to assess electronic and mobile offers. The theory of informational added values was extended by the definition of technology-specific properties that are advantageous when using them to build up business models or other solutions based on information and communication techniques. These so called electronic and mobile added values are the cause of informational added values. In order to identify particular dependencies between EAV/MAV and IAV in real business models a methodology was proposed. First, a business model is categorized into basic business model types, and then each basic offer is evaluated in respect of the existence of EAV and resulting IAV. Thus, with the help of this methodology one can clearly describe cause and result of an electronic offer. In order to build a comprehensive framework for comparison of business models, resulting IAV have to be quantified based on some criteria e.g. cost savings, extent of data redundancy, number of variants or willingness to pay. Up to now, only an estimation of influence is given.

References

[1]   Afuah, A., Tucci, C., *Internet Business Models and Strategies*, McGraw Hill, Boston, 2001.
[2]   Bartelt, A., Lamersdorf, W., *Geschäftsmodelle des Electronic Commerce: Modell-bildung und Klassifikation, Verbundtagung Wirtschaftsinformatik*, Shaker, 2000.
[3]   Fedewa, C. S., *Business models for Internetpreneurs*, 1996.
       http://www.gen.com/iess/articles/art4.html
[4]   Gordijn, J., Akkermans, J., van Vliet, J., *Designing and Evaluating E-Business Models*, IEEE Intelligent Systems, 16 (2001), pp. 11-17.
[5]   Hamel, G., *Leading the revolution*, Harvard Business School Press, Boston, 2000.
[6]   Heinkele, C., *Überblick und Einordnung ausgewählter Mobile Payment-Verfahren*, Report, Chair of Business Informatics and Systems Engineering, University of Augsburg, Augsburg, 2003.
[7]   iAnywhere, http://www.ianywhere.com/avantgo/aboutus/index.html, accessed 16.04.2004.
[8]   Kuhlen, R., *Informationsmarkt: Chancen und Risiken der Kommerzialisierung von Wissen*, Universitätsverlag Konstanz, Konstanz, 1996.
[9]   Mahadevan, B., *Business Models for Internet based E-Commerce: An Anatomy*, California Management Review, 42 (2000).
[10]   Osterwalder, A., *An e-Business Model Ontology for the Creation of New Management Software Tools and IS Requirement Engineering*,
       http://www.hec.unil.ch/aosterwa/Documents/eBusinessModels/Publications/CR_CAISE02_PHD_02.pdf.
[11]   Pateli, A., Giaglis, G. M., *A Domain Area Report on Business Models*, Athens University of Economics and Business, Athens, Greece, 2002.
[12]   Pousttchi, K., Turowski, K., Weizmann, M., *Added Value-based Approach to Analyze Electronic Commerce and Mobile Commerce Business Models*, in R. Andrade, J. Gómez, C. Rautenstrauch and R. Rios, eds., *International Conference Management and Technology in the New Enterprise*, CUJAE, La Habana, 2003, pp. 414-423.
[13]   Rappa, M., *Managing the digital enterprise - Business models on the Web*, http://digitalenterprise.org/models/models.html, accessed 14.06.2004.

[14]   Rayport, J. F., Jaworski, B. J., *E-Commerce*, McGraw-Hill/Irwin, New York, 2001.
[15]   Schlachter, E., *Generating revenues from websites*, *Board Watch*, 1995.
        http://boardwatch.internet.com/mag/95/jul/bwm39.htm
[16]   Schwickert, A. C., *Geschäftsmodelle im Electronic Business - Bestandsaufnahme und Relativierung*, Professur BWL-Wirtschaftsinformatik, Justus-Liebig-Universität, Gießen, 2004.
[17]   Tapscott, D., Lowi, A., Ticoll, D., *Digital Capital - Harnessing the Power of Business Webs*, Harvard Business School Press, Boston, 2000.
[18]   Timmers, P., *Business models for Electronic Markets*, Electronic Markets, 8 (1998), pp. 3-8.
[19]   Turowski, K., Pousttchi, K., *Mobile Commerce - Grundlagen und Techniken*, Springer Verlag, Heidelberg, 2003.
[20]   TVinfo, http://www.tvinfo.de, accessed 16.04.2004.
[21]   Weill, P., Vitale, M. R., *Place to Space: Migrating to eBusiness Models*, Harvard Business School Press, Boston, 2001.
[22]   Wirtz, B., Kleineicken, A., *Geschäftsmodelltypen im Internet*, WiSt, 29 (2000), pp. 628-636.

A Decomposition Based Approach for Design of Supply Aggregation and Demand Aggregation Exchanges

Shantanu Biswas[1], Y. Narahari[1], and Anish Das Sarma[2]

[1] Electronic Enterprises Laboratory, Computer Science & Automation
Indian Institute of Science, Bangalore, India
{biswas,hari}@csa.iisc.ernet.in
[2] Computer Science & Engineering
Indian Institute of Technology, Bombay, India
anish@cse.iitb.ac.in

Abstract. Combinatorial exchanges are double sided marketplaces with multiple sellers and multiple buyers trading with the help of combinatorial bids. The allocation and other associated problems in such exchanges are known to be among the hardest to solve among all economic mechanisms. In this paper, we study combinatorial exchanges where (1) the demand can be aggregated, for example, a procurement exchange or (2) the supply can be aggregated, for example, an exchange selling excess inventory. We show that the allocation problem in such exchanges can be solved efficiently through decomposition when buyers and sellers are single minded. The proposed approach decomposes the problem into two stages: a forward or a reverse combinatorial auction (stage 1) and an assignment problem (stage 2). The assignment problem in Stage 2 can be solved optimally in polynomial time and thus these exchanges have computational complexity equivalent to that of one sided combinatorial auctions. Through extensive numerical experiments, we show that our approach produces high quality solutions and is computationally efficient.

1 Introduction

1.1 Combinatorial Exchanges

Combinatorial exchanges are two sided combinatorial mechanisms involving multiple buyers and multiple sellers. Combinatorial exchanges (CEs) have major economic advantages due to the power of combinatorial bidding and highly expressive bidding languages. However, they are, at the same time notoriously complex from a computational angle. There are two main computational problems associated with CEs:

- Allocation problem (also called winner determination problem or trade determination problem): Choosing an optimal subset of bids so as to optimize a chosen performance metric (such as revenue maximization, cost minimization, surplus maximization, etc.).

M. Núñez et al. (Eds.): FORTE 2004 Workshops, LNCS 3236, pp. 58–71, 2004.

– Pricing problem: Determining the actual payments to be made by the buyers and actual payments to be made to the sellers, so as to induce truthful bidding by the buyers and sellers.

The above problems have been shown to be NP-hard [1, 2]. Researchers have therefore been seeking computationally efficient ways of solving these problems exactly or approximately.

Numerous industrial applications have been reported in the literature for combinatorial exchanges. These include: collaborative planning [3], logistics and transportation exchanges [4, 5, 6], bandwidth exchanges [7], steel exchanges (for example, www.esteel.com), supply chain formation [8], e-procurement exchanges [9, 10], stock exchanges, and exchanges for sale of excess inventory.

1.2   Combinatorial Exchanges with Aggregation

Our motivation in this paper is to study combinatorial exchanges where:

– the demand can be aggregated, for example, a procurement exchange where the buyers' demands can be aggregated,
– the supply can be aggregated, for example, an exchange selling excess inventory where the sellers' bids can be aggregated.

1.3   Contributions and Outline

We show that when agents are single minded the aggregated combinatorial exchanges can be decomposed into two separate stages.

– Stage 1: A combinatorial auction
– Stage 2: An assignment problem

Since the problem in Stage 2 can be solved exactly in polynomial time, therefore these exchanges have computational complexity equivalent to one sided combinatorial auctions. We show that the iterative Dutch auction schemes proposed in [11] can be extended to solve the problem in stage 1 in a computationally efficient way to obtain near optimal allocations.

The rest of the paper is organized as follows. Section 2 presents a review of relevant work to put our contributions in perspective. In Section 3, we present a mathematical formulation of the allocation problem for both demand aggregation and supply aggregation combinatorial exchanges and show that these exchanges can be decomposed into a two stage problem. In Section 4, we present generalized combinatorial Dutch auction mechanisms for solving the combinatorial auction problem in stage 1. In Section 5, we present numerical experiments. We summarize the contributions of the paper in Section 6.

2   Review of Relevant Work

Combinatorial exchanges (CE) are generalizations of combinatorial auctions. Also, CEs are multi-item exchanges, so they are more general than single item, multi-unit exchanges. Several survey papers have appeared on combinatorial auctions. These include the papers by de Vries and Vohra [2], and Narahari and Pankaj [12]. Similarly, there are several papers on single item, multi-unit exchanges, which are summarized in [1].

The paper by Smith, Sandholm, and Simmons [13] presents a design for a market maker to construct and clear a combinatorial exchange for trading single units of multiple items. Pankaj and Narahari [14] have applied a decomposition idea to solve electronic exchanges trading multiple units of a single homogeneous item. The paper by Kothari, Sandholm, and Suri [15] considers a multi-unit, multi-item combinatorial exchange where acceptance of partial bids is allowed. Parkes, Kalagnanam, and Eso [16, 17] design a combinatorial exchange that is approximately efficient and approximately truthful.

Iterative or indirect mechanisms are those where multiple rounds of bidding and allocation are conducted and the problem is solved in an iterative and incremental way [1]. Such an approach has several advantages: incremental information revelation, reduction in the complexity of the allocation problem, and practical appeal in industrial applications. There are several iterative mechanisms proposed for combinatorial auctions [1, 16]. The use of iterative mechanisms for clearing combinatorial exchanges has been proposed by Biswas [18]. The mechanisms proposed include auction mechanisms, Dutch auction mechanisms, and tâtonnement mechanisms.

Biswas and Narahari [11] have proposed the use of combinatorial Dutch auctions as an iterative mechanism for combinatorial auctions. They use the weighted set packing structure of forward combinatorial auctions to suggest an iterative forward Dutch auction algorithm for forward combinatorial auction problems, using generalized Vickrey auctions (GVA) with reserve prices in each iteration. They prove the convergence of the proposed algorithm and derive worst case bounds for the algorithm. Similarly, they use the set covering structure of reverse combinatorial auctions to suggest an iterative reverse Dutch auction algorithm for reverse combinatorial auction problems. They also show that the proposed algorithms produces near optimal quality solutions and are computationally efficient. In this current paper, we will be using these combinatorial Dutch auction algorithms in the first stage of solving aggregated combinatorial exchanges.

3   Formulation of the Exchange Problems

We consider two special cases of combinatorial exchanges: Demand aggregation combinatorial exchanges and supply aggregation combinatorial exchanges. We assume that the goods can be freely disposed, that is, the supply is greater than or equal to the demand.

Table 1. Notation used for the demand and supply aggregation exchange models

$M = \{1, 2, ..., m\}$	Set of seller agents
$i \in M$	Seller agent
$N = \{1, 2, ..., n\}$	Set of buyer agents
$j \in N$	Buyer agent
$K = \{1, 2, ..., l\}$	Set of items
$k \in K$	Any item
$G = \{S_1, S_2, ...\}$	Collection of all multi-sets over K.
$S \subseteq G$	Any subset of G
$a(S, k)$	Quantity of item k in the subset S
$v(S, i)$	Value of the subset S to seller agent i
$v(S, j)$	Value of the subset S to buyer agent j
$y(S, i)$	Boolean variable indicating whether or not seller i gets the set S
$y(S, j)$	Boolean variable indicating whether or not buyer j gets the set S

3.1 Demand Aggregation Combinatorial Exchanges

Buyers submit their requirements, that is, the set of items and the quantities they want to procure. We assume that

- the buyers are single minded i.e. they are interested only in a single subset.
- the buyers submit atomic (all-or-nothing) bids i.e. they are interested only in a single set The buyers also submit their maximum willingness to pay for the set.

The exchange pools the demand and accepts bids from the interested sellers for the aggregated demand. The allocation problem can be formulated as follows. We give the notation used in Table 1.
The integer programming formulation of the exchange problem is:

$$V = \max \left\{ \sum_{j \in N} \sum_{S \subseteq G} v(S, j) y(S, j) - \sum_{i \in M} \sum_{S \subseteq G} v(S, i) y(S, i) \right\}$$

s.t.

$$\sum_{S \subseteq G} y(S, i) \leq 1 \ \ \forall i \in M$$

$$\sum_{S \ni k} \sum_{j \in M} a(S, k) y(S, j) \leq \sum_{S \ni k} \sum_{i \in M} a(S, k) y(S, i) \ \ \forall k \ \ \forall S \subseteq G$$

$$y(S, i) = 0, 1 \ \ \forall S \subseteq G, \forall i \in M$$

$$y(S, j) = 0, 1 \ \ \forall S \subseteq G, \forall j \in N$$

Since the demand is aggregated we can decompose the above problem into two stages. In Stage 1, knowing the aggregated demands, we solve a combinatorial procurement problem to procure the demanded items at minimum cost by choosing from the bids submitted by the sellers. In Stage 2, the procured items are sold to the buyers so as to generate maximum revenue by choosing from the bids submitted by the buyers. This is described more formally below.

Stage 1: We have assumed that the buyers are single minded. Therefore, we can aggregate the buyers' demand. Let q_k be the aggregate demand of item k, where

$$q_k = \sum_{S \ni k} \sum_{j \in N} a(S,k) y(S,j)$$

The allocation problem for Stage 1 becomes:

$$V_1 = \min \sum_{i \in M} \sum_{S \subseteq G} v(S,i) y(S,i)$$

s.t.

$$\sum_{S \subseteq G} y(S,i) \le 1 \ \forall i \in M$$

$$\sum_{S \ni k} \sum_{i \in M} a(S,k) y(S,i) \ge q_k \ \forall k \ \forall S \subseteq G$$

$$y(S,i) = 0,1 \ \forall S \subseteq G, \forall i \in M$$

This is precisely the formulation for reverse combinatorial auction for procurement as in [11] and in [7].

Stage 2: The problem in the second stage is to allocate to the buyers the items procured in the first stage to maximize the revenue of the exchange. The integer programming formulation of this stage is:

$$V_2 = \max \sum_{j \in N} \sum_{S \subseteq G} v(S,j) y(S,j)$$

s.t.

$$\sum_{S \ni k} \sum_{j \in N} a(S,k) y(S,i) \le q_k \ \forall k \ \forall S \subseteq G$$

$$y(S,j) = 0,1 \ \forall S \subseteq G, \forall j \in N$$

We can immediately note that the above is an assignment problem and therefore can be solved exactly in polynomial time.

We have thus decomposed the allocation problem of a demand aggregation combinatorial exchange into a reverse combinatorial procurement auction followed by an assignment problem.

3.2 Supply Aggregation Combinatorial Exchanges

Here the sellers declare to the exchange their individual total supplies and corresponding reserve prices. We assume that

- the sellers are single minded.
- the sellers submit atomic asks. But this can be generalized to other bidding languages such as XOR or OR*.

Then the exchange asks the interested buyers to submit their bids for the aggregated supply.

The notation for the supply aggregation exchange problem is given Table 1. The exchange can now be formulated as given below.

$$V = \max \left\{ \sum_{j \in N} \sum_{S \subseteq G} v(S,j)y(S,j) - \sum_{i \in M} \sum_{S \subseteq G} v(S,i)y(S,i) \right\}$$

s.t.

$$\sum_{S \subseteq G} y(S,j) \leq 1 \ \forall j \in N$$

$$\sum_{S \ni k} \sum_{j \in N} a(S,k)y(S,j) \leq \sum_{S \ni k} \sum_{i \in M} a(S,k)y(S,i) \ \forall k \ \forall S \subseteq G$$

$$y(S,i) = 0,1 \ \forall S \subseteq G, \forall i \in M$$

$$y(S,j) = 0,1 \ \forall S \subseteq G, \forall j \in N$$

Since the aggregated supply is known, we can decompose the above problem into two stages. In Stage 1, knowing the aggregated supply, we solve a combinatorial selling problem to sell the items to maximize revenue by choosing from the bids submitted by the buyers. In Stage 2, we procure the sold items from the sellers so as to minimize procurement cost by choosing from the bids submitted by the sellers. This is described more formally below.

Stage 1: We have assumed that the sellers are single minded. Therefore, we can aggregate the total supply from all the suppliers. Let q_k be the aggregated supply of item k, where

$$q_k = \sum_{S \ni k} \sum_{i \in M} a(S,k)y(S,i)$$

The allocation problem for Stage 1 becomes:

$$V_1 = \max \sum_{j \in N} \sum_{S \subseteq G} v(S,j)y(S,j)$$

s.t.

$$\sum_{S \subseteq G} y(S,j) \leq 1 \ \forall j \in N$$

$$\sum_{S \ni k} \sum_{j \in N} a(S,k)y(S,j) \leq q_k \ \forall k \ \forall S \subseteq G$$

$$y(S,j) = 0,1 \ \forall S \subseteq G, \forall j \in N$$

This is precisely the formulation for forward combinatorial auction discussed in [11] and in [19, 2].

Stage 2: The problem in the second stage is to allocate to the sellers the items sold to the buyers in the first stage. The integer programming formulation of the stage stage is:

$$V_2 = \min \sum_{j \in N} \sum_{S \subseteq G} c(S, j) y(S, j)$$

s.t.

$$\sum_{S \ni k} \sum_{j \in N} a(S, k) y(S, j) \geq q_k \quad \forall k \quad \forall S \subseteq G$$

$$y(S, j) = 0, 1 \quad \forall S \subseteq G, \forall j \in N$$

Note that the above is an assignment problem which can be solved exactly in polynomial time.

We have thus decomposed the aggregation combinatorial exchanges into a combinatorial auction followed by an assignment problem. Different mechanisms have been proposed for combinatorial auction problems. We generalize the iterative Dutch auctions suggested in [11] for the aggregation exchange problems.

4   Combinatorial Dutch Auctions for Aggregation Exchanges

We can extend the iterative Dutch auctions suggested in [11] for the aggregation exchanges as follows.

4.1   Reverse Combinatorial Dutch Auction for Demand Aggregation Exchanges

The exchange aggregates demands of all the buyers and also computes the maximum price it is willing to pay for the entire bundle. Table 2 shows the notation used in the formulation. The proposed iterative mechanism consists of multiple bidding rounds denoted by $t = 0, 1, 2, ...$ ($t = 0$ is the initial round). The aggregated bundle of all the buyers is therefore B_0. The exchange sets the value for $W(B_t)$, maximum willingness to pay for the remaining bundle B_t to be procured in round t. The pricing of items is not linear, therefore the cost of the allocated bundles cannot be divided into price of individual items. Therefore we calculate p_t, the average willingness of the exchange to pay for each item in round t.

$$p_t = \frac{W(B_t)}{|B_t|}, \quad \text{where } B_t \neq \phi$$

Table 2. Notation for reverse Dutch combinatorial auction for demand aggregation exchanges

$t = 0, 1, 2, \ldots$	Iteration (or bidding round) number
B_t	Bundle to be procured in iteration t
B_0	Total aggregated bundle of all the buyers' demand
$W(B_t)$	Maximum willingness of the exchange to pay bundle B_t in iteration t
S_t	Bundle procured in round t
p_t	Average willingness of the exchange to pay for each item in round t
$V^*(S_t)$	Payment made by exchange for the subset S_t in iteration t. The payment is computed by solving GVA with reserve prices.
v_t	Average payment made for any item in iteration t
$\|S\|$	Cardinality of the set S
ϵ	Price increment per item in every iteration

These average prices p_t are not used in the auction mechanism but are used to prove the bounds given in Section 4.3. The payment made by the exchange for the subset S_t in iteration t is $V^*(S_t)$. The average price paid by the exchange for each item procured is

$$v_t = \frac{V^*(S_t)}{|S_t|}$$

We ignore the iterations in which no items are procured.

The exchange sets the reserve price of the seller for any bundle S in iteration t as $|S|v_{t-1}$. We use GVA with reserve prices [20] in each iteration to solve the allocation and payment problem efficiently. The bundle procured in round t is denoted by S_t. Therefore the integer programming formulation of the GVA problem with reserve prices in iteration t becomes

$$V^*(S_t) = \max \sum_{i \in M} \sum_{S \subseteq G} v(S, i) y(S, i) \tag{1}$$

s.t.

$$\sum_{S \subseteq G} y(S, i) \leq 1 \ \forall i \in M$$

$$\sum_{S \ni k} \sum_{i \in M} a(S, k) y(S, i) \geq q_k \ \forall k \ \forall S \subseteq G$$

$$\sum_{i \in M} \sum_{S \subseteq G} v(S, i) y(S, j) \leq W(B_t) \ \forall S \subseteq M$$

$$v(S, i) y(S, i) \geq |S| v_{t-1} \ \forall S \subseteq M, \forall j \in N$$

$$y(S, i) = 0, 1 \ \forall S \subseteq G, \forall i \in M$$

Table 3. Notation for the forward combinatorial Dutch auction for supply aggregation exchanges

$t = 0, 1, 2, \ldots$	Iteration (or bidding round) number
B_t	Bundle to be sold in iteration t
B_0	Total aggregated bundle available from of all the suppliers
$W(B_t)$	Minimum ask price of the exchange for pay bundle B_t in iteration t
S_t	Bundle sold in round t
p_t	Average ask price of the exchange for each item in round t
$V^*(S_t)$	Revenue earned by the exchange for the subset S_t in iteration t. The revenue is calculated by solving GVA with reserve prices.
v_t	Average revenue for any item in iteration t
ϵ	Price decrement per item in every iteration

4.2 Forward Combinatorial Dutch Auction for Supply Aggregation Exchanges

Here the exchange aggregates the supply from all the sellers and computes the total aggregated bundle and the minimum price at which it is willing to sell the aggregated bundle. Table 3 shows the notation for the formulation. In the combinatorial version of iterative forward Dutch auction ([11]), the seller starts with a high initial price and keeps on decreasing the price until the total bundle is sold. In the generalized Dutch mechanism for supply aggregation exchanges, the seller provides $W(B_t)$, total ask for the remaining bundle B_t to be sold in round t. We compute p_t, the average ask price of the exchange for each item in round t. The average ask prices p_t are not used in the auction mechanism but are used to prove the bounds given in Section 4.3. The payment earned by the exchange for the subset S_t in iteration t is $V^*(S_t)$. The average selling price for each item sold is

$$v_t = \frac{V^*(S_t)}{|S_t|}$$

We ignore the iterations in which no items are sold i.e. $S_t \neq \phi \; \forall t$.

The reserve price for the remaining bundle S_t in iteration t is $W(B_t)$. Also the maximum payment to the buyers for any bundle S in iteration t is $|S|v_{t-1}$. Therefore the integer formulation of the GVA problem with reserve prices in iteration t becomes

$$V^*(S_t) = \min \sum_{j \in N} \sum_{S \subseteq G} v(S, j) y(S, j) \qquad (2)$$

$$s.t.$$

$$\sum_{S \subseteq G} y(S, j) \leq 1 \;\; \forall j \in N$$

$$\sum_{S \ni k} \sum_{j \in N} a(S, k) y(S, j) \leq q_k \;\; \forall k \;\; \forall S \subseteq G$$

$$v(S,j)y(S,j) \leq |S|v_{t-1} \ \forall S \subseteq G, \forall j \in N$$

$$\sum_{j \in N} \sum_{S \subseteq M} v(S,j)y(S,j) \geq W(B_t) \ \forall S \subseteq G$$

$$y(S,j) = 0,1 \ \forall S \subseteq G, \forall j \in N$$

4.3   Bounds for the Algorithms

The second stage problem in both demand aggregation and supply aggregation exchanges can be solved optimally in polynomial time. Therefore the bounds for these problems depend only on the bounds of the first stage problems. Thus bounds for these mechanisms are same as the bounds given for iterative Dutch combinatorial auctions in [11].

Upper Bound for Reverse Dutch Auction and Demand Aggregation Problem: The upper bound for the iterative reverse Dutch auction is $(1 + \frac{1}{2} + \ldots + \frac{1}{r})V(N)$, where

$$V(N) = \min \sum_{j \in N} \sum_{S \subseteq G} v_j(S)y(S,j), \text{ and}$$

$$r = \max_{S \in K} |S|$$

Lower Bound for Forward Dutch Auction and Supply Aggregation Problem: The lower bound for the forward Dutch auction is $\frac{1}{l}V(N)$, where

$$V(N) = \max \sum_{i \in M} \sum_{S \subseteq G} v_i(S)y(S,i)$$

5   Numerical Experiments

We have derived the worst case (lower or upper) bounds for these iterative Dutch mechanisms. We have run our algorithms on some of the test cases suggested by various authors [21, 22, 2, 23]. We have used CPLEX^{TM} 8.0 to solve the various instances of GVA with reserve prices.

5.1   Experiments for a Demand Aggregation Exchange

We first conduct numerical experiments with demand aggregation exchanges by varying ϵ and the number of agents i.e. buyers and sellers. Since we solve the second stage problem exactly, the solutions vary according to the results of the first stage. The trends in the graphs are therefore very similar to those obtained in the reverse Dutch auctions discussed in [11].

The graph in Figure 1 shows that the solutions tend towards actual optimal solutions as ϵ tends towards unity. We also find the results of the approximate

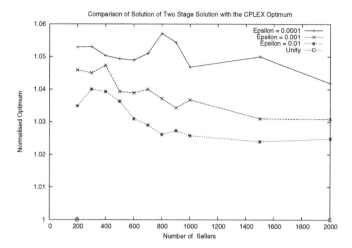

Fig. 1. Comparison of the demand aggregation results with the CPLEX optimum

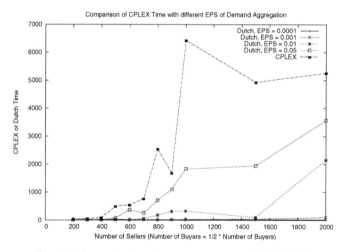

Fig. 2. Computation time comparison with CPLEX

solutions are very good even when ϵ is very small. However, we see from the graph in Figure 2 that the time taken to solve the problems grows exponentially when ϵ is very close to 1. This happens because when ϵ is close to 1 the problem we solve in the first iteration is almost the as hard as original problem.

5.2   Experiments for a Supply Aggregation Exchange

Numerical experiments with supply aggregation exchanges by varying ϵ and the number of agents i.e. buyers and sellers are discussed in this section. In these

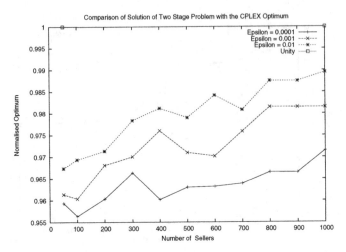

Fig. 3. Comparison of the supply aggregation results with the CPLEX optimum

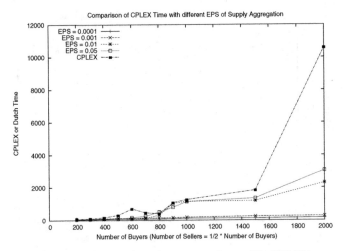

Fig. 4. Computation time comparison with CPLEX

experiments, we again solve the second stage problem exactly and therefore the solutions depend on the results of the first stage. The trends in the graphs are therefore very similar to those in the forward Dutch auctions discussed in [11].

The solutions tend towards the actual optimal solution as ϵ gets close to 1 (see Figure 3). But again the time taken grows exponentially when ϵ tends to 1 (see Figure 4).

6   Summary

In this paper, we have studied a useful class of combinatorial exchanges where we can have demand aggregation (for example, procurement exchanges) or supply aggregation (for example, exchanges selling excess inventory). We have shown that the allocation problem in these exchanges can be decomposed into two stages: (a) Stage 1: Combinatorial auction (forward or reverse). (b) Stage 2: Assignment problem. Since the assignment problem in stage 2 can be solved exactly in polynomial time, we studied only the problem in the first stage. We have shown that the the iterative Dutch auction schemes proposed in [11] can be used for for solving the allocation problem in stage 1. This results in a computationally efficient way of solving aggregation exchanges to obtain near optimal allocations. We have conducted numerical experiments to show that the proposed approach and algorithms perform very well and give results which are very close to the optimal solutions.

The proposed approach can be used in all applications where aggregation combinatorial exchanges are relevant. The computational efficiency and the high quality of solutions will ensure that the mechanisms can be deployed in all practical applications. Procurement exchanges, excess inventory exchanges, and stock exchanges are a few examples.

In this paper, we have not considered game theoretic issues such as Vickrey payments, truthful bidding, etc. These are important issues that need to be addressed in future research.

References

[1] Kalagnanam, J., Parkes, D.: Auctions, bidding, and exchange design. In Simchi-Levi, Wu, D., Shen, eds.: Supply Chain Analysis in the eBusiness Area. Kluwer Academic Publishers (2003) 59, 60

[2] de Vries, S., Vohra, R.: Combinatorial auctions, a survey. INFORMS Journal of Computing **15** (2003) 59, 60, 64, 67

[3] Hunsberger, L., Gross, B.J.: A combinatorial auction for collaborative planning. In: Proceedings International Conference on Multi-Agent Systems (ICMAS-00). (2000) 151–158 59

[4] Kameshwaran, S., Narahari, Y.: Innovative auction mechanisms for logistics marketplaces. In: Proceedings of the International Conference on Automation, Energy, and Information Technology, EAIT-2001, Indian Institute of Technology, Kharagpur. (2001) 59

[5] Song, J., Regan, A.C.: Combinatorial auctions for transportation since procurement : The carrier perspective. Technical report, Institutee of Transportation Studies, University of California, Irvine (2002) 59

[6] Ledyard, J.O., Olson, M., porter, D., Swanson, J.A., Torma, D.: The first use of a combined value auction for transprotation services. Technical Report 1093, California Institute of Technology (2000) 59

[7] Eso, M., Kalagnanam, J., Ladanyi, L., Li, Y.: Winner determination in bandwidth exchanges. Technical report, RC22219 (W0110-087), IBM TJ Watson Research Center (2001) 59, 62

[8] Walsh, W.E., Wellman, M.P., Ygge, F.: Combinatorial auctions for supply chain formation. In: ACM Conference on Electronic Commerce. (2000) 260–269 59

[9] Hohner, G., Rich, J., Ng, E., Reid, G., Davenport, A.J., Kalagnam, J.R., Lee, H.S., An, C.: Combinatorial and quantity discount procurement auctions provide benifits to mars and its suppliers. Technical report, IBM Research Report (2001) 59

[10] Elmaghraby, W., Keskinocak, P.: Combinatorial auctions in procurement. Technical report, Dept. of Industrial and Systems Engineering, Georgia Institute of Technology (2002) 59

[11] Biswas, S., Narahari, Y.: Iterative Dutch combinatorial auctions. Annals of Mathematics and Artificial Intelligence (2004) To appear in the special issue on the Foundations of Electronic Commerce. 59, 60, 62, 64, 66, 67, 69, 70

[12] Narahari, Y., Dayama, P.: Combinatorial auctions in electronic business. Technical report, Electronic Enterprises Laboratory, Department of Computer Science and Automation, Indian Institute of Science (2004) 60

[13] Smith, T., Sandholm, T., Simmons, R.: Constructing and clearing combinatorial exchanges using preference elicitation. In: Proceedings of National Conference on Artificial Intelligence (AAAI-02). (2002) 60

[14] Dayama, P., Narahari, Y.: Design of multi-unit electronic exchanges through decomposition. Technical report, Electronic Enterprises Laboratory, Department of Computer Science and Automation, Indian Institute of Science (2003) 60

[15] Kothari, A., Sandholm, T., Suri, S.: Solving combinatorial exchanges: Optimality via a few partial bids. In: AAAI. (2002) 60

[16] Parkes, D.: Iterative Combinatorial Auctions: Achieving Economic and Computational Efficiency. PhD thesis, Department of Computer and Information Science, University of Pennsylvania (2001) 60

[17] Parkes, D.C., Kalagnanam, J., Eso, M.: Achieving budget-balance with Vickrey-based payment schemes in exchanges. In: 17th International Joint Conference on Artificial Intelligence (IJCAI-01). (2001) 60

[18] Biswas, S.: Iterative Mechanisms for Combinatorial Auctions and Exchanges. PhD thesis, Department of Computer Science and Automation, Indian Institute of Science, Bangalore, India (2004) 60

[19] Bikchandani, S., Ostroy, J.M.: The package assignment model. Technical report, Anderson Graduate School of Management and Department of Economics, UCLA (2001) 64

[20] Ausubel, L., Cramton, P.: Vickrey auctions with reserve pricing. Technical report, Working Paper, University of Maryland (1999) 65

[21] Sandholm, T.: An algorithm for optimal winner determination in combinatorial auctions. In: Proceedings of International Joint Conference on Artificial Intelligence (IJCAI-99). (1999) 542–547 67

[22] Boutilier, C., Goldszmidt, M., B., S.: Sequential auctions for the allocation of resources with complementarities. In: International Joint Conferences on Artificial Intelligence. (1999) 67

[23] Kevin Leyton-Brown, Mark Pearson, Y.S.: Towards a universal test suite for combinatorial auction algorithm. In: ACM Conference on Electronic Commerce, 2000. (2000) 67

A Construction Kit for Modeling the Security of M-commerce Applications

Dominik Haneberg, Wolfgang Reif, and Kurt Stenzel

Lehrstuhl für Softwaretechnik und Programmiersprachen
Institut für Informatik, Universität Augsburg
86135 Augsburg Germany
{haneberg,reif,stenzel}@informatik.uni-augsburg.de

Abstract. In this article we present a method to avoid security problems in modern m-commerce applications. The security problems that we are addressing are breaches of security due to erroneous cryptographic protocols. We describe a specification technique that gives way to a formal, and thereby rigorous, treatment of the security protocols used in such applications. Security of communication is important in modern m-commerce applications. As parts of the specification of the security protocols, we describe how to specify the behavior of the agents, how to specify the attacker and how further aspects of the application reflect in the formal specification. The problem is that such formal specifications are difficult to get right, so we propose a construction kit for their development.

1 Introduction

1.1 Mobile-Commerce

Mobile-commerce applications appear in a large variety of forms. They can be customer-oriented (electronic selling of goods) or they can be intra-organizational (electronic business processes). Although the electronic selling is better known in the society, the mobile reorganization of business processes is getting more and more important. The devices used for m-commerce are manifold. Smart cards for high-secure applications, mobile phones or mobile digital assistants for smart mobile services or notebooks with mobile Internet access for heavyweight applications. Independent of the device used for the service, the requirements of m-commerce services are quite similar: Security of transmitted data, identification of the agents, exclusion of fraud. Yet these goals seem to be quite simple and even though they are claimed in all applications, realizing them properly is quite tricky. Differences in the application design, different possible forms of fraud in different applications and the large differences in the technical features of the mobile devices result in securing an m-commerce application being a challenging task.

M. Núñez et al. (Eds.): FORTE 2004 Workshops, LNCS 3236, pp. 72–85, 2004.

1.2   Security Protocols for Communication

One important aspect of innovative m-commerce applications is the transformation of business goods into digital data. Examples for such applications are electronic ticketing or electronic purses. It is crucial for such applications that the business goods cannot be manipulated or multiplied because this would permit fraud. For example, someone could increment the amount of money in an electronic purse. Another aspect is that m-commerce applications can require the transfer of customer data that must not be disclosed, e. g. credit card data or other personal information. Communication in m-commerce therefore means a lot of data that must be protected against different threats. The means for protecting data and ensuring authenticity are cryptographic methods. For the different functions of the application, security protocols (also called cryptographic protocols) must be developed that ensure the security of the data. The problem is that these protocols are very error prone [1].

There are quite a few well-known security protocols that can be used to ensure many of the more common security demands (e. g. non-disclosure of the transmitted data and authenticity of the agents). One such protocol, often used in WWW-based e-commerce applications, is SSL [6]. The problem is that such standard protocols are not usable in all scenarios because they do not necessarily guarantee the application specific security goals. In smart card based applications, which are the main focus of the work presented here, the additional problem arises that smart cards do not offer the resources necessary to execute such standard protocols.

Our work is a method for the specification and verification of cryptographic protocols for m-commerce applications and we therefore address the security problems arising from erroneously designed cryptographic protocols.

1.3   Designing Secure M-commerce Protocols

Cryptographic protocols are difficult to design. They may contain subtle errors that are not detected for several years (see [2] for examples). It is commonly agreed that formal methods give the highest assurance that the protocols are secure. This means that we can formally prove that a given protocol adheres to all required security properties (which must be given in a suitable mathematical description). As basis of such a formal treatment of security protocols, a specification that unambiguously describes the protocols is needed.

However, creating such specifications is quite complex. The commonly used specification techniques are unsatisfying because they are either to detailed, for example the full EMV standard [5] or they lack a lot of relevant information, e. g. treatment of errors or checks of the data exchanged [2]. The formal proofs are surprisingly difficult, because an informal argumentation necessarily contains holes. And there is a graver problem: If the formal specification does not adequately reflect the real world, a 'proof' that a protocol is secure may be possible, but in the real world the protocol is not secure: In [2] the security of a version of the Needham-Schroeder protocol is 'proven', but in fact the protocol was flawed [8]. Even an expert in formal methods is at risk.

Therefore we propose a 'construction kit' to design formal protocol specifications. While every application requires its own protocols and security properties, experience shows that the remaining parts of a formal specification can be standardized. Using standard components reduces the risk of errors and allows to reuse previous proofs.

1.4   A Construction Kit for Formal Protocol Specifications

We propose a *construction kit* to design correct formal protocol specifications without much effort. The kit contains the following building blocks:

1. A UML [10] class diagram for the agents in the application, and UML activity diagrams for the protocols (described in section 2).
2. Security properties (described in section 3).
   These can be either class invariants or formulas of the formal specification. Additionally, the formal specification should be validated, i. e. it should fulfill some properties. These properties are: a successful protocol run is possible; and a modified protocol is insecure. The diagrams and security properties are specific for every application and must be designed by the application designer.
3. One of three different attacker models (described in section 4):
   – An attacker that may receive and modify every message.
   – An attacker that receives every message, but cannot modify a message.
   – An attacker that cannot eavesdrop on or modify messages between other agents.
4. The communication structure (described in section 5).
   This includes the number of agents, and the manner of communication. The more realistic this aspect is modeled the more complex the specification and proofs will be. However, a too simple model may be not an adequate model of reality.

Some parts of the building blocks are generated automatically, some are taken from a library and a small part must be added by hand. The building blocks are unified in one large formal specification in which the correctness and security of the cryptographic protocols are proven.

2   Modeling Applications

In this section we describe our technique to specify the communication protocols and those parts of the application that contain data relevant for the security (most often the application logic but not the user interface). A specification of an application consists of two parts, the description of the agents and the protocols. The agents are all the entities that play an active role in the application. They are represented by their internal state. Unlike the common descriptions of security protocols we explicitly model the internal state of the agents. We therefore can describe which data is stored in each agent and when and how an agent modifies its state. Multiple agents of the same type are possible, similar to multiple objects that are different instances of the same class. The communication protocols of an application describe how the different agents work together, which messages are exchanged and which computations take place.

Specifications that are written in a way that they are usable for verification, e. g. algebraic specifications, are hard to develop and require expert knowledge in formal methods. Our goal was to enable the application developer to contribute to the specification by using an UML-based approach. The scenario and the protocols are described in a graphical notation and are automatically converted into an algebraic specification.

2.1 An Example

The example we use to illustrate the specification is a simplified electronic purse. A user of this service can use special terminals to load money onto his smart card by inserting the smart card and the money he wants to load. Then the smart card stores the amount of money in the electronic purse. The smart card with the stored money can be used for payments of small amounts, e. g. in a canteen or in public libraries for using the copying machines.

2.2 UML Diagrams

We use two kinds of diagrams for the specification of an application. The state of the agents and the methods used to manipulate data are described in a class diagram. Class diagrams are mainly used in a standard manner and not further discussed.

The protocols which describe the communication between the different agents are specified as activity diagrams. In general each function that is to be performed by the application requires its own protocol. The protocols define at what time what message is to be sent by which agent. Also the structure of the messages is defined by the protocols. Most important thereby is how the data is secured, i. e. what cryptographic primitives are used in what way. Figure 1 shows one of the protocols of the electronic purse, the *pay*-function. This function is used if the user wants to pay for goods or services and use the money on his card for it. The example application has another function, the function used to load money onto the card. This function has its own protocol which is omitted here. The diagram for *pay* contains two swimlanes, one for each agent participating in the protocol. The left swimlane represents the terminal, in the case of the *pay*-function this would be a merchant terminal, and the other swimlane stands for the smart card. The protocols all start at the start-node in the terminal swimlane. In smart card applications the communication is always initiated by a terminal, a smart card cannot begin an operation on its own. The course of events in the protocol is described by the control flow of the diagram. Activities stand for calculations being performed and for modifications of the

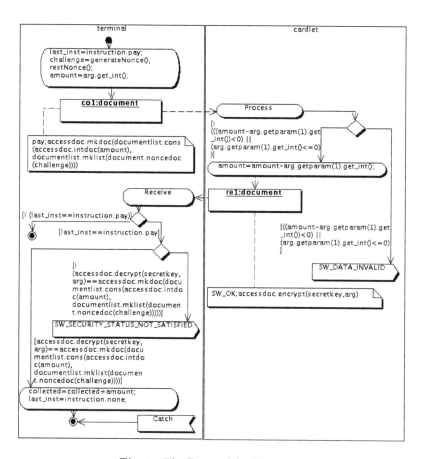

Fig. 1. The Protocol for Payments

state of the agent. A branch node is used for tests that have to be performed, e. g. correctness of received data, object nodes and the notes attached to them describe the exchanged messages. The path from the start node to the last end node describes the intended successful run of the protocol. Signal sending nodes and the other end nodes represent early ends of a protocol run, e. g. because of wrong data.

2.3   Algebraic Specifications

The graphical notation described in the last section is good for the specification process, because the notation enables non-experts in formal methods to contribute to the specification. Unfortunately, for the verification we need another description mechanism, one that contains the specification in the language of the theorem prover used. This theorem prover input is, in large parts, automatically generated from the diagrams. In our case we use the KIV theorem prover [3] which works with algebraic specifications [7] and therefore the generation of the formal specification currently targets on algebraic specifications. Of course it would be possible to use other specification techniques, e. g. temporal logics or state machines.

As a result of the automatic transformation process a structured algebraic specification is generated. An algebraic specification consists of a set of data type definitions, functions manipulating the data types and also predicate symbols. Combined with quantifiers we have a powerful formal description mechanism for software systems. The specification created from the diagrams contains the data types for the agents of the application, a document data type describing how messages are built in the communication and a function that describes the agents behavior in the protocols.

Each agent is represented by its internal state, i. e. the value of all fields of the data type. When generating the data type for an agent, the fields are taken from the agents description in the class diagram. This explicit model of the internal state of the agents participating in an application is a significant difference to the other approaches for modeling and verifying security protocols. As we are ultimately aiming at a verified implementation of the application, we think that a model that is close to the actual software is better than the stateless descriptions in other modeling techniques.

The function describing the agents behavior is the central part of the protocol specification. It defines for all agents how they react, i. e. what they answer and how they modify their state, if they receive a certain message. The function

$$agent - says : (agent, document) \rightarrow (agent, document)$$

takes the current state of an agent and the document the agent receives and returns the state of the agent after the modifications and the document the agent produces as answer. The axioms for this function are generated from the activity diagrams. Note that all the different activity diagrams are brought together in one function. This is due to the fact that each one of the activity diagrams only contains the information how the agents mentioned in the diagram behave in one specific function of the application, but for a description of an agent as a whole all these parts must be aggregated.

A great deal of the algebraic specification can be generated automatically, yet some parts must be added by hand. It is possible to use methods in the activity diagrams describing the protocols (e. g. generateNonce() in Figure 1). These methods must be present in the class diagram, but only the signature can be taken from the class diagram and added to the specification. The semantics of these functions has to be added by hand. They are usually functions that deal with the treatment of data, e. g. a function storeTicket() to store a ticket in an array.

3   Security Properties

Apart from the specification of the behavior of the agents in an m-commerce application we need two further ingredients in order to prove the security of the communication protocols. At first we need to know what exactly security of the protocols means in a specific application. This is discussed in this section. For the electronic purse the claim of the service provider would be that at no time the sum of the money spent with the cards is higher than the sum of all the money collected in the load stations. In the example, this property is expressed quite elegantly using two fields of the terminal to count the loaded and collected money:

$$term.collected \leq term.issued$$

This class invariant is translated into (the additional parts of the formula will be explained later)

$$sec\_glob: \qquad admissible(tr)$$
$$\rightarrow \forall n.tr[n].env.term.collected \leq tr[n].env.term.issued$$

This theorem guarantees that at no time more money is collected by the point-of-sales terminals than was issued by the load terminals. This rules out fraud because it cannot happen that money is spent that was not previously loaded on a card by a genuine load station. Other applications have completely different security claims. In an electronic shopping scenario, e. g. the customer would demand that his payment information (e. g. credit card data) is not disclosed to anyone other than the merchant.

Finding, respectively determining, the security goals for an m-commerce application is part of the application design. The security demands, most certain at first just as some informal ideas, must be put in rigorous formalization to allow for their formal verification. Therefore the informal demands become logical formulas in the verification process. The theorems representing the security goals are the main object of the protocol correctness proofs.

Besides the actual security goals some additional properties for the application should be proven. They can be seen as 'sanity' checks because they validate the specification. Most important are the following:

- It is possible to successfully execute the protocols. This ensures that the specification of the possible traces is not malformed in a way that entirely disables the communication.
- A insecure version of a protocol should be formulated and using this a successful attack should be proven. This ensures that the attacker is not accidently disabled by the specification of the possible traces.

4   Specifying the Attacker

The second building block that has to be added is the description of the threats the application is facing. The threats we are dealing with are not such unwanted events limiting the availability of the service, e. g. hardware failures. Our focus are the threats resulting from accidental or deliberate misuse by one or more individuals. In the design and analysis of security protocols such individuals are usually called the attackers. To what extent an attacker poses a threat to an application is determined by his abilities. In security protocol analysis in general an instance of the Dolev-Yao attacker [4] model is used. This attacker is the most powerful attacker that still permits secure protocols.

The problem is that such a powerful attacker is not realistic in all possible application scenarios. Designing the protocols in a way that they are secure against the Dolev-Yao attacker always guarantees that the application is also secure if the real attacker is less powerful. Therefore we do not have a security problem but we have an economical problem. A more powerful attacker usually means that the security protocols must be more elaborate. They are harder to design and use more advanced cryptographic features. To make things worse, more advanced cryptographic primitives (e. g. asymmetric instead of symmetric cryptography) can necessitate more capable hardware. Additionally the usage of public-key systems could require the build up of a public-key infrastructure, which means a great deal of administrative effort. This all results in increasing costs. For example a smart card that can only perform symmetric cryptography is cheaper than a smart card with support for an asymmetric cryptographic algorithm. All in all we have the problem that an application can become unnecessary complex and expensive if an attacker is selected who is too powerful and therefore inappropriate for the application.

Classical security protocol analysis generally assumes communication over a wide area network such as the Internet. Especially m-commerce scenarios make use of a wider range of possible communication channels:

- Infrared (IrDA),
- radio-based, e. g. Bluetooth for short-range and GSM for long-range communication,
- LANs and WANs,
- but also exclusive point-to-point connections, e. g. a smart card in a terminal.

The different characteristics of the communication channels should reflect in the attacker model. This is another reason why a limitation to the Dolev-Yao attacker is not adequate. We therefore developed several other attackers with different abilities. They represent different levels of realistic adversaries in real life applications.

4.1   Aspects Common to All Attacker Models

Certain aspects of the attacker are common to all the attacker models we use. The central idea of the attacker is that he collects as much information as possible and tries to use the information he gathered to cheat on other agents. The information the attacker has collected is called his knowledge. The attacker's knowledge is a set of documents that initially contains often just the attacker's personal cryptographic keys but it grows when the attacker intercepts new messages.

One common aspect of the attacker models is how they treat the messages they obtain. A document that is received by the attacker is always added to his knowledge. But some documents are made up of sub-documents, e. g. an encrypted document contains the plaintext of the message as sub-document. In case of compound documents special rules apply. Not all sub-documents may go into the attacker's knowledge. The process of adding additional documents to the attacker's knowledge is specified using several functions (similar to [11]), most important:

$$. \int + . : documentset \times document \rightarrow documentset$$

$\int+$ computes a new set of documents by adding a document to a given set of documents and adding all documents that can be derived. If an attacker, with present knowledge docset, receives a document his knowledge is extended to $docset_0$ = docset $\int+$ doc. Some other functions are used in the specification of $\int+$ and explain how the new knowledge can be computed. In this process, the knowledge of the attacker is extended with all documents derivable from his present knowledge. What the derivable direct sub-documents of a document are depends on the document and the knowledge. For example a document encrypted with key key, encdoc(key, doc), contains the plaintext as sub-document but this sub-document is derivable only if the knowledge contains the information necessary to decrypt messages encrypted with key:

sub-enc-yes :
  $can\_decrypt(key, docset) \rightarrow sub\text{-}docs(encdoc(key, doc), docset) = \{doc\};$
sub-enc-no :
  $\neg\, can\_decrypt(key, docset) \rightarrow sub\text{-}docs(encdoc(key, doc), docset) = \emptyset;$

Note that the algebraically specified abstract documents can contain additional information which their real counterparts do not contain, e. g. the key in an encrypted document. The information that is not contained in the real documents must of course not be a derivable sub-document.

Also common to all attacker models is how they build new messages from the knowledge they have collected so far. They can guess non-confidential data, but they cannot guess confidential data such as nonces or keys. This means they can only use keys and nonces that they acquired by eavesdropping. Otherwise it would be impossible to ensure most of the common security goals. The attacker's ability to derive documents is covered by a special predicate $\models$ with signature

$$. \models . : documentset \times document$$

docset $\models$ doc states that the document doc can be constructed from the set of documents $docset$ which contains the attacker's knowledge. There are axioms for all kind of documents describing if they can be built given a certain set of documents. As mentioned above the attacker cannot guess keys, therefore he can build an encrypted document only if he possesses the key. This is covered by the axiom

$$\begin{aligned}
\text{encdoc}: \quad \text{docset} &\models \text{encdoc(key, doc)} \\
&\leftrightarrow \text{encdoc(key, doc)} \in \text{docset} \\
&\lor \text{docset} \models \text{keydoc(key)} \land \text{docset} \models \text{doc};
\end{aligned}$$

and it states that the attacker can derive an encrypted document if the document is part of his knowledge or if the plaintext of the document and the used key can be derived from his knowledge.

4.2 Attacker Models

The Dolev-Yao Attacker The Dolev-Yao attacker model is the most powerful attacker model used. This attacker has complete control over the communication, i. e. he can eavesdrop into every data exchange and manipulate all messages traveling through the communication channels. The attacker decomposes all messages he intercepts and decrypts encrypted messages, provided that he has the necessary key. The attacker can arbitrarily generate messages from his knowledge.

It is easy to see that it is not very common that someone has the abilities of this attacker. The attacker must have access to all agents participating in the communication.

An Attacker with Limited Access to the Communication This attacker is developed from the Dolev-Yao model by limiting his access to the communication. First of all this attacker can only eavesdrop into the data exchanges but he cannot manipulate the messages sent. This does not mean that he cannot participate in the communication at all. This attacker can still generate his own messages and send them over a communication channel as a regular participant of the service. Another possible limitation is that the attacker cannot eavesdrop on all data exchanges but just a few, i. e. he does not have control over the complete communication infrastructure but on some systems with an installed Trojan horse program.

Prohibiting the attacker to manipulate messages is also necessary in order to prove certain reliability properties. For example it can only be guaranteed that an electronic railway ticket can successfully be presented to the conductor if the attacker cannot simply inhibit all communication by elimination of all messages. Availability of a service cannot be guaranteed with a Dolev-Yao attacker [9].

Attacker Without Access to the Communication This is the most restricted attacker we use. This attacker cannot eavesdrop on any communication taking place. What he can do is communicating with his own genuine device, e. g. his own smart card, and he can program a faked device, e. g. using a programmable smart card, that can be used to communicate with real agents and try to trick them into revealing interesting information. This is a quite realistic attacker. Every person with programming knowledge and a smart card reader is an instance of this attacker model. As the attacks that can be performed by this attacker do not require great effort and are not expensive, attacks of this kind must be expected in every m-commerce application, even if the possible gain of a successful attack is limited.

4.3   Further Aspects

What kind of attacker should be used in the verification of the application is a design decision that must be taken in an early step of the application development because it has a direct impact on the protocols and probably on the hardware selection. Some factors must be observed when trying to decide on the most realistic threat. In general one must anticipate more elaborate attacks if the result of a success is more severe. For example a smart card based credit card will attract more and technologically more advanced attacks than for example a loyalty card.

There is another aspect of the attackers that must be kept in mind. It has no direct consequence for the formalization of the attackers but for the design of the security protocols. It is generally assumed that an attacker is trying to achieve a personal benefit by attacking a service. This is not necessarily true. When designing a service one should keep in mind that the service may have to deal with attacks whose only purpose is to annoy others, see e. g. denial of service attacks on the Internet. Preparing for such attacks is especially important if the availability of the service is crucial.

4.4   In Brief

The attacker is a very important concept in our treatment of security protocols. There are different aspects to be considered. In brief the following things are important:

- How can the attacker decompose messages and build new ones.
- Which communication channels can be eavesdropped by the attacker, which cannot.
- Can the attacker replace messages in transfer by his own messages.
- Does the attacker participate as a normal user of the service. (This is the case in most scenarios.)
- Does the attacker use faked devices, e. g. a self-programmed smart card.
- Does one attacker suffice or should a set of attackers be considered.
- Is an 'annoy only' attacker relevant?

5   The Communication Structure

After modeling the protocols and the agents, and after selecting the attacker the communication structure remains to be modeled. This requires further choices:

1. The number of agents.

   It may be sufficient to consider only one attacker, one customer, and one merchant. This reduces the complexity of the specification and proofs considerably compared to one that considers an arbitrary number of agents. So this choice is desirable. On the other hand, there may be attacks against the protocol involving several agents, that are not possible otherwise. In this case the formal specification must consider an arbitrary number of agents. Otherwise the specification is not an adequate model of reality.

2. The manner of communication.

   This can be either broadcast (one to all for radio based communication) or one to one, and may contain one channel or several. For example, there may be an 'insecure' radio based channel like WAP and a 'secure' channel based on GSM. Again, the choice influences the complexity of the specification and proofs, and how adequate the formal model is.

3. Interleaving of operations.

   Is it adequate to assume that every software component immediately answers to a received message? Or is it necessary to assume that things can happen interleaved or even in parallel? Since we are dealing only with the logical properties of the protocols the first possibility is sufficient. However, one agent may have exclusive access to a communication partner. (E. g. a terminal to a smart card if an attacker without access to the communication is used.)

4. Occurrence of state changes.

   Every agent has an internal state. This is important when the specification is refined into an implementation. If interleaving is used an agent receives a message and some time later issues an answer. Usually, the internal state is modified. The question is when? When a message is received, when an answer is issued, or sometimes between?

With these choices the formal specification can be completed. An *environment* contains all agents with their internal state, an *event* consists of an environment and a communication between two or more agents, and a *trace* is a sequence of events. A trace is *admissible* if all agents adhere to their specified behavior. In the electronic purse example this means that the smart card, the load stations and the pay stations follow their protocols, and that the attacker sends only messages that are derivable from his knowledge. An admissible trace can be viewed as a sequence of events that can happen in the real world. Consequently the security properties must be proven for all admissible traces (see sec_glob in section 3). The definition of admissible can be divided into several parts that are to some degree independent of each other:

$$
\begin{aligned}
&\text{admissible(trace)}\\
\leftrightarrow\quad &\text{attacker\_admissible(trace)}\\
&\wedge\ \text{protocol\_admissible(trace)}\\
&\wedge\ \text{state\_admissible(trace)}\\
&\wedge\ \ldots
\end{aligned}
$$

For example, attacker_admissible(trace) may look like:

$$\text{attacker\_admissible}([ev, ev_0, trace])$$
$$\leftrightarrow \quad (ev.from = attacker \rightarrow ev.env.known \models ev.doc)$$
$$\land (ev_0.to = attacker \rightarrow ev.env.known = ev_0.env.known \int + ev_0.doc)$$
$$\land (ev_0.to \neq attacker \rightarrow ev.env.known = ev_0.env.known)$$
$$\land \text{attacker\_admissible}([ev_0, trace])$$

Here, a trace consisting of a last event ev, a previous event ev_0, and a remaining trace is considered. (For verification purposes the first element in a trace is the last event that occurred.) The first part of the axiom specifies that if a document is sent by the attacker ($ev.from = attacker$), he must be able to generate it from his knowledge ($ev.env.known \models ev.doc$); the second part specifies that if he received a document ($ev_0.to = attacker$) in the next to last event it is added to his knowledge and all derivable documents as well ($ev.env.known = ev_0.env.known$ $\int + ev_0.doc$) so that the knowledge is present in the last event; the third part specifies that if the document is not sent to the attacker his knowledge remains unchanged. This implies an attacker without access to the communication.

protocol_admissible(trace) specifies that if a normal agent issues a message in event ev it is the answer to a received document in some event ev_0 and follows the protocol as defined by agent-says:

$$\text{protocol\_admissible}([ev, trace])$$
$$\leftrightarrow \quad (\quad ev.from \neq attacker$$
$$\rightarrow \exists \ ev_0 \in trace: \text{agent-says}(ev_0.agent, ev_0.doc) = (ev.agent, ev.doc)$$
$$\land ev_0 = \text{matching\_event}([ev, trace]))$$
$$\land \text{protocol\_admissible}(trace)$$

If interleaving is used event ev_0 is not necessarily the next event, but can occur somewhere in the trace. This must be specified with matching_event. Furthermore, the axiom does not define the internal state of the agent between the two events, or when the state changes. The predicate state_admissible specifies that the state of all agents that do not participate in a communication remains unchanged. Further predicates are needed to specify the communication structure exactly.

The problem is that the different building blocks described so far cannot be specified completely separate. Actually, they are interwoven and may contain subtle interactions. This means it is very easy to introduce errors if the specification is written 'by hand'. A faulty specification is not an adequate model of the real world. In the best case it is not possible to prove that a protocol is indeed secure. In the worst case a 'proof' is possible for an insecure protocol. For example, the axioms used to describe admissible traces may be inadvertently contradictory (one axiom may say that a state change must occur, another that a state change may not occur). In this case there are no admissible traces (in the formal model) and every security property is trivially fulfilled. Especially the combination of interleaving and exclusive access to an agent is very difficult to specify correctly.

6   Conclusion

In this paper we discuss questions concerning the security of m-commerce applications. We introduce a method to avoid security problems by formally analyzing the application. The problem is that building a formal model is difficult and it is easy to introduce errors. Therefore we propose a 'construction kit' that allows an automatic generation of large parts of the specification. The kit consists of several parts: We describe how security protocols can be modeled. We also describe different attackers relevant for m-commerce applications. It is described what different abilities these attackers posses and how some of these abilities are represented in an algebraic specification. We also discuss further aspects that influence the modeling of the application and especially how these factors influence which traces (list of events) are possible and which not.

References

[1] R. Anderson and R. Needham. Programming satan's computer. In J. van Leeuwen, editor, *Computer Science Today: Recent Trends and Developments*. Springer LNCS 1000, 1995. 73

[2] M. Burrows, M. Abadi, and R. Needham. A logic of authentication. *ACM Transactions on Computer Systems*, 8(1), Feb 1990. 73

[3] M. Balser, W. Reif, G. Schellhorn, K. Stenzel, and A. Thums. Formal system development with KIV. In T. Maibaum, editor, *Fundamental Approaches to Software Engineering*, number 1783 in LNCS, pages 363–366. Springer-Verlag, 2000. 77

[4] D. Dolev and A. C. Yao. On the security of public key protocols. In *Proc. 22th IEEE Symposium on Foundations of Computer Science*, pages 350–357. IEEE, 1981. 79

[5] EMVCo LLC. *EMV 4.0 Specifications Book 1 – Application independent ICC to Terminal Interface requirements*, December 2000. http://www.emvco.com/documents/specification/view/book1.pdf. 73

[6] Alan O. Freier, Philip Karlton, and Paul C. Kocher. *The SSL Protocol Version 3.0*. Netscape Communications, November 1996. http://wp.netscape.com/eng/ssl3/. 73

[7] J. Loeckx, H. Ehrich, and M. Wolf. *Specification of Abstract Data Types*. Wiley-Teubner, 1996. 77

[8] Gavin Lowe. Breaking and fixing the Needham-Schroeder public-key protocol using FDR. In *Tools and Algorithms for the Construction and Analysis of Systems (TACAS)*, volume 1055, pages 147–166. Springer-Verlag, Berlin Germany, 1996. 74

[9] Catherine Meadows. Formal methods for cryptographic protocol analysis: Emerging issues and trends. *IEEE Journal on Selected Areas in Communication*, 21(1):44–54, January 2003. 81

[10] The Object Management Group (OMG). *OMG Unified Modeling Language Specification Version 1.5*, 2003. http://www.omg.org/technology/documents/formal/uml.htm. 74

[11] Lawrence C. Paulson. The inductive approach to verifying cryptographic protocols. *Journal of Computer Security*, 6:85–128, 1998. 80

A Minimal Market Model in Ephemeral Markets

Daniel Rolli, Dirk Neumann, and Christof Weinhardt

University of Karlsruhe, Information Management and Systems
Englerstr. 14, 76131 Karlsruhe, Germany
{rolli,neumann,weinhardt}@iw.uni-karlsruhe.de

Abstract. Peer-to-peer markets going mobile spur spontaneity in trading considerably. Spontaneity, however, imposes severe informational requirements on the market participants. Informational requirements are twofold: Firstly, participants have to agree on a common vocabulary for that spontaneous market. Secondly, they need precise information about how the trading process is organized. Due to the lack of a central market operator these common understandings must be determined by the market participants themselves. Prior to any market process, these terms and regulations must be distributed by the market participant that initiates the market process. This raises the question concerning the used ontology. Standards describing (business) processes are available in general, but are currently not suitable for ephemeral markets. Electronic markets are extremely context sensitive, making the establishment of common understandings crucial as well as difficult. This paper uses structural similarities of markets and creates a Minimal Market Model. Since this model is for all conceivable markets constituent, it can be used as the core component. As any market is founded on this minimal model, it can be systematically extended to capture the peculiarities of each particular market. The derivation of the Minimal Market Model is founded on a solid ground of economic theory and refined such that it can be expressed in a formal way.

1   Introduction

With the rapid technological progress of mobile ad hoc networks (MANET) [1] and wireless devices with sizeable graphical user interfaces (GUI) (like Smartphones, PDAs communicating wirelessly, etc.) mobility in markets has recently become a very important and attractive issue. The innovation and technology affinity of electronic market participants and the continuing trend towards total mobility in work and lifestyle only add to this significance. Yet, most electronic markets still rely on client-server-technology with a persistent infrastructure. Just rudimentary attempts have been made to establish mobile markets. Transferring the market GUI to mobile clients that still access the same steady server can only be considered a first start.

Ephemeral markets are markets that arise and fade spontaneously. They are typically short-lived and often based on a peer-to-peer (P2P) structure as well as

M. Núñez et al. (Eds.): FORTE 2004 Workshops, LNCS 3236, pp. 86–100, 2004.
© Springer-Verlag Berlin Heidelberg 2004

MANETs. The combination of the latter two paradigms enables truly decentralized mobile market structures that challenge the client-server-approach. They show promise to add to the variety of markets and to develop new application areas, but still require substantial research.

To advance the establishment of mobile markets, this paper provides a theoretical fundament for market models applicable to ephemeral markets. This brings together Economics with Computer Science concepts. Section 2 introduces ephemeral markets and identifies their economic challenges relevant for application. After related work is presented in section 3, section 4 presents the Minimal Market Model and the methodology for market modeling it implies. Section 5 proposes and examines the application of respective market models to ephemeral markets in order to tackle the crucial aspects of section 2. Section 6 briefly summarizes the presented work and gives an outline for future work.

2   Economic Characteristics of Ephemeral Markets

Traditionally, the discipline of Economics has been devoted to the study of markets. From the beginning, markets have been viewed as a coordination mechanism [2]. However, Coase concludes that in modern economic theory the market itself has "[...] an even more shadowy role than the firm. [...] In the modern textbook, the analysis deals with the determination of market prices, but discussion of the market itself has entirely disappeared" [3]. Characterizing markets as theoretical constructs in neoclassical tradition is not sufficient, as it provides only a functional definition of the market (a market is what a market does). It especially ignores the notion of transaction costs that exist in real-world markets. Based on this intuition, New Institutional Economics has bred out a more comprehensive definition than Neoclassical Theory. Accordingly markets describe the institutional rules how the market price is formed. With this definition in mind, economists have developed a causal theory about the working of markets including informational asymmetries and principal-agent problems.

When markets turn mobile, providing contextuality becomes crucial[1]. Contextuality comprises in what way and in what circumstances mobile agents act [4]. It is the mobility dimension most relevant for the economic challenges in ephemeral markets. These challenges arise from three major aspects of P2P markets based on MANETs:

1. Spontaneous participation
   Participants arbitrarily enter and leave a market. They appear without any prior market knowledge and leave taking all their information with them.
2. Spontaneous evolution
   Markets are created spontaneously by any participant and fade when every involved individual leaves the particular market.

---

[1] Kakihara and Sørensen identify three dimensions of mobility, namely spatiality, temporality and contextuality. [4]

3. Lack of a distinguished persistent entity
There is no distinguished entity that could continuously cache and provide information.

These three aspects combined hamper the establishment and maintenance of a constant and common contextuality. The biggest challenge is to inform an agent about the structure of the concrete market he is about to join.

In traditional markets a distinguished persistent entity usually exists and is trusted by all participants. This solves the problems arising from spontaneous participation and prevents spontaneous evolution. Information about the respective market – especially for new participants – is provided by the trusted distinguished entity. To a great extend, this information is presented and only exists in an implicit or informal way: Traditionally, the description of an electronic market is communicated as a combination of rules buried in code and one or several natural language documents. The software confronts the user with most market requirements by the entries it accepts and the information it reveals. The underlying structure is implicit and requires a lot of user experience to be extracted. An eventual additional description in natural language relies on the description skills and willingness of the author as well as a competent interpretation by the participants that can hardly be automated. As such, it supports no coherent theoretical foundation that guarantees or at least promotes a complete coverage of all relevant market aspects. In particular, the implicitness of information severely hampers an explicit analysis and comparison of the implied market specifications.

Since market participants always base their strategies on their understanding for one market, an explicit, formal, coherent and well-founded description for the market conditions is desirable in any kind of market. For ephemeral markets, however, such a representation is indispensable, because agents can hardly rely on a closed, rigid and untraceable implementation without further specification. They rather require easy perceivability of any particular aspect of trade with as little previous knowledge required as possible and rapid reconciliation of market protocols.

3   Related Work

A multitude of different terminologies as well as description approaches for market structure exists, both in the research and the industry sector. Taking part in markets – either electronic or face-to-face – always requires from all market participants to share a common understanding of trading specific terms and structure. Principally, there are not that many basic concepts and interrelations required, but the parallel development of proprietary standards in different fields and domains has bred out the mentioned multitude of variants.

eBay as one well-studied realization example of a market model requires from each participant to understand the underlying terms (buyer, seller, bid, etc.) used on its web pages[2] and the rules of the auction (bids with increasing

---

[2] http://www.ebay.com/

price, fixed time closing rule, etc.). A market model in general defines all institutional rules that regulate the functioning of an electronic market (e.g. bidding language, bidding process rules, price and allocation rules). For eBay at least three different approaches to terminology and structure description of the auction market model existfrom the research side. They range from "English auction with proxy bidding" [5] over "Second price auction" [6] to parametric description of components, like matching and allocation [7]. These descriptions - although totally different – all refer to the same market model. Even more difficult, the used terms and interrelations of market models are context-sensitive and often differ from industry to industry.

Principally, the problem of reconciling and coherently describing a common market model in ephemeral markets resembles the interoperability problem known from B2B electronic commerce. The interoperation between systems of different corporations requires a common understanding of the exchanged data and an agreed-upon protocol for data exchange. This requires syntactic as well as semantic interoperability.

On the syntactic level a mutually agreed-on vocabulary is needed to build the market model on this foundation. In B2B electronic commerce, the marketplace providers mostly dictate their own languages like xCBL (Commerce One), cXML (Ariba) or OAGIS (Open Application Group) [8, 9]. Those standards, however, do not encourage the reconciliation of conflicting terms from different backgrounds. They are mainly aimed at the interconnection of terminology-compliant ERP systems and not towards the use in spontaneous markets.

On the semantic level a common understanding of (business) processes and interrelation between terms is necessary for all market participants. Starting out with the open-edi initiative in 1988, the business transaction was split into two views – one for business properties and another for technical properties. Both views help different companies to define the same product in exactly the same way. In the open-edi tradition the RosettaNet Implementation Framework defines an exchange protocol, and the Message Guidelines, while the latter give instructions on how to encode individual partner interface processes into specific packages [10]. While RosettaNet is domain-specific for the IT industry, ebXML contributes a domain-independent global standard for communication between businesses and specifications for business processes. In essence, ebXML provides an open architecture to define business messages, communicate messages, conduct trading, and define and register business processes. By means of ebXML companies can describe their business processes in a specified manner and register them (i.e. XML documents). ebXML also provides a mechanism to match companies with the same business processes [11, 8].

In essence, a market model can also be perceived as providing a business process, namely for the market operator [12]. In ephemeral markets there does, however, not exist a central market operator. As such the market participants must themselves agree upon a market model. Current attempts to provide a common market model definition are mainly on the syntactical level. For example Wurman et. al decompose auctions into their institutional rules, which are treated as parameters [13, 14]. To define an auction a list of parameters needs to be specified for configuring the market model. By varying the specifications of the parameters other auction formats can be configured. As such, the configuration space of auctions that can be described parametrically is rather huge. Ströbel and Weinhardt extend Wurman's work from auctions to negotiations [15]. An abstract version of those definitions can be found at Maekioe and Weber [16]. The definition of the market models typically follows a top-down approach trying to encompass every imaginable market detail a priori. All parameters in a list that is given beforehand must be specified for a valid market model. Even if parameters are oblivious for a specific market, these approaches require every parameter in the list to be regarded. On the one hand, this hampers the spontaneous establishment of new market models essential for ephemeral markets. On the other hand, even an extensive parametrization approach still limits the number of market models that can be configured.

Thus, in the following, a bottom-up approach is motivated. Instead of identifying all conceivable parameters of the market model on the syntactical level, only a minimal set of interrelated core concepts – the Minimal Market Model – is presented. This merely needs to be refined in the – possibly few – aspects particular for one spontaneously initiated market, since the basic semantics remain the same for all particular market models. In this manner, the Minimal Market Model can be systematically extended to cover any market imaginable. The functional structure of this bottom-up approach makes a multitude of – potentially synonymous – tags or verbal descriptions obsolete as identifiers. For instance, the "English auction with proxy bidding" on eBay will be represented by a model identical with the one for the "Second price auction" that also refers to eBay. Thus, the ambiguities between existing standards are eliminated.

4   The Minimal Market Model

The Minimal Market Model (MMM) offers a semantic perspective on markets and a core of market conditions. Its structure suffices to capture the essential aspects within a market. But, beyond that, it forms the basis for systematically developing more specific market models. The MMM is presented as a theoretical approach in this section. The formalization aims at computer processing. But only in the following section 5 will the MMM be introduced to implementation. The main contribution is the theoretical look below the surface in order to identify the underlying structures of markets. This paper abstracts from any execution, enforcement, representation and media aspects including the actual realization of market communication, the technical infrastructure, etc.

The MMM is based on the following notion of intentional reasoning [17]: Trading occurs, because the participating agents perceive a trade as beneficial. Their intentions and the intrinsic motivation to realize these are the driving force for trade. In this context, a market is the impartial structured condensation of participants' intentions into exchange agreements. Therefore, intentions have to be uttered. The market process is characterized by patterns and market models intend to capture the structure of these patterns. Besides this descriptive aspect, market models can also be used to prescribe patterns for markets. Some patterns are required for every market, namely that intentions are characterized by their associated participant and the products the latter intends to give away and receive in exchange. Products are described by – potentially complex – attribute structures. Agreements can only be reached, when the constituting intentions match. These essential requirements are common to all markets and reveal their very essence. When assembling a market model, they can serve as a starting point and always outline the minimum conditions. The minimal structural description is tightened in the Minimal Market Model that is presented in the following subsection 4.1. Our notion of minimality implies that a market based strictly on the MMM has the least restrictions required for a market. This also means minimum restrictions on the strategy space of market participants and therefore maximum freedom for them. It implies that every essential aspect of markets is included and no superfluous or redundant information is represented. That leads to a very compact model with all of its elements indispensable. It appears in a manageable guise, but nevertheless its instances contain a wealth of dense information. Thus, the crucial function of the Minimal Market Model is to provide a complete, compact and coherent representation of the characteristics of the market nature.

4.1 Statics of the Minimal Market Model

Building on the deliberations above, we shape the heart of the MMM. The five elementary concepts, also called classes, within a market are the following:

- **intention**
  An intention represents the smallest closed entity of purpose within a market. It can be binding, which means that it is committed to the exact fulfillment of the expressed purpose. If it is not binding, it merely reveals information relevant for the market and does not in any way represent commitment nor the will to commitment.
  An intention is specified by adjacent instances of the three following classes.
- **participant**
  A participant represents an agent of any kind that takes part in the market. This can be a software agent, a human individual or any other entity capable of having intentions.
  Participants must have at least one intention in a market, but can have more.
- **product**
  A product can represent any good (including physical and digital ones, transferable rights, money, engagements like those for employment, ...) or service that can be traded within a market.
  It is associated with exactly one intention. And it always has either the role of an incomingProduct or an outgoingProduct, while incoming and outgoing refer to the perspective of the participant that is connected to the product via an intention. Every intention is associated with one or more incoming and one or more outgoing products.

- **attribute**

  One or several attributes describe the properties of products. Complex structures are accounted for by allowing attributes to have subattributes, since product description can be a very elaborate and crucial task in market modeling.

  An attribute can be declared forMatching. This means that the respective attribute is considered when matching the underlying intention with others. This requires other potentially matching intentions to also represent the statement of the respective attribute in a forMatching state. An attribute that is not forMatching provides information about the respective product but is not regarded for the matching in the market. An attribute is associated with at least one product. If it connects several products they must be associated with the same intention. Attributes spanning more than one product are used to represent interdependencies between the products.

- **agreement**

  An agreement is always derived from two fully specified intentions that are declared binding. It indicates that the two associated intentions match and that the respective participants have committed themselves to exchanging the products of the involved intentions.

These five concepts and the respective interrelations constitute the core of any market structure. Conditions for further interrelations are the following: Existing products and participants are always connected to one or more intentions, and an intention always needs one participant and one or more products associated. Every product connected with an intention is classified as either an incomingProduct or an outgoingProduct. Incoming and outgoing indicate whether the associated participant intends to give a product away or to receive it. Combining incoming and outgoing products in one intention means that the respective participant wants to trade all outgoingProducts for all incomingProducts in one deal. This allows for product bundles. It appears that the attributes only refer to products. Of course, the other concepts' properties are also described with attributes, but they can simply be embedded in the respective classes. The complex attribute-subattribute structure is generally not required for these concepts. If need be, though, it can also be attached to them.

It is crucial to keep in mind the distinction between the theoretical level of the MMM and the perceivable layer of markets in practice. For example, an intention, abstract by nature, can manifest in a multitude of ways ranging from vegetables with a price tag on a stall, over printed catalogs, or purchasable files presented on a website, to offers in structured electronic documents. The sheer raising of a hand for bidding in a real-life English auction epitomizes a full intention. It implies that the person attached to this raised hand intends and signals that she is willing to take the product at stake in exchange for the announced amount of money. The intention per se is, of course, not visible in the practical setting, but precisely defined in the context of the market model and the history of preceding intentions. The vivid variety of real life is brought down to the intention structure in theory.

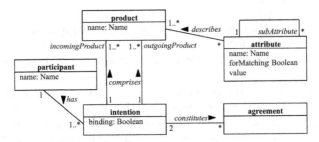

Fig.1. UML Class Diagram for Market Statics

Although intentions can represent preferences[3] – that are also theoretical in nature - they are not identical with these. A preference is internal, passive and not necessarily associated with the immediate will to act that is necessary for markets. An intention, however, is an active element that is consciously brought into a market. It does not have to represent a fully specified preference, but can leave some aspects, namely attributes, open for completion. Fully specified intentions, however, always express preferences, since the respective participant is willing to give away the specified outgoingProduct(s) in exchange for the incomingProduct(s). For rational agents this implies that they prefer what they receive over what they give away. All these aspects are static since their instantiation can only capture the state of a market at one given moment in time. Any aspect that is related to change over time is not regarded, yet.

To give an overview of the static aspects, the Unified Modeling Language (UML)[4] class diagram of Figure 1 depicts the static hull of a market, namely its elementary class types and their associations including cardinalities and role names.

In addition to Figure 1 some static axioms apply that implicitly have been introduced above. The following list pulls them together and gives a short explanation for each:

- **Intentions must be binding to be able to constitute an agreement**
  The binding-flag in the intention class must be set to true before an intention can constitute an agreement.
- **Intentions must exactly match when constituting an agreement**
  Agreements require matching in general:
  - The outgoingProduct of one intention must be equal to the incomingProduct of the partner intention and vice versa.
  - Every aspect specified by the attributes of a product with forMatching set to true must also be specified for the corresponding product of the other intention involved.
  Agreements further requrire exact matching in the following sense:

---

[3] In Economics preferences are used to express how alternatives are related to one another. For instance, an agent might prefer bundle a to b. [18]

[4] http://www.uml.org

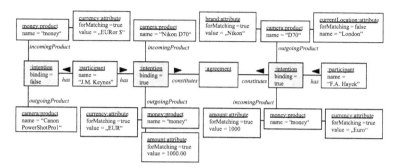

Fig.2. UML Object Diagram of Market Snapshot

- Every attribute must make one statement and not allow for any choice of alternatives. E.g. it must represent one single value as opposed to a range or set of values.
- The unequivocal statement of one attribute forMatching must be identical to its equivalent describing the corresponding product of the other intention involved.

Aspects specified by an attribute-subattribute combination do not necessarily have to appear in the same shape; only the meaning as well as the forMatching status must be equivalent. This may require rather complex matching methods. Yet, they can be kept simple by predefining the structure of attributes for concrete settings.

Figure 2 depicts a UML object diagram to give an example of what instances of the class diagram look like. According to the UML specification [19] it "shows a snapshot of the detailed state of a system at a point in time". Some association names and all attribute names are not displayed for the sake of clarity.

The exemplary snapshot in Figure 2 depicts two participants in a market for digital photo cameras. They have just accepted the agreement that F.A. Hayek will give his product D70, manufactured by Nikon and currently located in London, to J.M. Keynes in exchange for 1000 euros. J.M. Keynes has the non-binding intention to sell his camera Canon PowerShot Pro1. He would therefore accept euros or dollars.

A complete snapshot of a market comprises every instance of every class that is relevant at the time of the exposure. Naturally, not all instances have to be connected via association instances.

4.2   Dynamics of the Minimal Market Model

The static aspect is not sufficient for tracing the action within markets. It takes a series of snapshots that results in a market movie – to stay in the image. Every such market movie covers all information available in theory for the respective market. Therefore, it must contain a snapshot with a time stamp for every update

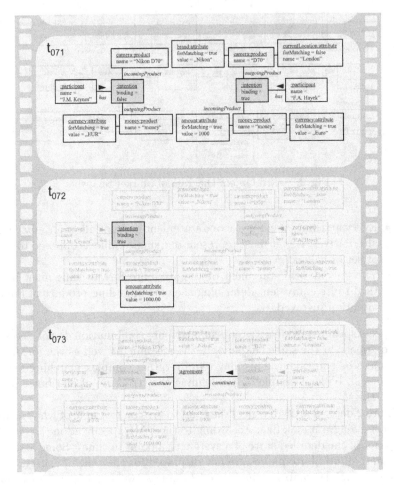

Fig.3. Exemplary Market History Excerpt

within the market. An update event is triggered whenever a new intention arises, an old one fades, an existing one shifts, an agreement is reached, etc. So, a market is represented by a history of instances of the class diagram as shown in the following Figure 3.

Figure 3 shows an example of three subsequent market snapshots t_{071}, t_{072} and t_{073}. All information new in a snapshot is shown in black; the remaining relevant information from the preceding step(s) is displayed in grey.

At t_{071} the market participant F.A. Hayek has made a binding offer for a camera he is willing to sell for 1000 euros. The camera is located in London, has the name D70 and the brand Nikon. J.M. Keynes signals his non-binding intention to buy a Nikon D70 camera and to pay for this in euros. At t_{072} J.M. Keynes concretizes the amount of euros he is willing to pay to 1000 and declares his intention binding. At t_{073} both participants reach an agreement based on their intentions which therefore must and do match.

Within the time dimension markets gain profile as the evolution of the snapshots also follows certain patterns. The structures for the development of intentions and agreements over time have to be added to a market model to describe the respective market's character as thoroughly as possible. They imply a restricted strategy space of the market participants and thereby limit the set of possible market movies within a more concrete market model. Consequently, these conditions go beyond the scope of just one market snapshot and (logically) span several snapshots within the history of one market. The static aspect of the MMM provides a closed basis for the dynamic market conditions. The concepts in section 4.1 plus the time are all the variables needed for any market microstructural specification. For the case of minimality only one very simple dynamic condition applies: **Ex post, at least one agreement between two different participants must exist in the history of market instances**

No strategy space restrictions exist beyond the ones presented so far. Thus, in a completely unconstrained – that is minimal – market, any participant can express any model-compliant intention at any time.

5   Implications

The MMM as presented is a concluded specification of the essential market conditions and captures the nature of markets. Any snapshot movie complying with the MMM depicts a market. Any instance that fits in a specific market model belongs to the respective market.

Furthermore, the MMM is a fundament for deriving the models for specific markets. On the static level, subclasses can inherit from the concepts of the MMM, to introduce the product categories, participant groups, etc. of one specific market. When talking about a domain market, for example the "camera market", a camera market model could derive the subclass "digital photo camera" from the product concept in the MMM. The European camera market model could further derive an explicit and mandatory location attribute for products and restrict its values to European cities. On the dynamic level, the most interesting phase lies between the stages where multiple intentions match and where the agreement based on two of the matching intentions is reached. This phase is called allocation.

In the minimal setting any agreement requires the explicit acceptance of the involved participants. In some specific market models, allocation rules automate the acceptance of the participants when the latter commit themselves to these rules. In contrast to the matching conditions that merely scrutinize intentions, allocation rules can actually concretize alter intentions. For the minimal setting we will further assume that allocation merely means explicitly accepting an agreement. But for specific markets, the matching conditions can be refined and allocation rules added. This can result in the specification of auction types.

Again, more structure will narrow the use of the resulting model to a subset of markets, for example a class of auctions.

The MMM does not restrict the visibility of information for any participant, since information revelation is not limited in a minimal market. However, information in concrete markets is often explicitly restricted for most (groups of) market actors and respective rules will have to be included in specific market models.

6 Application Issues for Market Models in Ephemeral Markets

For the application of market models this section will examine the challenges that occur when implementing any market model – including the MMM – in practice, independent from domain specifics. Addressing the issues of market model refinement and specific domains is beyond the scope of this paper.

For general implementation issues of market models the notion of *marketplaces* has to be regarded. A marketplace can be seen as an imaginary delimited container that restricts the matching of intentions. In theory (section 4) an omniscient auctioneer sees all instances within a market and can identify matching intentions, etc. However, the marketplace notion restricts the overall view for the matching and that of any agent to one container. What an agent can do is observe several containers, but joining the information gathered as well as possible functionality spanning multiple containers is up to him. To post intentions in a container, they are made explicit in offers. Only intentions whose offers meet within the same container can practically match. One intention can be expressed with more than one offer and the latter can be sent to different containers. So, it is possible to either distribute one intention to multiple offers, e.g. for bundles, or to express an intention repeatedly. If independent intentions that underlie offers in different containers match according to a given market model, they belong to the same market. Yet, the respective offers do not match in practice due to the separation between the marketplaces. Consequently, agreements can only be reached based on two intentions that are in the same container, i.e. on the same marketplace. So, the market, cohesive in theory, is usually distributed to several marketplaces in practice. In ephemeral markets we regard all nodes that share the market specification and are connected in a communication network as one marketplace.

Distributing the MMM to all potential market participants suffices to deliver a common understanding of the essential market notion. For the characteristics of a certain market, a specific market model including refined products, additional matching and allocation conditions, etc. can be derived from the MMM. This specific model alone delivers a common understanding for markets – as it includes all minimal information from the MMM – and at the same time informs the potential participants about the concrete market details. For transmission, the models need to be formalized in a serializable way. Ontologies [20] are one representation method suitable for all aspects of the MMM. They also provide the possibility to describe synonyms and homonyms that tackle the problems of conflicting terminologies (cp. section 3). Ontologies can be represented in the web ontology language[5] (OWL) that is XML[6] based and therefore serializable. Instances can be created from an ontology representing the MMM. They can be sent as offers and used for matching.

So, the required knowledge about market processes and the interfaces is clearly defined and formalized by the ontology in a machine-readable way. Any kind of client can now be used for the market as long as it complies with the provided specification. The self-concluded specification allows for everything from individual clients for each participant developed in proprietary environments to a light-weight and flexible common client automatically and traceably adapting to different specifications.

Yet, we still have to take a closer look at the three aspects crucial for contextuality in ephemeral markets, namely spontaneous participation, spontaneous evolution and the lack of a distinguished persistent entity (cp. section 2).

Spontaneous participation is supported by the introduced methodology of modeling markets. Firstly, a concrete market model that is a systematic refinement of the MMM contains a comprehensive market description. This provides the information necessary for market participants to adapt their strategies – and possibly clients – to the market conditions. Compared to the implementation a specification is much lighter and can be transferred more easily. Secondly, making the specification explicit and presentable in a formal way allows for systematic analysis and comparison of market models that can also be automated. Software agents, for example, could automatically adapt their strategies based on such specifications.

Spontaneous evolution profits from the MMM when one peer creates a new market. Again, a specific market model derived from the MMM is sure to contain a comprehensive description of this market. This is the origin for passing on this information as described above for the issue of spontaneous participation. To enable this, the MMM and a method for systematic refinement must be provided for every market creator.

The distinguished persistent entity missing in the ephemeral setting takes on the matching in traditional markets. The lack of this entity is made up for by passing on the market model, as the latter also contains the matching conditions. Their specification suffices to directly derive a matching implementation. This corresponds to the functionality of the central (matching) server in traditional markets. In the ephemeral setting one or more peers have to substitute this service.

The first case of a single peer providing the matching is most proximate with the traditional setting in mind. So, the one peer initiating a market could implement the matching conditions first, collect all offers in the corresponding imaginary container and match. As the initiator leaves, or at a time before that, he could pass on the responsibility for matching to another participant.

---

[5] http://www.w3.org/TR/owl-features/
[6] http://www.w3.org/XML/

The counterpart to the first approach is a completely decentralized matching where every participant matches all offers she sees – possibly only the ones interesting for herself. With several matching instances, the issue of multiple offers representing one intention must be resolved. One way is to technically ensure authenticity, integrity and that offers cannot be duplicated. Then one can interpret every offer as unique and the associated participant could always be accounted for it. Since this is hardly possible in a decentralized setting with possible freedom of implementation, we will look at a second way. The acceptance of an agreement can simply be kept explicit. Then, the participant associated with an offer implicitly confirms any offer when she accepts an agreement based on it.

In a decentralized market it is not possible to immediately and reliably delete one or several offers that represent an intention. Yet, it is desirable to be able to express that an offer is not valid anymore. Therefore we propose adding an attribute construct to the intention class that describes the validity period of one intention, respectively every offer.

7   Conclusion and Outlook

The Minimal Market Model epitomizes the methodology of bottom-up market modeling, which offers a new perspective on markets. Furthermore, the MMM is an explicit, coherent specification of the market essence and presentable in a formal way. We elaborated on the economic challenges of ephemeral markets and proposed the MMM to tackle these challenges.

The presented theoretical approach will be implemented in the project SESAM[7] and there be examined and tested in several applications. This will lead to refinement of this methodology and further research into its qualities and potentials. We will have to take a much closer look at the connection between the theoretical level and the practical details.

Moreover, we will elaborate on the systematic transition from the abstraction to concrete markets. We will, in particular, look at the integration of matching and allocation processes into market models. This effort includes the elaboration on information revelation. Making progress in this aspect would enhance the representation capabilities for auctions. Since the minimality in representation eliminates redundancy within the MMM, the information content is very dense. So, a wealth of contained information can be derived from the resulting market movies. This information extraction will also be subject to future research.

References

[1] Bruno, R., Conti, M., Gregori, E.: Wlan technologies for mobile ad hoc networks. In: 34th Annual Hawaii International Conference on System Sciences (HICSS-34). Volume 9., Maui, Hawaii (2001) 86

---

[7] SESAM - Self Organization and Spontaneity in Liberalized and Harmonized Markets – is funded by the German Federal Ministry of Education and Research.

[2] Smith, V.: Markets, institutions and experiments. In Nadel, L., ed.: Encyclopedia of Cognitive Science. Nature Pr (2002) 87

[3] Coase, R. H.: The Firm, the Market and the Law. University of Chicago Press, Chicago (1988) 87

[4] Kakihara, M., Sørensen, C.: Mobility: An extended perspective. In Sprague, R. H. J., ed.: Thirty-Fifth Hawaii International Conference on System Sciences (HICSS-35), Big Island, Hawaii, IEEE (2002) 87

[5] Wang, T. J.: Is last minute bidding bad? Working Paper (2003) 89

[6] Roth, A. E., Ockenfels, A.: Last-minute bidding and the rules for ending second-price auctions: Evidence from ebay and amazon on the internet. American Economic Review **92** (2002) 1093–1103 89

[7] Wolfstetter, E.: Auctions: An introduction. Journal of Economic Surveys **10** (1995) 367–420 89

[8] Hofreiter, B., Huemer, C.: B2b integration – aligning ebxml and ontology approaches. In: Eurasian Conference on Advances in Information and Communication Technology, Shiraz, Iran (2002) 339–349 89

[9] Li, H.: Xml and industrial standards for electronic commerce. Knowledge and Information Systems **2** (2000) 89

[10] Gosain, S., Malhotra, A., Sawy, O. A. E., Chehade, F.: The impact of common e-business interfaces. Communication of the ACM **46** (2003) 186–195 89

[11] Graham, I., Pollock, N., Smart, A., Williams, R.: Institutionalisation of e-business standards. In King, J. L., Lyytien, K., eds.: Workshop on Standard Making: A Critical Research Frontier for Information Systems, Seattle, WA (2003) 1–9 89

[12] Picot, A., Bortenländer, C., Röhrl, H.: The automation of capital markets. Journal of Computer-Mediated Communication **1** (1995) 89

[13] Wurman, P., Wellman, M. P., Walsh, P.: Specifying rules for electronic auctions. AI Magazine **23** (2002) 15–23 90

[14] Wurman, P., Wellman, M. P., Walsh, W. E.: A parametrization of the auction design space. Games and Economic Behavior **35** (1998) 271–303 90

[15] Ströbel, M., Weinhardt, C.: The montreal taxonomy for electronic negotiations. Group Decision and Negotiation **12** (2003) 143–164 90

[16] Maekioe, J., Weber, I.: Component-based specification and composition of market structures. In al., B.e., ed.: Coordination and Agent Technology in Value Networks. GITO, Berlin (2004) 127–137 90

[17] Elster, J.: Ulysses and the Sirens: Studies in rationality and irrationality. Cambridge University Press, Cambridge (1979) 90

[18] Debreu, G.: The coefficient of resource utilization. Econometrica **19** (1951) 273–292 93

[19] OMG: Unified modeling language specification (2003) 94

[20] Uschold, M., Gruninger, M.: Ontologies: Principles, methods and applications. Knowledge Engineering Review **11** (1996) 93–155 97

A Process-Oriented Approach Towards Structured Market Modelling

Juho Mäkiö[1]

University of Karlsruhe, Information Management and Systems
Englerstrasse 14, 76131 Karlsruhe, Germany
juho.maekioe@iw.uni-karlsruhe.de

Abstract. Our approach to market modelling is based on analysis of the negotiation process execution tasks. We use this for extraction of the offer life cycle, which provides tasks to be modelled. Combined, these tasks constitute the process. In addition to the offer life cycle, the information flow in the market also needs to be modelled. For each task, we propose the use of components that can be concatenated to concrete market models, whereby each component encapsulates one or more functional parts forming the complete process. We arrive at a structured approach to market modelling that is reduced in complexity because of the fragmentation of the modelling tasks. This approach is promising as it raises the modelling task to a high level of abstraction freeing the modeller from the implementation details. By way of example, we demonstrate how this approach can be employed to complete market models by using appropriate components.

1 Introduction

The progress of information technology has profoundly changed the structure of trading over the past two decades. A corollary of new forms of trading based on advancing computer technologies is a new organization of the exchange of goods and services in electronic markets. Electronic markets are commonly defined as inter-organizational information systems that allow buyers and vendors to exchange information about prices and product offerings [1]. They support electronic transaction processes, enabling multiple buyers and sellers to trade with technical aids, such as computers, to fulfil the needs of buyers, sellers, and other information carriers in respect of information dissemination and exchange.

The setting of the market structure parameters determinates the market design. Since the needs and demands of market participants require a market design that induces market efficiency and the setting of market structure parameters affects the market outcome, electronic markets have to be carefully designed. Central questions concerning market design are what parameters, rules, and criteria are necessary to compose a market, how such components can be defined, and how they can be composed to build a market.

This paper presents a process-oriented approach to the design and implementation of electronic markets. The approach is based on the offer life cycle,

M. Núñez et al. (Eds.): FORTE 2004 Workshops, LNCS 3236, pp. 101–113, 2004.

defined by the stages each offer in electronic markets usually goes through. The benefit of process-orientation lies in facilitation of a higher level of abstraction in the design and implementation of electronic markets, which eases both of these tasks dramatically.

Section 2 presents and discusses various researches in the context of auction and negotiation classification in respect of electronic markets. Section 3 presents a process-oriented approach to describe electronic markets that is needed to simplify and to clarify the design and implementation of electronic markets. Section 4 shows that the process-oriented approach leads to component-based specification and composition of electronic markets. Section 5 examines a concrete application scenario and shows how the process-oriented approach presented here – together with the components and their composition – can be used to design electronic markets. Finally, a possible implementation for the concepts presented here is discussed and conclusions and presentation of the ambit of future work is presented in section 6.

2   Related Work

Since all auctions are negotiations, (but not vice versa, cf. [1]) we consider works from both fields of research in this section. McAfee and McMillan define an auction as "a market institution with an explicit set of rules determining resource allocation and prices on the basis of bids from the market participants." According to [2], a microeconomic system consists of two distinct component elements: an environment and an institution, whereby the environment is defined as a "set of initial circumstances which can not be altered by the agents or the institutions within which they interact" [2].

An economic environment consists of economic agents (market participants), commodities (transaction object), and agent characteristics. The institution defines the language of the market, the communication rules for agents, and the condition under which the communication takes place [3]. The rules that define an institution can be subdivided into market microstructure, business structure, and infrastructure. The market microstructure defines the trading rules, the business structure defines rules for the fee structure of the market, and the infrastructure defines rules given by the computerization of markets. The disjunction between market microstructure and infrastructure is particularly relevant for electronic markets. Figure 1 illustrates the elements described above.

The definitions outlined above describe microeconomic systems by giving a general survey of the elements that constitute a microeconomic system. Further considerations need to be made in order to clarify the various functions of these elements. Various schemata and ontologies for the classification of electronic markets, electronic negotiations, and electronic auctions [4, 5] have been presented in scientific literature that aims to consider and describe them at an abstract level. For the most part, these schemata focus on a limited sub field of markets and do not provide a classification for markets in general.

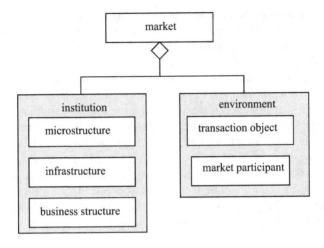

Fig.1. Microeconomic system component elements based on [2]

[6] presents a price-based general platform for electronic negotiation that supports multiple simultaneously running auctions. The authors mention that the "task of designing negotiation rules is that of designing auctions." For this purpose, they define a classification of auctions in the form of a parameterisation of the auction design space focusing on the operational perspective of auctions. The authors categorize the parameters in three groups according to the basic activities common to all auctions: (1) receiving bids, (2) clearing, and (3) revealing intermediate information. Each of these activities is further subdivided into message types defining the communication process between agents and the auction server, and the handling of bids in it. According to this categorization, the authors have created a XML schema implementation of the parameterisation [7].

The agent communication language (ACL) defined by the Foundation of Intelligent Physical Agents (FIPA) provides a process-oriented view of the modelling of agent communication. ACL provides various message types explicitly intended to support negotiation. Nevertheless, it is inappropriate for defining the properties of negotiation protocols because ACL is intended to be used by agents during the negotiation.

An approach for the definition of the agent communication in unified modelling language (UML) [8] – included into the FIPA'99 standard – is presented in [9]. The authors define an agent interaction protocol (AIP) that describes a communication pattern with an allowed sequence of messages between agents having different roles, constraints on the content of the messages, and a semantic that is consistent with the communicative acts (CAs) within a communication pattern. However, the granularity of the modelling is very fine and would lead to a modelling task that requires detailed knowledge about the communication process of the negotiation. Hence, AIP is inappropriate for market modelling at a higher abstract level.

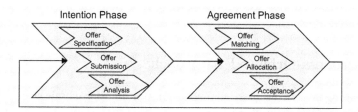

Fig.2. Negotiation process execution tasks according to [5]

[10] presents an ontology for automated negotiation. The task of this ontology is to "provide the shared vocabulary permitting agents to negotiate in any kind of marketplace regardless of the negotiation mechanism that is used." The authors see the advantages of their approach firstly in its flexibility and secondly in that it "provides a common terminology to reason in terms of negotiation protocols, their components, and the constraints regulating them" [10].

A further classification, "The Montreal Taxonomy" (MT) [5], is based on the media reference model (MRM) presented in [11]. The MRM identifies four phases of interaction: 1) knowledge; 2) intention; 3) agreement and 4) settlement (cf. [7]).

MT states that "an agreement process represents the complete agent interaction in the intention and agreement phase for the coordination of one or more transactions" and thus it focuses on the intention phase and on the agreement phase of electronic transactions. The authors subdivide both of these phases into tasks related to the offer exchange in the electronic negotiation, whereby the final execution does not implicitly correspond to the given process model, and some tasks can be omitted. The intention phase has three subtasks: offer specification, offer submission, and offer analysis, whereby the subtasks of an agreement phase are: offer matching, offer allocation, and offer acceptance (cf. Figure 2).

In summary, the classifications in [3] and [6] are based on similarities amongst negotiation protocols. [3] offers a 'snapshot' description of microeconomic systems or negotiation scenarios, whereby [6] also take into account operational perspectives of auctions – e.g. how they function. The classification given in [5] and the ontology introduced in [10] are more general approaches providing a terminology for electronic negotiations.

It is of note that all the works referred to above consider the market as a system. However, in order to define and specify electronic markets we propose a change of paradigm in market modelling. Instead of focusing solely on the market as a system, we introduce an offer-oriented methodology for the market definition and description. The offer lifecycle stands in the foreground of the offer-oriented methodology and the modelling task is oriented to the phases in the offer lifecycle, from the offer specification till the offer execution. These phases are common to all negotiations, and particularly all auctions . The phases define a process of offer handling in the market that forms a skeleton for the offer-oriented approach.

3   A Process-Oriented Approach

The preceding section discussed classifications for microeconomic systems and for electronic negotiations and proffers an offer-oriented approach of market modelling. This section presents a process-oriented approach to describe auction-based electronic markets. The intention of the approach presented here is the attainment of a high abstraction level of market modelling in order to free the market designer from implementation details. Our approach adapts to the negotiation process execution tasks (cf. Figure 2) and extracts functionalities needed to describe an electronic market. The objective of this section is the determination of these functionalities. Note that we assume the transaction object type – which describes the objects of the negotiation – as pre-defined. Objects can be both material and immaterial goods that are transferred after an agreement in the negotiation is reached. In addition to the functionalities illustrated in Figure 2, two further fields need to be modelled: information revelation and strategy (cf. [5, 6]). As these fields cannot be assigned to any certain functionality in the process oriented approach, they will be discussed briefly in section 3.2 (cf. [5]).

In the following scenario, we consider a client-server based trading system where multiple clients are able to define and send offers (bids and asks) to a single electronic market system. Note that we do not focus on the implementation of such a system, but on the functionalities required for the process-oriented approach to describe electronic markets. The process-oriented approach is defined and structured as a reusable process. This means that the basic structure of the process is usable for similar transaction processes in electronic markets. In the abstraction level of modelling the basic transaction process is domain-independent: it is detached from the domain and from the transaction object as well as from the domain-specific behaviour of market participants. In addition, new auction types can be easily generated by specification of values of the basic activities within the transaction process.

The diagram in Figure 3 illustrates the offer life cycle from the specification to the acceptance and shows both of the phases relevant to our approach (intention phase and agreement phase) from the negotiation process execution tasks. The client is responsible for the specification and submission of the offers (combined as "Client side"). The offer analysis, matching, allocation, and acceptance are executed in the server (combined as "Server side"). The starting point for the process-oriented approach is the life cycle of an offer, e.g. what happens with an offer from the moment of its definition in the trading client until its execution in the trading server. After an offer analysis the offer can be whether matched (Offer Matching) or not (Offer Matching). For example in continuous double auction the matching is executed directly an order inserted in a trading system.

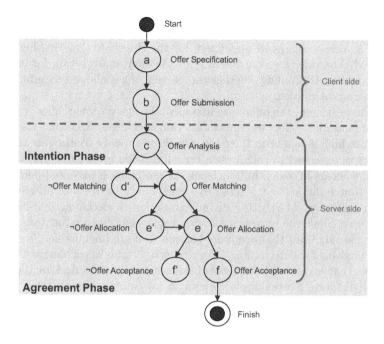

Fig.3. The offer life-cycle

3.1   The Process

Firstly, on the client side, the agent participating in the negotiation specifies the offer. The offer describes one single combination of values associated to the negotiation attributes. Note that each attribute is not necessarily used firsthand for the negotiation. Some attributes contain information necessary for the offer flow management. The offer specification indicates the constraints towards the transaction object. The process of the offer specification functionality does not need to be modelled independently of the negotiation. Irrespective of the various attributes, the process of the offer specification can be considered equal for all electronic markets.

In the second step, the client submits the offer to the trading server. From a functional point of view, an agent requires a mechanism for the submission of an offer. Irrespective of the technical mode of communication, the submission mechanism can be considered equal in any electronic market system and thus need not be modelled separately for each single market. On the server side, the offer is first analysed, meaning that the offer is checked in respect of certain conditions or rules. For example, in an English auction, the value of the new offer has to be higher than the current best bid. Since each auction potentially varies in offer analysis rules, these must be explicitly modelled. The modelling provides a set of functions or rules to proof the offers invented into the current auction. Together, all these functions and rules build the functionality of offer analysis. The number of various functions is limited. MT specifies only two rules: value and threshold. MT names three signs in both instances – for the value: ascending, descending, and undefined; for the threshold: low-cut, high-cut, and undefined. The rules given in the MT for the offer analysis can, for instance, be extended towards proofing whether the participant is allowed to submit an offer into the current market.

In the next step, the offers are matched. The goal of matching is to find potential counterpart offers for the transaction execution. Note that the execution of the matching depends on the current auction type. In continuous auctions the matching is executed in each case after submission of an offer into the current auction, whereas in sealed bid auctions the matching is executed periodically in defined time intervals or triggered by events. Various distance functions can be used for matching. Mostly, the distance function in electronic markets is based on the price. Since the price is a numeric value, the distance function is a simple one but also auctions that are more complicated are imaginable. Since auctions are mechanisms for determining price and other terms of exchange [12], distance functions that use other parameters besides the price are used for the measurement of distance. For example, price can be combined with other properties like period of supply, or duration of the credit. Such multidimensional distance functions are used for the determination of quality rankings between offers and requests in electronic coordination scenarios, and are discussed in depth in [13]. For combinatorial auctions – which allow an expression of offers for combinations of goods and determine an allocation maximizing overall revenue – a detailed insight is delivered in [12].

The result of any price-based business negotiation process is a transaction, which specifies a certain transaction object at a certain price. The price determination for the transaction is done during the offer allocation. Thus, any implementation of an electronic market contains at least one mechanism for price-determination or price-generation. There are two conceivable ways to accomplish the price-determination: (1) sealed-bid or (2) out-cry. In the first case a number of bids and requests are collected. The price is determined automatically according to predefined rules, e.g. the maximisation of total transaction volume. Examples for this kind of price-determination are the Vickrey-auction and the call market. In the second case, the price determination process is continuously executed to compute the "best" available price at any moment for the transaction. The "best price" is the lowest possible price for the buyers and the highest possible price for the sellers. Auction forms such as the English auction, Dutch auction, and continuous double auction have an out-cry price-determination mechanism. Like the execution of the matching, the execution of the offer allocation also depends on the current auction form. For example, in the standard English auction and Dutch auctions the allocation is done only once, namely at the point when the auction ends. Thus, the offer allocation must also be modelled explicitly.

3.2   The Process Independent Criteria

As mentioned above, the information revelation and the strategy must also be modelled for electronic markets. Since both of these aspects are not bound with any specific state in the order life cycle and thus not bound with any phase in the process, they need to be modelled independently.

Information Revelation   The rules for information revelation define the amount, kind, and timing of information used for the communication during a negotiation, whereby sealed bid auctions do not reveal any information per definition. In [6] and [14] Wurman et al. identify four kinds of information that can be supplied to the participating auction agents: order book, price quotes, transaction history, and schedule information. Information supply can easily be defined by auction parameters according to these. An extensive presentation of criteria for the information revelation is given in the MT. Since the MT proposes a taxonomy for electronic negotiation, some criteria presented in it overlap with those discussed in [6] and [14].

An order book is used to list current bids [14]. The authors state: "Many online auction sites have a policy of revealing all of the bids." Beyond this, they note that auctions can reveal more differentiated information. The revelation of the information can be differentiated in various ways. In addition to those criteria given in the MT, we identify two further criteria of information revelation: the breadth and the depth. The breadth declares attributes of bids visible from the order book for the agents and the depth specifies the number of the bids visible from the order book.

The Strategy   The strategy rules define the fees for the services that the market platform supplies to the participants. Electronic markets are exposed to competition among the customers. Accordingly, market place operators need to offer better and more differentiated services to the customers. Thus, offered services vary in fees customers need to pay for their usage. Therefore, fees need to be modelled. For example, the order book breadth and the order book depth can be concatenated with fees. A more detailed discussion about fees is available in [15].

4   Components

Some basic concepts for the implementation of the process-oriented approach with components are discussed in this section. In the software engineering domain components are defined as "a physical and replaceable part of a system that conforms to and provides the realization of a set of interfaces...[component] typically represents the physical packaging of otherwise logical elements, such as classes, interfaces, and collaborations" [8]. This general definition focuses both the software conception and its implementation. The component definition given below considers both of these aspects, whereby the conceptual level of the market modelling is in the foreground.

4.1 Component Definitions

Firstly, we consider components as a set of rules $R = \{R_1, R_2, \ldots, R_k\}$ with R_i, $i \in \{1, \ldots, k\}$, k mutual independent rules, and a set of algorithms $A = \{A_1, A_2, \ldots, A_l\}$ with A_j, $j \in \{1, \ldots, l\}$, l mutual independent algorithms. We define a component C as a set of rules R and a set of algorithms A that is $C = \{R, A\}$. For instance an auction with one seller, multiple buyers, and winner determination according to lowest bid contains following components: $C_1 = \{\text{Participation(two-sided)}\}$, $C_2 = \{\text{Agents(n bidders:1 auctioneer)}\}$, and $C_5 = \text{Provision(offer-dependent)}$.

For the concatenation of these components to new components and finally to new market structures [16] defines a logic composition operation ∘ for two or more components. For example, the components C_1 and C_2 can be used to build a new component $C = C_1 \circ C_2$. In this case, C_1 and C_2 are subcomponents of C.

The recursive definition of components and their composition lead directly to a definition for a component based market structure: $M = C_1 \circ C_2 \circ \ldots \circ C_n = \{R_1, A_1\} \circ \{R_2, A_2\} \circ \ldots \circ \{R_n, A_n\}$. This definition enables us to build up a market structure from components using the composition.

For the structured market modelling it is useful to adjust the component definition such that it takes into account the process-oriented approach. Note that our component definition differentiates from the definition in [8] (p. 343) in that it considers not solely the "physical packaging of otherwise logical elements, such as classes, interfaces, and collaborations" but also their parameterisation. For example, the rules to control the admission of market participants into one electronic market can be defined by agents and groups of agents whom the admission is prohibited or allowed. In the example above we defined an auction with one seller and multiple buyers with following components: $C_1 = \text{Participation(two-sided)}$, $C_2 = \text{Agents(n bidders:1 auctioneer)}$. A further component $C_3 = (\text{Admission([list of agents allowed to admit into the market])})$ leads together with C_1 and C_2 to an two-sided auction with 1 auctioneer and n bidders, whereby only bidders given in the component C_3 are allowed to take part.

4.2 Component Classes

Components are based on rules and algorithms that customarily govern the process in a market. The offer life cycle defines the main component in the process-oriented approach. As mentioned above, the current auction type determines the order life cycle. [6] provides a classification of traditional auction types. These are illustrated in Figure 4.

Each auction type defines a basic structure of communication with agents. Hence, these types can be used as a skeleton for the definition of the offer life cycle and consequently for the definition of the communication components. Each auction type follows the negotiation process execution tasks (cf. Figure 2). Consequently, an order life cycle according to Figure 3 exists for each auction type. Thus, components for the communication mechanisms can easily be defined for further auction types.

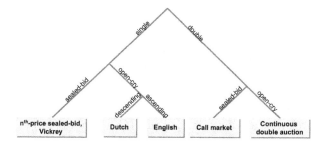

Fig.4. A classification of classic auction types [6]

Further components can be identified and deduced from phases of the order life cycle (cf. Figure 3). For each single phase, characteristic components can be defined according to the relevant tasks that need to be executed. For example, corresponding components are needed for the offer matching or for the offer analysis.

As mentioned above, process independent criteria cannot be modelled based on order life cycle. Thus, components to implement the information revelation and fees have to be provided separately.

5   Composition of Components

This section demonstrates how concrete market models can be assembled using components and the process-oriented approach presented in this work. Consider therefore a Reverse 1st Price Sealed Auction (C_1) for eProcurement where one buyer (C_2) wants to buy a computer system and multiple sellers (C_3) offer in a one round bidding (C_4) auction. The winner will be determined according to lowest bid (C_5). The price and the bidder name of the five best offers will be published at the end of the auction (C_6). All bids must be submitted online, no later than 5:00 p.m., Friday November 14, 2003 (C_7). Bids received after the designated date and time will not be considered. Bidding will commence at 10:00 a.m., Tuesday December 2 2003 (C_8). If there are two or more identical high bids, the apparent high bidder will be determined by the earliest date-received stamp (C_9). Withdrawal of offers is not allowed (C_{10}).

5.1   Modelling of the Process

As above mentioned the auction form used is a Reverse 1st Price Sealed Auction. In the process-oriented approach, first step to do is the selection of the component for the communication. Note that the definition of the communication component $C = C_1 \circ C_2 \circ C_3 \circ C_4$ determinates the order life cycle. Having in mind the order life cycle presented in Figure 3 and assuming that the definition of the transaction object is already done (a computer system), the relevant part of the order life cycle starts with the offer analysis.

Analysis: For this auction there are no limits for the participation or no rules for the value and threshold given. The only limitation given is that all bids must be submitted online, no later than 5:00 p.m., Friday November 14, 2003 and bids received after the designated date and time will not be considered (C_7).

Matching: The bids will be opened beginning at 10:00 a.m., Tuesday, December 2, 2003 means that the matching will be started at that time (C_8). For the matching relevant attribute is the price (C_5). From there, two components need to be created: one to define at what time the matching will start (C_8) and another to implement the matching according to the lowest bid (C_5). Note that the matching is here used to sort the bids in the current auction according to the price and date-received, because by identical high bids, the apparent high bidder will be determined by the earliest date-received stamp.

Allocation: All bids will be opened beginning at 10:00 a.m., Tuesday, December 2, 2003. This means that the allocation starts at that time and can be defined with the component (C_8). The winner is the submitter of the offer with the lowest bid (C_5). For two or more identical bids, the apparent high bidder will be determinated by the earliest date-received stamp (C_9). For the allocation, two components are needed: one to control the starting of the allocation and the second one to determine the winner according to the lowest bid.

Acceptance: Because the withdrawal of the offers is not allowed (C_{10}), the last component to create permits the withdrawal of submitted offers. Composing these components together leads to a component based market structure: $M = C \circ C_5 \circ C_7 \circ C_8 \circ C_9 \circ C_{10}$. New component based market structures can be reached just by changing one of the components or by insertion/deletion of components into/from the existing market structures.

5.2 Modelling of the Information Flow

In addition to the process modelling, the process independent criteria (cf. Section 3.2) also need to be modelled. According to the rules for the auction outlined above, the bidder names of the five best offers will be published at the end of the auction (C_6). This means that from the first five bids in the order book the bidder name and the offered price will be published at the end of the auction (therewith it is obvious that the information flow is a process independent criteria: the timing of the information publishing can be chosen free irrespective of the offer life cycle). Consequently, three components need to be defined: firstly, component C_a that defines the breadth declares attributes visible in the auction for the agents (here the name and the price), secondly the component C_b that defines the depth to specify the number of the visible bids (here five), and thirdly the component C_c that defines the timing for the information revelation. This means that the component C_6 is a composition of the components C_a, C_b, and C_c.

6 Conclusions and Future Work

A rise in the level of interest in computer supported electronic markets is characteristic of the past few years. Theoretical foundations for the design and implementation of such systems are given among other things by systematic analysis of the nature of microeconomic systems, negotiations, and auctions. In this paper, we first presented an overview of research in these fields and ascertained that (electronic) markets and (electronic) negotiations are analysed as systems. Having identified the difficulties for market design, we proposed a process-oriented approach towards structured market modelling. The process-orientation that we presented is based on the offer life cycle, from which we deduced a common process for offers in any negotiation system. This process consists of six phases: specification, submission of the offer (processed on the "Client side") and offer analysis, matching, allocation, and acceptance (processed on the "Server side"). We stated that each of these phases contains specific functions that need to be modelled. In addition to the modelling of the offer life cycle, we showed the need for the separate modelling of information revelation and strategy because both cannot be assigned to any certain functionality in the order life cycle.

Subsequent to the definition of components and their composition, we demonstrated using a concrete example how the process-oriented approach based on the order life cycle could be effectively used to define a market structure.

A further aspect, not featured in this paper, but which we are working on, is the market modelling language MML – a semi-formal component-based language for the modelling and specification of electronic markets. The MML is based on the process-oriented approach presented in this work and on the parameterisation of that process. The MML contains components for the specification of the offer life cycle, the information revelation and the strategy, allowing the market designer easily to design new market structures. We consider that this frees the market designer from implementation details and that a higher level of modelling abstraction leads to better understanding of electronic markets and the mechanisms behind them.

References

[1] Kersten, G. E., Teich, J.: Are all e-commerce negotiations auctions? In: Fourth International Conference on the Design of Cooperative Systems, Sophia-Antipolis, France. (2000) 102
[2] Smith, V. L.: Microeconomic systems as an experimental science. The American Economic Review **72** (1982) 923–955 102, 103
[3] Smith, V.: Markets, institutions and experiments. In Nadel, L., ed.: Encyclopedia of Cognitive Science. Nature Pr (2002) 102, 104
[4] Lomuscio, A. R., Wooldridge, M., Jennings, N. R.: A Classification Scheme for Negotiation in Electronic Commerce. In: Agent Mediated Electronic Commerce. Springer (2001) 19–33 102
[5] Ströbel, M., Weinhardt, C.: The montreal taxonomy for electronic negotiations. Group Decision and Negotiation Journal **12** (2003) 143–164 102, 104, 105

[6] Wurman, P., Wellman, M. P., Walsh, W. E.: A parametrization of the auction design space. Games and Economic Behavior **35** (2001) 304–338   103, 104, 105, 108, 109, 110

[7] Schmid, B., Lindemann, M.: Elements of a reference model for electronic markets. In: Proceedings of the 31st Annual Hawaii International Conference on Systems Science HICSS'98, Vol. IV. (1998) 193–201   103, 104

[8] Booch, G., Rumbaugh, J., Jacobson, I.: The Unified Modelling Language User Guide. –. Addison Wesley (1998)   103, 108, 109

[9] Bauer, B., Mueller, J., Odell, J.: Agent uml: A formalism for specifying multiagent software systems. International Journal of Software Engineering and Knowledge Engineering **11** (2001) 207–230   103

[10] Tamma, V., Wooldridge, M., Dickinson, I.: An ontology for automated negotiation. In: Proceedings of the Workshop on Ontologies in Agent Systems, Bologna, Italy (2002)   104

[11] Schmid, B.: Elektronische Märkte – Merkmale, Organisation, Potentiale. In: Handbuch Electronic Commerce. Vahlen Verlag (1999)   104

[12] Reeves, D. M., Grosof, B. N.: Automated negotiations from formal contract descriptions. Computational Intelligence **18** (2002) 482–500   107

[13] Veit, D.: Terminology and Overview. In: Electronic Negotiations and Multidimensional Matchmaking – an Agent based Approach. University of Karlsruhe (2002) 21   107

[14] Wurman, P., Wellman, M. P., Walsh, P.: Specifying rules for electronic auctions. AI Magazine **23** (2002) 15–23   108

[15] Holtmann, C., Neumann, D., Weinhardt, C.: Market engineering – an interdisciplinary approach. Technical report, University of Karlsruhe, Karlsruhe (2002) 108

[16] Maekioe, J., Weber, I.: Component-based specification and composition of market structures. In al., B.e., ed.: Coordination and Agent Technology in Value Networks. GITO, Berlin (2004) 127–137   109

Formal Specification
of Symbolic-Probabilistic Systems*

Natalia López, Manuel Núñez, and Ismael Rodríguez

Dept. Sistemas Informáticos y Programación
Facultad de Informática
Universidad Complutense de Madrid
E-28040 Madrid, Spain
e-mail: {natalia,mn,isrodrig}@sip.ucm.es

Abstract. We consider the formal specification and validation of systems where probabilistic information is not given by means of fixed values but as sets of probabilities. These sets will be intervals contained in $(0, 1]$ indicating the possible value of the *real* probability. In order to specify this kind of systems we will introduce a suitable extension of the notion of finite state machine. Essentially, choices between transitions outgoing from a state and having the same input action are probabilistically resolved. We will also present some implementation relations to assess the conformance of an implementation to a specification. The first implementation relation will clearly present the probabilistic constraints of the specification, but it will be unfeasible from the practical point of view. The other relations will overcome the problems of the first one by introducing a notion of conformance *up to* a given level of confidence. These relations will assess the validity of an implementation with respect to a specification by considering a finite *sample* of executions of the implementation and comparing it with the probabilistic constraints imposed by the specification.

1 Introduction

During the last years we have seen an evolution in the kind of systems that formal methods are dealing with. In the beginning the main focus was on functional properties. The next step was to consider quantitative information such as the *time* underlying the performance of the system or the *probabilities* resolving the non-deterministic choices to be taken. Following this line, plenty of frameworks considering time and/or probabilistic aspects have been proposed (e.g. [1, 2, 3, 4, 5, 6, 7, 8, 9, 10]).

In this paper we concentrate on the formal specification and validation of a novel notion of probabilistic systems. One of the main criticisms about formal models including probabilistic information is the inability, in general, to

* Work supported by the Spanish MCyT project *MASTER* (TIC2003-07848-C02-01), the Junta de Castilla-La Mancha project *DISMEF* (PAC-03-001), and the Marie Curie project *TAROT* (MRTN-CT-2003-505121).

M. Núñez et al. (Eds.): FORTE 2004 Workshops, LNCS 3236, pp. 114–127, 2004.
© Springer-Verlag Berlin Heidelberg 2004

accurately determine the actual values of the involved probabilities. The usual inclusion of probabilities is given by (using a process algebraic notation) processes such as $P = a +_{\frac{1}{3}} b$. In this case, P may be thought as expressing that if the choice between a and b must be resolved then a has probability $\frac{1}{3}$ of being chosen while b has probability $\frac{2}{3}$. However, there are situations where it is rather difficult to be so precise when specifying a probability. A very good example is the specification of *faulty channels* (e.g. the classical ABP [11]). Usually, these protocols contain information such as "the probability of losing the message is equal to 0.05." However, two questions may be immediately raised. First, why would one like to specify the exact probability of losing a message? Second, how can the specifier be sure that this is in fact the probability? In other words, to know the exact value seems as a very strong requirement. It would be more appropriate to say "the probability of losing the message is smaller that 0.05." Such a statement can be interpreted as: "we know that the probability is low but we do not know the exact value." Moreover, our approach, that we call *symbolic probabilities*, allows us to use *successive refinements*. For example, let us suppose that after experimentation with the system we have detected that some messages are lost (so that we can discard that the probability of losing a message is equal to zero) but *not many* messages were lost. By using the appropriate statistics machinery (mainly hypothesis contrasts and Tchebyshev inequality) we may indicate information such as "with probability 0.95 the *real* probability of losing the message belongs to the interval $[0.01, 0.03]$."

In this paper we present a formalism to specify symbolic-probabilistic systems. We will consider a suitable extension of *finite state machines* where probabilistic information is included in the appropriate places. Intuitively, transitions in finite state machines indicate that if the machine is in a state s and receives an input i then it will produce an output o and it will change its state to s'. An appropriate notation for such a transition could be $s \xrightarrow{i/o} s'$. If we consider a probabilistic extension of finite state machines, transitions as $s \xrightarrow{i/o}_p s'$ indicate that the probability with which state s performs the output o after the input i is received and reaches state s' belongs to the range given by the expression p. For instance, p may be the interval $[\frac{1}{4}, \frac{3}{4}]$ while the *real* probability is in fact 0.53.

An important issue when dealing with probabilities consists in fixing how different actions/transitions are related according to the probabilistic information. In [5] a taxonomy, that has become classical, is given. In this paper we consider a variant of the *reactive* interpretation of probabilities since it is the most suitable for our framework. Intuitively, a reactive interpretation imposes a probabilistic relation among transitions labeled by the same action, but without quantifying how choices between different actions is resolved. In our case, our probabilistic finite state machines will be able to express probabilistic relations between transitions outgoing from a given state and having the same input action (while the output action may vary). In the following example we illustrate this notion of probabilities (the formal definition of our notation will be given in the next section).

Example 1. Let us consider that the unique transitions from a state s are

$$t_1 = s \xrightarrow{\quad i_1/o_1 \quad}_{p_1} s_1 \qquad t_2 = s \xrightarrow{\quad i_1/o_2 \quad}_{p_2} s_2 \qquad t_3 = s \xrightarrow{\quad i_1/o_3 \quad}_{p_3} s_2$$

$$t_4 = s \xrightarrow{\quad i_2/o_1 \quad}_{p_4} s_3 \qquad t_5 = s \xrightarrow{\quad i_2/o_3 \quad}_{p_5} s_1$$

If the environment offers the input action i_1 then the choice between t_1, t_2, and t_3 will be resolved according to some probabilities fulfilling the conditions p_1, p_2, and p_3. All we know about these values is that they fulfill the imposed restrictions, that they are non-negative, and that the sum of them equals 1. Something similar happens for the transitions t_4 and t_5. However, there does not exist any probabilistic relation between transitions labeled with different input actions (e.g. t_1 and t_4). □

In addition to the definition of our formalism, we have also developed appropriate implementation relations to try and determine whether an implementation conforms to the behavior indicated by the corresponding specification. We have to take into account that, in general, we will not be able to *see* the probabilities that the implementation has assigned to each of the choices. Thus, even though implementations will behave according to fixed probabilities, in contrast with specifications, the problem is that we will not be able to *read* their values. Following the approach presented in [12], in order to compute the probabilities associated with each choice of the implementation we will analyze some samples collected from the implementation. By comparing them with the symbolic probabilities of the specification we will be able to assess the validity of the implementation. This comparison will be performed by using *hypothesis contrasts*. These contrasts allow to (probabilistically) decide whether an observed sample follows the pattern given by a random variable.

The rest of the paper is organized as follows. In Section 2 we present our probabilistic finite state machines model. In Section 3 we introduce some basic statistical concepts that are (abstractly) used along the paper. In Section 4 we give our first implementation relation and show that, regardless its elegant definition, it is not adequate from the practical point of view. In Section 5 we present new implementation relations that can be checked in practice. The underlying idea is that these relations perform a hypothesis contrast to assess whether the observed behavior corresponds to the probabilistic behavior defined in the specification *up to* a certain confidence. Finally, in Section 6 we present our conclusions and some lines for future work.

2   Probabilistic Finite State Machines

In this section we introduce our notion of probabilistic finite state machines. As we have previously commented, probabilistic information will not be given by using fixed values of probabilities but by introducing certain constraints on the considered probabilities. By taking into account the inherent nature of probabilies we will consider that these constraints are given by intervals contained in $(0, 1] \subseteq \mathbb{R}$.

Definition 1. We define the set of *symbolic probabilities*, denoted by simbP, as the following set of intervals

$$\texttt{simbP} = \left\{ \$p_1, p_2\& \,\middle|\, \begin{array}{l} p_1, p_2 \in [0,1] \ \wedge \ p_1 \leq p_2 \ \wedge \ \$ \in \{\,(,[\,\} \ \wedge \ \& \in \{\,),]\,\} \ \} \ \wedge \\ 0 \notin \$p_1, p_2\& \ \wedge \ \$p_1, p_2\& \neq \emptyset \end{array} \right\}$$

If we have a symbolic probability as $[p, p]$, with $0 < p \leq 1$, we simply write p.

Let $\bar{p}_1, \ldots, \bar{p}_n \in \texttt{simbP}$ be symbolic probabilities such that for any $1 \leq i \leq n$ we have $\bar{p}_i = \$_i p_i, q_i \&_i$, with $\$_i \in \{\,(,[\,\}$ and $\&_i \in \{\,),]\,\}$. We define the *product* of $\bar{p}_1, \ldots, \bar{p}_n$, denoted by $\prod \bar{p}_i$, (respectively the *addition* of $\bar{p}_1, \ldots, \bar{p}_n$, denoted by $\sum \bar{p}_i$) as the symbolic probability $\& \prod p_i, \prod q_i \$$ (respectively $\& \sum p_i, \sum q_i \$$). The limits of the interval are defined in both cases as:

$$\& = \begin{cases} (& \text{if } \exists 1 \leq i \leq n : \&_i = (\\ [& \text{otherwise} \end{cases} \qquad \$ = \begin{cases}) & \text{if } \exists 1 \leq i \leq n : \$_i =) \\ ] & \text{otherwise} \end{cases}$$

□

The previous definition expresses that a symbolic probability $\bar{p}$ is a non-empty (open or closed) interval contained in $(0, 1]$. In particular, we will not allow transitions with probability 0 because this value would complicate (even more) our model since we would have to deal with priorities.[1] We have also defined how to *multiply* and *add* symbolic probabilities. The maximal (resp. minimal) bound of the resulting interval is obtained by operating over the respective maximal (resp. minimal) bounds of the intervals considered. Next, we introduce our notion of probabilistic finite state machine. In the following we consider that $|X|$ denotes the cardinality of the set X.

Definition 2. A *Probabilistic Finite State Machine*, in short PFSM, is a tuple $M = (S, I, O, \delta, s_0)$ where S is the set of states, I and O denote the sets of input and output actions, respectively, $\delta \subseteq S \times I \times O \times \texttt{simbP} \times S$ is the set of transitions, and s_0 is the initial state. Each transition belonging to δ is a tuple $(s, i, o, \bar{p}, s')$ where $s, s' \in S$ are the initial and final states, $i \in I$ is an input action, $o \in O$ is an output action, and $\bar{p} \in \texttt{simbP}$ is the symbolic probability associated with the transition. We will usually denote transitions as $(s, i, o, \bar{p}, s')$ by $s \xrightarrow{i/o}_{\bar{p}} s'$. Besides, we consider that for any $s \in S$, $i \in I$, and the set $\alpha_{s,i} = \{s \xrightarrow{i/o}_{\bar{p}} s' \mid \exists o \in O, \bar{p} \in \texttt{simbP}, s' \in S : s \xrightarrow{i/o}_{\bar{p}} s' \in \delta\}$ the following two conditions hold:

- If $|\alpha_{s,i}| > 1$ then for any $s \xrightarrow{i/o}_{\bar{p}} s' \in \alpha_{s,i}$ we have that $1 \notin \bar{p}$.
- $1 \in \sum \{\bar{p} \mid \exists o \in O, s' \in S : s \xrightarrow{i/o}_{\bar{p}} s' \in \alpha_{s,i}\}$.

□

---

[1] The interested reader can check [13] where different approaches for introducing priorities are reviewed.

Intuitively, a transition $s \xrightarrow{i/o}_{\overline{p}} s'$ indicates that if the machine is in state s and receives the input i then, with a probability belonging to the interval $\overline{p}$, the machine emits the output o and evolves into s'. As we pointed out in the introduction of the paper, this interpretation of the probabilistic information follows the *reactive* model as described in [5]. Let us comment the restrictions introduced at the end of the previous definition. The first constraint indicates that a symbolic probability such as $\overline{p} = \$p, 1]$ can appear in a transition like $s \xrightarrow{i/o}_{\overline{p}} s' \in \delta$ only if it is the unique transition for s and i. Let us note that if there would exist two transitions $s \xrightarrow{i/o}_{\overline{p}} s', s \xrightarrow{i/o'}_{\overline{p}'} s'' \in \delta$ and the probability of one of them (say $\overline{p}$) included 1, then the (real) probability associated to the other transition ($\overline{p}'$) could be 0, which is forbidden. Regarding the second condition, let us note that the *real* probabilities for each state $s \in S$ and for each input $i \in I$ should add 1. This is only possible if 1 is within the lower and upper bounds of the associated symbolic probabilities.

Next we define some additional conditions that we will sometimes impose on our probabilistic finite state machines.

Definition 3. Let $M = (S, I, O, \delta, s_0)$ be a **PFSM**. We say that M is *input-enabled* if for any state $s \in S$ and input $i \in I$ there exist $s' \in S$, $o \in O$, and $\overline{p} \in \text{simbP}$ such that $(s, i, o, \overline{p}, s') \in \delta$.

We say that M is *deterministically observable* if for any $s \in S$, $i \in I$, and $o \in O$ there do not exist two different transitions $(s, i, o, \overline{p}_1, s_1), (s, i, o, \overline{p}_2, s_2) \in \delta$.

□

First, let us remark that the previous concepts are independent of the probabilistic information appearing in the state machines. Regarding the notion of deterministically observable, it is worth to point out that it is different from the more restricted notion of deterministic finite state machine. In particular, we allow transitions from the same state labeled by the same input action, as far as the outputs are different.

Example 2. Let us consider the (probabilistic) finite state machines depicted in Figure 1. For the sake of clarity, we have not included probabilistic information in the graphs. Let us consider $M_3 = (\{1, 2, 3\}, \{i_1, i_2\}, \{o_1, o_2, o_3\}, \delta, 1)$. Next we define the set of transitions δ. For the first state, we have the transitions $(1, i_1, o_1, 1, 2)$, $(1, i_2, o_1, \overline{p}_1, 1)$, and $(1, i_2, o_2, \overline{p}_2, 3)$. Let us suppose that $\overline{p}_1 = (0, \frac{1}{2}]$ and $\overline{p}_2 = [\frac{1}{3}, 1)$, and let us remind that we denote the *interval* $[1, 1]$ simply by 1. We also know that the real probabilities associated with the last two transitions, say p_1 and p_2, are such that $p_1 + p_2 = 1$. A similar assignment of symbolic probabilities can be done to the rest of transitions appearing in the graph.

Regarding the notions of input-enabling and deterministically observable, we have that M_1 fulfills the first of the properties but not the second one (there are two transitions outgoing from the state 3 labeled by i_1/o_3). The first property does not hold in M_2 (there is no outgoing transition labeled by i_2 from the state 2) while the second one does. Finally, M_3 holds both properties.   □

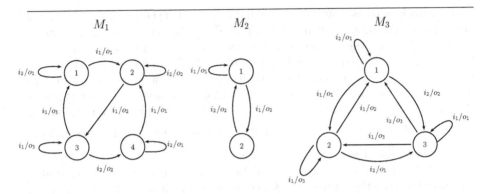

Fig. 1. Examples of PFSM

As usually, we need to consider not only single evolutions of a PFSM but also sequences of transitions. Thus, we introduce the notion of (probabilistic) trace. We will associate probabilities to traces. The probability of a trace will be obtained by multiplying the probabilities of all transitions involved in the trace.

Definition 4. Let $M = (S, I, O, \delta, s_0)$ be a PFSM. We write the *generalized* transition $s \xRightarrow[\overline{p}]{(i_1/o_1, \dots, i_n/o_n)} s'$ if there exist $s_1, \dots, s_{n-1} \in S, \overline{p}_1, \dots, \overline{p}_n \in$ simbP such that $s \xrightarrow[\overline{p}_1]{i_1/o_1} s_1 \xrightarrow[\overline{p}_2]{i_2/o_2} s_2 \cdots s_{n-1} \xrightarrow[\overline{p}_n]{i_n/o_n} s'$ and $\overline{p} = \prod \overline{p}_i$.

We say that $\rho = (i_1/o_1, \dots, i_n/o_n)$ is a *non-probabilistic trace*, or simply a *trace*, of M if there exist $s' \in S$ and $\overline{p} \in$ simbP such that $s_0 \xRightarrow[\overline{p}]{\rho} s'$.

Let $\rho = (i_1/o_1, \dots, i_n/o_n)$ and $\overline{p} \in$ simbP. We say that $\overline{p} = (\rho, \overline{p})$ is a *probabilistic trace* of M if there exists $s' \in S$ such that $s_0 \xRightarrow[\overline{p}]{\rho} s'$.

We denote by Traces(M) and pTraces(M) the sets of non-probabilistic and probabilistic traces of M, respectively. □

3   Statistical Concepts

In this section we introduce some statistical notions that will be used in our framework and a procedure to perform hypothesis contrasts. In the following definition we call *event* to any reaction we can detect from a system. For any set of events, a *sample* denotes the number of times we have detected each event along a set of observations. Besides, we associate a random variable with each set of events. Its purpose is to provide the theoretical (*a priori*) probability of each event belonging to the set. In our framework, these random variables will be inferred from the PFSMs denoting the (ideal) probabilistic behavior of systems, while the samples will be collected by interacting with the implementation to be validated. We will consider a variant of random variable allowing to deal with *symbolic* probabilities. Besides, we provide a function that returns the confidence we have that a sample of events has been produced according to a given random variable. This function encapsulates the contrast hypothesis in our framework.

Definition 5. Let $\mathcal{A} = \{a_1, \ldots, a_n\}$ be a set of *events*. A *sample* of $\mathcal{A}$ is a set $J = \{(a_1, m_1), \ldots, (a_n, m_n)\}$ where for any $1 \leq i \leq n$ we have that m_i represents the number of times that we have observed the event α_i.

Let $\xi : \mathcal{A} \rightarrow \texttt{simbP}$ be a function such that $1 \in \sum_{\alpha \in \mathcal{A}} \xi(\alpha)$. In this case we say that ξ is a *symbolic random variable* for the set of events $\mathcal{A}$. We denote the set of symbolic random variables for the set of events $\mathcal{A}$ by $\mathcal{RV}(\mathcal{A})$. We denote the set of symbolic random variables for any set of events by $\mathcal{RV}$.

Given the symbolic random variable ξ and the sample J we denote the *confidence* of ξ on J by $\gamma(\xi, J)$.   □

We assume that $\gamma(\xi, J)$ takes values in the interval $[0, 1]$. Intuitively, bigger values of $\gamma(\xi, J)$ indicate that the sample J is more likely to be produced by the symbolic random variable ξ. In the next definition we particularize the previous notions in the context of our framework. Basically, we give a sequence of inputs and consider the sequence of outputs that the system can return. Hence, the set of events are those sequences of outputs that could be produced in response. The random variable denoting the theoretical probability of each event is computed by considering the symbolic probability of the corresponding trace in the specification.

Definition 6. Let $M = (S, I, O, \delta, s_0)$ be a PFSM. Let $\pi = (i_1, \ldots, i_n)$ be a sequence of inputs. The *set of trace events* associated to M with respect to π, denoted by $\texttt{TraceEvents}(M, \pi)$, is defined as

$$\texttt{TraceEvents}(M, \pi) = \left\{ (o_1, \ldots, o_n) \,\middle|\, (i_1/o_1, \ldots, i_n/o_n) \in \texttt{Traces}(M) \right\}$$

The *symbolic random variable* associated to the previous events, denoted by ξ_M^π, is defined such that for any $(o_1, \ldots, o_n) \in \texttt{TraceEvents}(M, \pi)$ we have $\xi_M^\pi(o_1, \ldots, o_n) = \overline{p}$, where $((i_1/o_1, \ldots, i_n/o_n), \overline{p}) \in \texttt{pTraces}(M)$.   □

Now we introduce one of the standard ways to measure the confidence that a random variable has on a sample. In order to do so we will present a methodology to perform *hypothesis contrasts*. Intuitively, a sample will be *rejected* if the probability of observing that sample from a given random variable is low. In practice, we will check whether the probability to observe a *discrepancy* lower than or equal to the one that we have detected is low enough. We will present *Pearson's χ^2 contrast*. This contrast can be applied both to continuous and discrete random variables. The mechanism is the following. Once we have collected a sample of size n we perform the following steps:

- We split the sample into k classes covering all the possible range of values. We denote by O_i the *observed frequency* in class i (i.e. the number of elements belonging to the class i).
- We calculate, according to the proposed random variable, the probability p_i of each class i. We denote by E_i the *expected frequency* of class i, that is, $E_i = np_i$.

- We calculate the *discrepancy* between observed and expected frequencies as $X^2 = \sum_{i=1}^n \frac{(O_i - E_i)^2}{E_i}$. When the model is correct, this discrepancy is approximately distributed as a random variable χ^2.
- The number of freedom degrees of χ^2 is $k - 1$.
- We will *accept* that the sample follows the proposed random variable if the probability to obtain a discrepancy greater than or equal to the detected discrepancy is high enough, that is, if $X^2 < \chi_\alpha^2(k-1)$ for some α high enough. Actually, as such margin to accept the sample decreases as α increases, we can obtain a measure of the validity of the sample as $\max\{\alpha | X^2 \leq \chi_\alpha^2(k-1)\}$.

According to the previous steps, we can now present an operative definition of the function γ which has been presented before in Definition 5. Since we will use hypothesis contrasts to compare samples with *symbolic* random variables but the previous procedure refers to *standard* random variables, we must be carefull when applying the previous ideas in our framework. Let us note that symbolic random variables encapsulate a set of standard random variables (this set is in general infinite). For instance, let us consider the set of events $\mathcal{A} = \{a, b\}$ and the symbolic random variable $\xi : \mathcal{A} \to \texttt{simbP}$ with $\xi(a) = \xi(b) = (\frac{1}{4}, \frac{3}{4})$. Then, a possible standard random variable fitting into ξ is $\xi' : \mathcal{A} \to (0, 1]$ with $\xi'(a) = \frac{1}{3}$ and $\xi'(b) = \frac{2}{3}$. Another possibility is $\xi'' : \mathcal{A} \to (0, 1]$ with $\xi''(a) = \xi''(b) = \frac{1}{2}$. Since ξ embraces both possibilities, assessing the confidence of ξ on a sample should consider both of them. Actually, we will consider that the sample is adequate for ξ if it would be so for some standard random variable fitting into ξ. More generally, an *instance* of a symbolic random variable is a (standard) random variable where each probability fits into the margins of the symbolic random variable for the corresponding class. Besides, the addition of the probabilities must be equal to 1. In order to compute the confidence of a symbolic random variable on a sample we consider the instance of it that returns the highest confidence on that sample.

Definition 7. Let $\mathcal{A} = \{a_1, \ldots, a_k\}$ be a set of events, $\xi : \mathcal{A} \to \texttt{simbP}$ be a symbolic random variable, $\xi' : \mathcal{A} \to (0, 1]$ be a random variable, and J be a sample of $\mathcal{A}$. We say that the random variable ξ' is an *instantiation* of ξ, denoted by $\texttt{Instance}(\xi', \xi)$, if for any $a \in \mathcal{A}$ we have $\xi'(a) \in \xi(a)$ and $\sum_{a \in \mathcal{A}} \xi'(a) = 1$.

For any random variable $\xi' : \mathcal{A} \to (0, 1]$ let X^2 denote the discrepancy level of J on ξ' calculated as explained above by splitting the sampling space into the set of events $\mathcal{A}$. Let $\xi : \mathcal{A} \to \texttt{simbP}$ denote a symbolic random variable. We define the confidence of ξ on J, denoted by $\gamma(\xi, J)$, as follows:

$$\gamma(\xi, J) = \max \left\{ \alpha \; \middle| \; \begin{array}{l} \exists \, \xi' : \texttt{Instance}(\xi', \xi) \wedge \\ \alpha = \max\{\alpha' \mid X^2 \leq \chi_{\alpha'}^2(k-1)\} \end{array} \right\}$$

$\square$

4   Probabilistic Implementation Relation

In this section we introduce our first implementation relation. We will consider that both specifications and implementations are given by deterministically ob-

servable PFSMs. Moreover, we will assume that PFSMs representing implementations are input-enabled. We assume that implementations are *black-boxes*. Thus,
no information can be known about their internal behavior/structure. In addition, let us remark that the *symbolic* probabilities appearing in implementations
follow the pattern $[p, p]$ (or simply p), for some $p \in (0, 1]$. That is, they are indeed *fixed* probabilities. While specifications are abstract entities where symbolic
probabilities allow us to represent different scenarios (one for each probability
within the intervals) in a compact fashion, implementations represent concrete
machines. Hence, even though observations will not give us the actual probability associated to a transition in an implementation, we may rely on the fact that
the probability is indeed fixed.

   Regarding the performance of actions, our implementation relations follow
the classical pattern of formal conformance relations defined in systems distinguishing between inputs and outputs (see e.g. [14, 15]). That is, an implementa-
tion $\mathcal{I}$ conforms to a specification $\mathcal{S}$ if for any possible evolution of $\mathcal{S}$ the outputs
that the implementation may perform after a given input are a subset of those
for the specification. Besides, this relation will require that the probability of any
trace of the implementation is *within* the corresponding (symbolic) probability
of the specification for this trace.

Definition 8. Let $\mathcal{S}$ and $\mathcal{I}$ be PFSMs. We say that $\mathcal{I}$ *non-probabilistically conforms* to $\mathcal{S}$, denoted by $\mathcal{I}$ conf $\mathcal{S}$, if for any $\rho = (i_1/o_1, \ldots, i_n/o_n) \in \text{Traces}(\mathcal{S})$,
with $n \geq 1$, we have

$$\rho' = (i_1/o_1, \ldots, i_{n-1}/o_{n-1}, i_n/o'_n) \in \text{Traces}(\mathcal{I}) \text{ implies } \rho' \in \text{Traces}(\mathcal{S})$$

We say that $\mathcal{I}$ *probabilistically conforms to* $\mathcal{S}$, denoted by $\mathcal{I}$ conf$_p$ $\mathcal{S}$, if $\mathcal{I}$ conf $\mathcal{S}$
and for each $\bar{\rho} = (\rho, p) \in \text{pTraces}(\mathcal{I})$ we have

$$\rho \in \text{Traces}(\mathcal{S}) \text{ implies } (\rho, \bar{p}) \in \text{pTraces}(\mathcal{S}) \text{ for some } \bar{p} \text{ with } p \in \bar{p}.$$

$\square$

   Intuitively, the idea underlying the definition of the non-probabilistic conformance relation conf is that the implementation $\mathcal{I}$ does not *invent* anything for
those inputs that are *specified* in the specification (this notion has been previously used, with some variants, in [16, 12]). This condition is also required in the
probabilistic case: We check probabilistic traces only if they can be performed
by the specification.

   The problem underlying this implementation relation is that we have no access to the probabilities governing the transitions of the implementations. So, we
are not able to check whether a given implementation probabilistically conforms
to a specification. However, we may get *approximations* of the probabilities controlling the behavior of the implementation by collecting *samples* of its execution
and computing the empirical ratio associated with the different decision points
of the implementation.

5   Implementation Relations Based on Samples

In the previous section we presented an implementation relation that clearly expressed the probabilistic constraints an implementation must fulfill to conform to a specification. Unfortunately, this notion is useful only from a theoretical point of view since the correctness of the probabilistic behavior of an implementation with respect to a specification cannot be checked by using a finite number of observations. In this section we introduce new implementation relations that take into account the practical limitations to collect probabilistic information from a given implementation. We will present new versions of the relation defined in Section 4. These new relations allow us to claim the accurateness of the probabilistic behavior of an implementation with respect to a specification *up to* a given confidence level. Given a set of execution samples, obtained from the implementation, we will apply a hypothesis contrast to check whether the probabilistic choices taken by the implementation follow the patterns given by the specification.

In order to introduce our new relations, we need some notions to deal with samples collected from an implementation. The next definition presents some auxiliar predicates that we will use during the rest of the section. While the first two notions are easy to understand, the last one needs some additional explanation. Given a trace ρ and a set H of pairs (trace,natural number), $\texttt{IPrefix}(H, \rho)$ is another set of pairs including all traces such that its sequence of input actions matches that of ρ. The number attached to each trace corresponds with the number of traces belonging to H *beginning* with that trace. For instance, let us consider the set of pairs $H = \{((i_1/o_1, i_2/o_1), 1), ((i_1/o_2, i_1/o_2), 2), ((i_1/o_2, i_2/o_1), 3), ((i_2/o_1, i_2/o_2), 4)\}$ and let us apply the function to the trace (i_1/o_1). Then, the resulting set is $H' = \{((i_1/o_1), 1), ((i_1/o_2), 5)\}$. Let us remark that we discard the output of the trace considered as parameter. For instance, in the previous example we considered the trace (i_1/o_1) but the resulting set contained information for both (i_1/o_1) and (i_1/o_2). Given a sample of executions from an implementation, we will use this function to calculate the number of times that the implementation has performed each sequence of outputs in response to some sequence of inputs. Let us note that if we observe that the sequence of outputs $(o_1, \ldots, o_n)$ has been produced in response to the sequence of inputs $(i_1, \ldots, i_n)$ then, for any $j \leq n$, we know that the sequence of outputs $(o_1, \ldots, o_j)$ has been produced in response to $(i_1, \ldots, i_j)$. Hence, the observation of a trace is useful to compute the number of instances of any prefix of it.

Definition 9. Let $\sigma = (u_1, \ldots, u_n)$ and $\sigma' = (u'_1, \ldots, u'_m)$ be two sequences. We say that σ is *a prefix of* σ', denoted by $\texttt{Prefix}(\sigma, \sigma')$, if $n < m$ and for any $1 \leq i \leq n$ we have $u_i = u'_i$.

Let $\rho = (i_1/o_1, \ldots, i_m/o_m)$ be a sequence of input/output actions. We define the *input actions of the sequence* ρ, denoted by $\texttt{inputs}(\rho)$, as the sequence $(i_1, \ldots, i_m)$, and the *output actions of the sequence* ρ, denoted by $\texttt{outputs}(\rho)$, as the sequence $(o_1, \ldots, o_m)$.

Let $H = \{(\rho_1, r_1), \ldots, (\rho_m, r_m)\}$ be a set of pairs (trace, natural number) and $\rho = (i_1/o_1, \ldots, i_n/o_n)$ be a trace. The *set of input prefixes* of ρ in H, denoted by $\texttt{IPrefix}(H, \rho)$, is defined as

$$\texttt{IPrefix}(H, \rho) = \left\{ (\rho', r') \,\middle|\, \begin{array}{l} \texttt{inputs}(\rho) = \texttt{inputs}(\rho') \,\wedge\, r' > 0 \,\wedge \\ r' = \sum\{r'' \mid (\rho'', r'') \in H \,\wedge\, \texttt{Prefix}(\rho', \rho'')\} \end{array} \right\}$$

$\square$

Next we present the notions that we will use to denote that a given event has been detected in an implementation.

Definition 10. Let $\mathcal{I} = (S, I, O, \delta, s_0)$ be a PFSM. We say that $(i_1/o_1, \ldots, i_n/o_n)$ is an *execution* of $\mathcal{I}$ if the sequence $(i_1/o_1, \ldots, i_n/o_n)$ can be performed by $\mathcal{I}$.

Let $\rho_1, \ldots, \rho_n$ be executions of $\mathcal{I}$ and $r_1, \ldots, r_n \in \mathbb{N}$. We say that the set $H = \{(\rho_1, r_1), \ldots, (\rho_n, r_n)\}$ is an *execution sample* of $\mathcal{I}$. $\square$

Intuitively, a pair (ρ, r) denotes that the trace ρ has been observed r times.

Now we have the necessary notions to introduce our new implementation relations based on samples. In these relations, the non probabilistic constraint is exactly that of the previous one given in Definition 8. Thus, we require that the implementation does not *invent* any behavior that does not exist in the specification (i.e. the implementation does not show any output that cannot be performed by the specification). Let us remark that this constraint could be rewritten in probabilistic terms: The confidence we have on the fact that the implementation will not perform forbidden behaviors is 1. However, let us note that no hypothesis contrast can provide full confidence on the complete absence of a given event. So, it is preferable to keep the constraints over actions separated from the probabilistic constraints and deal with them in the classic way, that is, an implementation is incorrect with respect to forbidden behavior if such a behavior is detected.

Regarding the probabilistic constraints of the specification, the new relations will express them differently to the way we used in Definition 8. In the new setting we put together all the observations of the implementation. Then, the set of samples corresponding to each trace of the specification will be composed by taking all the observations such that the trace is a *prefix* of them. By doing so we will be able to compare the number of times the implementation has performed the chosen trace with the number of times the implementation has performed any other behavior. We will use hypothesis contrasts to decide whether the probabilistic choices of the implementation conform to the probabilistic constraints imposed by the specification. In particular, a hypothesis contrast will be applied to each sequence of inputs considered by the specification. This contrast will check whether the different sequences of outputs associated with these inputs are distributed according to the probability distribution of the random variable associated to that sequence of inputs in the specification. In the next definition we introduce our first implementation relation based on samples.

Definition 11. Let S be a specification and $\mathcal{I}$ be an implementation. Let H be an execution sample of $\mathcal{I}$ and let $0 \leq \alpha \leq 1$. We say that $\mathcal{I}$ $(\alpha, H)-probabilistically$ *conforms to* S, denoted by $\mathcal{I}\,\mathtt{confp}^{(\alpha,H)}\,S$, if $\mathcal{I}\,\mathtt{conf}\,S$ and for any $\rho \in \mathtt{Traces}(S)$ we have $\gamma(\xi_S^\pi, R) > \alpha$, where $\pi = \mathtt{inputs}(\rho)$ and $R = \{(\mathtt{outputs}(\rho'), r) \,|\, (\rho', r) \in \mathtt{IPrefix}(H, \rho)\}$. $\qquad\square$

In the previous relation, ξ_S^π denotes the symbolic random variable associated to the PFSM S and the sequence of input actions π given in Definition 6. Let us remind that this symbolic random variable shows the symbolic probability associated to the traces with the sequence of input actions π in the specification. Besides, each trace observed in the implementation will add one instance to the accounting of each trace being a prefix of it. We could consider an alternative procedure where traces are independently accounted and each observed trace does not affect the number of instances of other traces being prefix of it. However, this method would lose valuable information that might affect negatively the quality of the hypothesis contrasts. Let us note that the reliability of any hypothesis contrasts increases with the number of instances included in the samples. Besides, as we said before, an observation where $(o_1, \ldots, o_n)$ has been produced in response to $(i_1, \ldots, i_n)$ is indeed an observation where, in particular, $(o_1, \ldots, o_j)$ has been produced in response to $(i_1, \ldots, i_j)$, with $j \leq n$. So, by accounting prefixes we properly increase the number of instances processed by hypothesis contrasts, which makes them more precise (as well as the probabilistic implementation relation that takes them into account).

The previous idea induces the creation of a new implementation relation that is a refinement of the previous one. Let us note that the probability of observing a given trace decreases in general as the length of the trace increases. This is so because more probabilistic choices are taken in long traces. Besides, taking prefixes into account increases the number of instances of short traces more than the number of long traces. Thus, it is likely that the number of *short* traces applied to the hypothesis contrasts of the previous relation will outnumber that of longer traces. For example, let us suppose that the sequence of outputs (o_1, o_2) has been observed 51 times in response to (i_1, i_2), while the sequence (o_5, o_6) has been observed 49 times in response to the same input sequence (i_1, i_2). Then, it would be feasible that the number of times (o_1, o_2, o_3, o_4) was detected in response to (i_1, i_2, i_3, i_4) is 11, while (o_5, o_6, o_7, o_8) was detected 9 times. Similarly, the number of instances of other sequences of four outputs would be lower than those of two outputs. Let us note that statistical noise effects are higher when smaller sets of samples are considered. If we consider the previous example, a hypothesis contrast is more likely to be imprecise in the case of the traces having length four. Moreover, if we consider extremely long traces we could obtain a couple of instances or even none in each class of events to be considered by a hypothesis contrast, which would ruin the result of such contrast. Taking these factors into account, in the next definition we introduce a new implementation relation where the confidence requirement is *relaxed* as the length of the trace growths. This reduction is defined by a non-increasing function associating confidence levels to the length of traces.

Definition 12. Let $f : \mathbb{N} \to \mathbb{R}^+$ be a strictly non-increasing function. Let S be an specification and $\mathcal{I}$ an implementation. Let H be an execution sample of $\mathcal{I}$. We say that $\mathcal{I}$ $(f, H)-probabilistically\ conforms\ to\ S$, denoted by $\mathcal{I}\ \text{confp}^{(f,H)}\ S$, if $\mathcal{I}\ \text{conf}\ S$ and for any $\rho \in \text{Traces}(S)$ we have $\gamma(\xi_S^\pi, R) > f(l)$, where $\pi = \text{inputs}(\rho)$, l is the length of $\text{inputs}(\rho)$, and $R = \{(\text{outputs}(\rho'), r) \mid (\rho', r) \in \text{IPrefix}(H, \rho)\}$. □

6   Conclusions and Future Work

In this paper we have presented a validation methodology to check whether an implemention properly follows the behavior described by a specification. We have considered a framework where the specifications of systems contain probabilistic information. In order to improve the expressivity of specifications, this quantitative information is given in terms of symbolic probabilities. That is, *probabilities are intervals of values instead of fixed values*. This feature increases the complexity of the validation methodology, as it is impossible to infer the actual probabilities associated with implementations from a set of interaction samples. In order to cope with this problem we have defined two implementation relations based on samples. For any given trace performed by the implementation we compute the symbolic probability of the specification to perform it and we compare this value, by using hypothesis contrasts, with the number of times that a particular trace appears in the execution sample. The main difference between both implementation relations is how the hypothesis contrasts are applied.

We are developing a testing methodology so that our implementation relations can be checked by applying a set of tests derived from the specification to the implementation under test. Besides, we would like to study the integration of this framework within that presented in [12], where a testing methodology for stochastic-timed processes is introduced.

Acknowledgements

We would like to thank the anonymous referees of this paper for the careful reading and interesting suggestions. Besides, we would also like to thank Fernando Rubio for his comments and technical support during the development of this paper.

References

[1] Reed, G., Roscoe, A.: A timed model for communicating sequential processes. Theoretical Computer Science **58** (1988) 249–261   114
[2] Larsen, K., Skou, A.: Bisimulation through probabilistic testing. Information and Computation **94** (1991) 1–28   114
[3] Nicollin, X., Sifakis, J.: An overview and synthesis on timed process algebras. In: Computer Aided Verification'91, LNCS 575. (1991) 376–398   114

[4] Yi, W., Larsen, K.: Testing probabilistic and nondeterministic processes. In: Protocol Specification, Testing and Verification XII, North Holland (1992) 47–61 114

[5] Glabbeek, R.v., Smolka, S., Steffen, B.: Reactive, generative and stratified models of probabilistic processes. Information and Computation **121** (1995) 59–80 114, 115, 118

[6] Jonsson, B., Yi, W., Larsen, K.: Probabilistic extensions of process algebras. In Bergstra, J., Ponse, A., Smolka, S., eds.: Handbook of process algebra. North Holland (2001) 114

[7] Baeten, J., Middelburg, C.: Process algebra with timing. EATCS Monograph. Springer (2002) 114

[8] Cazorla, D., Cuartero, F., Valero, V., Pelayo, F., Pardo, J.: Algebraic theory of probabilistic and non-deterministic processes. Journal of Logic and Algebraic Programming **55** (2003) 57–103 114

[9] Núñez, M.: Algebraic theory of probabilistic processes. Journal of Logic and Algebraic Programming **56** (2003) 117–177 114

[10] Bravetti, M., Aldini, A.: Discrete time generative-reactive probabilistic processes with different advancing speeds. Theoretical Computer Science **290** (2003) 355–406 114

[11] Bartlett, K., Scantlebury, R., Wilkinson, P.: A note on reliable full-duplex transmission over half-duplex links. Communications of the ACM **12** (1969) 260–261 115

[12] Núñez, M., Rodríguez, I.: Towards testing stochastic timed systems. In: FORTE 2003, LNCS 2767, Springer (2003) 335–350 116, 122, 126

[13] Cleaveland, R., Lüttgen, G., Natarajan, V.: Priority in process algebra. In Bergstra, J., Ponse, A., Smolka, S., eds.: Handbook of process algebra. North Holland (2001) 117

[14] Tretmans, J.: Test generation with inputs, outputs and repetitive quiescence. Software – Concepts and Tools **17** (1996) 103–120 122

[15] Tretmans, J.: Testing concurrent systems: A formal approach. In: CONCUR'99, LNCS 1664, Springer (1999) 46–65 122

[16] Núñez, M., Rodríguez, I.: Encoding PAMR into (timed) EFSMs. In: FORTE 2002, LNCS 2529, Springer (2002) 1–16 122

How Synchronisation Strategy Approximation in PEPA Implementations Affects Passage Time Performance Results

Jeremy T. Bradley[1], Stephen T. Gilmore[2], and Nigel Thomas[3]

[1] Department of Computing, Imperial College London
180 Queen's Gate, London SW7 2BZ, United Kingdom
`jb@doc.ic.ac.uk`
[2] Laboratory for Foundations of Computer Science
The University of Edinburgh
Edinburgh EH9 3JZ, United Kingdom.
`Stephen.Gilmore@ed.ac.uk`
[3] School of Computing Science, University of Newcastle-upon-Tyne
Newcastle-upon-Tyne NE1 7RU, United Kingdom
`Nigel.Thomas@ncl.ac.uk`

Abstract. Passage time densities are useful performance measurements in stochastic systems. With them the modeller can extract probabilistic quality-of-service guarantees such as: the probability that the time taken for a network header packet to travel across a heterogeneous network is less than 10ms must be at least 0.95. In this paper, we show how new tools can extract passage time densities and distributions from stochastic models defined in PEPA, a stochastic process algebra. In stochastic process algebras, the synchronisation policy is important for defining how different system components interact. We also show how these passage time results can vary according to which synchronisation strategy is used. We compare results from two popular strategies.

1 Introduction

Probabilistic quality-of-service guarantees underpin most commercial SLAs (service level agreements): e.g. the probability that a 10-node cluster should be able to process 3000 database transactions in less than 6 seconds should be greater than 0.915; or a train service should not run more than 10 minutes late more than 20% of the time. Whether these commercial guarantees are met or broken depends on the aggregate time behaviour across a whole system of complex interactions.

It is frequently useful to model these systems with a process model and still further convenient to let individual process actions have random delay: this random delay might represent either incomplete or uncertain knowledge on the part of the modeller, or a good approximation to underlying aggregate complex but deterministic dynamics or genuine random behaviour.

M. Núñez et al. (Eds.): FORTE 2004 Workshops, LNCS 3236, pp. 128–142, 2004.

All these factors combined point to the conclusion that a stochastic process algebra (SPA) such as PEPA [1], EMPA [2] or IMC [3] is an appropriate modelling tool for many commercial and industrial problems. In this paper we use Hillston's Performance Evaluation Process Algebra (PEPA).

Traditionally, SPAs like PEPA have been analysed for mean statistics or steady-state values [4, 5, 6, 7, 8] with later extensions to transient (time-varying) measures with techniques such as uniformisation [9]. Here we not only show how complete passage time densities can be extracted but also how such passage times are affected by the choice of synchronisation strategy.

A synchronisation strategy defines how the components of a process algebra model interact. In SPAs which just employ Markovian transitions it is a distinguishing feature of the different SPAs [10]. Here we compare two popular strategies in PEPA:

minimum rate strategy from [4], which is easy to implement and understand and is used in most tool implementations. It can occasionally distort global rates of enabled actions. Also implemented in Möbius [11] and PRISM [12].

apparent rate strategy from [1], which has the benefit of making certain equivalences congruences and precisely represents the minimum rate at the global state space level. It is implemented in ipc [13].

Given that these strategies can have an effect on the end performance statistics of a model, it is important to quantify this effect and understand when differences may occur.

The paper is organised as follows: in Section 2 we discuss the background to the choice of synchronisation strategies; in Section 3, we describe the PEPA stochastic process algebra; in Section 4, we demonstrate passage time extraction from a PEPA model and in Section 5 we present a taxonomy of instances of when the synchronisation models differ in behaviour and results.

2   Background

In this section, we discuss the idea of a synchronisation strategy for stochastic process algebras. As described by Milner [14], sequential or serial modelling formalisms contrast with concurrent ones such as process algebras because the former use the *operator/operand* paradigm and the latter use the *cooperator/cooperand* paradigm. That is, concurrently active components are peers who cooperate and share work such that each participates actively in the shared activity. This naturally gives rise to questions such as "when P can perform α at rate r_1 and Q can perform α at rate r_2; and what is the rate at which α occurs when they cooperate to perform it?" The answer to this question is given by the synchronisation strategy of the process algebra.

There are many plausible definitions for a synchronisation strategy for a stochastic process algebra (see [15, 16] for a fuller discussion of this issue) but for a Markovian process algebra (MPA)—restricted to using only exponential distributions for rates—some possibilities are ruled out for the technical reason that an arbitrary combination of two exponential distributions is not necessarily an exponential distribution. For this reason some MPAs (such as TIPP [17]) chose functions for synchronisation strategies primarily because they satisfied the algebraic requirement that the chosen function produces an exponential distribution when applied to two exponentials. One such function is rate product, which was the choice of the designers of the TIPP language.

However, to use rate product as the synchronisation function does not accord well with our intuitions about the physical world and in fact essentially the only reason to choose rate product is because of its algebraic properties. To explain with an example, if we consider a print spooler which can spool PostScript files at a rate of a hundred pages per minute and a printer which can render them at a rate of ten pages per minute then the TIPP prediction is that when these components synchronise then the resulting assembly will be able to print a thousand pages per minute! The PEPA process algebra would instead say that the combination would print ten pages per minute (because the faster component is hindered by the slower one). This is in accord with our expectations and our experience of how the bottleneck device in the system limits the throughput of the whole.

Further, our spooler and printer illustration is not an isolated pathological example. An earlier study [16] showed that the performance results computed from the use of rate product as a synchronisation strategy could be arbitrarily wrong. The same paper went on to show that the strategy used by PEPA produced results which were in good agreement with a range of other reasonable synchronisation disciplines such as first-to-finish and last-to-finish.

The technical definition which provides PEPA with this intuitive behaviour when components synchronise is that of the *apparent rate* defined by Hillston [1] and adopted by other process calculi such as the Stochastic π-calculus [18]. Hillston's apparent rate calculation is perhaps the simplest function which simultaneously satisfies the two key requirements of:

1. building an exponential distribution when applied to two exponentials; and
2. computing numerical results which accord with our intuitions of synchronising timed activities.

However, the computation of the apparent rates of the transitions of a PEPA model must be performed efficiently if the (perhaps large) state-space of the model is to be derived effectively. In order to avoid the cost of this calculation it is tempting to approximate the apparent rate with the minimum rate. The novel contributions of this paper are the discussion of the cost of computing apparent rates and the comparison of the correct calculation of apparent rates with their approximation by minimum rates.

3   PEPA

PEPA [1] is a parsimonious stochastic process algebra that can describe compositional stochastic models. These models consist of components whose actions incorporate random exponential delays.

The syntax of a PEPA component, P, is represented by:

$$\mathbf{P} ::= (\mathbf{a}, \lambda).\mathbf{P} \mid \mathbf{P} + \mathbf{P} \mid \mathbf{P} \underset{S}{\bowtie} \mathbf{P} \mid \mathbf{P}/\mathbf{L} \mid \mathbf{A} \qquad (1)$$

$(\mathbf{a}, \lambda).\mathbf{P}$ is a prefix operation. It represents a process which does an action, $\mathbf{a}$, and then becomes a new process, $\mathbf{P}$. The time taken to perform $\mathbf{a}$ is described by an exponentially distributed random variable with parameter λ. The rate parameter may also take the value $\top$, which makes the action passive in a cooperation (see below).

$\mathbf{P_1} + \mathbf{P_2}$ is a choice operation. A race is entered into between components $\mathbf{P_1}$ and $\mathbf{P_2}$. If $\mathbf{P_1}$ evolves first then any behaviour of $\mathbf{P_2}$ is discarded and vice-versa.

$\mathbf{P_1} \underset{S}{\bowtie} \mathbf{P_2}$ is the cooperation operator. $\mathbf{P_1}$ and $\mathbf{P_2}$ run in parallel and synchronise over the set of actions in the set S. If $\mathbf{P_1}$ is to evolve with an action $\mathbf{a} \in S$, then it must first wait for $\mathbf{P_2}$ to reach a point where it is also capable of producing an $\mathbf{a}$-action, and vice-versa. In a cooperation, the two components then jointly produce an $\mathbf{a}$-action with a rate that reflects the slower of the two components (R in Figure 1).

$\mathbf{P}/\mathbf{L}$ is a hiding operator where actions in the set L that emanate from the component $\mathbf{P}$ are rewritten as silent τ-actions (with the same appropriate delays). The actions in L can no longer be used in cooperation with other components.

$\mathbf{A}$ is a constant label and allows, amongst other things, recursive definitions to be constructed.

Cooperation (Non-synchronising)

$$\frac{P \xrightarrow{(a,\lambda)} P'}{P \underset{S}{\bowtie} Q \xrightarrow{(a,\lambda)} P' \underset{S}{\bowtie} Q} \quad a \notin S$$

$$\frac{Q \xrightarrow{(b,\mu)} Q'}{P \underset{S}{\bowtie} Q \xrightarrow{(b,\mu)} P \underset{S}{\bowtie} Q'} \quad b \notin S$$

Cooperation (Synchronising)

$$\frac{P \xrightarrow{(a,\lambda)} P' \quad Q \xrightarrow{(a,\mu)} Q'}{P \underset{S}{\bowtie} Q \xrightarrow{(a,R)} P' \underset{S}{\bowtie} Q'} \quad a \in S$$

$$\text{where } R = \frac{\lambda}{r_a(P)} \frac{\mu}{r_a(Q)} \min(r_a(P), r_a(Q))$$

Fig. 1. An excerpt from the operational semantics for PEPA, showing only details of the cooperation operator

The synchronisation strategy effects the cooperation operator $\mathbf{P_1} \bowtie_S \mathbf{P_2}$. The difference between the *apparent rate strategy* and *minimum rate strategy* occurs when either $\mathbf{P_1}$ or $\mathbf{P_2}$ enable multiple a-transitions, where $a \in S$. In [1], the apparent rate semantics are defined as in Figure 1, where:

$$r_a(P) = \sum_{P \xrightarrow{(a,\lambda_i)}} \lambda_i \tag{2}$$

where $\lambda_i \in \mathbb{R}^+ \cup \{n\top \mid n \in \mathbb{Q}, n > 0\}$, $n\top$ is shorthand for $n \times \top$ and $\top$ represents a passive action rate that will inherit the rate of the coaction from the cooperating component. $\top$ requires the following arithmetic rules:

$$m\top < n\top : \text{for } m < n \text{ and } m, n \in \mathbb{Q}$$
$$r < n\top : \text{for all } r \in \mathbb{R}, n \in \mathbb{Q}$$
$$m\top + n\top = (m + n)\top : m, n \in \mathbb{Q}$$
$$\frac{m\top}{n\top} = \frac{m}{n} : m, n \in \mathbb{Q}$$

Note that $(r + n\top)$ is undefined for all $r \in \mathbb{R}$ in PEPA therefore disallowing components which enable both active and passive actions in the same action type at the same time, e.g. $(\mathbf{a}, \lambda).\mathbf{P} + (\mathbf{a}, \top).\mathbf{P}'$.

The minimum rate strategy is much simpler and is used in many tools [4, 11, 12] which implement PEPA. The semantics of the joint rate, R, in Figure 1 are rewritten as:

$$R = \min(\lambda, \mu) \tag{3}$$

for each instance of a cooperating action pair, where $\lambda, \mu \in \mathbb{R}^+ \cup \{\top\}$ and we only need to know that $r < \top$ for all $r \in \mathbb{R}^+$.

4   Extracting Passage Time Distributions

In this section, we briefly describe how passage time results are extracted from SPA models, so that the reader may better understand the analysis process and the sort of quantitative results that are obtained.

Passage time densities in stochastic models are defined by their source and target states, i.e. the time taken to get from one set of states to another. Process algebras use transitions or actions as their central descriptive philosophy with states only implicitly occurring "between" actions, so we need a technique for moving between these two paradigms: i.e. extracting the source and target states for the passage in a way that can be easily related to the action-model of the process algebra.

It is convenient to define passage time densities in PEPA models by means of fragments of process algebra known as *stochastic probes* [19]. These probes specify the actions that should be seen in order to start and stop the passage time measurement and they can easily be interrogated to identify source and target

$$A \stackrel{def}{=} (\textbf{run}, \lambda_1).(\textbf{stop}, \lambda_2).A$$
$$B \stackrel{def}{=} (\textbf{run}, \top).(\textbf{pause}, \lambda_3).B$$
$$Sys_0 \stackrel{def}{=} A \underset{\{run\}}{\bowtie} B$$

Fig. 2. PEPA description for model Sys_0—a simple two component system cooperating over the **run** action

$$Probe_{idle} \stackrel{def}{=} (\textbf{stop}, \top).Probe_{run}$$
$$Probe_{run} \stackrel{def}{=} (\textbf{stop}, \top).Probe_{idle}$$
$$Sys_1 \stackrel{def}{=} Probe \underset{\{stop\}}{\bowtie} Sys_0$$

Fig. 3. PEPA version of the stochastic probe for model Sys_0: toggles between started and stopped states according to whether it has observed a **stop** action or not

actions for the passage. It is important that the probe does not affect the time-behaviour of the model it is measuring, so it only presents passive actions for the model to synchronise with and it does not block actions it is not interested in.

In fact, stochastic probes are SPA-independent and can be tailored to any SPA which supports multi-way synchronisation between processes (so that one can probe the key passage activities). PEPA suited our needs here as it has an uncomplicated syntax which lends itself to describing the underlying concepts behind stochastic probes. As we will see, the probe is expressed as a single PEPA component, so that it can then be combined with the model being queried.

Figure 2 describes a very simple model with two components **A** and **B**. **A** can perform a **run** then a **stop** before becoming **A** again; whereas **B** can perform a **run** then a **pause** before becoming **B** again. The two components synchronise over the **run** action, with the overall rate of the **run** action being dictated by λ_1 from the **A** component (since **B**'s **run** action was passive, represented by the $\top$ symbol). We will briefly discuss the derivation of the passage time between successive **stop** actions in this model (a detailed discussion of passage times and stochastic probes can be found in [19, 20]).

Figure 3 shows the stochastic probe that is composed with the Sys_0 model. This simple version of a probe just toggles state every time it observes a **stop** action. When we examine the PEPA model of Figure 2 with the Imperial PEPA Compiler (ipc) [13], it automatically generates the probe of Figure 3 and inserts the state-based logic to define the passage time between successive **stop** actions.

ipc's output is in a form readable by Dingle and Knottenbelt's HYDRA tool [21, 22, 23] which can then compute both the probability density function (PDF) and the cumulative distribution function (CDF) shown in Figures 4 and 5.

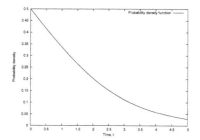
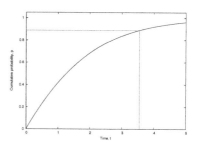

Fig. 4. Probability density function for time taken between successive **stop** actions in model **Sys₀**

Fig. 5. Cumulative distribution function for time taken between successive **stop** actions in model **Sys₀**. Shows that probability of successive stops occurring in less than 3.54 seconds is 0.8893

In this first example, there is only one possible **run** synchronisation (derived from exactly one active participant and exactly one passive participant) and the two synchronisation strategies considered in Section 3 (active and minimum) have identical behaviour in this situation.

In the next section, we will look at small variations of this model which add extra possibilities for synchronisation, in order to create a divergence in behaviour between the minimum rate and active rate strategies. It is this divergence we aim to study in the context of passage time analysis.

5 Results

For the analysis in this section we are going to need to compare passage times from different strategies. So given two random variables representing distinct passages, X_1 and X_2, we construct the quantity:

$$\psi(X_1, X_2, t) = \frac{F_{X_2}(t) - F_{X_1}(t)}{F_{X_1}(t)} \qquad (4)$$

to compare their CDFs, $F_{X_1}(t)$ and $F_{X_2}(t)$, at different t-values. For each of the models being considered in this section we will look at both the individual PDFs as well as the $\psi(\cdot)$ plot over the CDFs. This will give a good idea of the relative difference in CDF and thus passage time quantile result.

We consider three variations on the opening synchronisation example:

Model A multiple passive actions versus a single active action
Model B multiple passive actions versus multiple active actions
Model C multiple active actions versus a single active action

Passage times are then extracted using the same stochastic probe from Figure 3.

$$\mathbf{A} \stackrel{def}{=} (\mathbf{run}, \lambda_1).(\mathbf{stop}, \lambda_2).\mathbf{A}$$

$$\mathbf{B} \stackrel{def}{=} (\mathbf{run}, \top).(\mathbf{pause}, \lambda_3).\mathbf{B}$$

$$\mathbf{Sys_A} \stackrel{def}{=} \mathbf{A} \underset{\{run\}}{\bowtie} (\mathbf{B} \parallel \mathbf{B})$$

Fig. 6. PEPA description for model A

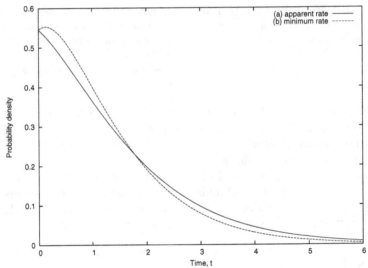

Fig. 7. Probability density functions for time taken between consecutive **stop** actions in model A for (a) the *apparent rate strategy* and (b) the *minimum rate strategy*

5.1   Model A

Now we consider a small variation on our first model from Figure 6. Here we have two copies of the component **B**. These act as clients of (the single) **A**, competing for its **run** activity. Thus there are two possible synchronisations: **A** with the left-hand **B**; and **A** with the right-hand **B**. Each of these has one active participant and one passive participant. This synchronisation metaphor has been termed an *implicit choice* because although the PEPA choice operator has not been used in the model definition still there is a choice of different partners for the **run** activity.

In this setting, the apparent rate and the minimum rate will produce different results. We plot the two PDFs from these strategies in Figure 7 as we probe the duration between consecutive **stop** actions in the model. In Figure 8, we plot the percentage difference between these, as carried through to the CDF function: $100\psi(X_{ars}, X_{mrs}, t)$ for X_{ars} being the passage variable for the apparent rate

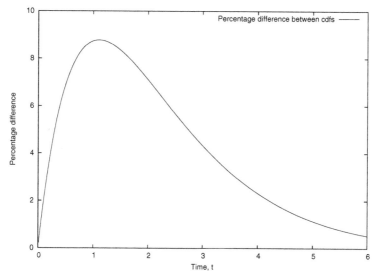

Fig. 8. Model A: Percentage difference from minimum rate strategy as carried through to the CDF

strategy and X_{mrs} being the passage variable for the minimum rate strategy. We note that it is never more than 9% and that it falls off rapidly as time increases, dropping under 1% within 6 seconds.

5.2   Model B

We consider a third variant on this simple model; Model B in Figure 9. We introduce additional copies of the **A** component, which plays the role of the server in the model. Now there are three servers (three copies of **A**), which is a change, and two clients (two copies of **B**), which is as it was in the previous version of the model. All of the servers are independent, as are all of the clients. Now there are six possible types of **run** action, with each of the **A**s synchronising with each of the **B**s.

$$\mathbf{A} \stackrel{def}{=} (\mathbf{run}, \lambda_1).(\mathbf{stop}, \lambda_2).\mathbf{A}$$
$$\mathbf{B} \stackrel{def}{=} (\mathbf{run}, \top).(\mathbf{pause}, \lambda_3).\mathbf{B}$$
$$\mathbf{Sys_B} \stackrel{def}{=} (\mathbf{A} \parallel \mathbf{A} \parallel \mathbf{A}) \underset{\{run\}}{\bowtie} (\mathbf{B} \parallel \mathbf{B})$$

Fig. 9.   PEPA description for model B

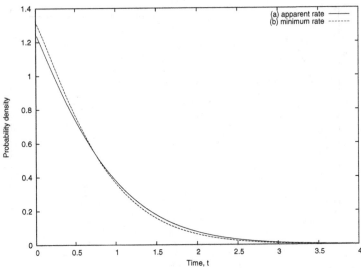

Fig. 10. Probability density functions for time taken between consecutive **stop** actions in model B for (a) an apparent rate strategy and (b) the *minimum rate strategy*

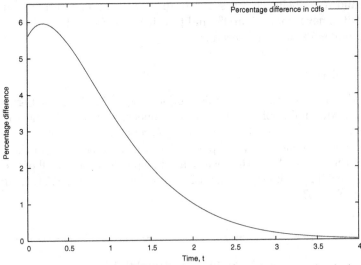

Fig. 11. Model B: Percentage difference between the *minimum rate strategy* and the *apparent rate strategy* as carried through to the CDF function

Again we plot the PDFs of both the model using the apparent rate computation and the model using the minimum rate (in Figure 10) and the percentage difference between these as carried through to the CDF (in Figure 11) as

$$\mathbf{A} \stackrel{def}{=} (\mathbf{run}, \lambda_1).(\mathbf{stop}, \lambda_2).\mathbf{A}$$
$$\mathbf{B} \stackrel{def}{=} (\mathbf{run}, \mu_1).(\mathbf{pause}, \lambda_3).\mathbf{B}$$
$$\mathbf{Sys_C} \stackrel{def}{=} \mathbf{A} \underset{\{run\}}{\bowtie} (\mathbf{B} \parallel \mathbf{B})$$

Fig. 12. PEPA description for Model C

$100\psi(X_{ars}, X_{mrs})$. Here the agreement is even more encouraging and the results are even better. The difference between the two plots is never more than 6% and the difference reduces to zero even more quickly (within about 4 seconds).

5.3   Model C

There is a final PEPA synchronisation idiom which we have not considered, which is when both of the partners in a synchronisation contribute actively to the result. Such a model is Model C, in Figure 12. Now **B** is an active participant in the **run** action and is no longer a client of **A**. Again the differences between the apparent rate calculation and the minimum rate calculation are computed (and plotted in Figures 13 and 14). The percentage difference between these is plotted in Figure 15. This time the calculations are repeated for five different values of the rate μ_1 while holding the value of $\lambda_1 = 1.0$ constant.

The difference between the two computations is greatest for slower rates (low values of μ_1) and least for faster rates (high values of μ_1). When μ_1 has the value 0.8 the difference between the two values is not more than 3% and again reduces to zero very quickly (within about 4 seconds) showing that even in this case the approximation provided by the minimum rate is acceptable. Not displayed is the passage difference, $\psi(\cdot)$, for $\mu_1 = 1.0$, which is 0 throughout, i.e. the strategies produce the same results when the synchronising rates are the same.

6   Conclusions

ipc [13] is a compiler for PEPA which carefully supports aspects of the PEPA language definition which have been approximated by other tools, in particular the crucial definition of apparent rate. ipc offers in addition the capability to specify and, with the aid of HYDRA [20], calculate passage time quantiles from PEPA models.

Using ipc, we have been able to compare different synchronisation strategies in PEPA. We have shown that when passive actions are involved, the minimum rate strategy tends to overestimate the global rate of action evolution. This translates into a slightly increased probability of early completion in passage time measures, as can be seen by the positive difference measure in Figures 8

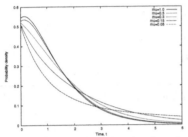

Fig. 13. Probability density functions for time taken between consecutive **stop** actions in Model C for $1.0 \geq \mu \geq 0.05$, using the *apparent rate strategy*

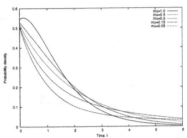

Fig. 14. Probability density functions for time taken between consecutive **stop** actions in Model C for $1.0 \geq \mu \geq 0.05$, using the *minimum rate strategy*

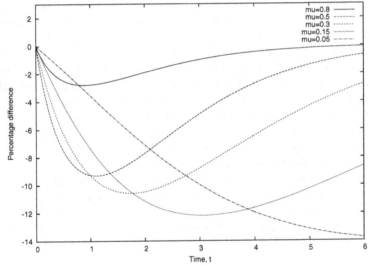

Fig. 15. Model C: Percentage difference between the *minimum rate strategy* and the *apparent rate strategy* as carried through to the CDF functions for 5 different values of μ_1

and 11. Conversely, in active synchronisations, we have shown that the minimum strategy results in a slightly decreased probability of early completion.

It would appear that, except in cases where the Markov chain is stiff (has rates of orders of magnitude difference), the differences in strategy are neither too large nor too long-lasting. It should be borne in mind that we have deliberately taken worst case scenarios of synchronisations that reoccur very frequently and that in larger models where the synchronisations are more separated, the differences in performance metrics are likely to be very small. As future work, we intend to look at how synchronisation affects larger models of system behaviour.

User experience tells us that the computation of apparent rates is a noticeable overhead on state-space generation time and so a reasonable methodological approach might be to work with the approximation to the apparent rate computation for swift initial investigation of the problem before progressing to the more accurate (but more expensive) calculation later. In this way, reasonable performance results can be obtained quickly while the PEPA model is being developed and debugged and the performance modeller can progress to a more careful calculation of performance metrics after this initial development phase has ended.

Acknowledgements

Stephen Gilmore is supported by the DEGAS (Design Environments for Global ApplicationS) project IST-2001-32072 funded by the FET Proactive Initiative on Global Computing and by the EPSRC grant GR/S21717/01 (Enhancing the Performance Predictability of Grid Applications with Patterns and Process Algebras). Jeremy Bradley is supported in part by the Nuffield Foundation under grant reference NAL/00805/G.

References

[1] Hillston, J.: A Compositional Approach to Performance Modelling. Volume 12 of Distinguished Dissertations in Computer Science. Cambridge University Press (1996) 129, 130, 132
[2] Bernardo, M., Gorrieri, R.: Extended Markovian Process Algebra. In Montanari, U., Sassone, V., eds.: CONCUR'96, Proc. of the 7th Int. Conference on Concurrency Theory. Volume 1119 of LNCS., Springer-Verlag (1996) 315–330 129
[3] Hermanns, H.: Interactive Markov Chains. PhD thesis, Univ. Erlangen-Nürnberg (1998) 129
[4] Gilmore, S., Hillston, J.: The PEPA workbench: A tool to support a process algebra-based approach to performance modelling. In Haring, G., Kotsis, G., eds.: Proc. of the 7th Int. Conf. on Modelling Techniques and Tools for Computer Performance Evaluation. Volume 794 of LNCS., Springer-Verlag (1994) 353–368 129, 132
[5] Clark, G., Gilmore, S., Hillston, J., Thomas, N.: Experiences with the PEPA performance modelling tools. In: UKPEW'98, Proceedings of the 14th UK Performance Engineering Workshop. (1998) 129
[6] de Alfaro, L.: How to specify and verify the long-run average behaviour of probabilistic systems. In: Proc. of the 13th IEEE Symp. on Logic in Computer Science, IEEE (1998) 129
[7] Bowman, H., Bryans, J. W., Derrick, J.: Analysis of a multimedia stream using stochastic process algebras. The Computer Journal 44 (2001) 230–245 129
[8] El-Rayes, A., Kwiatkowska, M., Norman, G.: Solving infinite stochastic process algebra models through matrix-geometric methods. [24] 41–62 129

[9] Wan, F.: Interface engineering and transient analysis for the PEPA Workbench. Master's thesis, School of Computer Science, The University of Edinburgh (2000) 129

[10] Hermanns, H., Herzog, U., Hillston, J.: Stochastic process algebras—A formal approach to performance modelling. Tutorial, Dept. of Computer Science, Univ. of Edinburgh (1996) 129

[11] Clark, G., Sanders, W.: Implementing a stochastic process algebra within the Möbius modeling framework. In de Alfaro, L., Gilmore, S., eds.: Proc. of the 1st joint PAPM-PROBMIV Workshop. Volume 2165 of LNCS., Aachen, Germany, Springer-Verlag (2001) 200–215   129, 132

[12] Kwiatkowska, M., Norman, G., Parker, D.: Probabilistic symbolic model checking with PRISM: A hybrid approach. In: TACAS'02, Proceedings of Tools and Algorithms for Construction and Analysis of Systems. Volume 2280 of Lecture Notes in Computer Science., Grenoble, Springer-Verlag (2002) 52–66   129, 132

[13] Bradley, J. T., Dingle, N. J., Gilmore, S. T., Knottenbelt, W. J.: Derivation of passage-time densities in PEPA models using ipc: the Imperial PEPA Compiler. In Kotsis, G., ed.: MASCOTS'03, Proceedings of the 11th IEEE/ACM International Symposium on Modeling, Analysis and Simulation of Computer and Telecommunications Systems, University of Central Florida, IEEE Computer Society Press (2003) 344–351   129, 133, 138

[14] Milner, R.: Communication and Concurrency. Prentice Hall (1989) 129

[15] Hillston, J.: The nature of synchronisation. In Herzog, U., Rettelbach, M., eds.: Proc. of the 2nd Int. Workshop on Process Algebras and Performance Modelling, Erlangen (1994) 51–70 129

[16] Bradley, J. T., Davies, N. J.: Reliable performance modelling with approximate synchronisations. [24] 99–118   129, 130

[17] Götz, N., Herzog, U., Rettelbach, M.: TIPP—Introduction and application to protocol performance analysis. In König, H., ed.: Formale Beschreibungstechniken für verteilte Systeme. FOKUS, Saur-Verlag (1993) 130

[18] Priami, C.: A stochastic π-calculus. In Gilmore, S., Hillston, J., eds.: Process Algebra and Performance Modelling Workshop. Volume 38(7) of Special Issue: The Computer Journal., CEPIS (1995) 578–589   130

[19] Argent-Katwala, A., Bradley, J. T., Dingle, N. J.: Expressing performance requirements using regular expressions to specify stochastic probes over process algebra models. In Almeida, V., Lea, D., eds.: WOSP'04, Proceedings of the 4th International Workshop on Software and Performance, Redwood City, California, ACM (2004) 49–58   132, 133

[20] Bradley, J. T., Dingle, N. J., Gilmore, S. T., Knottenbelt, W. J.: Extracting passage times from PEPA models with the HYDRA tool: a case study. In Jarvis, S. A., ed.: UKPEW'03, Proceedings of 19th Annual UK Performance Engineering Workshop. (2003) 79–90   133, 138

[21] Harrison, P. G., Knottenbelt, W. J.: Passage-time distributions in large Markov chains. In Martonosi, M., e Silva, E.d.S., eds.: Proc. of ACM SIGMETRICS 2002. (2002) 77–85   133

[22] Dingle, N. J., Harrison, P. G., Knottenbelt, W. J.: Response time densities in Generalised Stochastic Petri Net models. In: Proceedings of the 3rd International Workshop on Software and Performance (WOSP'2002), Rome (2002) 46–54   133

[23] Dingle, N. J., Knottenbelt, W. J., Harrison, P. G.: HYDRA: HYpergraph-based Distributed Response-time Analyser. In Arabnia, H. R., Man, Y., eds.: PDPTA'03, Proceedings of the 2003 International Conference on Parallel and Distributed

Processing Techniques and Applications. Volume 1., Las Vegas, NV (2003) 215–
219   133

[24] Hillston, J., Silva, M., eds.: PAPM'99, Proceedings of the 7th International Workshop on Process Algebra and Performance Modelling. In Hillston, J., Silva, M.,
eds.: Process Algebra and Performance Modelling Workshop, Centro Politécnico
Superior de la Universidad de Zaragoza, Prensas Universitarias de Zaragoza (1999)
140, 141

A Bounded True Concurrency Process Algebra for Performance Evaluation*

M. Carmen Ruiz, Diego Cazorla, Fernando Cuartero,
J. José Pardo, and Hermenegilda Macià

Escuela Politécnica Superior de Albacete
Universidad de Castilla-La Mancha. 02071 Albacete, Spain
{Juan.Pardo,Hermenegilda.Macia}@uclm.es
{MCarmen.Ruiz,Diego.Cazorla,Fernando.Cuartero}@uclm.es

Abstract. A *True Concurrency Timed Process Algebra* which takes into account the number of resources/processors that processes have at disposal is presented. Both its syntax and its operational semantics are defined. An algorithm which allows us to estimate the required time to evolve between states and which allows us to evaluate the performance of a system is also presented. A simple example is used to illustrate how a system can be specified by means of our language and how the performance evaluation algorithm works.

1 Introduction

It is a well-known fact that concurrency involves a radical increase in the complexity of a system. Theoretical models to study these systems at a formal level became of great importance. The first models abstract many real properties of concurrent systems which are considered non essential for them, such as duration and structure of actions, properties of communication networks, distribution of system components, number of processors and so on. By leaving these non essential properties aside, it is easier to study the behaviour of processes at a formal level due to a clearer design specification. However, these simplifications have a cost which is the loss of all the information which has been abstracted. This fact can be observed in early formal models such as *Petri nets* and *process algebras*.

Once the basic models have been thoroughly studied, it is necessary to extend them to deal with these other aspects, usually quantitative ones, which have been lost in the abstraction. Extended models have been proposed to represent aspects such as fairness [1, 2], timed models [3, 4], Markovian timed models [5, 6] and probabilistic models [7, 8, 9].

The aim of this paper is to introduce a timed process algebra, called **BTC** (for Bounded True Concurrency), which allows us to evaluate the performance

---

* This work has been partially supported by the MCyT project "Description and Performance of Distributed Systems and Application to Multimedia Systems" (Ref. TIC2003-07848-c02-02) and the JCCM project "Design and Implementation of Efficient Multimedia Systems by using Formal Techniques" (Ref. PAC-03001).

M. Núñez et al. (Eds.): FORTE 2004 Workshops, LNCS 3236, pp. 143–155, 2004.

of a system, considering that the (limited amount of) available processors have to be shared by all the processes. We can generalised this approach and consider systems that share homogeneous resources of any kind (processors, buses, disks, etcetera). Nevertheless, we cannot consider yet processes that need to use heterogeneous resources (e.g. one processor unit and two disk units). This extension of the process algebra is left for future work.

The most important consequence of this approach is that if there are more processes than resources then not all of them can be simultaneously executed. A process has to wait until it allocates the resources needed to continue its execution. This means that we can find two kinds of delays in the execution of a process: delays related to the synchronization of processes, and delays related to the allocation of resources. The former is usual in a (theoretical) concurrent context, but the latter is only taken into account if we consider a limited amount of available resources.

In order to present our model, it is worth to review an important characteristic of the currents formal models of concurrency. They can be roughly divided into two groups: *Interleaving* based models, in which the independent execution of two processes is modelled by specifying the possible interleaving of their actions; and *true concurrency* models, in which the causal relations between actions are explicitly represented. Our process algebra is based on the notion of true concurrency where concurrent behaviour can be distinguished from interleaving one by considering that $(a|b) \not\equiv (a.b + b.a)$

Furthermore, the bounded true concurrency approach we present in this paper considers all the cases between interleaving based models and true concurrency based models. In particular, if we consider only one resource unit, we will be considering an interleaving approach, while if we consider infinite resources we will have a true concurrency approach. From this point of view, our model extends both interleaving and true concurrency based models.

The performance of a system may be different depending on the number of available resources. If we denote by $[P]_N$ a process which is executed in the scope of N resources, we will have that $[a|b]_1 \equiv [a.b + b.a]_1$ but $[a|b]_n \not\equiv [a.b + b.a]_n$ $\forall n > 1$. In general, given a process P, $\forall n, m \in \mathbb{N}$ with $n \neq m$, we have that the performance of $[P]_n$ may be (or may be not) different from the performance of $[P]_m$. Actually, one of the main applications of this process algebra consists in finding a natural number n such that $\forall i \in \mathbb{N}, i \geq n$, $[P]_i$ is *equivalent* (from a performance point of view) to $[P]_n$, i.e., n represents the maximal degree of parallelism we can exploit in the system, and as a result, we obtain the optimum number of resources needed in order to speed up the performance of the system.

BTC is based on CSP [10]. We have extended its syntax in order to consider duration of actions by means of a timed prefix operator. The operational semantics has been also extended in order to consider the context (number of resources) in which processes are executed. A notion of timed bag of actions is also introduced to represent the concurrent (simultaneous) execution of processes.

In the literature we may find several theoretical models that consider the notion of resource consuming. Timed process algebras that consider resources are presented in [11, 12, 13, 14, 15, 16]. In [11, 12] a discrete timed process algebra for limited parallelism (CCSLP) is presented. Time is associated to actions by considering special actions t_n where n represents the consumption of n (homogeneous) resource units. This means that, if we want to specify an action that lasts 2 units of time, we have to write $a.t_1.t_1.NIL$, where a does not represent the execution of the action but just the moment in which the action starts its execution. From our point of view, the main problem of that model is that it may be difficult to know when an action finishes. If we consider three actions (a, b, c) with duration 2 (i.e., $a.t_1.t_1.NIL$, $b.t_1.t_1.NIL$, $c.t_1.t_1.NIL$), and two resources (processors), a possible sequence of actions is $a.b.t_2.c.t_2.t_2$, where the first t_2 represents the execution of the first unit of a and b, the second t_2 represents the execution of the first unit of c and the second unit of a or b, and the last t_2 represents the execution of the second unit of c and the second unit of b or a. Thus, it is difficult to analyse the performance of a system because it may be impossible to know when the system has reached a state.

In [13] a process algebra for shared processors is presented. The paper is focused on processes sharing a single processor scheduled according to some scheduling strategy. Multi-processors systems can be described but only with static allocation of processes to processors. This situation does not happen in our model where there is no assignment of processes to processors, i.e., a sequential process may be interrupted and later on it can continue its execution in a different processor.

ACSR, a process algebraic approach to the specification and analysis of resource-bound real-time systems is introduced in [14]. In that process algebra, the use of shared (heterogeneous) resources is represented by timed actions and synchronization is supported by instantaneous events. Timed actions are always executed for one time unit (*tick*) and they consume a set of resources during that time. ACSR supports also priorities which are used to decide among processes (actions) competing for resources. In [15] an extension of ACSR considering dense time is presented. In that model, timed actions have a duration given by a positive and finite real number u, where A^u represents the execution of a resource-consuming action A for a time u. Synchronization between timed actions is allowed but only in the case that both actions have the same duration and they use disjoint sets of resources. Other extensions of ACSR are presented in [16] where PACSR (probabilistic ACSR) and ACSR-VP (ACSR with value passing) are introduced.

The approach taken in ACSR and extensions is slightly different from ours. In ACSR, a timed action is a set of pairs $(resource, priority)$, and two (or more) timed actions may be executed simultaneously only if they use different resources. Let us consider a system with two processors. If we have three processes that use different resources, then the three processes may be executed simultaneously, but, actually, we have only two processors. In order to consider that there are only two available processors, we need to consider two resources, cpu1 and cpu2, each one representing one processor (in ACSR it is not allowed to have two units of a resource). As an example we can consider the following three processes (in ACSR syntax): $P = \{(cpu1, 1)\}^1 : NIL$, $Q = \{(cpu2, 1)\}^1 : NIL$ and $R = \{(cpu1, 1)\}^1 : NIL$. Then we have that in the first step P and Q or R and Q may evolve simultaneously, but not P and R because they share the resource cpu1. In other words, resources are statically assigned to processes. This does not occur in our model where resources are dynamically assigned to processes.

A different approach is considered in [17] where a process algebra for the management of resources in concurrent systems (**PARM**) is presented. In that paper a heterogeneous resource context and a resource trading policy (based on utility functions) are introduced. The main idea is that several processes can exchange resources in order to improve the performance of the global system, provided that none of them can get worse after the exchange. Although this is a very interesting work, it is not very closed to our approach because no quantification about the performance of a system is considered. A related approach is considered in [18] where an optimal resource allocation in multi-class networks scheme is presented.

The rest of the paper is organised as follows. First, we present the syntax of **BTC** and some basic notations. Next, the operational semantics of the language is defined by means of a set of inference rules. Building on it, we define an algorithm for performance evaluation and illustrate it with a simple example of how a system can be specified and how the performance algorithm works. Then we present our conclusions and outline some lines for current and future work.

2   Introducing the Language BTC

In this section we introduce the process algebra **BTC** by means of its syntax and an intuitive interpretation of the operators.

Definition 1. *Let Act_T be a finite set of timed actions and Act_U a finite set of untimed actions, $Act_U \cap Act_T = \emptyset$. The syntax of **BTC** is defined by the following BNF expression:*

$$P ::= stop \mid a.P \mid <b, \alpha>.P \mid P \oplus P \mid P + P \mid P \parallel_A P \mid recX.P$$

where $A \subseteq Act_U$, $a \in Act_U$, $b \in Act_T$, and $\alpha \in \mathbb{N}$, where $\mathbb{N}$ represents the set of natural numbers. Furthermore we assume a set of process variables Id ranged over by X, X', a set of processes $\mathcal{P}$ ranged over by P, Q, R, and a set of actions $Act = Act_U \cup Act_T$.

Let us now informally describe the interpretation of these operators. Later we will provide them with an operational semantics, so the meaning of each operator and the relationship among them will be completely formalised.

stop. This represents a deadlock, that is, no action can be executed.
Prefix. This is the classical prefix operator. It will we use to represent a process P prefixed by an untimed action. As usual, the process $a.P$, once the

action a has been executed, behaves like the process P. Mainly, we will use the (untimed) prefix operator to represent a possible synchronization of a process.

Timed prefix. The classical prefix operator has been enriched with information about the amount of time the action b takes in its execution (the value α). The process $<b, \alpha>.P$, once the action b has been executed, behaves like the process P.

Internal choice. This is essentially the classical internal choice operator. Given two processes P_1 and P_2, $P_1 \oplus P_2$ represents the process that behaves like P_1 or like P_2 as the result of an internal decision of the system.

External choice. This is also interpreted in the usual way. Given two processes P_1 and P_2, $P_1 + P_2$ represents the process that behaves like P_1 or like P_2 as the environment requests.

Parallel composition. $P_1 \parallel_A P_2$ represents the parallel execution of the processes P_1 and P_2, where they synchronize on the actions in A. We will denote by $P_1 \parallel P_2$ the parallel execution of P_1 and P_2 without synchronization, that is, $P_1 \parallel_{\{\}} P_2$.

Recursion. The process $recX.P$ represents the classical recursion operator where occurrences of X are substituted by $recX.P$. This operator allows us to define infinite behaviours.

During the rest of the paper we will use the following notation to deal with multisets (bags). We will use the convention that $B = \{2.x_1,\ 3.x_2,\ 5.x_3\}$ represents the multiset defined over the set $X = \{x_1,\ x_2,\ x_3,\ x_4\}$ by:

$$B : \{x_1,\ x_2,\ x_3,\ x_4\} \longrightarrow \mathbb{N}$$

$$B(x_1) = 2,\ \ B(x_2) = 3,\ \ B(x_3) = 5,\ \ B(x_4) = 0$$

We will use capital letters B, B_1, B_2, C, C_1, C_2 to denote multisets, while capital letters such us A, A_1, A_2 will represent sets. Both the empty multiset and the empty set will be represented by $\emptyset$. We will also use the following operations:

- $B_1 \cup B_2$: Union of multisets.
- $|B|$: Number of actions in the multiset, that is, $|B| = \sum_{x \in X} B(x)$.
- $B \cap A$: Multiset obtained by taking from B the actions belonging to A, that is,

$$(B \cap A)(x) = \begin{cases} B(x) & \text{if } x \in A \\ 0 & \text{otherwise} \end{cases}$$

Definition 2. *Let $\mathcal{B}(X) = \{B \mid \forall x \notin X, B(x) = 0\}$ be the set of multisets over the set X. A timed bag is a pair (B, α), where $B \in \mathcal{B}(X)$, and $\alpha \in \mathbb{N}$ is the duration of every element in B. The set of timed bags over the set X, denoted by $TB(X)$, is defined as $TB(X) = \{(B, \alpha) \mid B \in \mathcal{B}(X) \wedge \alpha \in \mathbb{N}\}$.*

Intuitively, a timed bag relates a multiset to a unique natural number that represents the time every action (element) in the multiset needs to finish its execution.

3   Operational Semantics

In this section we present an operational semantics. By means of this mechanism, we provide the language operators with a meaning and an accurate interpretation by describing how a process is able to turn into another. This evolution is represented by using labelled transition systems.

We will have that *transitions* are triples $(P, Q, (B, \alpha))$. We will usually denote transitions by $P \xrightarrow{B, \alpha} Q$.

Intuitively, the meaning of the previous transition is that the process P executes the actions belonging to the multiset B and then it behaves like the process Q. The execution of each action belonging to the same multiset takes α units of time.

In order to consider internal (non observable) evolutions of a process, we consider a new kind of action, $\tau \notin \mathcal{A}ct$, which represents an internal action. This action is used to define the evolution of the internal choice of two processes, and it has duration 0.

In Table 1 we can find the rules of the operational semantics. We assume that $\alpha, \alpha' \in \mathbb{N}$, $a \in \mathcal{A}ct_U$, $b \in \mathcal{A}ct_T$, $B_i \in \mathcal{B}(\mathcal{A}ct \cup \{\tau\})$ and $B' \in \mathcal{B}(\mathcal{A}ct_U)$. We also consider a constant $\mathcal{N}$ that represents the amount of processors/resources at disposal.

The rule $R1a$ is the classical one for the prefix operator. The rule $R1b$ states that given a process P and an action b with an execution time α, b is firstly executed and, after α units of time, the process behaves like P. In rule $R1c$ a partial execution of the timed action b is allowed, i.e., action b is executed for α' units of time and the remaining time $(\alpha - \alpha')$ will be performed later on.

The rule $R1c$ allows a prefix operator transition to be split into any number of consecutive transitions. This rule is very similar to the rule **ActT** presented in [15]. The only difference is that, in that case, a dense time domain is considered and, consequently, an infinite number of transitions are derived. In our model this does not occur because we work in a discrete time domain.

The rules $R2$ and $R3$ are the classical ones for the internal and external choice operators.

The rule $R4$ represents the basic synchronization mechanism. We only consider those synchronization actions that may be performed by processes P and Q. As synchronization actions are untimed actions, the whole process evolves in 0 units of time to $P' \parallel_A Q'$.

The rule $R5a$ captures the simultaneous execution of, at most, $\mathcal{N}$ no synchronization actions. Although we have considered as premises that both processes may perform different timed bags with the same time α, this does not represent a loss of generality because applying rule $R1c$ we can split transitions in order to have the same time in both premises.

The rules $R5b$ and $R5c$ are similar to $R5a$ but consider that only one of the two processes (P or Q) evolves.

Finally, the rule $R6$ captures the semantics for recursion in the usual fashion.

Definition 3. *The operational semantics of* **BTC** *is defined as the least multiset of transitions we can derive by using the rules in Table 1.*

Table 1. Operational Semantics

R1a)
$$a.P \xrightarrow{\{a\},0} P$$

R1b)
$$(b,\alpha).P \xrightarrow{\{b\},\alpha} P$$

R1c)
$$\cfrac{0 < \alpha' < \alpha}{(b,\alpha).P \xrightarrow{\{b\},\alpha'} (b,\alpha - \alpha').P}$$

R2a)
$$P \oplus Q \xrightarrow{\{\tau\},0} P$$

R2b)
$$P \oplus Q \xrightarrow{\{\tau\},0} Q$$

R3a)
$$\cfrac{P \xrightarrow{B,\alpha} P'}{P + Q \xrightarrow{B,\alpha} P'}$$

R3b)
$$\cfrac{Q \xrightarrow{B,\alpha} Q'}{P + Q \xrightarrow{B,\alpha} Q'}$$

R4)
$$\cfrac{P \xrightarrow{B',0} P' \wedge Q \xrightarrow{B',0} Q' \wedge B' = B' \cap A \neq \emptyset}{P \parallel_A Q \xrightarrow{B',0} P' \parallel_A Q'}$$

R5a)
$$\cfrac{P \xrightarrow{B_1,\alpha} P' \wedge Q \xrightarrow{B_2,\alpha} Q' \wedge B_i \cap A = \emptyset \wedge |B_1| + |B_2| \leq \mathcal{N}}{P \parallel_A Q \xrightarrow{B_1 \cup B_2,\alpha} P' \parallel_A Q'}$$

R5b)
$$\cfrac{P \xrightarrow{B,\alpha} P' \wedge B \cap A = \emptyset}{P \parallel_A Q \xrightarrow{B,\alpha} P' \parallel_A Q}$$

R5c)
$$\cfrac{Q \xrightarrow{B,\alpha} Q' \wedge B \cap A = \emptyset}{P \parallel_A Q \xrightarrow{B,\alpha} P \parallel_A Q'}$$

R6)
$$\cfrac{P\{recX.P/X\} \xrightarrow{B,\alpha} P'}{recX.P \xrightarrow{B,\alpha} P'}$$

4   Performance Evaluation Algorithm

With the formal resource-aware model that we have just defined, the timed characteristics of the system have been captured. Now we are concerned with defining an algorithm which allows us to estimate the minimum time needed to reach a given state.

By applying the rules of the operational semantics, we build a transition graph where we can abstract the information about actions and consider only the information about time (duration of actions). This graph is a weighted directed graph, where weights are always positive numbers, and finding the shortest path from the initial node is the problem we want to solve, problem which is solved by using Dijkstra algorithm.

Let T_{S_i} be the expected time to evolve from the *initial state* S_0 to a state S_i, and $In(S_i)$ the set of predecessor nodes of S_i. For every state $S_j \in In(S_i)$ an edge labelled by α_{ji} which represents the time to evolve from S_j to S_i exists.

Then, T_{S_i} may be obtained by computing recursively the following equation

$$T_{S_i} = \begin{cases} 0 & \text{if } S_i = S_0 \\ \min\{T_{S_j} + \alpha_{ji} \mid S_j \in In(S_i)\} & \text{otherwise} \end{cases} \quad (1)$$

In order to compute (1), we number the n nodes of the graph from 0 to $n-1$, and we assume it is represented by an adjacency matrix where $cost[i][j]$ is defined as follows

$$cost[i][j] = \begin{cases} \alpha_{ij} & \text{if } S_i \in In(S_j) \\ \infty & \text{otherwise} \end{cases}$$

Finally, the performance evaluation algorithm is shown in Fig. 1.

5   A Simple Example

In this section, we present a simple example of specification using **BTC** (addition of two matrices). We show the transition graph we obtain by applying the rules of the operational semantics, and we compute the minimum and maximum time needed to finish the operation depending on the size of the matrices and the available processors.

We assume, without loss of generality, that we have the same number of threads/processes as rows (columns) in the matrices to sum. This system can be modelled as follows:

$$\text{System} \equiv P_1 \parallel P_2 \parallel \ldots \parallel P_i \parallel \ldots \parallel P_n$$
$$P_i \equiv (rd_i, 4).(add_i, 1).(wr_i, 2).stop$$

where rd_i is an action meaning "read a row", add_i is "add a row" and wr_i is "write a row".

Figure 2 shows the transition graph we obtain when we consider two matrices with just three rows in a system with two processors ($\mathcal{N} = 2$). Taking into account the symmetry in the three possible paths from the initial node, just one

```
MinTime(int v, int cost[][], int n, int dist[], bool S[]) {
// v: initial node
// cost: adjacency matrix with weights
// n: number of nodes in the graph
// dist: shortest known path from initial node
// S: true if shortest path is known
// big_number: constant which value is a~big number
int u, minimum;

for (int i=0; i<n; i++) {
    S[i] = false; dist[i] = cost[v][i];
}
S[v] = true; dist[v] = 0;
for (int num=0; num<n; num++) {
// Choose u from among nodes not in S such that dist[u] is minimum.
    minimum = big_number;
    for (int i=0; i<n; i++)
      if (!S[i] && (dist[i]<minimum))
          minimum=dist[i]; u=i;
    S[u]=true;
    for (int w=0; w<n; w++) // Update distances
        if (!S[w] && (dist[w]>dist[u]+cost[u][w]))
            dist[w] = dist[u] + cost[u][w];
    }
}
```

Fig. 1. Performance evaluation algorithm

of them has been depicted. For the sake of clarity, we have always chosen the biggest number of actions we can execute simultaneously.

There are several paths in which the required time to do this addition is minimum. In the transition graph in Fig. 2 we have marked with dotted lines one of them. Every node in this shortest path has a representation in terms of **BTC** as follows:

$N_0 = (rd_1, 4).(add_1, 1).(wr_1, 2)||(rd_2, 4).(add_2, 1).(wr_2, 2)||(rd_3, 4).(add_3, 1).(wr_3, 2)$
$N_1 = (add_1, 1).(wr_1, 2)||(add_2, 1).(wr_2, 2)||(rd_3, 4).(add_3, 1).(wr_3, 2)$
$N_3 = (add_1, 1).(wr_1, 2)||(wr_2, 2)||(rd_3, 3).(add_3, 1).(wr_3, 2)$
$N_9 = (add_1, 1).(wr_1, 2)||(rd_3, 1).(add_3, 1).(wr_3, 2)$
$N_{15} = (wr_1, 2)||(add_3, 1).(wr_3, 2)$
$N_{21} = (wr_1, 1)||(wr_3, 2)$
$N_{23} = (wr_3, 1)$
$N_{26} = STOP$

We observe that the minimum time needed to do this addition of matrices is 11 units of time while if we were to work in a sequential way (or interleaving) we would have needed 21 units of time.

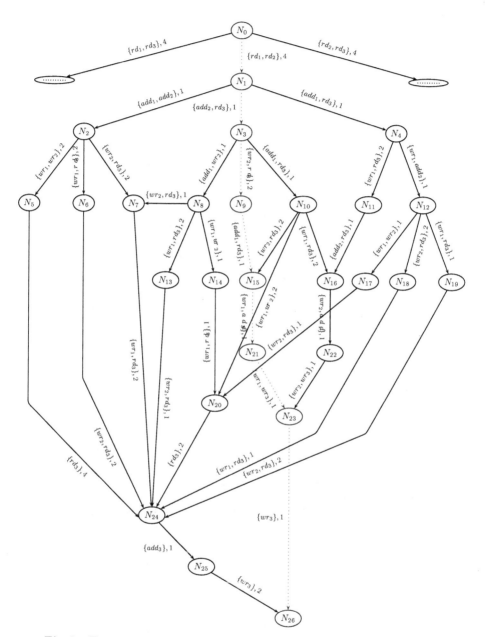

Fig. 2. Transition graph for the addition of two matrices 3x3 with $\mathcal{N} = 2$

The same example of the addition of matrices has been developed for various matrix sizes and different number of processors, obtaining the results displayed in Table 2.

Table 2. Sum of two matrices with various matrix sizes and different number of processors

Matrix size	Processors	T. Min	T. Max
3	2	11	21
3	3	7	21
4	2	14	28
4	3	10	28
4	4	7	28
6	2	21	42
6	3	14	42
6	4	11	42
6	6	7	42
10	2	35	70
10	3	24	70
10	4	18	70
10	5	14	70
10	6	12	70
10	7	11	70
10	8	11	70
10	9	11	70
10	10	7	70

6   Conclusions

In this paper we have presented a timed extension of CSP, called **BTC**, which allows us to evaluate the performance of a system, taking into account that the available resources have to be shared by all the processes. In this first approach to the model we have only considered homogeneous resources.

This algebra can be used for two main different tasks. On one hand, given a fixed number of resources, we are able to evaluate the performance of a system. On the other hand, if we start with some specification, we can find the appropriate number of resources that we need to fulfil some time requirements. We can even calculate the minimum number of resources needed to obtain the best performance of a system. This is particularly important in some applications (e.g. MPEG2 encoding compression algorithm [19]) where the performace of parallel algorithms is *measured* considering different experimental settings (2, 4, 8, ... processors) [20].

Although we have found in the literature different approaches to the problem, none of them seems to cover the main topic of our model: performance evaluation of processes that share resources.

7 Future Work

Our future work is related to extend **BTC** in order to consider heterogeneous resources. In order to define this extension we consider that some of the ideas presented in ACSR [14, 15] could be of interest.

From an application point of view, it would be interesting to link our resource-aware model to a tool for standard timed models making the analysis amenable. If it were impossible we will consider to design a new tool.

Another goal is to model (and analyse) a real system. For this aim, we are considering some parallel algorithms for image and video compression based on Wavelet methods. Compression of visual data is a computationally expensive task where large volumes of data have to be processed; therefore compression algorithms can greatly benefit from the use of parallel systems. In this setting, our algebraic language can be used to find the most appropriate number of needed processors for optimum performance.

Finally, our model suffers from the *state explosion problem*. We think that it could be useful to include some kind of reduction techniques (maybe scheduling) in our model which allows the reduction of the graphs.

Acknowledgements

The authors would like to thank the anonymous referees for their very careful reading and useful suggestions. We would like to thank also Manuel Nuñez for his always right suggestions and comments.

References

[1] Costa, G., Stirling, C.: Weak and Strong Fairness in CCS. Information and Computation **73** (1987) 207–244 143
[2] Rutten, J., Zucker, J.: A Semantics Approach to Fairness. Fundamenta Informaticae **XVI** (1992) 1–38 143
[3] Reed, G., Roscoe, A.: A Timed Model for Communicating Sequential Processes. Theoretical Computer Science **58** (1988) 249–261 143
[4] Moller, F., Tofts, C.: A Temporal Calculus of Communicating Systems. In: Proc. of CONCUR'90, LNCS 458, Springer (1990) 401–415 143
[5] Hillston, J.: A Compositional Approach to Performance Modelling. Cambridge University Press (1996) 143
[6] Hermanns, H., Herzog, U., Katoen, J. P.: Process algebra for performance evaluation. Theoretical Computer Science **274** (2002) 43–86 143
[7] Giacalone, A., Jou, C. C., Smolka, S.: Algebraic Reasoning for Probabilistic Concurrent Systems. In: Proc. of Working Conference on Programming Concepts and Methods, IFIP TC 2. (1990) 143
[8] Núñez, M., de Frutos, D., Llana, L.: Acceptance Trees for Probabilistic Processes. In: Proc. of CONCUR'95, LNCS 962, Springer (1995) 249–263 143
[9] Cuartero, F., de Frutos, D., Valero, V.: A sound and complete proof system for probabilistic processes. In: Proc. of 4th International AMAST Workshop on Real-Time Systems (ARTS'97), LNCS 1231, Springer (1997) 143

[10] Hoare, C.: Communicating Sequential Processes. Prentice Hall (1985) 144
[11] Gruska, D. P.: Process Algebra for Limited Parallelism. In: Proc. of Concurrency, Specification and Programming (CS&P'96). (1996) 61–74 145
[12] Gruska, D. P.: Bounded Concurrency. In Chlebus, B. S., Czaja, L., eds.: Proc. of 11th International Symposium on Fundamentals of Computation Theory (FCT'97), LNCS 1279, Springer (1997) 198–209 145
[13] Buchholtz, M., Andersen, J., Løvengreen, H. H.: Towards a Process Algebra for Shared Processors. Electronic Notes in Theoretical Computer Science **52** (2002) 145
[14] Lee, I., Brémond-Grégoire, P., Gerber, R.: A process algebraic approach to the specification and analysis of resource-bound real-time systems (1994) 145, 154
[15] Brémond-Grégoire, P., Lee, I.: A Process Algebra of Communicating Shared Resources with Dense Time and Priorities. Theoretical Computer Science **189** (1997) 179–219 145, 148, 154
[16] Lee, I., Choi, J. Y., Kwak, H. H., Philippou, A., Sokolsky, O.: A Family of Resource-Bound Real-Time Process Algebras. In: Proc. of FORTE'01, Kluwer Academic Publishers (2001) 443–458 145
[17] Núñez, M., Rodríguez, I.: PAMR: A Process Algebra for the Management of Resources in Concurrent Systems. In: Proc. of FORTE'01, Kluwer Academic Publishers (2001) 169–185 146
[18] Kalyanasundaram, S., Chong, E., Shroff, N.: Optimal resource allocation in multi-class networks with user-specified utility functions. Computer Networks **38** (2002) 613–630 146
[19] Pelayo, F. L., Cuartero, F., Valero, V., H.Macia, Pelayo, M. L.: Applying Timed-Arc Petri Nets to Improve the Performance of the MPEG-2 Encoding Algorithm. In: Proc. of the 10th IEEE International Conference on Multi-Media Modelling (MMM'2004), IEEE CS (2004) 49–56 153
[20] Olivares, T., Quiles, F., Cuenca, P., Orozco, L., Ahmad, I.: Study of Data Distribution Techniques for the Implementation of an MPEG-2 Video Encoder. In: Proc. of the 11th IASTED Int. Conference on Parallel and Distributed Computing Systems (PDCS'99). (1999) 537–542 153

Branching Time Equivalences
for Interactive Markov Chains

Guangping Qin[1] and Jinzhao Wu[1,2,*]

[1] Chengdu Institute of Computer Applications
Chinese Academy of Science, Chengdu 610041, China
qgp_max@163.com
[2] Fakultät für Mathematik und Informatik
Universität Mannheim, D7, 27, 68131 Mannheim, Germany
wu@pi1.informatik.uni-mannheim.de

Abstract. Interactive Markov chains (IMCs) are powerful models of concurrent systems, and branching time equivalences are useful to compare the behaviour of concurrent systems. In this paper we define various branching time relations on IMCs, including strong and weak (bi)simulations, and investigate connections among these relations. These relations are defined as an orthogonal extensions of classical labelled transition systems and pure stochastic settings. The logical characterizations of them are also studied by using an action-based logic aCSL. We show that for IMCs, bisimulation equivalence coincides with aCSL-equivalence, and simulation preorder weakly preserves aCSL safety and liveness formulae.

1 Introduction

Bisimulation and simulation relations are used widely to compare the behaviour of concurrent systems. They are both known as branching time relations. Bisimulations are equivalences that relate two states if they exhibit identical stepwise behaviour while simulations are preorders requiring one state to mimic another state in a stepwise manner, but the reverse does not necessarily hold. Typically, there are two distinct types of both simulation and bisimulation, i.e., strong (bi)simulations and weak (bi)simulations. Strong (bi)simulations require each individual step needs to be mimicked whereas weak (bi)simulations consider only observable steps and ignore internal behaviour.

Originally, simulation and bisimulation relations are defined on labelled transition systems (LTS) [20, 21], and their relationship has been studied intensively [14, 15]. The logical characterizations of these relations are also investigated based on classical transition systems. For example, strong bisimulation coincides with CTL-equivalence [10] and strong simulation agrees with a "preorder" on the universal (or existential) fragment of CTL [11]. Similar results hold for weak (bi)simulation where typically the next operator is omitted [22].

---

* Partially supported by National Science Foundation of China (NSFC) under Grant No. 60373113.

During the last decade, many (bi)simulation relations have been defined on probabilistic systems [3, 8, 9, 12, 19, 23], and various logics to reason about such systems have been proposed [1, 2, 16]. In the probabilistic framework, Markov chains are widely used as system models, including discrete-time and continuous-time models. In such frameworks, bisimulation and simulation relations are efficient means to aggregate the state space, and therefore can be useful to solve the well-known *state space explosion problem* occurring when using Markov chains as system models. Bisimulation and simulation relations for discrete-time Markov chains (DTMCs) and continuous-time Markov chains (CTMCs) have been developed respectively. A logic termed PCTL [16], which extends CTL with probability, is proposed to characterize DTMCs. For CTMCs, another extension of CTL called CSL (*Continuous Stochastic Logic*), first proposed in [1] and then refined in [4, 5, 6], is dedicated to characterize such models. However, these works are developed in isolation, and the connections among each other have received scant attention.

This paper attempts to study these branching time relations for stochastic system in a uniform framework, especially their interrelation. Furthermore, we consider these relations on a more powerful model — interactive Markov chains (IMCs) [17]. An IMC is the combination of CTMCs and *interactive process*, and treats interactive transitions and Markovian transitions in a separate way. Due to the distinctive representation of action and Markovian transitions, IMCs can preserve most advantages of both interactive processes and CTMCs. This makes IMCs also a powerful model of performance evaluation.

The logical characterizations of these relations are also considered in this paper. We use an action-based logic called aCSL to specify the logical characterization of IMCs. This logic is a variant of the language using in [18] except that the steady-state operator is omitted. The main results are that the strong bisimulation coincides with aCSL-equivalence while strong simulation preserves aCSL safe and live formulae. For weak relations, the similar results also hold where the internal action is ignored. Such coincidences with logics are very useful to help simplify model checking stochastic models. See e.g. [4, 6].

The rest of this paper is organized as follows: Section 2 introduces our system model, interactive Markov chains. In Section 3, we define various branching time relations on IMCs and investigate connections among these relations. The logic characterizations of these branching time relations are studied in Section 4. Section 5 concludes this paper.

2 Interactive Markov Chains

Interactive Markov chains are proposed by H. Hermanns [17], which combine interactive processes and CTMCs together and aim at compositional performance evaluation. This section gives a brief introduction to IMCs, serving as our underlying model.

2.1   Continuous-Time Markov Chains

IMCs are an extension of continuous-time Markov chains, we therefore first recall
the basic concept of CTMCs. Let AP be a fixed finite set of atomic propositions,
and $\mathbb{R}_{\geq 0}$ denote the set of non-negative reals.

Definition 1. A (labelled) *CTMC* is a tuple $C = (S, \mathbf{R}, L)$ where:

- S is a countable set of states,
- $\mathbf{R} : S \times S \to \mathbb{R}_{\geq 0}$ is a *rate matrix*, and
- $L : S \to 2^{AP}$ is a labelling function which assigns to each state $s \in S$ the set
  $L(s)$ of atomic propositions that are valid in s.

Intuitively, $\mathbf{R}(s, s') > 0$ iff there is a transition from s to s' and the probability
of this transition taking place within t time units is $1 - e^{-\mathbf{R}(s,s') \cdot t}$, an exponential
distribution with rate $\mathbf{R}(s, s')$. If $\mathbf{R}(s, s') > 0$ for more than one state s', a *race*
between the outgoing transitions from s exists, and the probability of which
the state s' wins the race is given by $\mathbf{P}(s, s') = \mathbf{R}(s, s')/E(s)$ where $E(s) = \sum_{s' \in S} \mathbf{R}(s, s')$, denoting the *total rate* at which any transition outgoing from
state s is taken. More precisely, $E(s)$ specifies that the probability of leaving s
within t time units is $1 - e^{-E(s) \cdot t}$. If $E(s) = 0$, we call s an *absorbing state*,
and define $\mathbf{P}(s, s') = 0$. Consequently, when there exists race condition, the
probability to move from s to s' within t time units is given by $\mathbf{P}_t(s, s') = \mathbf{P}(s, s') \cdot (1 - e^{-E(s) \cdot t})$.

2.2   Interactive Markov Chains

Let Act denote the universal set of actions, ranged over by $a, b, \cdots$. $\tau \in Act$,
denoting the internal action.

Definition 2. An *interactive Markov chain (IMC)* is a quadruple
$M = (S, \mathcal{A}, \longrightarrow, \dashrightarrow)$, where

- S is a nonempty set of states,
- $\mathcal{A} \subseteq Act$ is a countable set of actions,
- $\longrightarrow \ \subset S \times \mathcal{A} \times S$ is a set of so called *interactive transitions*, and
- $\dashrightarrow \ \subset S \times \mathbb{R}_{\geq 0} \times S$ is a set of so called *Markovian transitions*.

Here, we restrict the Markovian transitions to further satisfy that for each
pair of states (s_1, s_2) there is at most one Markovian transition between them.
We can see that IMCs combine actually the interactive processes and CTMCs as
orthogonal to each other as possible except that the labelling function of CTMC
is absent. This means that IMCs are no longer state-based but action-based. The
interactive transitions correspond to the action transitions of classical labelled
transition systems, and the Markovian transitions are in fact equivalent to the
rate matrix $\mathbf{R}$ of the CTMC (cf. Definition 1.). Figure 1 is an example IMC.

In the sequence, we also use $\mathbf{R}(s, s')$ to denote the rate of exponential distribution when there exists a Markovian transition between s and s' such that
$(s, \mathbf{R}(s, s'), s') \in \dashrightarrow$. For $C \subseteq S$, let $\mathbf{R}(s, C) = \sum_{s' \in C} \mathbf{R}(s, s')$ and $\mathbf{P}(s, C) = \sum_{s' \in C} \mathbf{P}(s, s')$ for simplicity.

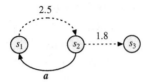

Fig. 1. An example of interactive Markov chain

3   Bisimulation and Simulation Relations

Bisimulation and simulation are the most important and useful branching time relations in concurrency theory. Our purpose is to lift these notions to IMCs. We consider both strong and weak relations on this model.

3.1   Bisimulation

As defined in the definition of IMCs, there are two different kinds of transitions in an IMC. How these two different transitions perform when they are both present is important. In fact, the executions are governed by the so called *maximal progress assumption* [17]: if the interactive transition is an internal transition, then it prevent the Markovian transition. While for observational action, its execution may rely on the sojourn time of the state, which is determined by the total rate of the state.

We use $s \not\xrightarrow{\tau}$ to denote the absence of such internal transitions. Let $M = (S, \mathcal{A}, \longrightarrow, \dashrightarrow)$ be an IMC. Strong bisimulation on IMCs is defined as follows:

Definition 3. An equivalence relation $\mathcal{B}$ on S is a *strong bisimulation* iff for all $s_1 \mathcal{B} s_2$:

1. $s_1 \xrightarrow{a} s'_1, a \in \mathcal{A} \Rightarrow \exists s'_2 \in S, s_2 \xrightarrow{a} s'_2$ and $s'_1 \mathcal{B} s'_2$, and
2. $s_1 \not\xrightarrow{\tau} \Rightarrow \mathbf{R}(s_1, C) = \mathbf{R}(s_2, C)$ for all equivalence classes C of $\mathcal{B}$.

s_1 and s_2 are strongly bisimilar, denoted $s_1 \sim s_2$, if there exists a strong bisimulation $\mathcal{B}$ on S with $s_1 \mathcal{B} s_2$.

Example 1. Figure 2 shows a strong bisimulation equivalence on the given IMC, where the states with the same shade are strongly bisimilar.

Strong bisimulation relation treats internal actions as special only in Markovian transitions. It does not abstract internal actions from sequence of interactive transitions, as weak bisimulation relation on classical labelled transition systems does. So we want to lift such weak bisimulation relation to the context of IMCs.

Let $\xRightarrow{\tau}$ represents the reflexive and transitive closure of $\xrightarrow{\tau}$, and $\xRightarrow{a}$ denotes $\xRightarrow{\tau}\xrightarrow{a}\xRightarrow{\tau}$. Note that $\xRightarrow{\tau}$ is possible without actually performing an internal action, but $\xRightarrow{a}$ must perform exactly one transition $\xrightarrow{a}$ proceeded and followed by arbitrary (possibly empty) internal actions.

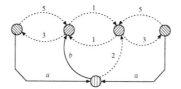

Fig. 2. Strong bisimulation equivalence

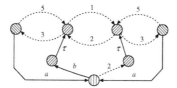

Fig. 3. Weak bisimulation equivalence

Definition 4. An equivalence relation $\widetilde{\mathcal{B}}$ on S is a *weak bisimulation* iff for all $s_1\widetilde{\mathcal{B}}s_2$:

1. $s_1 \xLongrightarrow{a} s_1', a \in \mathcal{A}\backslash\{\tau\} \Rightarrow \exists s_2' \in S, s_2 \xLongrightarrow{a} s_2'$ and $s_1'\widetilde{\mathcal{B}}s_2'$, and
2. $s_1 \xLongrightarrow{\tau} s_1', s_1' \not\xrightarrow{\tau} \Rightarrow \exists s_2' \in S, s_2 \xLongrightarrow{\tau} s_2', s_2' \not\xrightarrow{\tau}$ and $\mathbf{R}(s_1', C) = \mathbf{R}(s_2', C)$
   for all equivalence classes C of $\widetilde{\mathcal{B}}$ with $C \neq [s_1]_{\widetilde{\mathcal{B}}}$.

s_1 and s_2 are weakly bisimilar, denoted $s_1 \approx s_2$, if there exists a weak bisimulation $\widetilde{\mathcal{B}}$ on S with $s_1\widetilde{\mathcal{B}}s_2$.

Note that the second condition is not required to hold for all equivalent class but only the equivalent class C with $C \neq [s_1]_{\widetilde{\mathcal{B}}}$. This consideration is similar to the weak bisimulation on LTS, where we abstract the internal actions from observation. Intuitively, The Markovian transitions in the same equivalent class can be seen as internal moves and thus their cumulated rate do not need to be calculated.

Example 2. In contrast with Fig. 2, Fig. 3 shows a weak bisimulation equivalence on the given IMC, where the states with the same shade are weakly bisimilar.

It is not hard to see that in Fig. 3 the weakly bisimilar states are not strongly bisimilar. However, in Fig. 2, the strongly bisimilar states can also be considered weakly bisimular according to Definition 4. Thus we have:

Proposition 1. For any IMC and any state $s_1, s_2 \in S, s_1 \sim s_2$ implies $s_1 \approx s_2$.

$\square$

3.2   Simulation

Simulation for classical labelled transition systems is defined in terms of simulation of successor states, i.e., state s' simulates s if for each successor t of s there

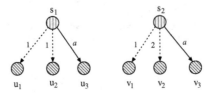

Fig. 4. Strong simulation preorder

is a successor t' of s' that simulates t. For the stochastic behaviours of IMCs, we follow the same ideal of [3, 19] to define the simulation relation by means of *weight functions*. Let $\mathsf{Dist}(S)$ denote the set of all distributions on the set S.

Definition 5. Let $\mu, \mu' \in \mathsf{Dist}(S)$, $R \subseteq S \times S$. A *weight function* for μ and μ' with respect to R is a function $\Delta : S \times S \to [0, 1]$ such that:

1. $\Delta(s, s') > 0$ implies sRs',
2. $\mu(s) = K_1 \cdot \sum_{s' \in S} \Delta(s, s')$ for any $s \in S$, and
3. $\mu'(s') = K_2 \cdot \sum_{s \in S} \Delta(s, s')$ for any $s' \in S$,

where $K_1 = \sum_{s \in S} \mu(s), K_2 = \sum_{s' \in S} \mu'(s')$. We write $\mu \sqsubseteq_R \mu'$ iff there exists a weight function for μ and μ' with respect to R.

Relation $\sqsubseteq_R$ is symmetric if μ and μ' are both *stochastic* [3]. A weight function is indeed a probability distribution on $S \times S$ such that the probability to select (s, s') with sRs' is 1. In addition, the probability to select an element in R whose fist component is s equals $\mu(s)$, and the probability to select an element in R whose second component is s' equals $\mu'(s')$.

Definition 6. A preorder $\mathcal{S}$ on S is a *strong simulation* iff for all $s_1 \mathcal{S} s_2$:

1. $s_1 \xrightarrow{a} s_1', a \in \mathcal{A} \;\Rightarrow\; \exists s_2' \in S, s_2 \xrightarrow{a} s_2'$ and $s_1' \mathcal{S} s_2'$, and
2. $s_1 \not\xrightarrow{\tau} \;\Rightarrow\; \mathbf{P}(s_1, \cdot) \sqsubseteq_{\mathcal{S}} \mathbf{P}(s_2, \cdot)$ and $E(s_1) \leqslant E(s_2)$.

s_2 strongly simulates s_1, denoted $s_1 \precsim s_2$, iff there exists a strong simulation $\mathcal{S}$ on S with $s_1 \mathcal{S} s_2$.

Example 3. Figure 4 illustrates a strong simulation relation on the given IMC. We have $s_1 \precsim s_2$. The simulation for interactive transitions is obvious. For Markovian transitions, note that $E(s_1) = 2 < E(s_2) = 3, \mathbf{P}(s_1, u_1) = \mathbf{P}(s_1, u_2) = \frac{1}{2} = \frac{3}{6}, \mathbf{P}(s_2, v_1) = \frac{1}{3} = \frac{2}{6}, \mathbf{P}(s_2, v_2) = \frac{2}{3} = \frac{4}{6}$, and the weight function is defined by $\Delta(u_1, v_1) = \frac{2}{6}, \Delta(u_1, v_2) = \frac{1}{6}, \Delta(u_2, v_2) = \frac{3}{6}$.

Proposition 2. [7] For any IMC and any state $s_1, s_2 \in S$

(1) $s_1 \sim s_2$ implies $s_1 \precsim s_2$.
(2) $\precsim \cap \precsim^{-1}$ coincides with $\sim$. $\square$

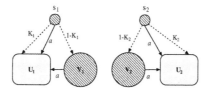

Fig. 5. Scenario of weak simulation relation on IMCs

Definition 7. A preorder $\widetilde{\mathcal{S}}$ on S is a *weak simulation* iff for all $s_1\widetilde{\mathcal{S}}s_2$:

1. $s_1 \overset{a}{\Longrightarrow} s_1', a \in \mathcal{A}\backslash\{\tau\} \;\Rightarrow\; \exists s_2' \in S, s_2 \overset{a}{\Longrightarrow} s_2'$ and $s_1'\widetilde{\mathcal{S}}s_2'$, and
2. $s_1 \overset{\tau}{\Longrightarrow} s_1', s_1' \not\overset{\tau}{\rightarrow} \;\Rightarrow\; \exists s_2' \in S, s_2 \overset{\tau}{\Longrightarrow} s_2', s_2' \not\overset{\tau}{\rightarrow}$ and there exist functions $\Delta : S \times S \rightarrow [0,1], \delta_i : S \rightarrow [0,1]$ and sets $U_i, V_i \subseteq S(i = 1, 2)$ given by

$$U_i = \{u_i \in S \mid \mathbf{R}(s_i', u_i) > 0 \wedge \delta_i(u_i) > 0\} \text{ and}$$
$$V_i = \{v_i \in S \mid \mathbf{R}(s_i', v_i) > 0 \wedge \delta_i(v_i) < 1\}$$

such that:
   - $v_1\widetilde{\mathcal{S}}s_2'$ for any $v_1 \in V_1$ and $s_1'\widetilde{\mathcal{S}}v_2$ for any $v_2 \in V_2$,
   - $\Delta(u_1, u_2) > 0$ implies $u_1 \in U_1, u_2 \in U_2$ and $u_1\widetilde{\mathcal{S}}u_2$,
   - $K_1 \cdot \sum_{u_2 \in U_2} \Delta(w, u_2) = \delta_1(w) \cdot \mathbf{P}(s_1', w)$ and
     $K_2 \cdot \sum_{u_1 \in U_1} \Delta(w, u_1) = \delta_2(w) \cdot \mathbf{P}(s_2', w)$ for all $w \in S$, and
   - $K_1 \cdot E(s_1') \leqslant K_2 \cdot E(s_2')$.
   where $K_i = \sum_{u_i \in U_i} \delta_i(u_i) \cdot \mathbf{P}(s_i', u_i)$ for $i = 1, 2$.

s_2 weakly simulates s_1, denoted $s_1 \overset{\sim}{\precsim} s_2$, iff there exists a weak simulation $\widetilde{\mathcal{S}}$ on S with $s_1\widetilde{\mathcal{S}}s_2$.

Figure 5 gives an intuitive imagination of weak simulation relation. The successor states of weakly similar ones (e.g., $s_1 \overset{\sim}{\precsim} s_2$ in the figure) are grouped into two subsets according to the function δ_i, denoted by U_i and V_i respectively (Note that the sets U_i and V_i are not necessarily disjoint). The transitions to the V_i-states are viewed as "internal" moves and such transitions are taken totally with probability $1 - K_i$. Accordingly, the transitions to the U_i-states are considered as "observable" moves and such transitions are taken totally with probability K_i. The U_1-states and U_2-states are related by a weight function Δ. It is a weight function for the probability distributions $\delta_i(\cdot) \cdot \mathbf{P}(s_i, \cdot)/K_i$.

Proposition 3. For any IMC and any state $s_1, s_2 \in S$

(1) $s_1 \overset{\sim}{\precsim} s_2$ implies $s_1 \overset{\sim}{\precsim} s_2$.
(2) $\overset{\sim}{\precsim} \cap \overset{\sim}{\precsim}^{-1}$ coincides with $\approx$.

Proof. (1) follows directly from the definitions, where for the strongly similar states s_1 and s_2, their successor states can be considered to be all in set U_i, i.e., we can let $V_i = \varnothing, \delta_i(u_i) = 1$ and $\delta_i(v_i) = 0$ in Definition 7 so that the strong simulation can be viewed as such a special case of weak simulation. To certify (2), we see that the coincidence of interactive transition is straightforward, and the coincidence of stochastic behaviours has been proved in [7].   □

4   Logical Characterizations

In this section, we investigate logical characterizations of simulation and bisimulation defined in the previous section. The logic we adopt is a variant of an action-based logic termed aCSL (action-based CSL), which is first proposed in [18] to characterize stochastic process algebra. The main difference between our logic and the logic in [18] is that there is no steady-state probability operator $\mathcal{S}$ in our logic. This is due to the separation of interactive and Markovian transitions. Since the execution of interactive transitions are not confined to the execution of Markovian transitions, interactive transitions may destroy the steady-state of Markov chains. Therefore, the steady state of IMCs can not be reached if there exist interactive transitions.

4.1   Action-Based CSL

When a transition is taken from one state in an IMC to another, there are two characters to be specified, the time spent in the previous state and the action it may interact with. In order to represent both these two characters in a uniform way, we use a pair (a, t), where the first component denotes the action and the second denotes the time. If the transition is just Markovian transition, i.e., it does not interact with any action, we denote it $(*, t)$.

Now let $Label = (Act \cup \{*\}) \times \mathbb{R}_{\geqslant 0}$ and $\mathbb{N}$ be the set of natural numbers. A *path* through an IMC is a sequence $\sigma = s_0 \xrightarrow{l_0} s_1 \xrightarrow{l_1} \cdots s_{k-1} \xrightarrow{l_{k-1}} s_k$ with $s_i \in S, l_i = (a_i, t_i) \in Label, i \in \mathbb{N}$ such that from s_i to s_{i+1} there exists an interactive transition or Markovian transition. If s_k is absorbing and it cannot take any interactive transition, we called it a *finite path*, otherwise it is called an *infinite path*. We use $Path(s)$ to denote the set of paths in an IMC starting from s.

For infinite path σ and $i \in \mathbb{N}$, let $\sigma[i] = s_i$, the $(i + 1)$-st state of σ, and $\delta(\sigma, i) = t_i$, denoting the time spent in s_i. For $t \in \mathbb{R}_{\geqslant 0}$ and i the smallest index with $t \leqslant \sum_{j=0}^{i} \delta(\sigma, j)$, let $\sigma@t = \sigma[i]$, the state in σ occupied at time t. For finite path σ that ends in s_k, $\sigma[i]$ and $\delta(\sigma, i)$ are only defined for $i \leqslant k$. For $L \subseteq Label$, we denote $\sigma[i] \xrightarrow{L} \sigma[i + 1]$ whenever $\sigma[i]$ can move to $\sigma[i + 1]$ by taking a Markovian or interactive transition specified by the element in L.

A Borel space constructed on paths is defined as in [6]. Since there are two different kinds of transitions in IMCs, the probabilistic measure on path must be revised slightly. Let $C(s_0, I_0, ..., I_{k-1}, s_k)$ denote the *cylinder set* consisting of all paths $\sigma \in Path(s_0)$ such that $\sigma[i] = s_i (i \leqslant k)$ and $\delta(\sigma, i) \in I_i \subseteq \mathbb{R}_{\geqslant 0} (i < k)$. The probability measure Pr on paths is defined by induction as:

(1) $Pr(C(s_0)) = 1$,

(2) For $k \geqslant 0, a \in Act$

$$Pr(C(s_0, I_0, ..., I_{k-1}, s_k, I', s'))$$
$$= \begin{cases} Pr(C(s_0, I_0, ..., s_k)) \cdot \mathbf{P}(s_k, s') \cdot \int_{I'} E(s_k) \cdot e^{-E(s_k) \cdot t} dt & \text{if } s_k \xrightarrow{(*, t')} s', \\ Pr(C(s_0, I_0, ..., s_k)) & \text{if } s_k \xrightarrow{(a, t')} s'. \end{cases}$$

The interactive transitions are ignored when computing the probability on paths.

Syntax. For $p \in [0, 1]$, $\bowtie \in \{\leqslant, <, \geqslant, >\}$, the state-formulae of aCSL are defined by the grammar

$$\Phi ::= true \mid \Phi \wedge \Phi \mid \neg \Phi \mid \mathcal{P}_{\bowtie p}(\varphi)$$

where path-formulae are defined for $t \in \mathbb{R}_{>0}$ and $A, B \subseteq Act$ by

$$\varphi ::= \Phi_A \mathcal{U}^{<t} \Phi \mid \Phi_A \mathcal{U}^{<t}{}_B \Phi.$$

Note that atomic propositions are absent in this logic. The state-formulae have the usual meanings as in CSL. The path-formula $\Phi_1 {}_A\mathcal{U}^{<t}\Phi_2$ is fulfilled by a path if a Φ_2-state is eventually reached via visiting only Φ_1-states before, while interacting only with actions in A; besides, going from the beginning of the path until reaching the Φ_2-state should last at most t time units. The formula $\Phi_1 {}_A\mathcal{U}^{<t}{}_B\Phi_2$ requires in addition that a move to a Φ_2-state is actually made and this transition is labelled by some action in B. The commonly used *next* operator can be derived as follows:

$$X_A^{<t}\Phi = true \; {}_\varnothing\mathcal{U}^{<t} {}_A\Phi.$$

Note that in this sense, the concept of "next step" in this logic is based on the interactive transition.

Semantics. Let $M = (S, \mathcal{A}, \longrightarrow, \dashrightarrow)$ be an IMC. The state formulae of aCSL are interpreted over the states of an IMC and the path formulae of aCSL are interpreted over the path of an IMC. We give aCSL formulae semantics by defining the following satisfaction relation $\models$ on states and paths.

Definition 8. (*Semantics of state formulae*) Let $Sat(\Phi) = \{s \in S \mid s \models \Phi\}$. The satisfaction relation $\models$ for aCSL state formulae is defined by:

$$\begin{aligned} s &\models true & &\text{for all } s \in S \\ s &\models \neg \Phi & &\text{iff } s \not\models \Phi \\ s &\models \Phi_1 \wedge \Phi_2 & &\text{iff } s \models \Phi_1 \wedge s \models \Phi_2 \\ s &\models \mathcal{P}_{\bowtie p}(\varphi) & &\text{iff } Prob(s, \varphi) \bowtie p \end{aligned}$$

Here

$$Prob(s, \varphi) = Pr\{\sigma \in Path(s) \mid \sigma \models \varphi\}.$$

Definition 9. (*Semantics of path formulae*) Let $L_A^* = (A \cup \{*\}) \times \mathbb{R}_{\geqslant 0}$, $L_A = A \times \mathbb{R}_{\geqslant 0}$, and $L_B = B \times \mathbb{R}_{\geqslant 0}$. The satisfaction relation $\models$ for aCSL path formulae is defined by:

$$\sigma \models \Phi_1\, {}_A\mathcal{U}^{<t}\Phi_2 \text{ iff } \exists k \geqslant 0. \quad (\sigma[k] \models \Phi_2$$
$$\wedge (\forall 0 \leqslant i < k - 1. \sigma[i] \models \Phi_1 \wedge \sigma[i] \xrightarrow{L_A^*} \sigma[i+1])$$
$$\wedge \sigma[k-1] \models \Phi_1 \wedge \sigma[k-1] \xrightarrow{L_A} \sigma[k]$$
$$\wedge \textstyle\sum_{i=0}^{k-1} \delta(\sigma, i)) < t$$
$$\sigma \models \Phi_1\, {}_A\mathcal{U}^{<t}{}_B\Phi_2 \text{ iff } \exists k > 0. \quad (\sigma[k] \models \Phi_2$$
$$\wedge (\forall 0 \leqslant i < k - 1. \sigma[i] \models \Phi_1 \wedge \sigma[i] \xrightarrow{L_A^*} \sigma[i+1])$$
$$\wedge \sigma[k-1] \models \Phi_1 \wedge \sigma[k-1] \xrightarrow{L_B} \sigma[k]$$
$$\wedge \textstyle\sum_{i=0}^{k-1} \delta(\sigma, i)) < t$$

Remark that $\delta(\sigma, i)$ denotes the sojourn time in state $\sigma[i]$. Clearly, the path formula $\Phi_1\, {}_A\mathcal{U}^{<t}\Phi_2$ is valid for a path where its first state (i.e., $\sigma[0]$) satisfies Φ_2 regardless of its next states it will pass through. But for the path formula $\Phi_1\, {}_A\mathcal{U}^{<t}{}_B\Phi_2$ we must consider at least one step — the last step must take an interactive transition which is labelled with some action in B.

4.2   Logical Characterization of Bisimulation

Strong bisimulation for CTMCs has been proved to coincide with CSL- equivalence [4, 13]. That is, if two states are strongly bisimilar, then they satisfy the same CSL formula, and vice versa. For weak bisimulation, [7] has proved that it coincides with $\text{CSL}_{\backslash X}$-equivalence, where $\text{CSL}_{\backslash X}$ is the fragment of CSL without the next-operator. In this section, we show the similar results of bisimulation for IMCs and aCSL.

We use $\equiv_L$ to denote the equivalence for some logic L, i.e., $s_1 \equiv_L s_2$ iff $\forall \Phi \in L, s_1 \models \Phi \Leftrightarrow s_2 \models \Phi$.

Let aCSL^- denote the subset of aCSL where in the path formula $\Phi_A\mathcal{U}^{<t}{}_B\Phi$ we further restrict that $\tau \notin B$. It then corresponds to the logic $\text{CSL}_{\backslash X}$. The relation between bisimulation and the logical equivalence in the context of IMCs is stated in the following theorem.

Theorem 1. Let $M = (S, \mathcal{A}, \longrightarrow, \dashrightarrow)$ be an IMC, and $s_1, s_2 \in S$, then

(1) $s_1 \sim s_2 \Leftrightarrow s_1 \equiv_{aCSL} s_2$.
(2) $s_1 \approx s_2 \Leftrightarrow s_1 \equiv_{aCSL^-} s_2$.

Proof. (1) "$\Rightarrow$": Similar to [18] and we only give the sketch here. The proof starts by an induction on aCSL formula Φ. The only non-trivial case is to prove the result holds for $\Phi = \mathcal{P}_{\bowtie p}(\varphi)$. Here we only give the proof of the path formula $\Phi_1\, {}_A\mathcal{U}^{<t}{}_B\Phi_2$. The other case is similar and simpler. By defining a set $B_n^s(t)^1$ that denotes the paths starting in s and reaching a Φ_2-state within t time units

---

[1] For the formal definition of $B_n^s(t)$ we refer the reader to [18].

in n steps, where in the first $n - 1$ steps it may only interact with actions in $A \backslash B$ and the last step must interact with some action in B, we can transfer the goal of proof to the following

$$\forall t > 0, \sum_{i=1}^{\infty} Pr\{\sigma \in B_i^{s_1}(t)\} = \sum_{i=1}^{\infty} Pr\{\sigma \in B_i^{s_2}(t)\},$$

which can be proved by induction on n by proving that for all $n > 0$,

$$Pr\{\sigma \in B_n^{s_1}(t)\} = Pr\{\sigma \in B_n^{s_2}(t)\}.$$

The base case is obvious. In the induction phase we have to distinguish two cases:

- *Case 1:* The first transition is an interactive transition. We have $Pr\{\sigma \in B_{n+1}^{s_1}(t)\} = Pr\{\sigma \in B_n^u(t - x)\}$ for $u \models \Phi_1$ and $0 \leqslant x \leqslant t$. Then by $s_1 \sim s_2$ and the outer induction hypothesis that bisimilar states satisfy the same aCSL formula Φ, we can take the same interactive transitions as s_1 from s_2 to v within x time units such that $v \sim u$ and have

$$\begin{aligned} Pr\{\sigma \in B_{n+1}^{s_2}(t)\} &= Pr\{\sigma \in B_n^v(t - x)\} \\ &= Pr\{\sigma \in B_n^u(t - x)\} \\ &= Pr\{\sigma \in B_{n+1}^{s_1}(t)\}. \end{aligned}$$

- *Case 2:* The first transition is a Markovian transition. This case is similar to [18], and we also have $Pr\{\sigma \in B_{n+1}^{s_1}(t)\} = Pr\{\sigma \in B_{n+1}^{s_2}(t)\}$.

"$\Leftarrow$": We need to show that if $s_1 \models \Phi$ and $s_2 \models \Phi$ for all $\Phi \in aCSL$, then $s_1 \sim s_2$. This can proceed by induction on aCSL formula. The only non-trivial case in the induction phase is that if $s_1 \models \mathcal{P}(\varphi) \wedge s_2 \models \mathcal{P}(\varphi)$, then $s_1 \sim s_2$. Here, again we present the proof of path formula $\Phi_1 \, _A\mathcal{U}^{<t}{}_B \Phi_2$. Using the above notation, we have

$$\forall n > 0, Pr\{\sigma \in B_n^{s_1}(t)\} = Pr\{\sigma \in B_n^{s_2}(t)\}.$$

If $n = 1$, σ consists of only one B-transition and obviously $s_1 \sim s_2$. If $n > 1$ and the first transition of σ is an interactive transition, i.e., s_1 and s_2 can both take an A-transition to the next state that also satisfies Φ_1. By induction hypothesis, these Φ_1-states are bisimilar. If, on the other hand, the first transition of σ is a Markovian transition, we have the similar transformations of $Pr\{\sigma \in B_n^{s_1}\}$ and $Pr\{\sigma \in B_n^{s_2}\}$ as in [18]. These yield $\mathbf{R}(s_1, C) = \mathbf{R}(s_2, C)$ for any $C \in S/\sim$.

Following the definition of strong bisimulation, we get $s_1 \sim s_2$.

(2) Similar to (1), where we ignore the τ-actions when considering the interactive transitions. $\qquad \square$

Corollary 1. For any IMC and any state $s_1, s_2 \in S$,

$$s_1 \equiv_{aCSL} s_2 \text{ implies } s_1 \equiv_{aCSL}^{-} s_2.$$

$\qquad \square$

4.3   Logical Characterization of Simulation

The logical characterization of simulation relation for Markov chains have been studied in [3, 12]. It turns out that simulation preorder weakly preserves a subset of CSL formulae, i.e., the safety (or liveness) formulae of CSL. *Weak preservation* means if $s_1 \precsim s_2$ then for all safety formulae Φ it follows that $s_2 \models \Phi$ implies $s_1 \models \Phi$ but the converse does not hold necessarily. Here we show that in the context of IMCs and the logic aCSL, the result holds as well.

aCSL safety and liveness properties. Safety and liveness properties are two kinds of important properties. Safety properties assert that something bad never happens while liveness properties assert that something good will eventually happen. Since the safety and the liveness properties are dual, we only discuss the safety properties in the following. As usual, safety properties are negation-free, i.e., they are in positive normal form, and the probability bounds are restricted. Formally, the syntax of aCSL-safety formulae is defined as:

$$\Phi ::= true \mid false \mid \Phi \wedge \Phi \mid \Phi \vee \Phi \mid \mathcal{P}_{\leqslant p}(\neg\Phi_A \mathcal{U}^{<t}{}_B \neg\Phi) \mid \mathcal{P}_{\leqslant p}(\neg\Phi_A \mathcal{U}^{<t} \neg\Phi).$$

For example, a safety aCSL formula $\mathcal{P}_{\leqslant 0.01}(true_{\{Run\}} \mathcal{U}^{<100} false)$ expresses that the probability of which the system will down within 100 time units is at most 0.01.

We use in the following $\preccurlyeq_L$ to denote the weak preservation for some logic L, i.e., $s_1 \preccurlyeq_L s_2$ iff $\forall \Phi \in L, s_2 \models \Phi \Rightarrow s_1 \models \Phi$.

Now, let aCSL$_S$ denote the aCSL-safety formulae, and aCSL$_S^-$ denote the subset of aCSL-safety formulae where we further restrict that $\tau \notin B$ in the path formulae $\Phi_A \mathcal{U}^{<t}{}_B \Phi$. The following theorem shows the weak preservation results of simulation preorder on IMCs.

Theorem 2. Let $M = (S, \mathcal{A}, \longrightarrow, \dashrightarrow)$ be an IMC, and $s_1, s_2 \in S$, then

(1) $s_1 \precsim s_2 \Rightarrow s_1 \preccurlyeq_{aCSL_S} s_2$.
(2) $s_1 \approxsim s_2 \Rightarrow s_1 \preccurlyeq_{aCSL_S^-} s_2$.

Proof. The core of the proof is to show that if $s_1 \precsim s_2$ ($s_1 \approxsim s_2$) then $Prob(s_1, \varphi) \leqslant Prob(s_2, \varphi)$ for all aCSL$_S$ (aCSL$_S^-$) path formula φ. The result for CTMCs and CSL has been proved in [3]. We can adopt this result, following the same treatment of interactive transitions as we did in Theorem 1 and then get the result as required.   □

Corollary 2. For any IMC and any state $s_1, s_2 \in S$:

$$s_1 \preccurlyeq_{aCSL_S} s_2 \text{ implies } s_1 \preccurlyeq_{aCSL_S^-} s_2.$$

□

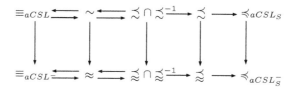

Fig. 6. Branching time relations for IMCs

5   Conclusions

In this paper we investigated the branching time equivalences for IMCs, a power-ful model of performance evaluation. We focused on simulation and bisimulation relations, and studied how to lift these concepts from classical labelled transition systems and pure stochastic settings to IMCs. Our notions of various branching time relations are rather natural extensions of those on both labelled transition systems and stochastic settings. It is clear that such extensions to labelled tran-sition systems and stochastic settings are orthogonal to each other. Therefore, our equivalent and preorder relations are compatible with the existing ones.

We also studied the logical characterizations of the branching time relations. The logic we use to characterize IMCs is the action-based logic aCSL. The results presented here subsume those correspond to the CTMCs and the logic CSL. This is not surprising because of the compatibility of our branching time relations on IMCs and those on CTMCs.

To summarize, we depict the interrelation of the branching time equivalences and preorders in Fig. 6, where $R \longrightarrow R'$ means that relation R implies rela-tion R'.

The results shown in this figure can be seen as a complement of those given in [7], where a branching time spectrum for DTMCs and CTMCs is presented. As mentioned in the introduction, bisimulation and simulation relations can be used to solve the state space explosion problem to a large extent. Such problem is the main obstacle of model checking approach in practice. Our future work is to investigate model checking of IMCs against aCSL. These branching time equivalences and preorders can be used to efficiently aggregate the state space of IMCs and to simplify the procedure of model checking.

References

[1] A. Aziz, K. Sanwal, V. Singhal and R. Brayton. Verifying continuous time Markov chains. In *CAV*, LNCS 1102: 269–276, 1996.   157
[2] A. Aziz, V. Singhal, F. Balarin, R. Brayton and A. Sangiovanni-Vincentelli. It usually works: the temporal logic of stochastic systems. In *CAV*, LNCS 939, pp. 155–165, 1995   157
[3] C. Baier, J.-P. Katoen, H. Hermanns and B. Haverkort. Simulation for continuous-time Markov chains. In *CONCUR*, LNCS 2421: 338–354 , 2002.   157, 161, 167

[4] C. Baier, B. R. Haverkort, H. Hermanns and J.-P. Katoen. Model checking continuous-time Markov chains by transient analysis. In *CAV*, LNCS 1855: 358–372, 2000. 157, 165

[5] C. Baier, B. R. Haverkort, H. Hermanns and J.-P. Katoen. On the logical characterization of performability properties. In *ICALP*, LNCS 1853: 780–792, 2000. 157

[6] C. Baier, J.-P. Katoen, H. Hermanns. Approximate symbolic model checking of continuous-time Markov chains. In *CONCUR*, LNCS 1664: 146–162, 1999. 157, 163

[7] C. Baier, H. Hermanns, J.-P. Katoen and Verena Wolf. Comparative branching-time semantics for Markov chains. In *CONCUR*, LNCS 2761, 2003. 161, 163, 165, 168

[8] C. Baier and H. Hermanns. Weak bisimulation for fully probabilistic processes. In *CAV*, LNCS 1254, pp. 119–130, 1997. 157

[9] M. Bravetti. Revisiting Interactive Markov Chains. *3rd Workshop on Models for Time-Critical Systems*, BRICS Notes NP-02-3, pp. 68–88, 2002. 157

[10] M. Brown, E. Clarke, O. Grumberg. Characterizing finite Kripke structures in propositional temporal logic. *Th. Comp. Sci.*, 59: 115-131, 1988. 156

[11] E. Clarke, O. Grumberg and D. E. Long. Model checking and abstraction. *ACM Trans. on Programming Language and Systems*, 16(5): 1512–1542, 1994. 156

[12] J. Desharnais. Logical characterisation of simulation for Markov chains. In *Proc. Workshop on Probabilistic Methods in Verification*, Tech. Rep. CSR-99-8, Univ. of Birmingham, 1999. 157, 167

[13] J. Desharnais and P.Panangaden. Continuous stochastic logic characterizes bisimulation of continuous-time Markov processes. *J. of Logic and Algebraic Programming*, 2003. 165

[14] R. van Glabbeek. The linear time - branching time spectrum I. The semantics of concrete, sequential processes. *LNCS*, 430: 267–300, 1990. 156

[15] R. van Glabbeek. The linear time - branching time spectrum II. The semantics of sequential processes with silent moves. In *CONCUR*, LNCS 715, pp. 66–81, 1993. 156

[16] H. Hansson and B. Jonsson. A logic for reasoning about time and reliability. *Form. Asp. of Comp.* 6: 512–535, 1994. 157

[17] H. Hermanns. Interactive Markov Chains. *PhD thesis, Universität Erlangen-Nürnberg*, 1998. 157, 159

[18] H. Hermanns, J.-P. Katoen, J. Meyer-Kayser and M. Siegle. Towards model checking stochastic process algebra. In *Integrated Formal Methods*, LNCS 1945: 420–439, 2000. 157, 163, 165, 166

[19] B. Jonsson and K. G. Larsen. Specifcation and refnement of probabilistic processes. In *IEEE Symp. on Logic in Computer Science*, pp. 266–277, 1991. 157, 161

[20] B. Jonsson. Simulations between specifications of distributed systems. In *CONCUR*, LNCS 527, pp. 346–360, 1991. 156

[21] R. Milner. Communication and Concurrency. *Prentice-Hall*, 1989. 156

[22] R. De Nicola and F. Vaandrager. Three logics for branching bisimulation. *J. of ACM*, vol. 42, no. 2, pp. 458–487, 1995. 156

[23] R. Segala and N. A. Lynch. Probabilistic simulations for probabilistic processes. *Nordic J. of Computing*, 2(2): 250–273, 1995. 157

System Contents Versus System Delay for Discrete-Time Queueing Systems with Renewal Arrivals

Bart Vinck and Herwig Bruneel

Ghent University, Department TELIN[*]
Research Group SMACS[**]
Sint-Pietersnieuwstraat 41, B-9000 Gent, Belgium
{bvinck,hb}@telin.ugent.be

Abstract. This paper concerns discrete-time queueing systems operating with a first-come-first-served (FCFS) queueing discipline. Customers arrive in the system according to a renewal process; the inter-arrival times form a family of independent and identically distributed (i.i.d.) random variables. We establish a relationship between the probability generating function (pgf) of the system delay of an arbitrary customer and the pgf of the system contents during an arbitrary slot. Based on this result we derive relationships between the mean and variance, the mass function and the tail probabilities of the respective distributions. These relationships are valid irrespective of the characteristics of the servicing process, i.e., irrespective the number of servers, the distribution of the service times and possible correlation between the service times of consecutive customers.

1 Introduction

Queueing occurs in many nodes of communication networks and in many IT-elements. Buffers are typically introduced where multiple data streams, applications or connections make use of common resources. Examples of such are communication links and computational resources. Queueing is especially abundant in packet-oriented networks such as the Internet. When resources are shared between a large number of applications, and packets streams are multiplexed, those resources are used more efficiently. However, sharing comes at the expense of the resource not permanently being available to arriving or new user; some of them will have to wait because the resource is busy and hence experience a delay. With the advent and growing popularity of delay-sensitive services (e.g. multi-media services) over the World Wide Web, tight control over the delay has become more important than it was when the Internet was predominantly providing services such as e-mail and browsing of static content.

---

[*] TELIN: Telecommunications and Information Processing
[**] SMACS: Stochastic Modeling and Analysis of Communication Systems

M. Núñez et al. (Eds.): FORTE 2004 Workshops, LNCS 3236, pp. 170–183, 2004.
© Springer-Verlag Berlin Heidelberg 2004

Queueing processes are typically studied from two perspectives: that of the user (or customer) and that of the provider. The user's primary concern lies with the delay that he or she experiences. IN a communication setting: how much delay and delay variation can the application tolerate and how much delay should the receiving end expect and be prepared to accept? The primary concern for the provider lies with the queue contents – for instance, how much buffer space should she provide such that the probability of packet loss is sufficiently small. The buffer space itself may be a resource that is shared by multiple queues. In this paper we derive a relationship the delay experienced by an arbitrary customer and the number of customers present during an arbitrary time slot. We assume renewal arrivals and a first-come-first-served queueing discipline.

Little's Theorem [1, 2, 3, 4] is probably the best-known result of queueing theory. It relates the first-order moment of the system contents during an arbitrary slot to the first moment of the system delay of an arbitrary customer. The relationship holds regardless of the nature of the arrival and servicing/departure process. Where authors have generalized the result to higher-moments they have imposed restrictions on either the arrival process or the servicing process. Marschal [5] obtained a relationship between the moments of the waiting time and the queue contents for continuous-time multi-server queueing systems operating with a FCFS queueing discipline, Poisson arrivals and general service times (i.e., $M/G/c$). Brumelle [6] derived expressions for the moments of the queue contents for the more general $G/G/c$ queueing system but not explicitly in terms of moments of the waiting-time distribution. Tight relationships between the probability mass functions (pmf's) of the system delay (of an arbitrary customer) and the system contents (during an arbitrary slot) have been derived for discrete-time queueing systems with service times of 1 slot, both for the single-server case [7] and for the multi-server case [8]. A similar relationship between the probability generating functions (pgf's) was derived recently for the multi-server queueing system with geometric service times [9]. This paper establishes a formula that allows to derive the pgf of the system contents from the pgf of the system delay. We assume a renewal arrival process, i.e., whereby the *interarrival times* are independent and identically distributed (i.i.d.) random variables.

The relationships established in this paper are restricted to renewal arrivals, but allow a wide range of servicing processes. Note however, that in order to apply the result, it must first be possible to obtain the pgf of the system delay of an arbitrary customer. The result can be applied on the queue, the servers or on the queue and the servers taken together. It does require however that customers depart from the system in the order of their arrival. Hence, the relationship is valid for the queue of a multi-server queues with i.i.d. service times, but not for the system (i.e., queue and servers) when the service times are non-deterministic. The proof does not require that a limiting (i.e., steady-state) distribution of system delay and system contents exist. The system contents, for instance, does not have a limiting distribution when the arrival process is periodical, i.e., when the interarrival times are always a multiple of a period that consists of more than one slot. The system delay, for instance, does not have a limiting distribution when customers are always served in n-tuples (e.g., pairs, trios, etc.). However, in both cases the system contents (during an arbitrary slot) and the system delay (of an arbitrary customer) remain well-defined; and the relationships derived here apply between their respective pgf's. However, in the event that the steady-state distributions exist (and usually they do), they are identical to the distributions for arbitrary slots or arbitrary customers.

The paper is organized as follows. In Sect. 2 we introduce our numerical example. We return to this numerical example after having derived our main result. Section 3 introduces the notation and Section 4 introduces further auxiliary variables and presents intermediate results. Those are used in the next section, in which we derive the main result of the paper in integral form. The next two sections then, are spent on two important special cases: in Sect. 6 the case of the system delay having a rational pgf and in Sect. 7 the case of the interarrival times having a rational pgf. Finally, in Sect. 8 we return to our numerical example and show how the result obtained in the paper can be applied on the numerical case. Finally we write conclusions and make suggestions for further research.

2   Application: Problem Setting

We consider the provider of a digital communication link that can transmit one data unit per time slot. Messages arrive according to a very regular pattern: every c time slots she receives c messages. The number of cells in a message, i.e., the message length is a stochastic variable. All message lengths are i.i.d. random variables with a Poisson distribution with parameter ρ, $0 \le \rho < 1$. The provider will queue the message in a buffer in front of the communication link. The queueing system is a single-server queue with deterministic interarrival times (of c slots) and service times (per message) with $B(z) = \exp(c\,\rho\,(z-1))$. For this type of queueing system the system delay of an arbitrary customer has been derived in [10] and is given by:

$$D(z) = \frac{c\,(1-\rho)\,(z-1)\,B(z)\,P(z)}{z^c - B(z)} \quad \text{with} \quad P(z) \doteq \prod_{n=1}^{c-1} \frac{z - \phi_n}{1 - \phi_n}\,, \qquad (1)$$

whereby $\{\phi_n \mid n = 1, \ldots, c-1\}$ are the $c-1$ distinct zeros of the denominator $z^c - B(z)$ inside and on the unit circle and not equal to 1. We now derive a result that allows to derive the pgf of the queue length from (1). We return to this numerical example in Sect. 8.

3   Model

We consider a discrete-time queueing system operating with a FCFS queueing discipline. Time is divided in fixed-length (time) slots separated by clock instants t, $\forall t \in \mathbb{N}$.

The customers arrive on clock instants according to a renewal process. Let a_n denote the *arrival instant* of the n-th customer and let $A_n \doteq a_{n+1} - a_n$, $\forall n \in \mathbb{N}_0$, denote the n-th *interarrival time*. The interarrival times are i.i.d. random variables with common pmf $\{a(k) \doteq \Pr[A_t = k], k \in \mathbb{N}\}$, corresponding pgf $\{A(z) \doteq \mathrm{E}[z^{A_n}], |z| < \mathcal{R}_A\}$ and expected value $\mathrm{E}[A_n] = 1/\lambda$. We assume that $\mathcal{R}_A$ is strictly larger than 1.

Let d_n, $\forall n \in \mathbb{N}_0$, denote the *departure instant* of the n-th customer. We require that customers depart from the system in the order of their arrival. Let $t_n \doteq \max\{d_{n-1}, a_n\}$ denote the start of the *service time* of the n-th customer. Then $B_n \doteq d_n - t_n$, $\forall n \in \mathbb{N}_0$, denotes the service time of the n-th customer (this service time may assume the value zero for some customers if more than one customer departs at the same clock instant). Let M_n denote the sum of the service times of the first n customers, i.e., $M_n \doteq B_1 + B_2 + \ldots B_n$. We assume that the limits $\sigma \doteq \lim_{n \to \infty} n/M_n$ exists with probability 1 and that $\lambda < \sigma$. The load ρ is defined as λ/σ and therefore equals the limit $\rho = \lim_{n \to \infty} M_n/a_n$ and satisfies $\rho < 1$.

Let U_t, $\forall t \in \mathbb{N}_0$, denote the *system contents*, i.e., the number of customers present, during the slot $(t - 1, t]$. We assume, without loss of generality, that we start with an empty system, i.e., that $U_1 = 0$. We define the pmf $\{u(k), k \in \mathbb{N}\}$ and pgf $\{U(z), |z| < \mathcal{R}_U\}$ of the system contents during an arbitrary slot as

$$u(k) \doteq \lim_{T \to \infty} \frac{1}{T} \sum_{t=1}^{T} \Pr[U_t = k] \quad \text{and} \quad U(z) \doteq \lim_{T \to \infty} \frac{1}{T} \sum_{t=1}^{T} \mathrm{E}[z^{U_t}] \ . \quad (2)$$

We assume that $\mathcal{R}_U$ is strictly larger than 1. From the above definitions it follows that $U(0) = 1 - \rho$. The *system delay* $D_n \doteq d_n - a_n$, $\forall n \in \mathbb{N}_0$, refers to the number of slots that the n-th customer spends in the system. We define the pmf $\{d(k), k \in \mathbb{N}\}$ and pgf $\{D(z), |z| < \mathcal{R}_D\}$ of the system delay of an arbitrary customer as

$$d(k) \doteq \lim_{N \to \infty} \frac{1}{N} \sum_{n=1}^{N} \Pr[D_n = k] \quad \text{and} \quad D(z) \doteq \lim_{N \to \infty} \frac{1}{N} \sum_{n=1}^{N} \mathrm{E}[z^{D_n}] \ . \quad (3)$$

4   Preliminary Results

We introduce the following auxiliary variables: the *waiting time* of a customer, the *idle time* following the servicing of a customer, and the *virtual waiting time* at a clock instant following a busy slot. We prove three lemma's that we will use to derive the main result in Sect. 5.

Let $W_n \doteq t_n - a_n$, $\forall n \in \mathbb{N}_0$, denote the *waiting time* of the n-th customer. We have that $W_1 = 0$ and for $\forall n \geq 2$: $W_n \doteq \max\{D_{n-1} - A_{n-1}, 0\}$. We define the pmf $\{w(k), k \in \mathbb{N}\}$ and pgf $\{W(z), |z| < \mathcal{R}_W\}$ of the waiting time of an arbitrary customer in the same way as the pmf and the pgf of the system delay were defined via (3). Note that $\forall n \in \mathbb{N}_0$: $W_n \leq D_n$ and hence that for $\forall x \in (0, \mathcal{R}_D)$: $\mathrm{E}[x^{W_n}] \leq \mathrm{E}[x^{D_n}]$. After averaging over all customers this yields that

$\forall x \in (0, \mathcal{R}_D)$: $W(x) \leq D(x)$ and hence that $W(z)$ converges on the open interval $(0, \mathcal{R}_D)$. Hence, $\mathcal{R}_D \leq \mathcal{R}_W$.

Let I_n denote the *idle time* after servicing the n-th customer, i.e., $I_n \doteq \max\{A_n - D_n, 0\}$. Note that if $W_{n+1} > 0$ then $I_n = 0$. Let $I(z)$ denote the pgf of the idle time before servicing an arbitrary customer arriving in an idle system, i.e.,

$$I(z) \doteq \lim_{N \to \infty} \frac{1}{N} \sum_{n=1}^{N} \mathrm{E}\left[z^{I_n} \mid W_{n+1} = 0\right] . \tag{4}$$

Note that $\forall t \in \mathbb{N}_0$: $I_n \leq A_n$ and hence that analogously $\mathcal{R}_I \geq \mathcal{R}_A$.

Lemma 1. *If $z \in \mathbb{C}$ and $\mathcal{R}_A^{-1} < |z| < \mathcal{R}_D$ then*

$$W(z) = D(z) A(1/z) + w(0) [1 - I(1/z)] . \tag{5}$$

Proof. The nature of the servicing process yields that $W_1 = 0$ and $\forall n \in \mathbb{N}_0$: $W_{n+1} = \max\{D_n - A_n, 0\}$. After Z-transformation and averaging over all customers this yields

$$W(z) = \lim_{N \to \infty} \frac{1}{N} \left(1 + \sum_{n=1}^{N} \mathrm{E}\left[\mathbf{1}\left(W_{n+1} > 0\right) z^{D_n - A_n} + \mathbf{1}\left(W_{n+1} = 0\right)\right]\right)$$

$$= \lim_{N \to \infty} \frac{1}{N} \sum_{n=1}^{N} \mathrm{E}\left[z^{D_n - A_n} + \mathbf{1}\left(W_{n+1} = 0\right)\left[1 - z^{-I_n}\right]\right] .$$

In view of the definitions of the pgf $D(z)$, $W(z)$ and $I(z)$ and the statistical independence of D_n and A_n this yields (5). The condition $\mathcal{R}_A^{-1} < |z|$ ensures that the power series of $A(1/z)$ and $I(1/z)$ converge. Likewise, the condition $|z| < \mathcal{R}_D$ follows from the requirement that the power series of $W(z)$ and $D(z)$ converge. □

Let b_m, $\forall m \in \mathbb{N}_0$, denote the end of the m-th busy slot. Let c_m, $\forall m \in \mathbb{N}_0$, denote the customer present during $(b_m - 1, b_m)$ having the smallest index, i.e., let $c_m \doteq \min\{n \in \mathbb{N}_0 \mid a_n < b_m \leq d_n\}$. Let $V_m \doteq b_m - a_{c_m}$, $\forall m \in \mathbb{N}_0$, denote the time spent by customer c_m in the system at clock instant b_m. We refer to V_m as the *virtual waiting time* at clock instant b_m. We define the pmf and pgf of the virtual waiting time at the end of an arbitrary busy slot as

$$v(k) \doteq \lim_{M \to \infty} \frac{1}{M} \sum_{m=1}^{M} \Pr\left[V_m = k\right] \quad \text{and} \quad V(z) \doteq \lim_{M \to \infty} \frac{1}{M} \sum_{m=1}^{M} \mathrm{E}\left[z^{V_m}\right] . \tag{6}$$

Lemma 2. *If $z \in \mathbb{C}$ and $|z| < \mathcal{R}_D$ then*

$$V(z) = \sigma z \frac{D(z) - W(z)}{z - 1} . \tag{7}$$

Proof. Where $V(z)$ converges, then also any subrow of (6) converges. Those subrows then each have the same limit value as the row in (6). We consider the subrow that consists of only those clock instants following busy slots that are departure instants. Hence,

$$V(z) = \lim_{N \to \infty} \frac{1}{M_N} \sum_{m=1}^{M_N} \mathrm{E}\left[z^{V_m}\right] = \lim_{N \to \infty} \frac{N}{M_N} \cdot \lim_{N \to \infty} \frac{1}{N} \sum_{n=1}^{N} \sum_{m=1}^{B_n} \mathrm{E}\left[z^{V_{M_{n-1}+m}}\right] .$$

The first factor converges to σ. Note that $D_n = W_n + B_n$, $\forall n \in \mathbb{N}_0$, and hence, that the virtual waiting times at clock instants in the interval $(t_n, d_n]$ are given by $W_n + 1$, $W_n + 2$, $\ldots$, and $W_n + B_n \equiv D_n$. This yields for the pgf of the virtual waiting time at the end of an arbitrary busy slot:

$$\sigma \lim_{N \to \infty} \frac{1}{N} \sum_{n=1}^{N} \mathrm{E}\left[z^{W_n+1} + \ldots + z^{D_n}\right] = \sigma \lim_{N \to \infty} \frac{1}{N} \sum_{n=1}^{N} \mathrm{E}\left[\frac{z^{D_n+1} - z^{W_n+1}}{z - 1}\right] ,$$

which in view of the definitions of $W(z)$ and $D(z)$ yields (7). Note that $V(z)$ converges where both $D(z)$ and $W(z)$ converge. In view of $\mathcal{R}_D \leq \mathcal{R}_W$ it follows that $\mathcal{R}_D$ is the radius of convergence of $V(z)$. □

Lemma 3. *If $z \in \mathbb{C}$ and $|z| < \mathcal{R}_U$, with $\mathcal{R}_U^{-1} \doteq A(\mathcal{R}_D^{-1})$, then*

$$\frac{U(z) - 1}{z - 1} = \frac{\rho}{2\pi \mathrm{i}} \oint_C d\zeta \, \frac{V(\zeta) - 1}{\zeta (\zeta - 1) [1 - z A(1/\zeta)]} , \tag{8}$$

with C being a contour around the origin such that $\forall \zeta \in C$: $|\zeta| < \mathcal{R}_D$ and $|zA(1/\zeta)| < 1$.

Proof. The system contents during the m-th busy slot exceeds k if and only if the virtual waiting time at clock instant b_m exceeds the sum of the first k interarrival times following the arrival of the customer c_m. This yields, $\forall k \in \mathbb{N}$:

$$U_{b_m} > k \quad \Leftrightarrow \quad V_m > A_{c_m} + \cdots + A_{c_m+k-1} ,$$

which yields

$$\sum_{s=k+1}^{\infty} \Pr\left[U_{b_m} = s\right] = \sum_{l=1}^{\infty} \sum_{r=0}^{l-1} \Pr\left[V_m = l\right] \Pr\left[A_{c_m} + \cdots + A_{c_m+k-1} = r\right] . \tag{9}$$

The interarrival times $\{A_n, n \in \mathbb{N}_0\}$ are a family of i.i.d. random variables. Hence, the pgf of $A_{c_m} + A_{c_m+1} + \cdots + A_{c_m+k-1}$ is given by $A(z)^k$. We write the last factor as a complex integral along a contour (i.e., a closed curve) around the origin (cf. [11]), $\forall k \in \mathbb{N}$:

$$\Pr\left[A_{c_m} + \cdots + A_{c_m+k-1} = r\right] = \frac{1}{2\pi \mathrm{i}} \oint_L d\xi \, A(\xi)^k \, \xi^{-r-1} ,$$

with i being the imaginary unit and L being a contour around the origin such that $\forall \xi \in L$: $|\xi| < \mathcal{R}_A$. After a change of integration variable from ξ to $\zeta = 1/\xi$, and integration along C, the image of L after inversion, this yields:

$$\Pr\left[A_{c_t} + \cdots + A_{c_t+k-1} = r\right] = \frac{1}{2\pi i} \oint_C d\zeta \, A(1/\zeta)^k \, \zeta^{r-1} \, ,$$

with C being a contour around the origin such that $\forall \zeta \in C$: $\mathcal{R}_A^{-1} < |\zeta|$. Substituting the latter result in (9) and averaging over all busy slots yields:

$$\frac{1}{\rho} \sum_{s=k+1}^{\infty} u(s) = \sum_{l=1}^{\infty} \sum_{r=0}^{l-1} \frac{1}{2\pi i} \oint_C d\zeta \, v(l) \, A(1/\zeta)^k \, \zeta^{r-1} \, .$$

Note that we have used that $u(0) = 1 - \rho$. Multiplying both sides by ρ and z^k and summing over k from 0 to ∞ yields

$$\sum_{k=0}^{\infty} \sum_{s=k+1}^{\infty} u(s) \, z^k = \sum_{k=0}^{\infty} \sum_{l=1}^{\infty} \sum_{r=0}^{l-1} \frac{\rho}{2\pi i} \oint_C d\zeta \, v(l) \, [z \, A(1/\zeta)]^k \, \zeta^{r-1} \, .$$

The left-hand side evaluates to $[U(z) - 1]/(z - 1)$ for $|z| < \mathcal{R}_U$, whereby $\mathcal{R}_U$ remains to be determined. On the right-hand side, the summations can be brought behind the integral if the contour C is properly chosen. Convergence of the infinite summations over k and l require that $\forall \zeta \in C$: $|z \, A(1/\zeta)| < 1$ and $|\zeta| < \mathcal{R}_D$. The condition $|z \, A(1/\zeta)| < 1$ imposes an upper-bound for $|A(1/\zeta)|$ and hence a lower bound on $|\zeta|$ that depends on z and the argument of ζ. This lower bound is most severe along the positive real axis. A proper contour C can be constructed if and only if $|z| < 1/A(\mathcal{R}_D^{-1})$. Hence, $\mathcal{R}_U^{-1} = A(\mathcal{R}_D^{-1})$. If $|z| < \mathcal{R}_U$ the summations converge and after rearranging factors the expression reduces to (8).   □

5   Integral Forms

Using the lemma's we derive a relationship between the pgf of the system contents during an arbitrary slot and the pgf of the system delay of an arbitrary customer. We verify that our findings are in agreement with Little's Theorem and establish an integral form for the variance of the system contents during an arbitrary slot.

Theorem 1. *If $z \in \mathbb{C}$ and $|z| < \mathcal{R}_U$, with $\mathcal{R}_U^{-1} = A(\mathcal{R}_D^{-1})$, then*

$$\frac{U(z) - 1}{z - 1} = \frac{\lambda}{2\pi i} \oint_C d\zeta \, \frac{D(\zeta) \, [1 - A(1/\zeta)]}{(\zeta - 1)^2 \, [1 - z \, A(1/\zeta)]} \, , \tag{10}$$

with C being a contour around the origin such that $\forall \zeta \in C$: $1 < |\zeta| < \mathcal{R}_D$ and $|z A(1/\zeta)| < 1$.

Proof. Substituting the result of Lem. 2 in the result of Lem. 3 and eliminating $W(\zeta)$ using the result of Lem. 1 yields, for $|z| < \mathcal{R}_U$:

$$\frac{U(z) - 1}{z - 1} = \frac{\lambda}{2\pi i} \oint_C d\zeta \, \frac{\zeta \, D(\zeta) \, [1 - A(1/\zeta)] - w(0) \, \zeta \, [1 - I(1/\zeta)] - (\zeta - 1)/\sigma}{\zeta \, (\zeta - 1)^2 \, [1 - z \, A(1/\zeta)]}$$

with C being a contour around the origin such that $\forall \zeta \in C : \mathcal{R}_A^{-1} < |\zeta| < \mathcal{R}_D$ and $|z \, A(1/\zeta)| < 1$. Note that $\zeta = 1$ is not a pole (or otherwise a singularity) of the integrand of (8). Hence, it is not a singularity of the integrand in the expression above. The right-hand side can be split in two terms:

$$\frac{\lambda}{2\pi i} \oint_C d\zeta \, \frac{D(\zeta) \, [1 - A(1/\zeta)]}{(\zeta - 1)^2 \, [1 - z \, A(1/\zeta)]} - \frac{\lambda}{2\pi i} \oint_C d\zeta \, \frac{w(0) \, [1 - I(1/\zeta)] + (1 - 1/\zeta)/\sigma}{(\zeta - 1)^2 \, [1 - z \, A(1/\zeta)]} \, .$$

The integrands of both terms have a pole at $\zeta = 1$. We choose the contour C such that this pole lies inside C by imposing that $\forall \zeta \in C : 1 < |\zeta|$. This choice is possible regardless of the value of z. We now change the integration variable in the second term, replacing ζ by $\xi = 1/\zeta$, and integrating along a contour L which is the image after inversion of C. The last term then becomes:

$$-\frac{\lambda}{2\pi i} \oint_L d\xi \, \frac{w(0) \, [1 - I(\xi)] + (1 - \xi)/\sigma}{(\xi - 1)^2 \, [1 - z \, A(\xi)]} \, ,$$

with L being a contour around the origin such that $\forall \xi \in L : \mathcal{R}_D^{-1} < |\xi| < 1$ and $|z \, A(\xi)| < 1$. Since $|\xi| < 1$ along and inside L, the functions $I(\xi)$ and $A(\xi)$ remain analytical inside and on L and the pole $\xi = 1$ lies outside L. Along L, the condition $|z \, A(\xi)| < 1$ holds. This implies, by the Theorem of Rouché [12, p. 123], with $f(\xi) = 1$ and $g(\xi) = z \, A(\xi)$, that $1 - z \, A(\xi)$ has no zeros inside and on L. The integrand of the last term is therefore an analytical function inside and on L. An application of Cauchy's Residue Theorem [12, p.120] then yields that the second term is zero. Hence, $U(z)$ is given by the first term only of the last expression, i.e., by (10). $\qquad\square$

Using the moment-generating property of pgf's allows deriving expressions for the moments of the distribution of the system contents during an arbitrary slot by evaluating the derivatives after z of $U(z)$ at $z = 1$.

Corollary 1 (Little's Theorem). *There holds* $\mathrm{E}[U] = \lambda \, \mathrm{E}[D]$.

Proof. Evaluating both sides of (10) at $z = 1$ yields

$$U'(1) = \frac{\lambda}{2\pi i} \oint_L d\zeta \, \frac{D(\zeta)}{(\zeta - 1)^2} = \lambda \, D'(1) \, .$$

On the left-hand side we used de l'Hôpital's Rule; on the right-hand side we used Cauchy's Residue Theorem. $\qquad\square$

Corollary 2. *There holds*

$$\mathrm{var}[U] + \mathrm{E}[U]^2 = \frac{\lambda}{2\pi i} \oint_C d\zeta \, \frac{D(\zeta) \, [1 + A(1/\zeta)]}{(\zeta - 1)^2 \, [1 - A(1/\zeta)]} \, , \tag{11}$$

with C being a contour around the origin such that $\forall \zeta \in C : 1 < |\zeta| < \mathcal{R}_D$.

Proof. Evaluating (10) and its first derivative after z at $z = 1$ and using $U''(1) + U'(1) = \text{var}[U] + \text{E}[U]^2$ immediately yields (11). $\qquad\qquad\qquad\qquad\square$

The expressions in the right-hand side of (10) and (11) are in the form of a contour integral with $D(z)$ appearing in the integrand. Those expressions can be evaluated by means of numerical methods, see for instance [13]. Alternatively, and when possible more conveniently, the expressions can be converted to algebraic expressions with the help of Cauchy's Residue Theorem. This is the case when either $D(z)$ or $A(z)$ is a rational function. In Sect. 6 we discuss the special case of rational $D(z)$; in Sect. 7 we discuss the special case of $A(z)$ being rational.

6   System Delay with Rational PGF

In this section we consider the case where the pgf $D(z)$ of the system delay during an arbitrary slot is rational and only has simple poles. Since $D(z)$ is the pgf of a non-negative random variable, all poles of $D(1/z)$ lie inside the unit circle. Let $\{\mu_n \mid n = 1, \ldots, d\}$ denote the d distinct poles of $D(1/z)$. The partial fraction expansion of $D(1/z)$ then reads

$$D(1/z) = \sum_{n=1}^{d} \frac{K_D(n)}{z - \mu_n} \ . \tag{12}$$

The poles μ_n are either real or occur in complex conjugate pairs. If μ_n and $\mu_{n'}$ are each other's complex conjugate, then necessarily also $K_D(n)$ and $K_D(n')$, are each other's complex conjugate.

Theorem 2. *If $D(z)$ is rational and $D(1/z)$ has partial fraction expansion (12) then also $U(z)$ is rational and $U(1/z)$ has partial fraction expansion*

$$U(1/z) = 1 - \rho + \sum_{n=1}^{N} \frac{K_U(n)}{z - \theta_n} \ . \tag{13}$$

with $\forall n = 1, \ldots, d$:

$$\theta_n = A(\mu_n) \quad and \quad K_U(n) = \lambda \left(\frac{1 - \theta_n}{1 - \mu_n} \right)^2 K_D(n) \tag{14}$$

Proof. In view of $U(0) = 1 - \rho$, substitution of $z = 0$ in the result of Theorem 1 yields

$$\rho = \frac{\lambda}{2\pi i} \oint_C d\zeta \ \frac{D(\zeta) \left[1 - A(1/\zeta) \right]}{(\zeta - 1)^2} \ ,$$

Subtracting both sides of this equation from both sides of (10) yields

$$U(z) = 1 - \rho + z \frac{\lambda}{2\pi i} \oint_C d\zeta \ \frac{D(\zeta) \left[1 - A(1/\zeta) \right]^2}{(\zeta - 1)^2 \left[1 - z \, A(1/\zeta) \right]} \ ,$$

with C being a contour around the origin such that $\forall \zeta \in C \colon 1 < |\zeta| < \mathcal{R}_D$ and $|z\, A(1/\zeta)| < 1$. Substituting $1/z$ for z, changing the integration variable from ζ to $\xi = 1/\zeta$ and then integrating along a contour L which is the image after inversion of the contour C yields:

$$U(1/z) = 1 - \rho + \frac{\lambda}{2\pi i} \oint_L d\xi \, \frac{D(1/\xi)\,[1 - A(\xi)]^2}{(1 - \xi)^2\,[z - A(\xi)]} \, ,$$

with L being a contour around the origin such that $\forall \xi \in L \colon \mathcal{R}_D^{-1} < |\xi| < 1$ and $|A(\xi)| < |z|$. The condition $|\xi| < 1$ yields that $A(\xi)$ remains analytical inside L and that $\xi = 1$ lies outside L. The condition $|A(\xi)| < |z|$ yields, by the Theorem of Rouché, that the factor $z - A(\xi)$ has no zeros inside L. The condition $\mathcal{R}_D^{-1} < |\xi|$ yields that all poles of $D(1/\xi)$ lie inside L. Substitution of (12) then yields:

$$U(1/z) = 1 - \rho + \sum_{n=1}^{d} \frac{\lambda}{2\pi i} \oint_L d\xi \, \frac{K_D(n)\,[1 - A(\xi)]^2}{(\xi - \mu_n)\,(1 - \xi)^2\,[z - A(\xi)]} \, .$$

An application of Cauchy's Residue Theorem then yields (13).   □

Corollary 3. *If $D(z)$ is rational and $D(1/z)$ has partial fraction expansion (12) then also*

$$\operatorname{var}[U] + \mathrm{E}[U]^2 = \lambda \sum_{n=1}^{N} \frac{K_D(n)\,[1 + A(\mu_n)]}{(\mu_n - 1)^2\,[1 - A(\mu_n)]} \, . \tag{15}$$

Proof. Changing the integration variable in (11) in Cor. 2 from ζ to $\xi = 1/\zeta$ yields

$$\operatorname{var}[U] + \mathrm{E}[U]^2 = \frac{\lambda}{2\pi i} \oint_L d\xi \, \frac{D(1/\xi)\,[1 + A(\xi)]}{(\xi - 1)^2\,[1 - A(\xi)]} \, ,$$

with L being a contour around the origin such that $\forall \xi \in L \colon \mathcal{R}_D^{-1} < |\xi| < 1$. The only singularities inside L are the poles of $D(1/\xi)$. Substitution of (12) in this equation yields

$$\operatorname{var}[U] + \mathrm{E}[U]^2 = \sum_{n=1}^{d} \frac{\lambda}{2\pi i} \oint_L d\xi \, \frac{K_D(n)\,[1 + A(\xi)]}{(\xi - \mu_n)\,(\xi - 1)^2\,[1 - A(\xi)]} \, ,$$

An application of Cauchy's Residue Theorem then yields (15).   □

7 Interarrival Times with Rational PGF

In this section we consider the case where the pgf $A(z)$ of the interarrival times is rational. If the pgf $A(z)$ is a rational function, we define the unique mutually prime polynomial functions $P_A(z)$ and $Q_A(z)$ such that

$$A(1/z) = \frac{P_A(z)}{Q_A(z)}, \quad \gcd\{P_A(z), Q_A(z)\} = 1 \quad \text{and} \quad Q_A(1) = P_A(1) = 1 \, . \tag{16}$$

Let $c \doteq \deg Q_A$. From $\lim_{z \to \infty} A(1/z) = a(0) \in [0, 1)$ it follows that $\deg P_A \le \deg Q_A$.

Theorem 3. *If $A(z)$ is rational and the characteristic function $Q_A(\zeta) - z\, P_A(\zeta)$ has c distinct simple zeros $\{\gamma_n(z) \,|\, n = 1, \ldots c\}$ for some $z \in \mathbb{C}$ then*

$$U(z) = \lambda \sum_{n=1}^{c} \frac{D(\gamma_n(z))}{A'(1/\gamma_n(z))} \left(\frac{(z-1)\,\gamma_n(z)}{z\,[\gamma_n(z) - 1]} \right)^2 . \tag{17}$$

Proof. Substitution of (16) in (10) of Theorem 1 yields

$$\frac{U(z) - 1}{z - 1} = \frac{\lambda}{2\pi i} \oint_C d\zeta \, \frac{D(\zeta)\,[Q_A(\zeta) - P_A(\zeta)]}{(\zeta - 1)^2\,[Q_A(\zeta) - z\,P_A(\zeta)]} , \tag{18}$$

with C being a contour around the origin such that $\forall \zeta \in C\colon 1 < |\zeta| < \mathcal{R}_D$ and $|z\,A(1/\zeta)| < 1$. The condition $|\zeta| < \mathcal{R}_D$ implies that $D(\zeta)$ is an analytical function inside C. The condition $1 < |\zeta|$ yields that $\zeta = 1$ lies inside C. Unless $z = 1$, the numerator of the integrand has a simple zero and the denominator has a double zero at $\zeta = 1$. Hence, unless $z = 1$, the integrand has a simple pole at $\zeta = 1$. The contribution to the right-hand-side from the residue of the integrand at $\zeta = 1$ equals $-1/(z-1)$. The condition $|z\,A(1/\zeta)| < 1$ yields, after multiplication by $|Q_A(\zeta)|$, that $\forall \zeta \in C\colon |z\,P_A(\zeta)| < |Q_A(\zeta)|$. Note that $Q_A(\zeta)$ has c zeros inside the unit circle (counting with multiplicity), and hence also inside C. This implies, by the Theorem of Rouché, with $f(\zeta) = Q_A(\zeta)$ and $g(\zeta) = z\,P_A(\zeta)$ that the characteristic function $Q_A(\zeta) - z\,P_A(\zeta)$ has c zeros (counting with multiplicity) inside C. Note that since $\deg Q_A = c$ and $\deg P_A \le \deg Q_A$ those are the only zeros of the characteristic function. An application of Cauchy's Residue Theorem and some algebraic re-arranging then yields (17). □

Note that (17) still contain the zeros of the characteristic function and those depend on z. For general distributions of the interarrival time it is not possible to derive a closed-form expression for the $\gamma_n(z)$. Nor is it so that the $\gamma_n(z)$ are necessarily rational functions.

Corollary 4. *If $A(z)$ is rational and the polynomial function $Q_A(\zeta) - P_A(\zeta)$ has $c - 1$ distinct simple zeros $\{\beta_n \,|\, n = 1, \ldots, c-1\}$ inside or on the unit circle and not equal to 1 then*

$$\mathrm{var}[U] = 2\lambda \sum_{n=1}^{c-1} \frac{D(\beta_n)}{A'(1/\beta_n)} \left(\frac{\beta_n}{\beta_n - 1} \right)^2$$
$$+ \lambda^2 \, \mathrm{var}[D] + \lambda^3 \, \mathrm{E}[D]\,\mathrm{var}[A] - \frac{\lambda^3}{3}\,\mathrm{skew}[A] + \frac{\lambda^4}{2}\,\mathrm{var}[A]^2 + \frac{1 - \lambda^2}{6} . \tag{19}$$

Proof. Substitution of (16) in (11) in Cor. 2 yields that

$$\mathrm{var}[U] + \mathrm{E}[U]^2 = \frac{\lambda}{2\pi i} \oint_C d\zeta \, \frac{D(\zeta)\,[Q_A(\zeta) + P_A(\zeta)]}{(\zeta - 1)^2\,[Q_A(\zeta) - P_A(\zeta)]} ,$$

with C being a contour around the origin that fulfills $\forall \zeta \in C\colon 1 < |\zeta| < \mathcal{R}_D$. The condition that $1 < |\zeta|$ along C implies that along C holds $|A(1/\zeta)| < 1$ and hence that $|P_A(\zeta)| < |Q_A(\zeta)|$. An application of the Theorem of Rouché with $f(\zeta) = Q_A(\zeta)$ and $g(\zeta) = P_A(\zeta)$ then yields that the polynomial function $Q_A(\zeta) - P_A(\zeta)$ has c zeros (counting with multiplicity) inside C. Note that since C can be chosen arbitrarily close to (but larger than) the unit circle, those zeros lie inside or on the unit circle. One of those zeros is a simple zero at $\zeta = 1$, which is a third-order pole of the integrand. The contribution of this third-order pole to the right-hand side of the previous expression is given by

$$\lambda^2 \, \mathrm{var}[D] + \lambda^3 \, \mathrm{E}[D] \, \mathrm{var}[A] - \frac{\lambda^3}{3} \, \mathrm{skew}[A] + \frac{\lambda^4}{2} \, \mathrm{var}[A]^2 + \frac{1 - \lambda^2}{6} \; .$$

An application of the Residue Theorem and Little's Theorem yields (19).   □

8   Application: Result

We now return to the application introduced in Sect. 8 and apply the general result of Theorem 3. Deterministic interarrival times of c slots correspond with the special case $A(z) = z^c$ with $c \in \mathbb{N}_0$ and $\lambda = 1/c$. After substituting z^c for z, the characteristic function becomes $\zeta^c - z^c$. For $z \neq 0$ this function has c distinct zeros $\{\gamma_n(z^c) \,|\, n = 0, \ldots, c-1\}$ with $\gamma_n(z^c) = a^n z$ and $a \doteq \exp(2\pi i/c)$. An application of Theorem 3 for this special case then yields

$$U(z^c) = \frac{1}{c^2} \sum_{n=0}^{c-1} \frac{a^n D(a^n z)}{z^{c-1}} \left(\frac{1 - z^c}{1 - a^n z} \right)^2 . \tag{20}$$

Substitution of (1) thus yields the expression for the pgf of the system contents. The variance of the system content is then given by (in view of Cor. 4):

$$\mathrm{var}[U] = \frac{1}{c^2} \, \mathrm{var}[D] + \frac{c^2 - 1}{6 \, c^2} - \frac{2}{c^2} \sum_{n=1}^{c-1} \frac{D(a^n)}{|a^n - 1|^2} . \tag{21}$$

We study the behavior of expected value and standard deviation of the system contents (in terms of cells) during an arbitrary slot as a function of the load, for the cases whereby the message size $c = 1, 2, 4, 8$ and 16. Figure 1 shows the expected value of the number of cells present during an arbitrary slot as a function of the load. The figure shows that as the expected value of the system contents increases with the load and with the message size. Figure 2 shows that also the standard deviation of the system contents grows with the message size. These results show that for this queueing model reducing the message size (and the interarrival time) reduces both the expected value and the standard deviation of the system contents.

For this particular example with deterministic interarrival times it is possible to conduct explicitly the inverse Z-transformation of (20). This yields a relationship between the pmf of the system delay and the pmf of the system contents. Equation (20) is equivalent to

$$U(z^c) = \frac{1}{c^2} \sum_{n=0}^{c-1} \sum_{k=0}^{\infty} \sum_{l=0}^{c-1} \sum_{m=0}^{c-1} d(k) \, z^{k+l-m} \, a^{n(k+l-m)} \; ,$$

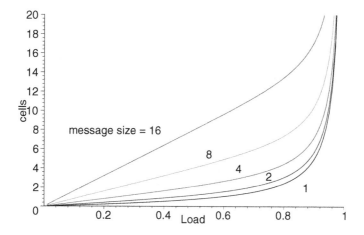

Fig. 1. System Contents, Expected Value

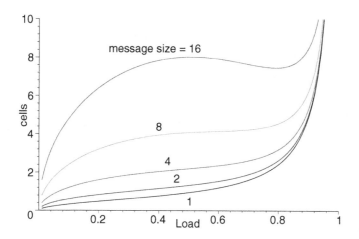

Fig. 2. System Contents, Standard Deviation

which in view of $\sum_{n=0}^{c-1} a^{nk} = c\,\mathbf{1}$ (n is a mutliple of c) reduces to, $\forall k \in \mathbb{N}$:

$$u(k) = \frac{1}{c^2} \sum_{l=0}^{c-1} \sum_{m=0}^{c-1} d(ck + l - m) = \sum_{l=-c+1}^{c-1} \frac{c - |l|}{c^2} d(ck + l) \ , \qquad (22)$$

whereby $d(k) = 0$ for negative values of k. We observe that $u(k)$ is a weighted average of the $u(k)$ in the immediate neighborhood of $u(ck)$. The result obtained here is similar to the result obtained in [8] in which a relationship between the pmf of the system contents and of the system delay was established without first establishing a relationship between the pgf, for multi-server queueing system with deterministic service times of 1 slot.

9 Conclusion

The paper extends Little's relationship between the first moment of sojourn time and queue contents to a relationship between the pgf of those performance measures, for the case of renewal arrivals and FCFS-scheduling. Algebraic expressions are obtained when either the interarrival times or the system delay have a rational pgf. From that expression a similar expression for the variance is derived; in a similar manner such relationships may be derived for higher-order moments. Further research might focus on establishing similar relationships for more complicated arrival processes. Alternatively, one could focus on estimates for the higher-order central moments of the system contents, given (estimates of) some central moments and some characteristics of the system delay and the distribution of the interarrival times, but not the entire pgf of the system delay.

References

[1] Little, J.: A proof of the queueing formula: $L = \lambda W$. Operations Research **28** (1961) 983–994   171

[2] Stidham, S.: $L = \lambda W$: A discounted analogue and a new proof. Operations Research **20** (1972) 115–1126   171

[3] Stidham, S.: A last word on $L = \lambda W$. Operations Research **22** (1974) 417–421   171

[4] Fiems, D., Bruneel, H.: A note on the discretization of little's result. Operations Research Letters **30** (2002) 17–18   171

[5] Marschall, K., Wolff, R.: Customer average and time average queue lengths and waiting times. Journal of Applied Probability **8** (1971) 535–542   171

[6] Brumelle, S.: On the relation between customer and time averages in queues. Journal of Applied Probability **8** (1971) 508–520   171

[7] Vinck, B., Bruneel, H.: Relationship between delay and buffer contents in ATM queues. Electronics Letters **31** (1995) 952–954   171

[8] Vinck, B., Bruneel, H.: Delay analysis of multiserver ATM buffers. Electronics Letters **32** (1996) 1352–1353   171, 182

[9] Gao, P., Wittevrongel, S., Bruneel, H.: Delay against system contents in discrete-time G/Geom/c queue. Electronics Letters **39** (2003) 1290–1292   171

[10] Van Ommeren, J.: The discrete-time single-server queue. Queueing Systems **8** (1991) 279–294   172

[11] Flanigan, F.: Complex Variables; Harmonic and Analytic Functions. Dover Publications, New York (1972/1983)   175

[12] Bak, J., Newmann, D.: Complex Analysis. 2nd edn. Springer-Verlag, New York (1996)   177

[13] Abate, J., Whitt, W.: The fourier-series method for inverting transforms of probability distributions. Queueing Systems **10** (1992) 5–87   178

Delay Analysis
for a Discrete-Time GI-D-c Queue
with Arbitrary-Length Service Times

Peixia Gao, Sabine Wittevrongel, and Herwig Bruneel

SMACS** Research Group
Department of Telecommunications and Information Processing
Ghent University, Sint-Pietersnieuwstraat 41, B-9000 Gent, Belgium
{pg,sw,hb}@telin.ugent.be
http://telin.ugent.be/smacs

Abstract. In this paper, we consider a discrete-time GI-D-c queueing system with general independent arrivals, deterministic service times of arbitrary length, multiple servers, an infinite buffer size and a first-come-first-served queueing discipline. A relationship between the probability distributions of the system contents and the packet delay is established. By means of this relation, an explicit expression for the generating function of the packet delay is obtained from the known generating function of the system contents, derived in previous work. In addition, some important characteristics of the packet delay, namely the mean, the variance and the tail distribution of the packet delay, are derived through some mathematical manipulations. Numerical examples are presented to illustrate the analysis.

1   Introduction

Discrete-time queueing models play an important role in the performance evaluation of packet-based telecommunication networks, where buffers are used for the temporary storage of information packets which cannot be transmitted to their destination immediately. In discrete-time queueing models, the time axis is divided into fixed-length intervals, referred to as slots, and the service (transmission) of packets can start or end at slot boundaries only. The latter implies that the service times of the packets consist of an integer number of slots. Usually, the performance of a queueing system is expressed in terms of such quantities as the system contents (i.e., the total number of packets present in the queueing system) and the delay of a packet (i.e., the time (in slots) spent by a packet in the system). Many results have been obtained for the analysis of both quantities in a single-server environment. In case systems with multiple servers are considered, fewer results are available. Most studies of multiserver systems assume constant service times equal to one slot, see for instance [1] and [2]. Multiserver systems with geometrically distributed service times have been considered in [3]-[6]. In [7]

** SMACS: Stochastic Modeling and Analysis of Communication Systems

M. Núñez et al. (Eds.): FORTE 2004 Workshops, LNCS 3236, pp. 184–195, 2004.
© Springer-Verlag Berlin Heidelberg 2004

and [8], discrete-time queueing models with multiple servers and constant service times of multiple slots have been studied, but only results in connection with the system contents have been derived.

In the present paper, we will extend the analysis of [7] in order to investigate the delay characteristics. A relationship between the distributions of the packet delay and the system contents is established first. Then, from the results for the system contents derived in [7], the probability generating function (pgf) of the packet delay is obtained. Finally, from this pgf the delay-related characteristics, i.e., the mean delay, the variance of the delay and the probability that the delay exceeds a given threshold, are calculated. To the best of the authors' knowledge, no such study has been reported before.

The paper is organized as follows. In Sect. 2, we describe the class of discrete-time queueing systems under study and introduce some notations. Some results of [7], which will be used in the paper, are also summarized there. For the considered class of queueing systems, we establish a relationship between the steady-state pgf's of the system contents and the packet delay in Sect. 3. In Sect. 4, the performance measures for the packet delay are presented. In Sect. 5, some numerical examples are given to illustrate the analysis. Finally, the paper is concluded in Sect. 6.

2   System Description, Notations and Preliminary Results

We consider a discrete-time multiserver queueing system with c ($c \geq 1$) servers (output channels). Time is divided into fixed-length slots. Packets arrive at the input of the system according to a general independent arrival process, i.e., the numbers of packet arrivals during the consecutive slots are assumed to be independent and identically distributed (i.i.d.) random variables; we denote their common pgf by $A(z)$. Packets are then queued in a buffer until they can be transmitted via one of the c output channels based on a first-come-first-served (FCFS) discipline. The buffer has an infinite storage capacity for packets. The service (or transmission) of a packet can start or end at slot boundaries only. In this paper, the service times of the packets are assumed to be constant equal to s ($s \geq 1$) slots. Moreover, the service and arrival processes are assumed to be mutually independent. Finally, in the analysis that follows it is assumed that the system can reach a steady state. Such a steady state exists if the mean number of packet arrivals during an arbitrary slot is strictly less than the mean number of packets that can be transmitted from the buffer per slot, i.e., if the load

$$\rho \stackrel{\triangle}{=} sA^{'}(1)/c < 1. \tag{1}$$

Let us denote by v_k the system contents (i.e., the total number of packets in the buffer system, including the packets under transmission, if any) at the beginning of slot k and by a_k the number of packet arrivals during slot k. Furthermore, let $u_{j,k}$ ($0 \leq j \leq s - 1$) indicate the total number of packets in the system at the beginning of slot k whose service has progressed for at most j

slots. Note that no packets in the system have received more than $s - 1$ slots of service due to the constant nature of the service times (packets who have received s slots of service are no longer in the system). In [7], it was shown that the following set of system equations can then be established:

$$v_k = u_{s-1,k};$$
(2)

$$u_{j,k+1} = u_{j-1,k} + a_k, \text{ for } 1 \le j \le s - 1,$$
(3)

and

$$u_{0,k+1} = (u_{s-1,k} - c)^+ + a_k,$$
(4)

where $(\cdots)^+ = max(0, \cdots)$. We moreover introduce the notation $u_{-1,k} = (u_{s-1,k} - c)^+$ to indicate the number of packets in the system at the beginning of slot k and not being served during slot k. In the steady state the distributions of the random variables v_k and $u_{j,k}$ become independent of the time index k. We denote by $V(z)$ and $U_j(z)$ the equilibrium pgf's of v_k and $u_{j,k}$, respectively. Equations (2)-(4) were used in [7] to derive the following expressions for the pgf's $V(z)$ and $U_j(z)$:

$$V(z) = c(1 - \rho) \frac{(z - 1)A(z)^s}{z^c - A(z)^s} \prod_{i=1}^{c-1} \frac{z - z_i}{1 - z_i},$$
(5)

where z_i ($1 \le i \le c - 1$) are the $c - 1$ zeros inside the unit disk $\{z : |z| < 1\}$ of $z^c - A(z)^s$, and

$$U_j(z) = \frac{V(z)}{A(z)^{s-j-1}}, \text{ for } -1 \le j \le s - 1.$$
(6)

In this paper, we will study the delay characteristics for the considered GI-D-c queueing model.

3   Relationship Between System Contents and Delay

We define the delay of a packet as the total number of slots between the end of the slot during which the packet arrived in the system and the end of the slot where the service (transmission) of the packet finishes and the packet leaves the system. In this section, we will derive a relationship between the steady-state probability distributions of the system contents at the start of an arbitrary slot and the delay of an arbitrary packet. For this purpose, let us consider an arbitrary packet P (referred to as the tagged packet), that arrives in the queueing system during some slot J in the steady state. Let d with pgf $D(z)$ denote the delay of P. Also define the waiting time of a packet as the number of slots between the end of the packet's arrival slot and the beginning of the slot where the service of the packet starts. Then it is clear that the delay of a packet is equal to the sum

of the waiting time and the service time of the packet. Hence, we can express
the pgf $D(z)$ as

$$D(z) = z^s W(z), \qquad (7)$$

where $W(z)$ denotes the pgf of the waiting time w of P.

We now concentrate on the derivation of the pgf $W(z)$. We let q denote the
total number of packets present in the system right after slot J with service
priority over the tagged packet P. Note that, in view of the FCFS discipline, q
consists of the packets that arrived before slot J and have not yet finished service
at the end of slot J on the one hand, and the packets that arrived in slot J but
before the packet P on the other hand. In order to derive $W(z)$, we follow the
relationship between q and w.

- Let us first observe the first frame of length s slots after slot J. If $q < c$, it is
  clear that P will get into service at the beginning of slot $J + 1$; otherwise, if
  $q \geq c$, P will have to wait at least 1 slot. At the end of slot $J + 1$, there will
  be $(u_{s-2,J} - u_{s-3,J})$ packets leaving the system, which is the total number
  of packets that have received exactly $s - 2$ slots of service at the beginning
  of slot J. In case P didn't get into service at the beginning of slot $J + 1$, an
  analogous reasoning holds for slot $J + 2$: either the packet P will get into
  service at the beginning of slot $J + 2$, if $q - (u_{s-2,J} - u_{s-3,J}) < c$, or the
  waiting time of P will be at least 2 slots otherwise. In the meanwhile, there
  will be $(u_{s-3,J} - u_{s-4,J})$ packets leaving the system at the end of slot $J + 2$.
  We see that the tagged packet will still be waiting for service during slot $J+i$,
  or in other words the waiting time of P will be at least i slots $(1 \leq i \leq s)$,
  only if $q - (u_{s-2,J} - u_{s-3,J}) - (u_{s-3,J} - u_{s-4,J}) - \cdots - (u_{s-i,J} - u_{s-i-1,J}) =$
  $q - u_{s-2,J} + u_{s-i-1,J} \geq c$.
- Next, let us observe the second frame of s slots after slot J. In case $q \geq c$,
  exactly c packets will leave the system during the first frame after slot J, and
  there will be $q - c$ packets left in the system at the beginning of slot $J + s + 1$
  to be served before P. Hence, in case P didn't yet get into service during the
  first frame after slot J, we note the following. If $q - c < c$, P will get into
  service at the beginning of slot $J + s + 1$; otherwise, if $q \geq 2c$, the waiting time
  of P will be at least $s + 1$ slots. At the end of slot $J + s + 1$, all packets whose
  service started at the beginning of slot $J + 2$ will leave the system; the number
  of these packets is $(u_{s-2,J} - u_{s-3,J})$. Then if $q - c - (u_{s-2,J} - u_{s-3,J}) \geq c$,
  P will have to wait at least $s + 2$ slots before getting service. Similarly, if

  $$q - c - (u_{s-2,J} - u_{s-3,J}) - (u_{s-3,J} - u_{s-4,J}) - \cdots - (u_{s-i,J} - u_{s-i-1,J})$$
  $$= q - c - u_{s-2,J} + u_{s-i-1,J} \geq c,$$

  the waiting time of P will be at least $s + i$ slots $(1 \leq i \leq s)$.
- In case P didn't get into service during the second frame after slot J, there
  will be $q - 2c$ packets in the system to be served before P at the start of the
  third frame, and we can repeat the former reasoning.

From the above survey, we conclude that the following relationship between the waiting time w of P and the random variable q holds:

$$w \geq ls + i \iff q - u_{s-2,J} + u_{s-i-1,J} \geq lc + c, \text{ for } l \geq 0, \ 1 \leq i \leq s. \quad (8)$$

According to the definition of q, we have

$$q = v_J + f - (u_{s-1,J} - u_{s-2,J}) = f + u_{s-2,J}, \quad (9)$$

where f is the number of packets arriving during the arrival slot of P (slot J), but before P. Then (8) can be further expressed as

$$w \geq ls + i \iff f + u_{s-i-1,J} - c \geq lc,$$

or equivalently

$$w \geq ls + i \iff \widetilde{q}_i \geq lc, \text{ for } l \geq 0, \ 1 \leq i \leq s, \quad (10)$$

with

$$\widetilde{q}_i \overset{\triangle}{=} f + u_{s-i-1,J} - c. \quad (11)$$

The next step is now to transform the relationship (10) between the random variables w and $\widetilde{q}_i$ ($1 \leq i \leq s$) into a relationship between their pgf's. To this end, we use the identity

$$\sum_{n=1}^{\infty} \text{Prob}[w \geq n] z^n = \frac{z[W(z) - 1]}{z - 1}.$$

From this identity and equation (10), it follows that

$$\frac{z^c[W(z^c) - 1]}{z^c - 1} = \sum_{n=1}^{\infty} \text{Prob}[w \geq n] z^{cn}$$

$$= \sum_{i=1}^{s} \sum_{l=0}^{\infty} \text{Prob}[w \geq ls + i] z^{c(ls+i)} \quad (12)$$

$$= \sum_{i=1}^{s} \sum_{l=0}^{\infty} \text{Prob}[\widetilde{q}_i \geq lc] z^{slc + ci}.$$

This can also be written as

$$\frac{z^c[W(z^c) - 1]}{z^c - 1} = \sum_{i=1}^{s} z^{ci} \sum_{m=0}^{\infty} \text{Prob}[\widetilde{q}_i \geq m] z^{sm} \sum_{l=0}^{\infty} \delta(m - lc), \quad (13)$$

where $\delta(\cdot)$ is the Kronecker delta function, which is zero unless its argument is zero, in which case it is equal to 1. Since $m \geq 0$ in the above expression, the lower limit of the sum over l in (13) can be replaced by $-\infty$ without any influence on

the result. We can then eliminate the Kronecker delta functions from (13) by
using the following identity:

$$\frac{1}{c}\sum_{n=0}^{c-1}\beta^{Kn} = \sum_{l=-\infty}^{\infty}\delta(K-lc), \text{ with } \beta \triangleq \exp(2\pi I/c),\qquad(14)$$

and where I is the imaginary unit ($I^2 = -1$). This identity expresses that the
left-hand side of (14) equals zero unless the integer K is a multiple of c, in which
case it is equal to 1. By using (14) in (13), we obtain

$$\frac{z^c[W(z^c)-1]}{z^c-1} = \frac{1}{c}\sum_{i=1}^{s}z^{ci}\sum_{j=0}^{c-1}\sum_{m=0}^{\infty}\text{Prob}[\tilde{q}_i \geq m](z^s\beta^j)^m$$

$$= \frac{1}{c}\sum_{j=0}^{c-1}\sum_{i=1}^{s}\frac{1-\beta^j z^s \widetilde{Q}_i(\beta^j z^s)}{1-\beta^j z^s}z^{ci},\qquad(15)$$

where $\widetilde{Q}_i(z)$ is the pgf of $\tilde{q}_i$, and where we have also used the identity

$$\frac{1-z\widetilde{Q}_i(z)}{1-z} = \sum_{m=0}^{\infty}\text{Prob}[\tilde{q}_i \geq m]z^m.$$

What remains now is to relate the pgf's $\widetilde{Q}_i(z)$, $1 \leq i \leq s$, to the pgf $V(z)$ of
the system contents v at the start of an arbitrary slot. This can be done based
on the definition (11) of $\tilde{q}_i$. In view of the uncorrelated nature of the packet
arrival process, the random variables f and $u_{s-i-1,J}$ on the right-hand side of
(11) are statistically independent. Hence, we get

$$\widetilde{Q}_i(z) = \frac{F(z)U_{s-i-1}(z)}{z^c},\qquad(16)$$

where $F(z)$ is the pgf of f, which can be shown to be (see e.g. [9])

$$F(z) = \frac{A(z)-1}{A'(1)(z-1)}.\qquad(17)$$

Combination of (16) and (6) yields

$$\widetilde{Q}_i(z) = \frac{F(z)V(z)}{z^c A(z)^i}, \text{ for } 1 \leq i \leq s.\qquad(18)$$

Substituting (18) into (15), working out the sum over i, using the property that
$\beta^{jc} = 1$ regardless of the value of j and the identity

$$\frac{1}{c}\sum_{j=0}^{c-1}\frac{1}{1-\beta^j z^s} = \frac{1}{1-z^{cs}},$$

which is easily shown based on equation (14), we finally obtain

$$W(z^c) = \frac{1-z^c}{cz^{cs}} \sum_{j=0}^{c-1} \frac{\beta^j z^s}{1-\beta^j z^s} \frac{[A(\beta^j z^s)^s - z^{cs}]F(\beta^j z^s)V(\beta^j z^s)}{A(\beta^j z^s)^s[A(\beta^j z^s) - z^c]}. \tag{19}$$

Combination of (19) with (7) then leads to the desired relationship between the steady-state pgf's of the system contents v at the beginning of an arbitrary slot and the delay d of an arbitrary packet.

4   Delay Characteristics

From the above relationship between system contents and delay and the known expression (5) for the pgf $V(z)$ of the system contents, we find the following explicit formula for the pgf of the delay experienced by an arbitrary packet in the steady state:

$$D(z^c) = z^{cs}W(z^c) = \frac{1-\rho}{A'(1)} \sum_{j=0}^{c-1} \frac{1-z^c}{1-(\beta^j z^s)^{-1}} \frac{A(\beta^j z^s)-1}{A(\beta^j z^s)-z^c} \prod_{i=1}^{c-1} \frac{\beta^j z^s - z_i}{1-z_i}. \tag{20}$$

In the rest of this section, we will use the expression for $D(z^c)$ to derive some important characteristics of the packet delay.

4.1   Moments of the Delay

The mean value of the packet delay can be found by evaluation of the first-order derivative of the pgf $D(z^c)$ with respect to z at $z = 1$. Specifically,

$$E[d] = D'(1) = \frac{1}{c} \frac{dD(z^c)}{dz}\Big|_{z=1}, \tag{21}$$

where $D(z^c)$ is given in (20). After some mathematical manipulations, we find

$$E[d] = \frac{E[v]}{A'(1)}, \tag{22}$$

which proves that our result fully agrees with Little's theorem ([10]). In a similar way, we can also obtain higher-order moments of the packet delay from (20), by calculating the appropriate higher-order derivatives of $D(z^c)$ at $z = 1$. For instance, the variance of the packet delay (delay jitter) can be expressed as

$$Var[d] = D''(1) + D'(1) - D'(1)^2, \tag{23}$$

where $D''(1)$, the second derivative of $D(z)$ in $z = 1$, can be obtained from (20) as

$$D''(1) = \frac{1}{c^2} \frac{d^2 D(z^c)}{dz^2}\Big|_{z=1} - \frac{c-1}{c} D'(1).$$

4.2   Tail Probabilities of the Delay

The aim of this section is to determine the tail distribution of the packet delay, i.e., the probability that the delay equals a given value n, for a sufficiently large value of n. In principle, the tail distribution of a discrete random variable can be determined by applying the inversion formula for z-transforms and Cauchy's residue theorem from complex analysis (see e.g. [11]) on its generating function and keeping only the contribution of the pole (or poles) of the pgf with smallest modulus outside the unit disk, as explained in [9]. From the expression (20) for $D(z^c)$, we find that $D(z^c)$ has c poles with the same smallest modulus. These poles are given by

$$z_d(m) = \beta^{-m} z_v^{1/s}, \text{ for } m = 0, \cdots, c-1, \tag{24}$$

where z_v is the dominant pole of the pgf $V(z)$ of the system contents, i.e., the zero of $z^c - A(z)^s$ outside the unit disk with the smallest modulus. Indeed, it is easy to show that $z_d(0) = z_v^{1/s}$ is the zero with minimal modulus outside the unit disk of the factor $[z^c - A(z^s)]$ in the denominator of $D(z^c)$. Moreover, since z^c remains unchanged when z is multiplied by β^{-m}, it is clear that $z_d(m) = \beta^{-m} z_v^{1/s}$ is also a pole of $D(z^c)$ with the same modulus $z_v^{1/s}$. In particular, it can be shown that the pole $z_d(m)$ is a zero of the factor $[A(\beta^j z^s) - z^c]$ in the denominator of $D(z^c)$ for which $j = (ms)$ mod c, i.e., for which j equals the remainder of the division of ms by c. Taking into account all the poles $z_d(m)$ of $D(z^c)$ with minimal modulus and keeping in mind that $\text{Prob}[d = n]$ is the coefficient of z^{cn} in the series expansion of $D(z^c)$, we finally obtain the following expression for $\text{Prob}[d = n]$ for sufficiently large n:

$$\begin{aligned}
\text{Prob}[d = n] &\approx -\sum_{m=0}^{c-1} \frac{b_m}{z_d(m)} [z_d(m)]^{-cn} \\
&= -\sum_{m=0}^{c-1} \frac{b_m}{z_d(m)} z_v^{-cn/s} \\
&= -C_d \, z_v^{-cn/s},
\end{aligned} \tag{25}$$

where b_m is the residue of $D(z^c)$ in the point $z = z_d(m)$ and where we have used the property that $\beta^{mc} = 1$. The residue b_m is given by

$$b_m = \frac{N_m(z_d(m))}{R_m{}'(z_d(m))},$$

where $N_m(z)$ and $R_m(z)$ are the numerator and the denominator, respectively, of the term of (20) corresponding with the index value $j = (ms)$ mod c. Using the expression (20), we find

$$C_d = \sum_{m=0}^{c-1} \frac{b(m)}{z_d(m)} = \frac{c(1-\rho)}{A'(1)} \frac{1 - z_v^{c/s}}{1 - (z_v)^{-1}} \frac{A(z_v) - 1}{s z_v A'(z_v) - c z_v^{c/s}} \prod_{i=1}^{c-1} \frac{z_v - z_i}{1 - z_i}. \tag{26}$$

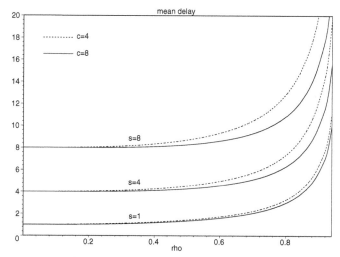

Fig. 1. Mean packet delay versus load ρ

The probability that the packet delay exceeds a given threshold T can be easily derived from (25) as

$$\text{Prob}[d > T] \approx -C_d \frac{z_v^{-cT/s}}{z_v^{c/s} - 1}. \tag{27}$$

5　Numerical Results

In order to illustrate the results obtained above, let us consider a number of numerical examples. Throughout this section, we assume the number of packets that arrive during a slot has a geometric distribution, i.e.,

$$A(z) = \frac{1}{1 + \lambda - \lambda z},$$

where λ denotes the mean number of packet arrivals per slot.

In Fig. 1, the mean packet delay is plotted versus the load ρ for various values of the number of servers c and the length of the service times s. For given values of c and s, we observe that the mean packet delay increases with increasing values of ρ. We also note that all the curves have a vertical asymptote at $\rho = 1$. For a given ρ, the mean delay increases as the service times become longer, although a higher number of servers can compensate this effect to some extent.

In Fig. 2, the variance of the packet delay is shown versus ρ, for $c = 4$ and for $s = 1$, 4 and 8. We see that for given values of c and ρ, the variance of the packet delay also increases as the length of the service times increases.

In Fig. 3, the probability that the delay exceeds some given threshold T is plotted versus T for $\rho = 0.8$, $s = 5$ and for three different numbers of servers, namely $c = 1$, 4 and 8. Clearly, the probability of having long delays decreases as the number of servers increases, in accordance with our intuitive feeling.

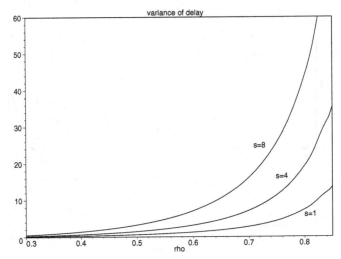

Fig. 2. Variance of the packet delay versus load ρ, for $c = 4$

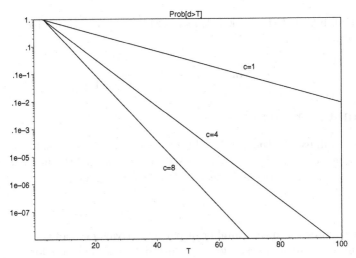

Fig. 3. Tail distribution of packet delay, $\mathrm{Prob}[d > T]$, versus T, for $\rho = 0.8$ and $s = 5$

6   Conclusion

In this paper, we have studied the delay performance of a discrete-time GI-D-c queueing system with multiple servers, constant service times of arbitrary length and a general independent arrival process. The study is an extension of previous work ([7]), which was concerned with the analysis of the system contents for this type of multiserver queueing system. In the present paper, we have established a relationship between the pgf's of the packet delay and the system contents, using an analytical technique based on generating functions. Then from the result for the pgf of the system contents, known from [7], we have obtained an explicit expression for the pgf of the packet delay, as well as closed-form expressions for the mean value, the variance and the tail distribution of the packet delay. The obtained results are easy to evaluate numerically. Some numerical results have been presented to illustrate the analysis.

The analyzed queueing model has practical applications in the domain of digital communication networks, such as traffic concentrators, ATM switching elements and circuit-switched TDMA systems. Let us take a traffic concentrator as an example to see how the modeling works. A concentrator is used to merge a large number of low-speed lines (inputs) to a smaller number (say c) of high-speed lines (outputs). Fixed-length messages enter the concentrator via the inputs and are temporarily stored in the buffer inside the concentrator until they can be transmitted via one of the outputs. In case the transmission time is s slots for each message, the concentrator can be described as the model we studied, where the pgf $A(z)$ describes the accumulated numbers of message arrivals via all the inputs of the concentrator. Readers are recommended to refer to [7] and [9] (Chapter 1) for more details and more applications. We note that besides the characteristics of the system contents studied in [7] for the considered model, the derived results for the packet delay (i.e., performance measures like the mean delay, the delay jitter and the probability that the packet delay exceeds a given threshold) are also very important for a network designer to guarantee the quality of service of the network.

References

[1] Bruneel, H., Steyaert, B., Desmet, E., Petit, G. H.: An analytical technique for the derivation of the delay performance of ATM switches with multiserver output queues. International Journal of Digital and Analog Communication Systems **5** (1992) 193-201   184

[2] Vinck, B., Bruneel, H.: Delay analysis of multiserver ATM buffers. Electronics Letters **32** (1996) 1352-1353   184

[3] Rubin, I., Zhang, Z.: Message delay and queue-size analysis for circuit-switched TDMA systems. IEEE Transactions on Communications **39**(6) (1991) 905-914   184

[4] Gao, P., Wittevrongel, S., Bruneel, H.: Discrete-time multiserver queues with geometric service times. Computers & Operations Research **31**(1) (2004) 81-99

[5] Gao, P., Wittevrongel, S., Bruneel, H.: Delay against system contents in discrete-time G/Geom/c queue. Electronics Letters **39**(17) (2003) 1290-1292

[6] Gao, P., Wittevrongel, S., Bruneel, H.: Discrete-time multiserver buffer systems with correlated arrivals and geometric service times. In: Proc. Conference on Design, Analysis, and Simulation of Distributed Systems, DASD 2003. Orlando (30 March - 3 April 2003) 27-34   184

[7] Bruneel, H., Wuyts, I.: Analysis of discrete-time multiserver queueing models with constant service times. Operations Research Letters **15** (1994) 231-236   184, 185, 186, 193, 194

[8] Chaudhry, M. L., Kim, N. K.: A complete and simple solution for a discrete-time multi-server queue with bulk arrivals and deterministic service times. Operations Research Letters **31**(2) (2003) 101-107   185

[9] Bruneel, H., Kim, B. G.: Discrete-time models for communication systems including ATM. Kluwer Academic Publishers, Boston (1993) 189, 191, 194
[10] Fiems, D., Bruneel, H.: A note on the discretization of Little's result. Operations Research Letters **30** (2002) 17-18 190
[11] Kleinrock, L.: Queueing systems, Volume I: Theory. Wiley, New York (1975) 191

Adaptive Fuzzy Queue Management and Congestion Avoidance in TCP/AQM Networks

Mahdi Jalili-Kharaajoo

Young Researchers Club, Islamic Azad University, Tehran
P.O. Box: 14395/1355, Tehran, Iran
mahdijalili@ece.ut.ac.ir

Abstract. Active Queue Management (AQM) takes a trade-off between link utilization and delay experienced by data packets. From control point of view, it is rational to regard AQM as a typical regulation system. Recently many AQM algorithms have been proposed to address performance degradations of end-to-end congestion control. However, these AQM algorithms show weaknesses to detect and control congestion under dynamically changing network situations. In this paper, an adaptive fuzzy AQM is designed to congestion avoidance in TCP/AQM networks. This kind of control action has robust performance, which is suitable for time varying and complex systems such as computer and communication networks. A candidate Lyapunov function is employed in the adaptive law synthesis to ensure convergence. A simulation study over a wide range of IP traffic conditions shows the effectiveness of the proposed controller in terms of the queue length dynamics, the packet loss rates, and the link utilization. Also, a complete comparison between the proposed fuzzy adaptive controller and classic Proportional-Integral (PI) controller is made, which the former has superior performance.

1 Introduction

TCP congestion control mechanism, while necessary and powerful, are not sufficient to provide good service in all circumstances, specially with the rapid growth in size and the strong requirements to Quality of Service (QoS) support, because there is a limitation to how much control can be accomplished at end system. It is needed to implement some measures in the intermediate nodes to complement the end system congestion avoidance mechanisms. Active Queue Management (AQM), as one class of packet dropping/marking mechanism in the router queue, has been recently proposed to support the end-to-end congestion control in the Internet [1-5]. It has been a very active research area in the Internet community. The goals of AQM are (1) reduce the average length of queue in routers and thereby decrease the end-to-end delay experimented by packets, and (2) ensure the network resources to be used efficiently by reducing the packet loss that occurs when queues overflow. AQM highlights the tradeoff between delay and throughput. By keeping the average queue size small, AQM will have the ability to provide greater capacity to accommodate nature-occurring burst without dropping packets, at the same time, reduce the delays seen by flow, this is very particularly important for real-time interactive applications. RED [6,7] was originally proposed to achieve fairness among sources with different

M. Núñez et al. (Eds.): FORTE 2004 Workshops, LNCS 3236, pp. 196-208, 2004.
© Springer-Verlag Berlin Heidelberg 2004

burst attributes and to control queue length, which just meets the requirements of AQM. However, many subsequent studies verified that RED is unstable and too sensitive to parameter configuration, and tuning of RED has been proved to be a difficult job [8-10].

Fuzzy logic controllers have been developed and applied to nonlinear system for the last two decades [11]. The most attractive feature of fuzzy logic control is that the expert knowledge can be easily incorporated into the control laws [12-14]. In [15,16] an adaptive fuzzy controllers has been proposed for robust control performance, which will be used in our controller design.

The intuition and heuristic design is not always scientific and reasonable under any conditions. Of course, since Internet is a rather complex huge system, it is very difficult to have a full-scale and systematic comprehension, but importance has been considerably noted. The mathematical modeling of the Internet is the first step to have an in-depth understanding, and the algorithms designed based on the rational model should be more reliable than one original from intuition. In some of the references, the nonlinear dynamic model for TCP flow control has been utilized and some controllers like PI and Adaptive Virtual Queue Algorithm have been designed for that [17-21].

Although PI controller successfully related some limitations of RED, for instance, the queue length and dropping/marking probability are decoupled, whenever the queue length can be easily controlled to the desired value; the system has relatively high stability margin. The shortcomings of PI controller are also obvious. The modification of probability excessively depends on buffer size. As a result, for small buffer the system exhibits sluggishness. Secondly, for small reference queue length, the system tends to performance poorly, which is unfavorable to achieve the goal of AQM because small queue length implies small queue waiting delay. Thirdly, the status of actual network is rapidly changeable, so we believe that it is problematic and unrealistic, at least inaccurate, to take the network as a linear and constant system just like the designing of PI controller. Affirmatively, the algorithm based on this assumption should have limited validity, such as inability against disturbance or noise. We need more robust controller to adapt complex and mutable network environment, which will be our motivation and aim in this study.

In the paper, we will apply an adaptive fuzzy controller to design the AQM system for congestion avoidance. First, a fuzzy logic based controller is designed and them the adaptive law will be applied to the designed controller. A candidate Lyapunov function is employed in the adaptive law synthesis to ensure convergence. The performance of the proposed fuzzy adaptive controller is compared with that of classic PI controller. The simulation results show the superior performance of the proposed controller in comparison with classic PI controller.

The rest of the paper is organized as follows: Section 2 presents the nonlinear dynamic model for TCP flow control and the state space description of this model. In Section 3, the basic principles of adaptive fuzzy controller are presented. Some simulations are provided using MATLAB package in Section 4 and the performance of the various controllers are compared. Finally, the paper is concluded in section 5.

2   TCP Flow Control Model

In [17], a nonlinear dynamic model for TCP flow control has been developed based on fluid-flow theory. This model can be stated as follows

$$
\begin{cases}
\dfrac{dW(t)}{dt} = \dfrac{1}{R(t)} - \dfrac{W(t)W(t-R(t))}{2R(t)} p(t-R(t)) \\[2mm]
\dfrac{dq(t)}{dt} = \dfrac{N(t)}{R(t)} W(t) - C(t)
\end{cases}
\tag{1}
$$

The above nonlinear and time-varying system was approximated as a linear constant system by small-signal linearization about an operating point [20,21] (Fig. 1). In the block diagram, $C(s)$ and $G(s)$ are the controller and the plant, respectively. The meaning of parameters presented in Fig. 1 are as following

$$
K(t) = \frac{[R(t)C(t)]^3}{[2N(t)]^2}, \quad T_1(t) = R(t), \quad T_2(t) = \frac{R^2(t)C(t)}{2N(t)}
\tag{2}
$$

where
$C(t)$: Link capacity (packets/sec)
q_o : Queue reference value
$N(t)$: Load factor, i.e., number of active sessions
$R(t)$: Round-trip time (RTT), $R(t) = 2\big(q(t)/C(t) + T_p\big)$, T_p is the fixed propagation delay
$p(t)$: Dropping/marking probability
$q(t)$: Instantaneous queue

We believe that the AQM controller designed with the simplified and inaccurate linear constant model should not be optimal, because the actual network is very changeful; the state parameters are hardly kept at a constant value for a long time [2,5]. Moreover, the equations (1) only take consideration into the fast retransmission and fast recovery, but ignore the timeout mechanism caused by lacking of enough duplicated ACK, which is very usual in burst and short-lived services. In addition to, there are many non-respective UDP flows besides TCP connections in networks; they are also not included in equations (1). These mismatches in model will have negative impact on the performance of controller designed with the approach depending with the accurate model. For the changeable network, the robust control should be an appropriate choice to design controller for AQM.

To describe the system in state space form, suppose that $x_1 = e$, $x_2 = de/dt$, so the plant depicted in Fig. 1 is described by a second order system as

$$
\begin{cases}
\dfrac{dx_1}{dt} = x_2 \\[2mm]
\dfrac{dx_2}{dt} = -a_1(t)x_1 - a_2(t)x_2 - b(t) + F(t)
\end{cases}
\tag{3}
$$

$$a_{1\min} \leq a_1 \leq a_{1\max}, a_{2\min} \leq a_2 \leq a_{2\max}, 0 < b_{\min} \leq b \leq b_{\max} \qquad (4)$$

where

$$a_1(t) = \frac{1}{T_1(t)T_2(t)}, a_2(t) = \frac{T_1(t) + T_2(t)}{T_1(t)T_2(t)}, b(t) = \frac{K(t)}{T_1(t)T_2(t)}$$

$$F(t) = \frac{d^2}{dt^2}q_o + \frac{T_1(t) + T_2(t)}{T_1(t)T_2(t)}\frac{d}{dt}q_o + \frac{1}{T_1(t)T_2(t)}q_o \qquad (5)$$

$F(t)$ is regarded as the system disturbance.

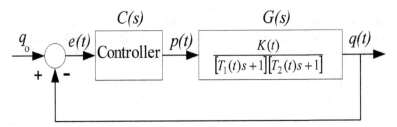

Fig. 1. Block diagram of AQM control system

3   Fuzzy Adaptive Controller Design

3.1 Fuzzy Control Design

Fuzzy logic control (FLC) has been demonstrated to solve some practical problems that have been beyond the reach of conventional control techniques. Fuzzy logic control is a knowledge-based control that uses fuzzy set theory, fuzzy reasoning and fuzzy logic for knowledge representation and inference [11,12,16]. The apparent success of FLC can be attributed to its ability to incorporate expert information and generate control surfaces whose shape can be individually manipulated for different regions of the state space with virtually no effects on neighboring regions.

In this paper a fuzzy system consisting of a fuzzifier, a knowledge base (rule base), a fuzzy inference engine and defuzzier will be considered. The knowledge base of the fuzzy system is a collection of fuzzy IF-THEN rules. Fuzzy logic control is ideal for the AQM problem, since there is no complete mathematical model. However, human experience and experimental results, can be used in the control system, design.

The controller has two inputs, the error (e) and its derivative $(\dot{e})$ and the control input (p). Five triangular membership functions are defined for error (Fig. 2), namely, Negative Large (NL), Negative Small (NS), Zero, Positive Small (PS), and Positive Large (PL). Similarly three triangular membership functions are defined for derivative of the error (Fig. 3) and there are as follows, Negative Small (NS), Zero, and Positive Small (PS). Also five triangular membership functions are defined for the control input (Fig. 4) and there are Zero, Small, Medium, Large and Very Large. The complete fuzzy rules are shown in Table 1. The first rule is outlined below,

Rule 1:

   If (*e*) is **PL** *AND* (*ė*) is **Zero** *THEN* (*p*) is **Large**.

The rest of the rules are derived similarly. The label names used here give an intuitive sense of how the rules apply. Through experimentation and tuning of the membership functions it was determined that the number of rules was sufficient to encompass all realistic combinations of inputs and outputs. This fuzzy logic controller is implemented using product inference and a center-average defuzzifier.

Table 1. Fuzzy Rules

e $\dot{e}$	NS	ZERO	PS
NL	ZERO	ZERO	ZERO
NS	SMALL	SMALL	SMALL
ZERO	ZERO	ZERO	ZERO
PS	SMALL	LARGE	MEDIUM
PL	MEDIUM	VERY LARGE	LARGE

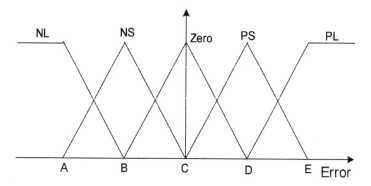

Fig. 2. Error membership function

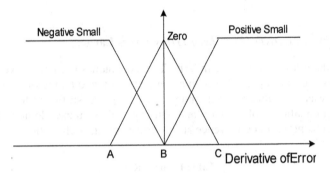

Fig. 3. Membership function for the derivative of Error

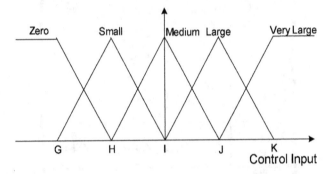

Fig. 4. Control input membership function

3.2 Adaptive Fuzzy Control

Assume that the rule base consists of multiple-input single-output (MISO) rules of the form

$$R^{(j)} : \text{IF } x_1 \text{ is } A_1^j \text{ and} \ldots \text{and } x_n \text{ is } A_n^j \text{ THEN } y_j \text{ is } C^j \qquad (6)$$

where $\underline{x} = (x_1 \ldots x_n) \in N$, y denotes the linguistic variables associated with inputs and outputs of the fuzzy system. A_i^j and C^j are linguistic values of linguistic variables x and y in the universes of discourse N and S respectively, $j = 1,2 \ldots Q_R$ (number of rules). A fuzzy system consisting of a singleton fuzzifier, product inference, center-average defuzzifier and triangular membership functions can be written as [14]

$$f(x) = \frac{\sum_{j=1}^{Q_R} \bar{y}^j \left(\prod_{i=1}^{n} \mu_{A_i^j}(x_i) \right)}{\sum_{j=1}^{Q_R} \left(\prod_{i=1}^{n} \mu_{A_i^j}(x_i) \right)} \qquad (7)$$

where $f : N \subset \Re^n \rightarrow \Re$, $\underline{x} = (x_1 ... x_n)^T \in N$ and $\mu_{A_i^j}(x_i)$ is a triangular membership function and $\bar{y}^j$ is the point in S were μ_{C^j} is maximum or equal to 1.If the $\mu_{A_i^j}(x_i)$'s and $\bar{y}^j$'s are free (adjustable) parameters, then (7) can be written as

$$f(\underline{x}) = \underline{\vartheta}^T \underline{\Psi}(\underline{x}) \tag{8}$$

where $\underline{\vartheta} = (\bar{y}^1, ... \bar{y}^{Q_R})$ is a parameter vector and $\underline{\Psi}(\underline{x}) = (\psi^1(x), ... \psi^{Q_R}(x))^T$ is a regression vector with the regressor given by

$$\psi_i(x) = \frac{\prod_i^n \mu_{A_i^j}(x_i)}{\sum_{j=1}^{Q_R} \left(\prod \mu_{A_i^j}(x_i) \right)} \tag{9}$$

Equation (8) is referred to as adaptive fuzzy systems [14-16].There are two main reasons for using adaptive fuzzy systems as building blocks for adaptive fuzzy controllers. Firstly, it has been proved in [14] that they are universal function approximators. Secondly, all the parameters in $\Psi(x)$ can be fixed at the beginning of adaptive fuzzy systems expansion design procedure, so that the only free design parameters are $\underline{\vartheta}$. In this case $f(x)$ is linear in the parameters. This approach will be adopted in synthesizing the adaptive control law in this paper. The advantage of this approach is that very simple linear parameter estimation methods can be used to analyze and synthesize the performance and robustness of adaptive fuzzy systems. If no linguistic rules are available, the adaptive fuzzy system reduces to a standard nonlinear adaptive controller.

3.3 Adaptive Law Synthesis

The mathematical model given by equation (3) can be expressed as

$$\dot{z} = Az + Bu + E(z) \tag{10}$$

where A is Hurwitz. Therefore there exists a unique positive definite matrix P that satisfies the Lyapunov equation.

$$A^T P + PA = -Q \tag{11}$$

If the control input, u, is expressed as an adaptive fuzzy system then (10) becomes,

$$\dot{z} = Az + B\vartheta^T \psi(z) + E(z) \tag{12}$$

Let [15,16],

$$\dot{\hat{z}} = A\hat{z} + B\vartheta^{*T}\psi(\hat{z}) \tag{13}$$

be the ideal systm model with no uncertainty (identification model) with $\varepsilon = z - \hat{z}$, where ϑ^* denotes the optimal ϑ defined as,

$$\vartheta^* \equiv \arg\min_{|u|\leq M}\left[\sup_{z\in\Omega}\left|u(z\,|\,\vartheta^*) - u(z\,|\,\vartheta)\right|\right] \tag{14}$$

Therefore,

$$\dot{\varepsilon} = A\varepsilon + B\phi^T\psi(\varepsilon) + \hat{E} \tag{15}$$

where $\phi = \vartheta - \vartheta^*$. To derive a control law that ensures that $\varepsilon \to 0$ as $t \to \infty$ a candidate Lyapunov function is defined as [14,16];

$$V = \frac{1}{2}\left(\varepsilon^T P\varepsilon + \frac{\phi^T\phi}{\gamma\|\hat{E}\|}\right) \tag{16}$$

where $\gamma > 0$ is a design parameter. The time derivative of V is

$$\dot{V} = -\varepsilon^T Q\varepsilon + \varepsilon^T PB(\hat{E} + \phi^T\psi(\varepsilon)) + \frac{\phi^T\dot{\phi}}{\gamma\|\hat{E}\|} \tag{17}$$

Rearranging equation (17) yields

$$\dot{V} = -\varepsilon^T Q\varepsilon + \varepsilon^T PB\hat{E} + \phi^T\left(\gamma\|\hat{E}\|\|\varepsilon^T PB\|\psi(\varepsilon) + \dot{\phi}\right) \tag{18}$$

Now choosing the adaptive law (recalling that $\dot{\phi} = \dot{\vartheta}$)

$$\dot{\vartheta} = -\gamma\|\hat{E}\|\|\varepsilon^T PB\|\psi(\varepsilon) \tag{19}$$

The equation (18) reduces to

$$\dot{V} = -\varepsilon^T Q\varepsilon + \varepsilon^T PB\hat{E} \tag{20}$$

The equation (21) can be recast using vector norms;

$$\dot{V} = -\lambda_{min}(Q)\|\varepsilon\|^2 + \|\varepsilon^T PB\|\|\hat{E}\| \tag{21}$$

Let $\|\hat{E}\|$ be selected such that

$$\|\hat{E}\| \geq \frac{\lambda_{min}(Q)\|\varepsilon\|^2 - \alpha\|\varepsilon\|}{\|\varepsilon PB\|} \tag{22}$$

where $\alpha > 0$, substituting for $\hat{E}$ in equation (22) gives

$$\dot{V} \leq -\alpha\|\varepsilon\| \tag{23}$$

Therefore the control law of equation (19) will ensure that the state ε converges.

4   Simulation Results

The network topology used for simulation, is depicted in Fig. 5 [2,5]. The only bottleneck link lies between node A and node B. the buffer size of node A is 200 packets, and default size of the packet is 350 bytes. All sources are classed into three groups. The first one includes N_1 greedy sustained FTP application sources, the second one is composed of N_2 burst HTTP connections, each connection has 10 sessions, and the number of pages per session is 3. The thirds one has N_3 UDP sources, which follow the exponential service model, the idle and burst times are 10000msec and 1000msec, respectively, and the sending rate during "on" duration is 40kbps. We introduced short-lived HTTP flows and non-responsive UDP services into the router in order to generate a more realistic scenario, because it is very important for a perfect AQM scheme to achieve full bandwidth utilization in the presence of noise and disturbance introduced by these flows. The links between node A and all sources have the same capacity and propagation delay pair (L_1, τ_1). The pair (L_2, τ_2) and (L_3, τ_3) define the parameter of links AB and BC, respectively.

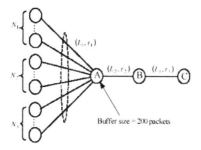

Fig. 5. The simulation network topology

In the first study, we will use the most general network configuration to testify whether the proposed Adaptive Fuzzy Logic Controller (AFLC) can reach the goals of AQM, and freely control the queue length to stabilize at the arbitrary expected value. Therefore, given that $(L_1, \tau_1) = (10Mbps, 15ms)$, $(L_2, \tau_2) = (15Mbps, 15ms)$, $(L_3, \tau_3) = (45Mbps, 15ms)$. $N_1 = 270$, $N_2 = N_3 = 0$. Let the expected queue length equal to 75 packets. To implement the control law, the fuzzy rule Table 1 is used and the insight gained from the non-adaptive fuzzy logic control is used to select the ϑ values to lie within the interval [1.0,2.0]. The remaining control parameters are set as: $Q = \text{diag}(3,3)$, $\hat{E} = 120$, $\gamma = 0.00025$. $\Psi(\varepsilon)$ is formulated using the IF part of fuzzy rule Table 1.

The instantaneous queue length using the proposed AFLC is depicted in Fig. 6. After a very short regulating process, the queue settles down its stable operating point. RED algorithm is unable to accurately control the queue length to the desired value [7,9]. The queue length varies with network loads. The load is heavier the queue length is longer. Attempting to control queue length through decreasing the interval between high and law thresholds, then it is likely to lead queue oscillation.

To investigate the performance of the proposed AFLC, we will consider a classic PI controller as

$$p(k) = (a-b)(q(k)-q_o) + b(q(k)-q(k-1)) + p(k-1) \qquad (24)$$

The coefficients a and b are fixed at $1.822e^{-5}$ and $1.816e^{-5}$, respectively, the sampling frequency is 500Hz, the control variable p is accumulative [5]. Because the parameter b is very small, and the sample interval is very short, the negative contribution to p made by the second item in the right can be omitted in initial process, then the positive contribution mainly come from the first item. The queue evaluation using PI controller is shown in Fig. 7. Although PI controller could regulate the queue to the fixed point, the integrated performance needs to be improved, such as the transient process is too long and the fluctuation in steady state is great, for small queue length, which lows the link utilization.

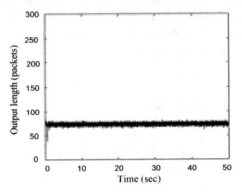

Fig. 6. Queue evaluation (AFLC)

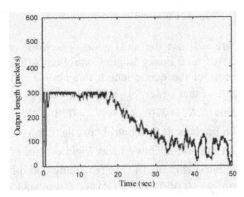

Fig. 7. Queue evaluation (PI)

In this section, Firstly, let $N_1 = 270, N_2 = 400, N_3 = 0$, the evaluation of queue size is shown in Fig. 8. As it can be seen, the proposed AFLC has better performance than that of PI one. Next, given that $N_1 = 270, N_2 = 0, N_3 = 50$, we further investigate performance against the disturbance caused by the non-responsive UDP flows. Fig. 9

shows the results, obviously, PI is very sensitive to this disturbance, while AFLC operates in a relatively stable state. The queue fluctuation increases with introducing the UDP flows, but the variance is too much smaller comparing with PI controller.

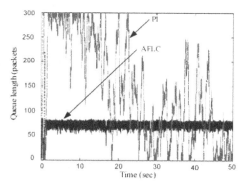

Fig. 8. Queue evaluation (FTP+HTTP)

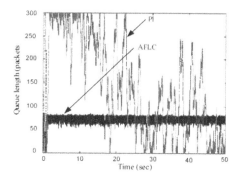

Fig. 9. Queue evaluation (FTP+UDP)

Finally, we evaluate the integrated performance of AFLC using one relatively real scenario, i.e., the number of active flows is changeable, which has 270 FTP flows, 400 HTTP connections and 30 UDP flows. Figs. 10 and 11 show the evaluation of queue controlled by AFLC and PI controllers, respectively. It is clear that the integrated performance of AFLC controller, namely transient and steady state responses is superior to that of PI controller. The AFLC controller is always keeping the queue length at the reference value, even if the network loads abruptly change, but PI controller has the inferior adaptability. In other words, the former is more powerful, robust and adaptive than the later one, which is in the favor of achievement to the objectives of the AQM policy.

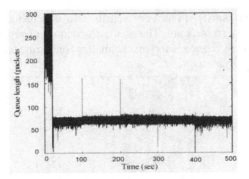

Fig. 10. Queue evaluation (AFLC)

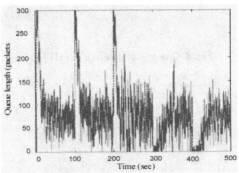

Fig. 11. Queue evaluation (PI)

5 Conclusions

In this paper, an adaptive fuzzy logic based controller was applied to TCP/AQM networks for the objective of queue management and congestion avoidance. For this purpose, a linearized model of the TCP flow was considered. A candidate Lyapunov function is employed in the adaptive law synthesis to ensure convergence. We took a complete comparison between performance of the proposed AFLC and classical PI controller under various scenarios. The conclusion was that the integrated performance of AFLC was superior to that of PI one.

References

[1]   Barden, B. et al., Recommendation on queue management and congestion avoidance in the internet, REC2309, April 1998.

[2]   Jalili-Kharaajoo, M., Application of robust fuzzy adaptive second-order sliding-mode control to active queue management, Lecture Notes in Computer Science, 2957, pp.109-119, 2004.

[3]   S. Ryu, C. Rump and C. Qiao, A Predictive and Robust Active Queue Management for Internet Congestion Control, in Proc. Eighth IEEE International Symposium on Computers and Communication (ISCC'03), Antalya, Turkey, 2003.

[4]   S. Ryu, C. Rump, and C. Qiao. Advances in Internet congestion control. *IEEE Communication Survey and Tutorial*, 2002.

[5]   R. Fengyuan, L. Chuang, Y. Xunhe, S. Xiuming, and W. Fubao, A Robust Active Queue Management algorithm based on Sliding Mode Variable Structure Control. in *Proc. INFOCOM'2002*, 21, pp.13–20, 2002.

[6]   Floyd, S. and Jacobson, V., Random early detection gateway for congestion avoidance, IEEE/ACM Trans. Networking, August 1993.

[7]   C. V. Hollot, V. Misra, D. Towsley, and W. Gong. A control theoretic analysis of RED. In *Proc. of INFOCOM'2001*, pages 1510–1519, April 2001.

[8]   Firoiu, V. and Borden, M., A study of active queue management for congestion control, in Proc. INFOCOM, March 2000.

[9]   May, M., Bonald, T. and Bolot, T., Analytic evaluation of RED performance, in Proc. INFOCOM, March 2000.

[10] S. Floyd and V. Paxson. Difficulties in simulating the Internet, *IEEE/ACM Transactions on Networking*, 9(4), pp.392–403, 2001.

[11] Zadeh, L.A., Fuzzy sets, Inf. Control (1965), 338-353.

[12] Jalili-Kharaajoo, M., and Ebrahimirad, H., Improvement of second order sliding mode control applied to position control of induction motors using fuzzy logic, Lecture Notes in Artificial Intelligence, 2715, 2003.

[13] Trebi-Ollennu, A., Robust output tracking for MIMO nonlinear systems: An adaptive fuzzy systems approach. IEE Proceedings, Control Theory and Applications 144(6): 537-544, 1997

[14] Li-Xin, W., Adaptive Fuzzy Systems and Control Design and Stability Analysis, Prentice Hall, 1994.

[15] Trebi-Ollennu, A. and J. M. Dolan, Adaptive Fuzzy Throttle Control for an All Terrain Vehicle, 2000.

[16] Trebi-Ollennu, A., Robust nonlinear control designs using adaptive fuzzy systems, Ph.D. Thesis. Department of Aerospace & Guidance Systems, Royal Military College of Science, Shrivenham, Cranfield University, 1996.

[17] Misra, V., Gong, W.B. and Towsley, D., Fluid-based analysis of network of AQM routers supporting TCP flows with an application to RED, in Proc. ACM/SIGCOMM, 2000.

[18] Hollot, C., Misra, V., Towsley, D. and Gong, W.B., On designing improved controllers for AQM routers supporting TCP flows, in Proc. INFOCOM, 2001.

[19] Misra, V., Gong, W.B. and Towsley, D., Analysis and design an adaptive virtual queue (AVQ) algorithm for active queue management, in Proc. ACM/SIGCOMM, 2001.

[20] Kelly, F.P., Maulloo, A. and Tan, D., Rate control in communication networks, Journal of the Operation research Society, 49, pp.237-252, 1998.

[21] Athuraliya, S., Lapsley, D.E. and Low, S.H., Random early marking for internet congestion control, in Proc. Globecom, 1999.

Modeling and Analysis
of Dual Block Multithreading

W.M. Zuberek

Department of Computer Science, Memorial University
St.John's, Canada A1B 3X5

Abstract. Instruction level multithreading is a technique for tolerating long–latency operations (e.g., cache misses) by switching the processor to another thread instead of waiting for the completion of a lengthy operation. In block multithreading, context switching occurs for each initiated long–latency operation. However, processor cycles during pipeline stalls as well as during context switching are not used in typical block multithreading, reducing the performance of a processor. Dual block multithreading introduces a second active thread which is used for instruction issuing whenever the original (main) thread becomes inactive. Dual block multithreading can be regarded as a simple and specialized case of simultaneous multithreading when two (simultaneous) threads are used to issue instructions for a single pipeline. The paper develops a simple timed Petri net model of a dual block multithreading and uses this model to estimate the performance improvements of the proposed dual block multithreading.

Keywords: Block multithreading, instruction issuing, pipelined processors, timed Petri nets, performance analysis, event–driven simulation.

1 Introduction

Continuous progress in manufacturing technologies results in the performance of microprocessors that has been steadily improving over the last decades, doubling every 18 months (the so called Moore's law [4]). At the same time, the capacity of memory chips has also been doubling every 18 months, but the performance has been improving less than 10% per year [5]. The latency gap between the processor and its memory doubles approximately every six years, and an increasing part of the processor's time is spent on waiting for the completion of memory operations [8]. Matching the performances of the processor and the memory is an increasingly difficult task [9].

Techniques which tolerate long–latency memory accesses include out–of–order execution of instructions and instruction–level multithreading. The idea of out–of–order execution is to execute, during the waiting for the completion of a long–latency operation, instructions which (logically) follow the long–latency one, but which do not depend upon the result of this long–latency operation. Since out–of–order execution exploits instruction–level concurrency using the

M. Núñez et al. (Eds.): FORTE 2004 Workshops, LNCS 3236, pp. 209–219, 2004.

existing sequential instruction stream, it conveniently maintains code–base compatibility [6]. In effect, the instruction stream is dynamically decomposed into micro–threads, which are scheduled and synchronized at no cost in terms of executing additional instructions. Although this is desirable, speedups using out–of–order execution on superscalar pipelines are not so impressive, and it is difficult to obtain a speedup greater than 2 using 4 or 8–way superscalar issue [11]. Moreover, memory latencies are so long that out–of–order processors require very large instruction windows to tolerate them. A cache miss to main memory costs about 128 cycles on Alpha 21264 [13] and 330 cycles on a Pentium-4–like processor [10]. Large instruction windows mean design complexity, verification difficulty and increased power consumption [7], so the industry is not moving toward the wide–issue superscalar model [1]. In effect, it is often the case that up to 60 % of execution cycles are spent waiting for the completion of memory accesses [7].

Instruction–level multithreading [2], [3] tolerates long–latency memory accesses by switching to another thread (if it is available for execution) rather than waiting for the completion of the long–latency operation. If different threads are associated with different sets of processor registers, switching from one thread to another (called "context switching") can be done very efficiently [12].

In block multithreaded processors, the pipeline is stalled occasionally for one or more processor cycles because of the instruction dependencies. Since the trend in modern microprocessors is to increase the depth of the pipelines [10], and deep pipelines increase the probability of pipeline stalls due to instruction dependencies, the effects of pipeline stalls on the performance of processors can be quite significant. This paper proposes a variant of block multithreading in which an additional active thread is used to issue instruction in those processor cycles in which the main thread is inactive. The proposed approach is called dual block multithreading.

The main objective of this paper is to study the performance of dual block multithreaded processors in order to determine how effective the addition of the second active thread can be. A timed Petri net [14] model of multithreaded processors at the instruction execution level is developed, and performance results for this model are obtained by event–driven simulation. Since the model is rather simple, simulation results can be verified (with respect to accuracy) by state–space–based performance analysis (for combinations of modeling parameters for which the state spaces remains reasonably small).

2   Petri Net Models

A timed Petri net model of a simple block multithreaded processor at the instruction execution level is shown in Fig.1 (as usually, timed transitions are represented by solid bars, and immediate ones, by thin bars). For simplicity, Fig.1 shows only one level of memory; this simplification is removed further in this section.

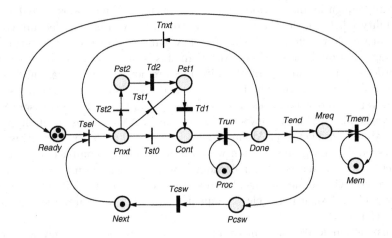

Fig. 1. Petri net model of a block multithreaded processor

Ready is a pool of available threads; it is assumed that the number of of threads is constant and does not change during program execution (this assumption is motivated by steady–state considerations). If the processor is idle (place *Next* is marked), one of available threads is selected for execution (transition *Tsel*). *Pnxt* is a free-choice place with three possible outcomes: *Tst0* (with the choice probability p_{s0}) represents issuing an instruction without any further delay; *Tst1* (with the choice probability p_{s1}) represents a single-cycle pipeline stall (modeled by *Td1*), and *Tst2* (with the choice probability p_{s2}) represents a two–cycle pipeline stall (*Td2* and then *Td1*); other pipeline stalls could be represented in a similar way, if needed. *Cont*, if marked, indicates that an instruction is ready to be issued to the execution pipeline. Instruction execution is modeled by transition *Trun* which represents the first stage of the execution pipeline. It is assumed that once the instruction enters the pipeline, it will progress through the stages and, eventually, leave the pipeline; since these pipeline implementation details are not important for performance analysis of the processor, they are not represented here.

Done is another free-choice place which determines if the current instruction performs a long–latency access to memory or not. If the current instruction is a non–long–latency one, *Tnxt* occurs (with the corresponding probability), and another instruction is fetched for issuing. If long–latency operation is detected in the issued instruction, *Tend* initiates two concurrent actions: (i) context switching performed by enabling an occurrence of *Tcsw*, after which a new thread is selected for execution (if it is available), and (ii) a memory access request is entered into *Mreq*, the memory queue, and after accessing the memory (transition *Tmem*), the thread, suspended for the duration of memory access, becomes "ready" again and joins the pool of threads *Ready*.

212   W.M. Zuberek

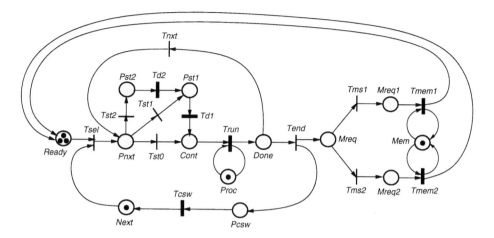

Fig. 2. Petri net model of a block multithreaded processor with a two–level memory

The choice probability associated with *Tend* determines the runlength of a thread, ℓ_t, i.e., the average number of instructions between two consecutive long–latency operations; if this choice probability is equal to 0.1, the runlength is equal to 10, if it is equal to 0.2, the runlength is 5, and so on.

The number of memory ports, i.e., the number of simultaneous accesses to memory, is controlled by the initial marking of *Mem*; for a single port memory, the initial marking assigns just a single token to *Mem*, for dual-port memory, two tokens are assigned to *Mem*, and so on.

In a similar way, the number of simultaneous threads (or instruction issue units) is controlled by the initial marking of *Next*. For a model of dual block multithreading, the initial marking of *Next* is 2.

Memory hierarchy can be incorporated into the model shown in Fig.1 by refining the representation of memory. In particular, levels of memory hierarchy can be introduced by replacing the subnet *Tmem–Mem* by a number of subnets, each subnet for one level of the hierarchy, and adding a free–choice structure which randomly selects the submodel according to probabilities describing the use of the hierarchical memory. Such a refinement, for two levels of memory, is shown in Fig.2, where *Mreq* is a free–choice place selecting either level-1 (submodel *Mem–Tmem1*) or level-2 (submodel *Mem–Tmem2*).

The effects of memory hierarchy can easily be compared with a uniform, non–hierarchical memory by selecting the parameters in such a way that the average access time of the hierarchical model (Fig.2) is equal to the access time of the non–hierarchical model (Fig.1).

For convenience, all temporal properties of the model are expressed in processor cycles, so, the occurrence times of *Trun*, *Td1* and *Td2* are all equal to 1 (processor cycle), the occurrence time of *Tcsw* is equal to the number of processor cycles needed for context switching (which is equal to 1 for many of the

Table 1. Block multithreading modeling parameters and their typical values

symbol	parameter	value
n_t	number of available threads	1,...,10
ℓ_t	thread runlength	10
t_{cs}	context switching time	1,5
t_m	average memory access time	10
p_{s1}	prob. of one–cycle pipeline stall	0.2
p_{s2}	prob. of two–cycle pipeline stall	0.1

following performance analyses), and the occurrence time of $Tmem$ is the average number of processor cycles needed for a long–latency access to memory.

The main modeling parameters and their typical values are summarized in Tab.1. The number of available threads, n_t, changes from 1 to 10 in order to check if a large number of threads has can provide a reasonable improvement of the processor's performance. Thread runlength, ℓ_t, equal to 10 corresponds to the (primary) cache miss of 10%. Context switching times equal to 1 and 5 are used to check the sensitivity of performance results on the duration of context switching. The average memory access time, t_m, of 10 processor cycles matches the thread runlength, ℓ_t, providing the balanced utilization of the processor and the memory; if $t_m > \ell_t$, the memory becomes the bottleneck which limits the performance of the system; if $\ell_t > t_m$, the memory has little influence on the system's performance. The probabilities of pipeline stalls, p_{s1} and p_{s2}, correspond to the probabilities of data hazards used in [5].

3 Performance Results

The utilization of the processor, as a function of the number of available threads, for a "standard" processor (i.e., a processor with a single instruction issue unit) is shown in Fig.3.

The asymptotic value of the utilization can be estimated from the (average) number of empty instruction issuing slots. Since the probability of a single–cycle stall is 0.2, and probability of a two–cycle stall is 0.1, on average 40 % of issuing slots remain empty because of pipeline stalls. Moreover, there is an overhead of $t_{cs} = 1$ slot for context switching. The asymptotic utilization is thus $10/15 = 0.667$, which corresponds very well with Fig.3.

The utilization of the processor can be improved by introducing a second (simultaneous) thread which issues its instructions in the unused slots. Fig.4 shows the utilization of a dual block multithreaded processor, i.e., a processor issuing instructions to a single instruction execution pipeline from two (simultaneous) threads.

The utilization of the processor is improved by about 40 %.

A more realistic model of memory, that captures the idea of a two–level hierarchy, is shown in Fig.2. In order to compare the results of this model with

214   W.M. Zuberek

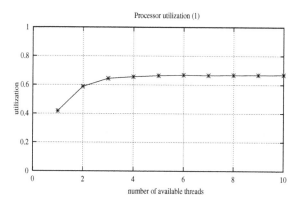

Fig. 3. Processor utilization for standard block multithreading; $l_t = 10$, $t_m = 10$, $t_{cs} = 1$, $p_{s1} = 0.2$, $p_{s2} = 0.1$

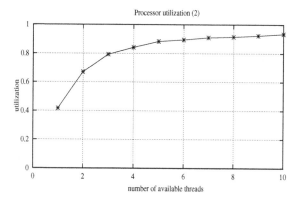

Fig. 4. Processor utilization for dual block multithreading; $l_t = 10$, $t_m = 10$, $t_{cs} = 1$, $p_{s1} = 0.2$, $p_{s2} = 0.1$

Fig.3 and Fig.4, the parameters of the two–level memory are chosen in such a way that the average memory access is equal to the memory access time in Fig.1 (where $t_m = 10$). Let the two levels of memory have access times equal to 8 and 40, respectively; then the choice probabilities are equal to 15/16 and 1/16 for level–1 and level–2, respectively, and the average access time is:

$$8 * \frac{15}{16} + 40 * \frac{1}{16} = 10.$$

The results for a standard block multithreaded processor with a two–level memory are shown in Fig.5, and for a dual block multithreaded processor in Fig.6.

The results in Fig.5 and Fig.6 are practically the same as in Fig.3 and Fig.4. This is the reason that the remaining results are shown for (equivalent) one-

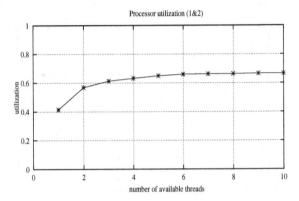

Fig. 5. Processor utilization for standard block multithreading with 2-level memory; $l_t = 10$, $t_m = 8 + 40$, $t_{cs} = 1$, $p_{s1} = 0.2$, $p_{s2} = 0.1$

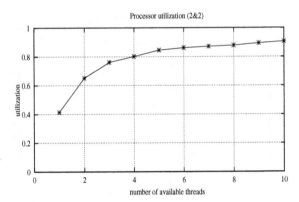

Fig. 6. Processor utilization for dual block multithreading with 2-level memory; $l_t = 10$, $t_m = 8 + 40$, $t_{cs} = 1$, $p_{s1} = 0.2$, $p_{s2} = 0.1$

level memory models; the multiple levels of memory hierarchy apparently have no significant effect on the performance results.

Dual multithreading is also quite flexible with respect to context switching times because the additional thread fills the instruction issuing slots which normally would remain empty during context switching. Fig.7 compares the utilization of the standard block multithreaded processor with $t_{cs} = 1$ (broken line) and $t_{cs} = 5$ (solid line). The reduction of the processor's utilization for $t_{cs} = 5$ is about 20 %, and is due to the additional 4 cycles of context switching which remain empty (out of 19 cycles, on average).

Fig.8 compares utilization of the dual block multithreaded processor for $t_{cs} = 1$ and $t_{cs} = 5$. The reduction of utilization is much smaller in this case and is within 10 %.

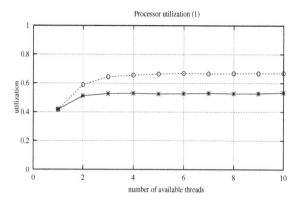

Fig. 7. Processor utilization for standard block multithreading; $l_t = 10$, $t_m = 10$, $t_{cs} = 1, 5$, $p_{s1} = 0.2$, $p_{s2} = 0.1$

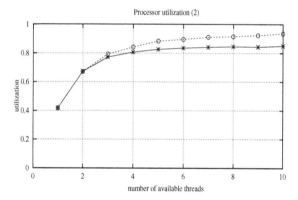

Fig. 8. Processor utilization for dual block multithreading; $l_t = 10$, $t_m = 10$, $t_{cs} = 1, 5$, $p_{s1} = 0.2$, $p_{s2} = 0.1$

4   Concluding Remarks

Dual block multithreading discussed in this paper is a means to increase the performance of processors by tolerating long–latency operations (block multi-threading) and pipeline stalls (dual multithreading). Its implementation is rather straightforward while the improvement of the utilization of processors can be quite significant, as shown in Fig.9.

However, the improved performance of dual multithreading can be obtained only if the system is balanced, or if the processor is the system's bottleneck. Fig.10 shows the utilization of the processor for standard (solid line) as well as dual multithreading (broken line); the utilizations of both processors are prac-tically identical because, in these particular cases, the memory is the system's bottleneck that restricts the performance of other components.

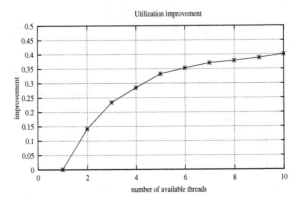

Fig. 9. The improvement of processor utilization due to dual block multithreading; $l_t = 10$, $t_m = 10$, $t_{cs} = 1$, $p_{s1} = 0.2$, $p_{s2} = 0.1$

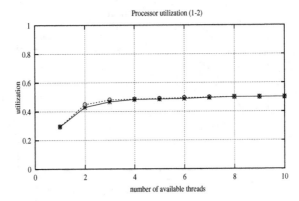

Fig. 10.   A comparison of processor utilization; $l_t = 10$, $t_m = 20$, $t_{cs} = 1$, $p_{s1} = 0.2$, $p_{s2} = 0.1$

All presented results indicate that the number of available threads, required for improved performance of the processor, is quite small, and is not greater than 4 threads. Performance improvement due to a larger number of available threads is rather insignificant.

Obtained processor utilization results are consistent with other studies of the performance of multithreaded architectures [16], [15]. The performance of distributed memory multithreaded multiprocessor systems can be compared with the results presented in this paper by assuming that the probability of accessing local nodes is equal to 1 (which means that the nodes can be analyzed in isolation).

The presented models of multithreaded processors are quite simple, and for small values of modeling parameters (n_t, n_p, n_s) can be analyzed by the explorations of the state space. The following table compares some results for the standard block multithreaded processor:

n_t	number of states	analytical utilization	simulated utilization
1	11	0.417	0.417
2	107	0.591	0.587
3	207	0.642	0.643
4	307	0.658	0.655
5	407	0.664	0.663

For a dual block multithreaded processor the comparison is:

n_t	number of states	analytical utilization	simulated utilization
1	11	0.417	0.417
2	130	0.672	0.670
3	320	0.793	0.793
4	642	0.848	0.841
5	972	0.878	0.883

The simulation–based results are very similar to the analytical results obtained from the analysis of states and state transitions. It should not be surprising that for more complex models the state space can become quite large. For example, the state space for the dual multithreaded processor increases by more than 300 state for each additional thread (above 3). Analytical solution of very large systems of linear equations (which describe the stationary probabilities of states) may require special numerical techniques to provide the necessary accuracy. Therefore, discrete–event simulation of net models is an attractive alternative to exhaustive state space exploration of complex models.

Finally, it should be noted that the presented model is oversimplified with respect to the probabilities of pipeline stalls and does not take into account the dependence of stall probabilities on the history of instruction issuing. In fact, the model is "pessimistic" in this regard, and the predicted performance, presented in the paper, is worse than the expected of real systems. On the other hand, the simplicity of the presented model is likely to outweight its simplification(s) as their effects are not expected to be significant.

References

[1] Burger, D., Goodman, J. R., "Billion–transistor architectures: there and back again"; IEEE Computer, vol.37, no.3, pp.22-28, 2004. 210

[2] Byrd, G. T., Holliday, M. A., "Multithreaded processor architecture"; IEEE Spectrum, vol.32, no.8, pp.38-46, 1995. 210

[3] Dennis, J. B., Gao, G. R., "Multithreaded architectures: principles, projects, and issues"; in "Multithreaded Computer Architecture: a Summary of the State of the Art", pp.1-72, Kluwer Academic 1994. 210

[4] Hamilton, S., "Taking Moore's law into the next century"; IEEE Computer, vol.32, no.1, pp.43-48, 1999. 209

[5] Hennessy, J. L., Patterson, D. A., "Computer architecture – a qualitative approach" (3 ed.), Morgan Kaufman 2003. 209, 213

[6] Jesshope, C., "Multithreaded microprocessors – evolution or revolution"; in "Advances in Computer Systems Architecture" (LNCS 2823), pp.21-45, 2003. 210

[7] Mutlu, O., Stark, J., Wilkerson, C., Patt, Y. N., "Runahead execution: an effective alternative to large instruction windows"; IEEE Micro, vol.23, no.6, pp.20-25, 2003. 210

[8] Sinharoy B., "Optimized thread creation for processor multithreading"; The Computer Journal, vol.40, no.6, pp.388-400, 1997. 209

[9] Sohi, G. S., "Microprocessors – 10 years back, 10 years ahead"; in "Informatics: 10 Years Back, 10 Years Ahead" (Lecture Notes in Computer Science 2000), pp.209-218, 2001. 209

[10] Sprangle, E., Carmean, D., "Increasing processor performance by implementing deeper pipelines"; Proc. 29-th Annual Int. Symp. on Computer Architecture, Anchorage, Alaska, pp.25-34, 2002. 210

[11] Tseng, J., Asanovic, K., "Banked multiport register files for high–frequency superscalar microprocessor"; Proc. 30-th Int. Annual Symp. on Computer Architecture, pp.62-71, 2003. 210

[12] Ungerer, T., Robic, G., Silc, J., "Multithreaded processors"; The Computer Journal, vol.43, no.3, pp.320-348, 2002. 210

[13] Wilkes, M. V., "The memory gap and the future of high-performance memories"; ACM Architecture News, vol.29, no.1, pp.2-7, 2001. 210

[14] Zuberek, W. M., "Timed Petri nets – definitions, properties and applications"; Microelectronics and Reliability (Special Issue on Petri Nets and Related Graph Models), vol.31, no.4, pp.627-644, 1991. 210

[15] Zuberek, W. M., "Analysis of pipeline stall effects in block multithreaded multiprocessors"; Proc. 16-th Performance Engineering Workshop, Durham, UK, pp.187-198, 2000. 217

[16] Zuberek, W. M., "Analysis of performance bottlenecks in multithreaded multiprocessor systems"; Fundamenta Informaticae, vol.50, no.2, pp.223-241, 2002. 217

Performance Evaluation of a SNAP-Based Grid Resource Broker

Iain Gourlay, Mohammed Haji, Karim Djemame, and Peter Dew

School of Computing, University of Leeds
Leeds, LS2 9JT, UK
{iain,mhh,karim,dew}@comp.leeds.ac.uk

Abstract. Resource brokering is an essential component in building effective Grid systems. The paper discusses the performance evaluation of a broker that is designed within the SNAP (Service Negotiation and Acquisition Protocol) framework and focuses on applications that require resources on demand. The performance evaluation is carried out using a combination of mathematical modelling and simulation. Initial results are presented, indicating that the simulation and modelling are in good agreement.

1 Introduction

The Grid offers scientists and engineering communities high performance computational resources in a seamless virtual organisation [1]. These resources are diverse and heterogeneous in nature, spanning across multiple domains and are not owned or managed by a single administrator.

A core component, which is desirable in order to insulate the user from the Grid middleware complexities, is a resource broker, which performs the task of mapping application requirements to resources that can meet those requirements. Specifically, brokering is defined as the process of making scheduling decisions involving resources over multiple administrative domains [2]. This can include searching multiple administrative domains to use a single machine or scheduling a single job to use multiple resources at a single site or multiple sites. A Grid broker must be capable of making resource selection decisions in an environment where it has no control over the local resources, the resources are distributed, and information about these resources is often limited or stale.

A key goal of Grid computing is to deliver utility of computation, as defined by users' Quality of Service (QoS) requirements. One approach to providing this functionality is to use SNAP (Service Negotiation and Acquisition Protocol) [3]. SNAP provides a modular structure for managing the access process to and use of resources in a distributed heterogeneous environment such as the Grid. This protocol is an appropriate choice in the design and implementation of a user-centric broker, since it provides the means to negotiate and acquire resources that meet the user's application requirements through Service Level Agreements (SLAs) [3]. Specifically, it defines a general framework within which resource acquisition, task submission and binding of task to resources can be carried out, as dictated by the ability of those resources to satisfy the needs of the user.

M. Núñez et al. (Eds.): FORTE 2004 Workshops, LNCS 3236, pp. 220-232, 2004.

In [5] the authors discussed the implementation of a simple SNAP-based resource broker and a more sophisticated SNAP broker, following a three-phase commit protocol. It was shown that, when certain specific scenarios occur, the use of the three-phase commit protocol provides a performance enhancement over the simple SNAP broker, in terms of the time it takes for a job to be successfully submitted and begin execution. However, the likelihood that these scenarios occur under realistic job traffic conditions was not addressed experimentally.

This paper presents an approach, based on mathematical modelling and simulation, to evaluating the performance of the SNAP resource brokers. This approach allows a wide range of possible traffic conditions to be considered. The traffic model on which the analysis is based is expressed using queueing theory [6].

The paper is organised as follows. Section 2 describes the architecture and protocols for the simple and three-phase commit SNAP brokers. Section 3 discusses the traffic model, used to provide the framework for modelling and simulation. Section 4 discusses the mathematical modelling, followed by a description of the simulation in section 5. Experiments and results are presented and discussed in section 6, followed by conclusions and indications of future work in section 7.

2   SNAP-Based Resource Brokers

SNAP is motivated by the requirement, in a Grid environment, to reconcile the needs of the users with those of the resource providers. This section presents a SNAP broker architecture and the broker protocols considered in this research. Details of SNAP can be found in [3].

2.1 SNAP Broker Architecture

Figure 1 shows the components that comprise the broker. In this architecture, the broker begins by parsing the user requirements submitted through a Grid portal. The second layer uses a *Matchmaker,* supplied with the parsed user requirements, to contact a Knowledge Bank (KB). The latter is a repository that stores static information on all resources. The broker can access this information on behalf of the user for each resource he/she is entitled to use. The information stored in the KB as attributes include the number of CPUs, the operating system, memory, storage capacity and past behaviour performance of a resource. This enables the broker to filter out all resources that could handle the job's needs prior to contact with the MDS, thereby avoiding contacting resources, which are unable to support the user's application. Further discussion on this can be found in [5].

Referring to Figure 1, on receiving the information the Matchmaker forwards the details to the *Decision Maker* that evaluates the information and categorises the potential resources into two categories by tagging them as either *blue* or *white.* This corresponds to their significance, i.e. that some resources are more 'desirable' (blue) than others (white). The issue of which attributes could be used to classify resources in this way is currently being addressed.

The *Resource Gatherer* based on the information received from the Decision Maker queries the information provider on each selected resource to gather dynamic information on their status. The Globus Monitoring and Directory Service [8] (MDS) is used in this architecture to gather dynamic information.

Once all queries have reported back to the broker the information is forwarded to the *Co-ordinator*, which nominates the resources to handle the tasks and secures them for utilisation through the use of immediate reservation. Once the resources are secured the final procedure is executed by the *Dispatcher* by submitting the task and binding it to the resources.

2.2 SNAP Broker Protocols

The simple SNAP broker works according to the following protocol:

1. Having received the user requirements, the matchmaker contacts the knowledge bank, which returns the attributes for the resources the user has access to and that are capable of supporting the job.
2. The matchmaker forwards the information to the decision maker, which prioritises resources, tagging them blue and white, corresponding to "high priority" and "adequate" respectively.
3. The decision maker passes this information onto the resource gatherer.
4. The resource gatherer contacts the MDS (the GRIS (Grid Resource Information Service) on each resource) to obtain up-to-date dynamic information about 'candidate' resources. In this step, probes are set up. This only occurs the first time step 4 is carried out. Probes do not need to be set up subsequently. These are only used in the simple SNAP broker, to support fast reservation of resources.
5. The dynamic information about the resources is passed to the co-ordinator, which makes a decision as to where the job should run. If insufficient resources are available, the co-ordinator informs the resource gatherer and step 4 is repeated. Otherwise the co-ordinator reserves the chosen resources. If this is unsuccessful (e.g. because another user has taken one or more of the chosen resources), return to step 4.

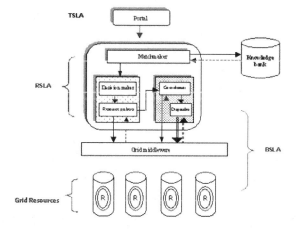

Fig. 1. A Grid resource broker architecture within the SNAP framework

Once resources have been secured, the simple SNAP broker can transfer any necessary data and submit the job for execution. However, as the following scenario illustrates, difficulties can arise in successfully securing resources.

Having received a user's request to run an application and details of the job requirements, a resource broker probes various sites that encompass resources, which could cater for the user's request. At the point of receiving a response from all providers, the broker begins co-allocating the task based on the information gathered. However time has elapsed since their last confirmation and other candidates (unknown to the broker) may have committed to some or all the resources it decided to use. If this occurs prior to reservation, alternative resources must be identified to replace those that are no longer available. This process could repeat itself and could lead into an oscillation between the broker and the resources without a successful job submission. Even if the job is eventually submitted successfully, such a scenario could significantly delay the execution start time. Consequently, the three-phase commit protocol was designed in order to reduce the likelihood of such a problem arising. The protocol is based on the idea of providing the broker with a vision of the resources through the use of probes. Hence the resources inform the broker when their status changes rather than the broker needing to contact resources to determine their current status. This is discussed in more detail in [5].

The three-phase commit broker works according to the following protocol (first three steps are as above):

4. The resource gatherer contacts the MDS (the GRIS on each resource) to obtain up-to-date dynamic information about 'candidate' resources. In this step, probes are set up. This only occurs the first time step 4 is carried out. Probes do not need to be set up subsequently. These probes listen for any changes in the status of resources. In addition they are used to support reservation.
5. The dynamic information about the resources is passed to the co-ordinator.
6. The co-ordinator makes a decision as to where the job should run. If insufficient resources are available, the co-ordinator waits until the probes inform it that sufficient resources are available to support the application.
7. If any resources are taken by other users, the broker is made aware of this by the probes. If this occurs, step 6 is repeated. Otherwise the co-ordinator reserves the chosen resources. If this is unsuccessful, return to step 6.

Once the resources are reserved, the dispatcher transfers any necessary files and submits the job.

3   Traffic Model

In order to model the behaviour of the SNAP-based resource brokers, a traffic model, which enables different realistic traffic conditions to be considered, is required. The approach taken here is based on queueing theory [6]. Initially a simple model was chosen, in order to enable a simple comparison between simulation and analytical results. This model is presented in section 3.1. The model was then extended to enable evaluation of the resource brokers under more realistic traffic conditions than was possible with the simple model. The extended model is presented in section 3.2.

3.1 Simple Traffic Model

It is assumed that each (single CPU) resource is a server and has a corresponding single-server queue. The queue capacity is initially set to infinity. Jobs are independently submitted to each queue, with random inter-arrival and service times (i.e. each queue is an M/M/1 queue). The broker needs to secure resources and submit jobs within this environment. The model is depicted in Figure 2.

The following parameters are used within this model:

Number of Processors (Servers)	P
Mean Service Time	T_s
Mean Arrival Rate	λ

Note that, with this model, the traffic on different resources does not display any correlation. Hence many realistic scenarios are not encapsulated by this model (e.g. users submitting jobs that require more than 1 resource). This is addressed in the extended model, discussed in the following section.

3.2 Extended Traffic Model

In order to account for correlations between traffic on different resources, a multi-server queue is introduced. As before, each server has an associated queue. However, incoming jobs to the system enter a multi-server queue. Each job has a service time (T_s) and number of resources (R) required associated with it. There are a number of possibilities regarding how jobs at the front of the multi-server queue are dealt with. For example:

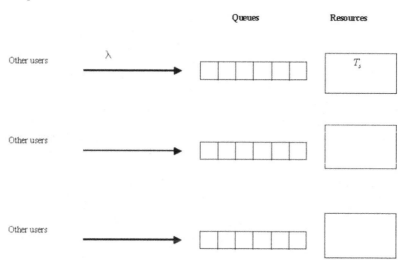

Fig. 2. Queueing system used in simple traffic model

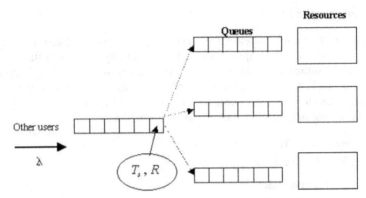

Fig. 3. Queueing system used in extended traffic model

1. When a job is at the front of the multi-server queue, it is sent to queues associated with those resources with the least items waiting in the local queue.
2. When a job is at the front of the multi-server queue, it is sent to local queues corresponding to randomly chosen resources.
3. When a job is at the front of the multi-server queues it is sent to local queues in a round-robin fashion, i.e. (for P resources) queue 1, queue 2, ...queue P, queue 1...

The jobs arriving in the multi-server queue have random inter-arrival and service times, while the number of resources required for a particular job is chosen at random from the set $\{1,2,4,8,16,32\}$. This is illustrated in Fig. 3.

4   Mathematical Modelling

This section presents a mathematical analysis, carried out in order to provide expressions that enable the performance of the SNAP based brokers to be evaluated. Specifically, expressions are obtained, enabling the average time taken (for each broker) between receiving user requirements and the job being submitted for execution. This is carried out using the simple traffic model, presented in section 3.1. These results enable the simulation and analytical results to be compared. If the results from these two approaches agree, this provides evidence to support the validity of further simulation results based on the extended traffic model, where the analytic approach would be impractical.

The following parameters are used in the analysis of the broker. The steps referred to are those given in section 2.3, where the SNAP broker protocols are presented.

J: Number of resources required by the job submitted.

t_{KB} :   The time taken for steps 1-3 of the broker protocols.

t_{mds} :   The time taken for step 4 of the broker protocols.

t_{dec} :   The time taken by the Co-ordinator to decide where the job should run.

t_{res} :   The time it takes to reserve resources.

The time taken to submit the job once resources have been reserved is not included in the analysis, since it is not dependent on which of the protocols (discussed in section 2.3) is used.

Section 4.1 presents the analysis for the simple SNAP broker and the corresponding analysis for the three-phase commit broker is given in section 4.2.

4.1 Simple SNAP Broker

Step 5 takes $t_{dec} + t_{res}$. It is assumed that

$$t_{mds} = t_{mds(1)} + t_{mds(2)} \tag{1}$$

Here $t_{mds(1)}$ is the time, for gathering resource information, during which any change to resource status (on any resource being contacted) will be picked up and $t_{mds(2)}$ is the time during which changes to status will not be identified.

The total time the broker takes, from receiving user requirements until resources are secured, in the absence of other traffic is,

$$E\big(t_{simple}\,(no\ traffic)\big) = t_{KB} + t_{mds} + t_{dec} + t_{res} \tag{2}$$

Note that the above time does not account for the possibility that certain steps may need to be repeated. Referring to the broker protocol, for step 5, there is an overhead associated with the possibility that step 4 needs to be repeated due to insufficient resources being available the first time the MDS is contacted. Each time this is carried out, the time taken is $(t_{mds} + t_{dec})$. Let the average time taken to complete this operation be $E(t_{mds/dec})$. Note that

$$E(t_{mds/dec}) = \overline{n}(t_{mds} + t_{dec}) \tag{3}$$

Here, $\overline{n}$ is the mean number of times that there are insuffient resources available when the MDS is contacted. This means that $(t_{mds} + t_{dec})$ must be replaced by $E(t_{mds/dec})$ in equation (2).

There is an additional overhead associated with the possibility that a chosen resource is taken prior to successful reservation. In order to explain the effect of this overhead on equation (2), consider the following scenario. Suppose an event, A occurs, taking time T_A. If the event fails, then it must be repeated until it succeeds. Let the probability that the event fails on a given trial be P_f. In that case, the entire process takes an average time given by,

$$E(t_{total}) = (1 - P_f)T_A \sum_{n=1}^{\infty} P_f^{n-1} n \tag{4}$$

The summation in equation (4) is equal to $1/(1-P_f)^2$. Hence,

$$E(t_{total}) = \frac{T_A}{(1-P_f)} \tag{5}$$

In the case under consideration, event A corresponds to contacting the MDS, making a decision as to where the job should run and reserving resources. The time taken (T_A) is therefore $(E(t_{mds/dec})+t_{res})$. Failure is caused by one or more chosen resources being taken by other users, prior to the completion of reservation. For the simple traffic model, the probability that a resource that is free at time t_0 is still free at time t_1 is $e^{-\lambda(t_1-t_0)}$ where λ is the mean arrival rate. Here the time interval Δt involved ranges from after the $t_{mds(1)}$, when the MDS is contacted, until reservation is successfully completed. Hence,

$$\Delta t = t_{mds(2)} + t_{dec} + t_{res} \tag{6}$$

Hence, the probability that one of the J resources chosen to run the job is taken prior to successful reservation is given by,

$$P_{fail} = 1 - e^{-\lambda J \Delta t} \tag{7}$$

This leads to the following expression for the average time the simple broker takes from receiving the users' requirements until resources are successfully reserved.

$$E(t_{simple}) = t_{KB} + e^{\lambda J \Delta t}(E(t_{mds/dec}) + t_{res}) \tag{8}$$

4.2 Three-Phase Commit Broker

In the case of the three-phase commit broker, the MDS is contacted only once, since the probes are used to provide the broker with a vision of the resources. However, there is still an overhead associated with the possibility that other users could take resources prior to the successful completion of the decision as to where the job should run. Hence t_{dec} is replaced with $E(t_{dec/three-phase})$. In addition, once the broker makes a decision, it may fail to successfully reserve resources, if another user takes one or more of the chosen resources, during the time interval t_{res}. Using the same reasoning as given above for the simple broker to calculate the effect of this overhead, leads to the following expression for the average time it takes the three-phase commit broker to successfully secure resources.

$$E(t_{three-phase}) = t_{KB} + t_{mds} + e^{\lambda J t_{res}}(E(t_{dec/three-phase}) + t_{res}) \tag{9}$$

5   Simulation

The discrete event simulation tool used in obtaining these results has been developed from scratch. This tool, written in Java, adopts the process interaction approach to discrete-event simulation. The resource broker objects (in the physical system) are represented by logical processes. Interactions among physical processes (events) are modelled by timestamped messages exchanged among the corresponding logical processes. The programs developed for the simulation are executed using the traditional sequential simulation protocol (Global Event List) [9].

The objectives of the simulation experiments are twofold: 1) an observation of the behaviour of the broker in terms of time to secure resources, and 2) a comparison between the analytical and simulation results. Specifically, the simulator can be used to consider a wide range of traffic conditions, using both the simple and extended traffic models presented in section 3. Experiments using the simple model can be used to assess the validity of the results through comparison with the analytical results. Experiments can then be carried out, using the extended traffic model, enabling the effect of correlation of traffic across resources to be evaluated. In each case, the performance of the three-phase commit broker relative to the simple SNAP broker is of significant interest.

6   Experiments and Results

This section presents the experiments designed to study the behaviour of the SNAP brokers under a range of traffic conditions. The approach taken is to compare analytic and simulation results, obtained using the simple traffic model. This is used to validate the results obtained using the simulator. A wider range of results will then be obtained through simulation using the extended traffic model.

6.1 Experimental Parameters

The following parameter values will be used in the experiments described below. These are based on values obtained on a Grid testbed, with machines connected over a local area network using 100Mbps fast Ethernet [5]. Some of these values would differ considerably in a geographically distributed Grid environment. In particular, the time taken to submit a job and the time taken to contact the MDS would typically be larger on average. In addition the time taken to contact the MDS may vary considerably across different machines and widely separated locations. The effect of this will be considered in future experiments.

- Time taken to connect to knowledge bank: 0.268 sec.
- Time taken to filter out resources: 0.017sec.
- Time taken for the broker to decide on resources to be contacted and tag them: 0.003 sec.
- Hence $t_{KB} = 0.288\ s$.

- Contacting the MDS takes 8 sec on average. It is assumed that changes to resource status are picked up in the first 4 sec. Hence, $t_{mds(1)} = t_{mds(2)} = 4\,s$
- The time taken to decide on where to submit the job is 0.007 sec. Hence, $t_{dec} = 0.007\,s$.
- Reservation takes 2.881 sec. Hence, $t_{res} = 2.881\,s$.

6.2 Experimental Design

6.2.1   Experiment 1

In this experiment, the entire scenario, involving the broker submitting a job into the system using the simple traffic model, is considered. For the initial run, the mean service time and mean inter-arrival time are 300s and 350s. The total number of processors is 128. It is assumed that all 128 processors are appropriate for the job to be submitted by the broker.

Firstly, simulation is used to obtain values for $E\left(t_{mds/dec}\right)$ and $E\left(t_{dec/three-phase}\right)$ in the simple SNAP and three-phase commit brokers respectively.

The average time each broker takes to submit the job is measured as a function of number of processors (1,2,3...) required by the job.

The simulation and modelling results, for the simple SNAP and the three-phase commit broker are then compared. If good agreement is obtained between simulation and modelling then this will support the validity of future results, obtained through simulation, for experiment 2 discussed below.

6.2.2   Experiment 2

This experiment is closely related to experiment 1, except that the extended traffic model is used in place of the simple traffic model. The mean inter-arrival time to the multi-server queue is

$$\frac{1}{\lambda} = \frac{350\overline{R}}{128} \tag{10}$$

Here $\overline{R}$ is the average number of resources required by the jobs being submitted to the multi-server queue. In this case, since R is randomly chosen from the set $\{1,2,4,8,16,32\}$, $\overline{R}$ is 10.5. The mean service time associated with these jobs is 300s.

6.3 Experimental Results and Discussion

The results for experiments 1 and 2 are presented in this section. Simulation results were obtained over 1000 runs, i.e. 1000 job submissions by the broker for each point in the plots presented below.

Fig. 4. shows a comparison, for experiment 1, of the simulation results with the analytic results for both the simple SNAP and three-phase commit brokers. The average time taken from receiving user requirements until resources are successfully reserved are plotted as a function of the number of resources required by the job. The average inter-arrival time is 350 seconds and the average service time is 300 seconds. As can be seen from the figures, the simulation and modelling show good agreement, with the only significant discrepancy occurring for the simple broker when 16 resources are requested.

In Figure 5, the same results are used to compare the performance of the three-phase commit and simple SNAP brokers. Both the simulation and the analytic results indicate that the three-phase commit broker protocol provides a significant performance enhancement, particularly as the number of resources increases to 12 or more.

Results for experiment 2 have been obtained, using the random and round-robin approaches to distributed jobs with the extended traffic model, i.e. approaches 2 and 3 discussed in section 3.2. Figure 6 shows these results, with mean inter-arrival time given by equation (10) and mean service time of 300s. The three-phase commit broker again outperforms the simple SNAP broker, although the performance enhancement is considerably less than that obtained in experiment 1, where the simple traffic model is used. The reasons for this are currently being investigated.

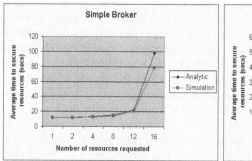 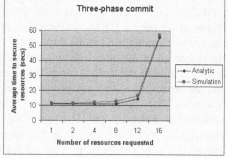

Fig. 4. Simulation vs. modelling results, showing the average time the simple SNAP and three-phase commit brokers take to secure resources. The mean inter-arrival time and mean service time are 350s and 300s respectively

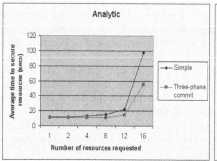 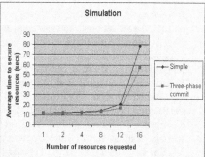

Fig. 5. Simulation and modelling results showing the average time the simple SNAP broker takes vs. the average time the three-phase commit broker takes to secure resources. The mean inter-arrival time and mean service time are 350s and 300s respectively

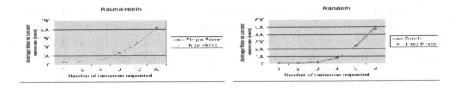

Fig. 6. Simulation results showing the average time the simple SNAP and three-phase commit brokers take secure resources when the extended traffic model is used. Results are shown for random selection and round-robin selection of local queues

7 Conclusions and Future Work

A simple SNAP broker and a strengthened three-phase commit protocol have been presented. An approach to evaluating the performance of these brokers, through modelling and simulation has been discussed. This is based on using a queueing theory to develop a traffic model. A simple traffic model has been used, in order to validate the simulation results through the use of mathematical modelling. The results for presented in this paper show good agreement between modelling and simulation. Results are also presented, comparing the performance of the simple SNAP broker and the three-phase commit broker in terms of the average time it takes to secure resources. The results indicate that the three-phase commit broker does provide a performance enhancement. The significance of this performance enhancement is to be investigated by considering a wider range of parameter values (e.g. varying inter-arrival and service times, number of resources in the system and time it takes to contact resources). In addition, more sophisticated traffic models are to be considered.

References

[1]   I. Foster, C. Kesselman, S. Tuecke. "The Anatomy of the Grid: Enabling Scalable Virtual Organizations". International Journal. Supercomputer Applications, 15(3), 2001.

[2]   J.M. Schopf. "A General Architecture for Scheduling on the Grid". Technical Report, Argonne National Laboratory ANL/MCS-P1000-10002.

[3]   K. Czajkowski, I. Foster, C. Kesselman, V. Sander, S. Tuecke. "SNAP: A Protocol for Negotiating Service Level Agreements and Coordinating Resource Management in Distributed Systems". In Proceedings of the 8th Workshop on Job Scheduling Strategies for Parallel Processing, Edinburgh, Scotland, July 2002.

[4]   K. Krauter, R. Buyya, and M. Maheswaran. "A Taxonomy and Survey of Grid Resource Management Systems". International Journal of Software: Practice and Experience, Vol. 32, No. 2, Wiley Press, USA, February 2002.

[5]   Mohammed H Haji, Peter M. Dew, Karim Djemame, Iain Gourlay. "A SNAP-based Community Resource Broker using a Three-Phase Commit Protocol". In Proceedings of 18th IEEE International Parallel and Distributed Processing Symposium, Santa Fe, New Mexico, April 2004.

[6]   L. Kleinrock, R. Gail, "Queueing Systems: Problems and Solutions", Wiley, 1996.

[7]   R. Buyya, D. Abramson and J. Giddy. "Nimrod/G: An Architecture for a Resource Management and Scheduling System in a Global Computational Grid". In Proceedings of the 4th International Conference on High Performance Computing in Asia-Pacific Region (HPC Asia 2000), May 2000, Beijing, China. IEEE Computer Society Press.

[8]   S. Fitzgerald, I. Foster, C. Kesselman, G. von Laszewski, W. Smith, S. Tuecke. "A Directory Service for Configuring High-Performance Distributed Computations". Proc. 6th IEEE Symposium on High-Performance Distributed Computing, pp. 365-375, 1997.

[9]   A.M. Law and W.D. Kelton, "Simulation Modelling and Analysis", McGraw-Hill, 2000.

Describing IEEE 802.11 Wireless Mechanisms by Using the π-Calculus and Performance Evaluation Process Algebra

K.N. Sridhar[1] and Gabriel Ciobanu[2]

[1] School of Computing, National University of Singapore
`sridhark@comp.nus.edu.sg`
[2] Romanian Academy, Institute of Computer Science
`gabriel@iit.tuiasi.ro`

Abstract. IEEE 802.11 protocols are formally expressed using the π-calculus process algebra and a performance evaluation process algebra. We first describe the handoff mechanism in wireless LANs, and then the IEEE 802.11 MAC, a medium access control mechanism which is a variant of CSMA/CA. A 4-way handshake mechanism of IEEE 802.11 with fixed network topology is expressed using the π-calculus. The verification process for the specified protocols is briefly described; Mobility Workbench and PEPA Workbench are used as software tools for verification.

1 Introduction

Wireless devices and applications are gradually becoming part of our daily lives. In order to achieve the goal of offering better communication services, and provide universal connectivity to increasingly mobile users, it is important that a suitable standard for Wireless Local Area Networks (WLANs) be designed, and an approach to interconnect these WLANs to existing wired LANs be adopted. IEEE 802.11 is the wireless LAN standard, developed under IEEE project 802. It defines both medium access control and physical layers. In contrast to wired devices, in wireless network we cannot adopt medium access control schemes such as Carrier Sense Multiple Access with Collision Detection (CSMA/CD) in order to prevent simultaneous transmission on the channel. Instead, the IEEE 802.11 standard uses the Carrier Sense Multiple Access with Collision Avoidance (CSMA/CA) mechanism for wireless networks. Formal models have been successfully employed to specify communication protocols and to verify their properties over the last two decades. A verification process can be viewed in two steps: specifying a protocol, which might result in a model, and verifying the properties of the protocol. A formal specification is the definition of an object, or a class of objects, using a description technique. Each defined object reflects a real world entity. It is important to precisely understand the basic concepts or construction elements from which the real world entities are composed. In this paper we concentrate on the process calculi and algebras for expressing the IEEE 802.11 protocols.

M. Núñez et al. (Eds.): FORTE 2004 Workshops, LNCS 3236, pp. 233–247, 2004.
© Springer-Verlag Berlin Heidelberg 2004

Process algebra is a formalism to specify the behavior of systems in a systematic, precise, modular and hierarchical way. The basic building blocks are processes and channels. Process algebra is compositional, providing scalability by composing larger processes out of smaller ones. We refer to process algebras like CCS [8], π-calculus [8], Performance Evaluation Process Algebra [3] etc. The Calculus of Communicating Systems (CCS) was originally developed by Robin Milner in 1980, and supports the analysis of interacting processes. We can draw diagrams of the processes as circles, and the interactions between them as connecting lines. In CCS, the processes can die, or split into two, but new linkages cannot be created. By contrast, the π-calculus is able to create new links. The π-calculus generalizes CCS by transmitting names rather than values across send-receive channels, while preserving matching as the control structure for communication. Since variables may be channel names, computation can change the channel topology, and by this process mobility is supported. Milner emphasized the importance of identifying the "elements of interaction" [7], and the π-calculus extends the general model of λ-calculus [1] with interaction. Performance Evaluation Process Algebra (PEPA) is similar to CCS in several aspects [2]; the operators and their semantics are similar. However, PEPA differs from CCS by adding stochastic rates to the actions.

The paper concentrates on the modelling of the handoff procedure from GSM and the CSMA/CA 4-way handshake mechanism of WI-FI protocol (IEEE 802.11). The paper presents a description in the π-calculus of these mechanisms of the IEEE 802.11 protocols, and further provide a verification of the obtained specifications using the Mobility Workbench tool. The quantitative analysis is given by using the Performance Evaluation Process Algebra and exploiting the facilities of the PEPA Workbench tool. The outline of the paper is as follows: Section 2 provides an introduction to the π-calculus. Section 3 describes the protocols and provides their π-calculus specifications. A brief introduction to the Mobility Workbench and verification aspects are presented in Section 4. Section 5 presents the quantitative analysis using the Performance Evaluation Process Algebra (PEPA) specifications of the protocols, and PEPA Workbench to determine the backoff-duration values and their corresponding collision probability. Section 6 presents the conclusion.

2 π-Calculus

The π-calculus is a widely accepted model of interacting systems with dynamically evolving communication topology. It allows channels to be passed as data along other channels, and this introduces a channel mobility. An important feature of the π-calculus is that mobility is expressed by the changing configuration and connectivity among processes. This mobility increases the expressive power enabling the description of many high-level concurrent features. The π-calculus has a simple semantics and a tractable algebraic theory. The computational world of the π-calculus contains just processes (also called agents) and channels (also called names or ports). It models networks in which messages are sent from one site to another site and may contain links to active processes, or to other sites. The π-calculus is a general model of computation which takes interaction as a primitive.

3   IEEE 802.11 Standard

The basic responsibility of a Medium Access Control (MAC) protocol is to ensure that all the end systems on a local area network cooperate. Ideally, it requires that only one station transmit at a time. In 1997, the IEEE adopted the first standard for wireless LANS (WLANs), namely IEEE Standard 802.11-1997 [5]. This standard defines MAC and physical layers. The scope of this paper is limited to 802.11 MAC. IEEE 802.11 architecture is built around a Basic Service Set (BSS). A BSS is a set of stations that communicate one another with the same MAC protocol and compete for accessing the same shared wireless medium. IEEE 802.11 broadly works in two modes: Distributed Coordinated Function (DCF) and Point Coordinated Function (PCF). DCF is the basis of the CSMA/CA standard access mechanism. Similar to Ethernet, it checks to see that the medium is clear before transmitting. Nodes uses random backoff after each frame to avoid collision. PCF can be viewed as an optional extension to DCF. PCF provides contention-free services, and is restricted to infrastructure networks. In the first part of this section we will concentrate on the PCF mode, and describe the handoff procedure using π-calculus. In PCF mode, Access Points (AP) act as a point coordinator. APs are also termed as Base Stations (BS). Each Mobile Node (MN) is controlled by a single AP at any given point of time, and AP could control more than one mobile nodes. We concentrate on the movement of a node from the control of one AP to another AP.

3.1   IEEE 802.11 Handoff

An AP broadcasts a beacon signal periodically: typically the period is around 100ms. An MN scans the beacon signal and associates itself with the AP having the strongest beacon. The MN keeps track of the Received Signal Strength (RSS) of the beacons transmitted by the associated AP. When the RSS becomes weak, MN starts to scan for stronger beacons from neighboring APs. The scanning process can be either active or passive. In passive scanning, MN scans the beacon signal and associates itself with the new AP. In active scanning, MN sends a probe request to a targeted set of APs that are capable of receiving its probe. Each AP that receives a probe replies with a probe response. The MN chooses the AP with the strongest beacon or probe response and sends a reassociation request to the new AP. The reassociation request contains information about MN and its old AP. In reply, the new AP sends a reassociation response that has information about bit rates, station ID, and other information needed to resume communication. Once the MN starts communicating with the new AP, the handoff process is accomplished. To clarify the distinction between beacons and probes, we describe them here:

- AP broadcasts beacon periodically. In passive scanning, MN scans the beacon signal and associates itself with the AP with the strongest beacon.

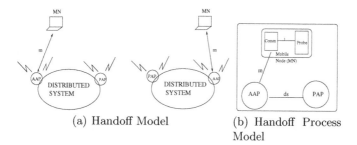

(a) Handoff Model   (b) Handoff Process
                               Model

Fig. 1. Handoff Mechanism and corresponding Process Model

- In active scanning, MN sends a probe request to a targeted set of APs
  that are capable of receiving its probe. Each AP that receives the probe
  responds with a probe response. MN chooses the AP with the strongest
  probe response.

Model. For simplicity, we will consider the case of only one mobile node, and two
access points. This allows us to concentrate on the essential features. Consider
the model as depicted in Figure 1a. The system consists of following objects: one
Active Access Point (AAP), one Passive Access Point (PAP), and one Mobile
Node (MN). Though AAP and PAP are access points with similar features, the
cycle of operations they perform are different. So, in our modelling we represent
them as different processes. The link Distributed System (DS) connects the
two access points. This link is fixed, in the sense that the name will not be
transmitted as objects in communications; intuitively this is part of a stationary
network. This is not accessible outside the system, so we consider it as local to
the system. In addition, each access point has one mobile link m representing
a radio channel. The AAP shares this m with the MN. This represents the fact
that AAP uses its m to communicate with the MN, while the m in PAP is unused
as yet. These m's are local names in a process and movement of channel m from
one process to another is considered.

The mobile node, as explained earlier, carries out probing to detect access
point, when it moves away from the current access point. This probing process
can be either active or passive. In our process model, as shown in Figure 1b, we
will not get into exact details of the probing mechanism, we just have a process
Probe. This process probes and obtains a channel for the process *Comm*, which
carries out the communication process. These two process communicate via the
channel l, which is local to MN. The *Probe* process, communicates with PAP
(either by beacons or probe packets), carries out reassociation and passes the
channel to *Comm* process which uses this to communicate with PAP. The handoff process is better understood by considering the specification in the π-calculus
and its corresponding MWB code.

Let us consider the specification of each component, one by one. A mobile
node is composed of two processes *Comm* and *Probe*. *Comm* communicates
with AAP, over the channel m, and with *Probe* over the channel l. It receives

the channel m from the *Probe* process and continues to communicate over the received channel.

$$Comm(l, m, data, disassoc) \stackrel{def}{=} \overline{m}\langle data \rangle.Comm(l, m, data, disassoc)$$
$$+l(mnew).\overline{m}\langle disassoc \rangle$$
$$.Comm(l, mnew, data, disassoc)$$

When mobility occurs, the *Probe* process carries out the probing and determines a passive access point. *Probe* and PAP share the channel, which is also termed as m. This m is passed to the *Comm* process over the local channel l. We have used same term m at both the places to indicate that only one m exist at any given point of time, and the nodes are sharing the same m.

$$Probe(l, m, reassoc) \stackrel{def}{=} \overline{m}\langle reassoc \rangle.\overline{l}\langle m \rangle.Probe(l, m, reassoc)$$

AAP receives data from MN and it might receive *disassoc* message at any time from the mobile node, when the node wants to disassociate itself from the AAP. When AAP receives *disassoc* message, it continues to behave as PAP.

$$AAP(m, data, disassoc) \stackrel{def}{=} m(c).([c = data]AAP(m, data, disassoc)$$
$$+[c = disassoc]PAP(m, data, disassoc))$$

Here the construction $[x = y]P + [x = z]Q$ is an extension with a matching operator of the π-calculus syntax presented in Section 2; it is similar to the usual "if-then-else" operator. The passive access point receives *reassoc* message from the *Probe* process of MN, and continues to behave as AAP.

$$PAP(m, data, disassoc) \stackrel{def}{=} m(reassoc).AAP(m, data, disassoc)$$

We now compose these processes to form a complete system and visualize how the handoff occurs. We will combine the process *Probe* of MN and PAP as P, which communicates over the channel m.

$$P(m, data, disassoc, l, reassoc) \stackrel{def}{=} (\nu m)(Probe(l, m, reassoc)|$$
$$PAP(m, data, disassoc))$$

Similarly, we will combine *Comm* process of MN with AAP as process Q, which communicates over channel m.

$$Q(l, m, data, disassoc) \stackrel{def}{=} (\nu m)(Comm(l, m, data, disassoc)|$$
$$AAP(m, data, disassoc))$$

Now, the complete system of handoff is the process P running in concurrent with process Q, where l is the local channel. The process P transfers the channel m to the process Q, and the state of access points get interchanged, from passive to active and vice versa.

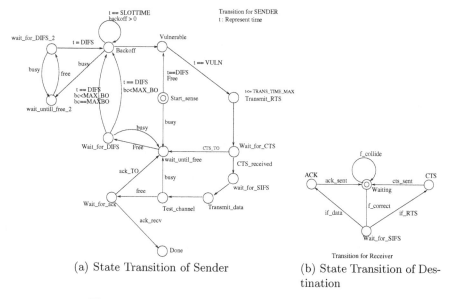

(a) State Transition of Sender

(b) State Transition of Destination

Fig. 2. State Transition for Sender and Destination

$$System(m, l, data, reassoc, disassoc) \stackrel{def}{=} (\nu l)(Q(l, m, data, disassoc)|$$
$$P(m, data, disassoc, l, reassoc))$$

In this model we do not consider the communication between access points. The decision criteria involved in probing mechanism, which results in identifying available links, is also not considered. However, these aspects can be directly added into the current specification, with few modifications and will not affect the formal representation of the handoff process.

3.2   DCF Mode: CSMA/CA

In this part, we concentrate on the DCF mode of IEEE 802.11. This mode is based on Carrier Sense Multiple Access-Collision Avoidance (CSMA/CA). The handshake mechanism involved in CSMA/CA can be either 2-way or 4-way. Here we consider the 4-way handshake mechanism. This mechanism has three components: sender, destination, and medium. We first consider the transition system of these components. These transition systems are extensions to the one used in [6]. Later, the model is described considering the specification of each and every component, and their subcomponents.

Transition System for Sender

Consider the transition system for sender as shown in Figure 2a. A sender with a new data packet to transmit monitors the channel activity. If the channel is idle for a period of time equal to DCF InterFrame Space (typically 128 μs), it transmits a control packet. Before actually transmitting the packet the node waits for small period VLUN. In this scheme, two small control packets are exchanged: Request To Send (RTS) and Clear To Send (CTS) packets. This exchange occurs before the data transmission process begins. The RTS packet contains information about the length of the frame, whereas the CTS acts as an acknowledgement for RTS. The sender sends the RTS packet and waits for the CTS acknowledgement. If the timeout occurs, or the channel is sensed busy, the sender goes to back off procedure. If the CTS is received before the timeout, the sender waits for Short InterFrame Space (SIFS) time, and sends the data. The time taken to send a packet is nondeterministic, and the success of transmission depends on whether collision has occurred or not.

DCF adopts an exponential backoff scheme. In this scheme, the sender first waits for the channel to be free for a period of DIFS, and sets its backoff value according to the random assignment backoff = RANDOM (bc), where bc is the backoff counter, which is updated (decremented by one) when the channel is idle for some standard duration (known as ASLOTTIME). However, if the channel is sensed busy in this slot, it waits until the channel is free, and then waits for DIFS before resuming its backoff procedure. When the backoff value reaches 0, the sender starts sending its packet. RANDOM (), is a uniformly distributed integer in $[0, (aCWmin + 1)2^{bc} - 1]$, where aCWmin is the initial value used (typically 15). The backoff process is highlighted in a dotted box in figure 2a. In our specification, we do not consider the timing aspects of the protocol. The state $Start\_sense$, covers both passive and active sense. The passive sense is described more in later subsections.

Transition System for Destination

Figure 2b shows the transition system for destination nodes. Each destination waits for an incoming packet. If the packet arrives correctly (event f_correct), then the destination waits for SIFS and subsequently sends either CTS packet or acknowledgement (ACK). CTS packet is sent in response to the RTS packet, whereas ACK is sent in response to the data packet. On the other hand, if the message arrives garbled (event f_collide), the destination node remains idle.

Transition System for Medium

The medium can be viewed as a communication line, whose end points are sender and destination. The transition system is as shown in Figure 3. In this transition system, we consider a medium with two senders and two destinations. This consideration is in accordance to our model which is explained in later subsections. Each node has the capability of sensing the medium. The medium will be initially in a free state, i.e., it is available for transmissions. From this point, receipt of a RTS or data packet from sender-1 or sender-2, triggers the transition to receive_DR_1 or receive_DR_2 respectively. This RTS or data packet can either finish successfully and return the medium to Medium_free state or collide with a transmission by another sender. Once a collision occurs, the medium enters into

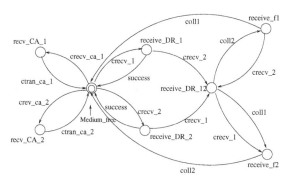

Fig. 3. State Transition of Medium

receive_DR_1_2 state, after which a collision event is sent to both the senders. This whole process can be viewed by considering the right-hand side of the state Medium_free in figure 3. The left-hand side of the state Medium_free of figure 3 explains the exchange of CTS and ACKs. The medium at state Medium_free can receive either CTS or ACK and carry out successful transmission of the same. We note that the situations where two CTS and ACKs collide are not modelled in this automaton. This is because we assume that such collisions are not possible.

Model. Now we are ready to specify the 4-way handshake mechanism of the 802.11 protocol, considering the components whose transition systems were described previously. We consider two senders and two destinations communicating over a channel MEDIUM. The complete system is described in Figure 4a.

Various components which constitute the handshake mechanism, and the way these components communicate with each other can be viewed as shown in the process model: Figure 4b. The functionalities are explained by considering each and every process.

The π-Calculus Expressions for the 802.11 Protocol

1. <u>Sender</u>
   The sender process is broken into three sub-processes: SenderSense, Sender-Transmit and PassiveSense. This definition of sender is the same for both Sender1 and Sender2. SenderSense queries the PassiveSense via channel psense and receives either true or false as a result. If it is true, it continues to query the medium. If the medium returns true for the query, it continues to behave as SenderTransmit. If any query results in false, then it continues to behave as SenderSense.
   We abbreviate SenderSense (psense,pctrl,sense,free,true,fals,cfre,ctru,cfls) and
   SenderTransmit (psense,pctrl,control, data,sense,free,true,fals,cfre,ctru, cfls,tran,coll,mesg,rts,dcts)

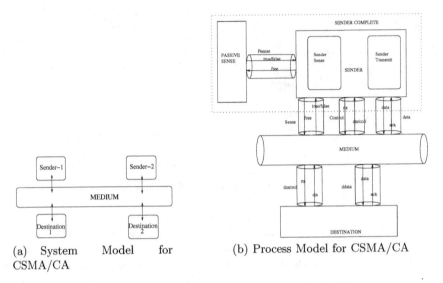

(a) System Model for CSMA/CA

(b) Process Model for CSMA/CA

Fig. 4. System and Process Model for CSMA/CA

$$SenderSense(psense, \ldots) \stackrel{def}{=} \overline{psense}\langle free \rangle . psense(pres).$$
$$([pres = fals]SenderSense(psense, \ldots)$$
$$+[pres = true]\overline{sense}\langle cfre \rangle . sense(cres).$$
$$([cres = cfls]SenderSense(psense, \ldots)$$
$$+[cres = ctru]SenderTransmit(psense, \ldots)))$$

SenderTransmit is the sub-process which handles the transmission part. This includes RTS/CTS, data and acknowledge exchanges. It communicates with the medium over two channels, *control* and *data*. Over the channel *control* it transmits RTS packets and receives either CTS packet or collision signal. Whereas, over *data* channel it transmits data packets and receives acknowledgement packets.

$$SenderTransmit(psense, \ldots) \stackrel{def}{=} \overline{control}\langle rts \rangle . control(tran).$$
$$([tran = coll]SenderSense(psense, \ldots)$$
$$+[tran = dcts]\overline{data}\langle mesg \rangle.$$
$$data(dack).SenderSense(psense, \ldots))$$

PassiveSense(psense, pctrl) subprocess receives the query from the Sender-Sense, and responds either true or false.

$$PassiveSense(psense, \ldots) \stackrel{def}{=} psense(free).\overline{psense}\langle true \rangle.$$
$$PassiveSense(psense, \ldots)$$
$$+psense(free).\overline{psense}\langle fals \rangle.$$
$$PassiveSense(psense, \ldots)$$

We compose the above subprocess into a single process called SenderComplete.

$$SenderComplete(psense, \ldots) \stackrel{def}{=} \nu psense(SenderSense(psense, \ldots)$$
$$|PassiveSense(psense, \ldots))$$

It is very important to note that in our definition of sender, we did not consider the backoff procedure. This helps us to concentrate only on the handshake mechanism, in which we are interested. Also, to include a backoff procedure we need the support of timers in π-calculus, which we consider in the next section. Passive sensing is another mechanism details of which are not considered.

2. Medium

The process Medium, is a little more complicated when compared to other processes. It communicates with both sender and destination. The definition below considers two senders and destinations. It shares channels, $sense, control$, and $data$ with sender, and channels, $dcontorl$, and $ddata$ with destination. The suffixes 1 and 2 refer to sender variables 1, 2 and destination variables 1, 2. We abbreviate

$$Medium(sense1, sense2, control1, control2$$
$$, data1, data2, dcontrol1, dcontrol2, ddata1, ddata2)$$
$$Medium(sense1, \ldots) \stackrel{def}{=} sense1(cfre1).(\overline{sense1}\langle ctru1\rangle.Medium(sense1, \ldots)$$
$$+\overline{sense1}\langle cfls1\rangle.Medium(sense1, \ldots))$$
$$+sense2(cfre2).(\overline{sense2}\langle ctru2\rangle.Medium(sense1, \ldots)$$
$$+\overline{sense2}\langle cfls2\rangle.Medium(sense1, \ldots))$$
$$+control1(rts1).(\overline{dcontrol1}\langle rts1\rangle$$
$$+control2(rts2).\overline{control1}\langle coll1\rangle.\overline{control2}\langle coll2\rangle.$$
$$Medium(sense1, \ldots))$$
$$+control2(rts2).(\overline{dcontrol2}\langle rts2\rangle$$
$$+control1(rts1).\overline{control1}\langle coll1\rangle.\overline{control2}\langle coll2\rangle.$$
$$Medium(sense1, \ldots))$$
$$+dcontrol1(dcts1).\overline{control1}\langle dcts1\rangle.$$
$$data1(mesg1).\overline{ddata1}\langle mesg1\rangle.$$
$$ddata1(dack1).\overline{data1}\langle dack1\rangle.Medium(sense1, \ldots)$$
$$+dcontrol2(dcts2).\overline{control2}\langle dcts2\rangle.$$
$$data2(mesg2).\overline{ddata2}\langle mesg2\rangle.$$
$$ddata2(dack2).\overline{data2}\langle dack2\rangle.Medium(sense1, \ldots)$$

3. Destination

$Destination(dcontrol, ddata)$ is the simplest of all processes. It communicates only with process Medium via $dcontrol$ and $ddata$. Like sender, the definition of destination is the same for both destination 1 and destination 2.

$$Destination(dcontrol, \ldots) \stackrel{def}{=} dcontrol(drts).\overline{dcontrol}\langle dcts\rangle.$$
$$Destination(dcontrol, \ldots)$$
$$+ddata(mesg).\overline{ddata}\langle dack\rangle.$$
$$Destination(dcontrol, \ldots)$$

4. **Complete System**
Once all the components are defined, we are now ready to define the complete system termed as

$$Mac(sense1, sense2, control1, control2, data1, data2, dcontrol1,$$
$$dcontrol2, ddata1, ddata2, psense2, pctrl2, psense1, pctrl1)$$

This is the combination of sender, medium and destination. The channels, *sense, control, data, dcontrol* and *ddata* are local to Mac.

$$Mac(sense1\ldots) \stackrel{def}{=} \nu sense1, control1, data1, dcontrol1, ddata1,$$
$$sense2, control2, data2, dcontrol2, ddata2$$
$$(SenderComplete1(psense1,\ldots)$$
$$|SenderComplete2(psense2,\ldots)$$
$$|Medium(sense1,\ldots)$$
$$|Destination1(dcontrol1,\ldots)$$
$$|Destination2(dcontrol2,\ldots))$$

4   Verification

Verification of software may be viewed as the process of checking some property P against either the software, or a model $\mathcal{M}$ of the software. For software in general, this is a hard problem, as the verification process may involve in-depth reasoning, perhaps requiring theorem provers to confirm parts of the verification. In this section we focus on a verification tool for the π-calculus, emphasizing on the bisimulation equivalences and properties as deadlocks.

Mobility Workbench (MWB) is a model checking tool for manipulating and analyzing mobile concurrent systems described in the π-calculus. It was developed by B.Victor, F.Moller, L-H.Eriksson and M.Dam [10]. It is written in Standard ML, and currently runs under the New Jersey SML compiler. An important functionality of the MWB is to decide the strong and weak open bisimilarity between two systems described as agents, as well as checking deadlocks and other properties of the agents (expressed as μ-calculus formulas).

In our work, we use this tool to carry out verification process. The π-calculus specifications of handoff process, and CSMA/CA 4-way handshake mechanism, which was described in the previous sections, was translated to MWB code. The syntax of MWB code is similar to that of the π-calculus, except for the fact that $\overline{m}\langle data\rangle$ is written $'m\langle data\rangle$. The handoff process is verified by stepping through the described agents. This stepping process allows the used to examine the state transitions. However, for CSMA/CA 4-way handshake mechanism we first verify properties such as deadlocks. The described system resulted in total size of 460 states and with deadlock free. We also carried out experiments for observational equivalence in which we show the equivalence of the described system with an ideal system, a system without any collisions and failures.

5   Quantitative Analysis

Performance Evaluation Process Algebra (PEPA) is similar to CCS in several aspects [2]; the operators and their semantics are similar. However, PEPA differs from CCS by adding rates to the actions. Each action has associated a stochastic delay which decides when an action takes place. With this addition of a stochastic delay, PEPA belongs to the class of stochastic process algebras. Syntactically, the composition symbol | of CCS is replaced by $\bowtie$ in PEPA; this new symbol is associated with a set of interacting ports. An action a of CCS is replaced in PEPA with (a, R), where R is the rate (delay) associated to a. The model generated by PEPA is a (continuous-time) Markov chain. The analysis of PEPA model consists of solving the probabilities of the states of the Markov chain.

PEPA Workbench is a software tool developed at the University of Edinburgh [9]. More information on the syntax used in PEPA Workbench can be found in [3]. PEPA Workbench is implemented in Standard ML, same as other workbenches like Concurrency Workbench and Mobility Workbench. A JAVA version of PEPA workbench is also available. We have used the JAVA version of PEPA workbench (TABASCO release).

First step in a performance analysis is to derive the model of the system under study using PEPA language. This model is loaded into PEPA workbench, and state space of the model is derived. Next step developed. This is a mandatory step to carry out state-based analysis. The last step is to carry out actual analysis using accompanying tools such as PEPA state finder, and PML_μ [4]. PEPA model for IEEE 802.11 is as shown in Table 1. The components of the model are similar to earlier model; two senders and receivers and a medium. The rate values indicating timeouts: ctsto and datato are set to 1. DIFS and SIFS are set to 2 and 1, respectively, and NAV value is set to 10. An important rate value to the analysis is the backoff duration. We vary this duration to carry out our analysis. For the sake of simplicity, we do not change this duration dynamically after every successful transmission. However according to IEEE 802.11 standard this duration depends on the transmission history. The specification given in Table 1 follows the syntax of PEPA Workbench.

The specification is loaded into the PEPA workbench and the corresponding state space is derived. The following steps are executed and confirmed: Parse successful. Exploring State Space. Number of States: 141. Calculating Transitions. Number of Transitions: 210. Approximate time to complete the derivation of the state space: 0.27sec.

The results show that there are no deadlocking states, and no zero or infinite-rate actions. The generated state space has 141 states and 210 transitions. As a consequence of these steps, the system generates three text files: `filename.table`, `filename.hash`, `filename.maple`. States of the model are associated with numbers, and they have associated a state table (`filename.table`), and a hash table (`filename.hash`). Using the `filename.maple`, the analysis can be carried out using a Maple tool. This can be used to solve steady state solutions corresponding to the underlying Markov chain. We have selected the linear Biconjugate Gradient method from the solvers options of the PEPA Workbench to derive the steady state solution. This results in the steady state probability values for all the states derived, and the values are stored in `filename.steadystates`.

5.1 State-Based Analysis

With the rate information associated with actions, we can see how long the system stays in each state and performing the actions. We use PEPA state finder

Table 1. PEPA Workbench description

```
retry=1.0; difs = 2.0; ctsto = 1.0; datato = 1.0;
sifs = 1.0; delay = 1.0; nav = 10; backoff-duration = 16;
//SENDER-1
sender10 = (gm, difs).sender11; sender11 = (rts1,nav).sender12;
sender12 = (c1,infty).sender13 + (coll1, infty). sender14;
sender13 = (data1, sifs).sender15;
sender14 = (rts1, backoff-duration). sender16;
sender15 = (a1,infty).sender10;
sender16 = (c1,infty).sender13 + (coll1, infty). sender11;
//SENDER-2
sender20 = (gm, difs).sender21; sender21 = (rts2,nav).sender22;
sender22 = (c2,infty).sender23 + (coll2, infty). sender24;
sender23 = (data2,sifs).sender25;
sender24 = (rts2, backoff-duration).sender26;
sender25 = (a2,infty).sender20;
sender26 = (c2,infty).sender23 + (coll2, infty).sender21;
//RECEIVER-1
recv10 = (r1,infty).recv11; recv11 = (cts1,sifs).recv12;
recv12 = (d1, datato).recv13; recv13 = (ack1,sifs).recv10;
//RECEIVER-2
recv20 = (r2,infty).recv21; recv21 = (cts2,sifs).recv22;
recv22 = (d2, datato).recv23; recv23 = (ack2,sifs).recv20;
//MEDIUM
medium0 = (rts1,infty).medium1 + (cts1,infty).medium2 +
+ (data1,infty).medium3+(ack1,infty).medium4+(rts2,infty).medium5 +
+ (cts2,infty).medium6+(data2, infty).medium7+(ack2,infty).medium8;
medium1 = (r1,delay).medium0 + (rts2,infty).medium9;
medium2 = (c1,delay).medium0; medium3 = (d1,delay).medium0;
medium4 = (a1,delay).medium0;
medium5 = (r2,delay).medium0 + (rts1, infty).medium9;
medium6 = (c2,delay).medium0; medium7 = (d2,delay).medium0;
medium8 = (a2,delay).medium0; medium9 = (coll1,delay).(coll2,
delay).medium0;
//COMPLETE SYSTEM
recv10 <r1,d1,cts1,ack1> (sender10 <rts1, data1, c1, a1,coll1>
medium0 <rts2, data2, c2, a2,coll2> sender20) <r2,d2,cts2,ack2>
recv20
```

Table 2. Collision probability with varying backoff-duration values

Backoff-duration	P_{coll}
8	0.117
16	0.147
24	0.161
32	0.170

tool provided with PEPA Workbench in order to carry out state-based analysis. This allows us to find the steady state probability associated with either a single state, or a set of states specified by a pattern (regular expression). The state finder matches the pattern, and then sums the probabilities of the fitting states. So, it is important to solve state values before carrying out analysis of single states. For example, in our work we carry out two simple quantitative analysis using the PEPA state finder tool. First we see the total probability value of Medium going into the state of collision (state medium9 from the above defined model). We term this value of collision probability (P_{coll}). We write a regular expression which matches any state in which medium is in $medium9$. The regular expression can be easily written in PEPA state finder, using "**", which denotes a wild-card and will match any of the derivatives. For this example, the regular expression; $** < rts1, c1, data1, coll1, a1, > medium9 **$ would suffice. The obtained value of result with backoff-duration set to 16 is 0.147. Next we vary the backoff-duration value and see the effect of this value on the collision probability:P_{coll}. Table 2 presents this result.

Such an analysis is useful in studying the effect of parameters on the performance of the communication protocol, and finding optimal values for effects of any parameter. For example, in our analysis we study the effect of the backoff-duration parameter on the collision probability metric, and it helps in finding an optimal value for this parameter. From the above analysis, if the backoff-duration is not changing dynamically, it can be seen that for higher values of backoff-duration the collision probability is also high. So the backoff-duration should be less to have less probability of collision. These kind of studies can be carried out to decide on optimal values for the parameters. More detailed analysis using other PEPA tools can be carried out.

6   Conclusion

The application of formal methods to the verification of protocol properties is an interesting research area. We have described some of the IEEE 802.11 mechanisms using few process algebras. We have considered the handoff mechanism in wireless LANs and the MAC mechanism. We have provided a refinement of the π-calculus specification with timers. Then we have used the Mobility Workbench to make simple verifications on the specified system. Finally, we did a quantitative analysis using a performance evaluation process algebra. The backoff procedure and timing aspects are considered with PEPA modelling and PEPA Workbench.

References

[1] H. P. Barendregt. The lambda calculus, its syntax and semantics, Elsevier, 1984. 234

[2] J.Edwards. Process algebras for protocol validation and analysis. In Proc. PREP 2001, pp. 1-20, 2001. 234, 244

[3] S.Gilmore, J.Hillston. The PEPA Workbench: A Tool to Support a Process Algebra-based Approach to Performance Modelling, In Proc. 7th Conf. on Modelling Techniques and Tools for Computer Performance Evaluation, LNCS, Springer, pp. 353-368, 1994. 234, 244

[4] S.Gilmore, J.Hillston. A survey of the PEPA tools. In Proc. 2nd PASTA Workshop, pp. 40-49, 2003. 244

[5] IEEE Standards Department. 802.11: IEEE Standard for Wireless LAN Medium Access Control (MAC) and Physical Layer (PHY) specifications, 1997. 235

[6] M. Z.Kwiatkowska, G.Norman, J.Sproston. Probabilistic model checking of the IEEE 802.11 wireless local area network protocol. PAPM-PROBMIV 2002: pp. 169-187, 2002. 238

[7] R.Milner. Elements of Interaction - Turing Award Lecture. CACM 36(1): pp. 78-89 1993. 234

[8] R.Milner. Communicating and Mobile Systems: The π-calculus, Cambridge University Press, 1999. 234

[9] PEPA Workbench, available at http://www.dcs.ed.ac.uk/pepa/ 244

[10] B.Victor, F.Moller. The Mobility Workbench: A tool for the π-calculus. LNCS 818, pp. 428-440, 1994. 243

An Analytical Design of a Practical Replication Protocol for Distributed Systems*

Luis Irún-Briz, Francisco Castro-Company,
Hendrik Decker, and Francesc D. Muñoz-Escoí

Instituto Tecnológico de Informática, Universidad Politécnica de Valencia
46022 Valencia, SPAIN
{lirun,fcastro,hendrik,fmunyoz}@iti.upv.es

Abstract. In replicated transactional systems, lazy update protocols have exhibited an undesirable behaviour, due to an increased abortion rate in scenarios with high degrees of access conflicts. In this paper, the abortion rate problem is studied from a statistical point of view. The resulting expressions describe the abortion problem, and were used to design a hybrid update database replication protocol, with performance similar to traditional lazy update protocols but with lower abortion rates. The protocol's algorithm has been validated analytically. Once implemented, performance measurements have confirmed the predicted results.

1 Introduction

Replicated transactional systems have a wide range of applications where it is often convenient or even necessary to replicate the information in a set of servers, each one attending its local clients. Replicas must then be interconnected, usually via a WAN. Moreover, a predominant locality of access patterns typically suggests a partitioning of the database [1, 2]. Replicated transactional systems enable a high degree of availability, as needed by many 24/7 services for network-internal or external clients. Efficiency and high availability of such services are key to their acceptance and success.

The MADIS project [3] provides a solution for database applications fitting the characteristics outlined above. Its architecture provides access to replicated databases, together with a standard API and a set of consistency protocols that maintain the coherence of the replicated data. Examples of these protocols were presented in [4, 5, 6], using different approaches for the update propagation.

When developing some protocols destined to cater for a high degree of data locality, we encountered that some applications' needs could be satisfied with *lazy update protocols* [2]. These protocols have a short transaction service time, but a high abortion rate, and replicas may become inconsistent due to lazy update propagation. To understand the problem, we performed a statistical study of the

---

* This work has been partially supported by the Spanish MCYT grant TIC2003-09420-C02-01.

M. Núñez et al. (Eds.): FORTE 2004 Workshops, LNCS 3236, pp. 248–261, 2004.

abortion rates obtaining a parametrized expression describing the behaviour. The use of the expression as an oracle to predict the *freshness state* of each accessed object allowed us to theoretically determine an improved basic lazy protocol. Theoretical analysis predicted that the protocol should yield, at low performance costs, a reduction on the abortion rates. The protocol includes the run-time computation of that expression, which can also be used to decrease the outdate time of replicated objects. Experimental validation of the predicted behaviour resulted in a modification of the protocol, to find dynamically its optimal tuning.

Section 2 includes the description of the modeled system and the results of the formal analysis of the abortion rate. Section 3 describes the proposed algorithm, together with a theoretical analysis for determining the achievable improvements. Section 4 describes the modification performed to automate the optimal tuning of the algorithm. Section 5 addresses related work, and section 6 conclusively summarizes the proposed protocol.

2 Modeling the Abortion Rate

The MADIS middleware provides transparent access to networked relational DBMSs, as if it were a single database. Thus, clients of each node are enabled by MADIS to access the data locally. A consistency protocol, plugged into each node, is in charge of propagating all local updates to all other database replicas.

2.1 The Modeled System

One of the problems solved by MADIS[7] is to ensure the consistency of transactions being executed in different database replicas. Depending on the needs of an application, different update propagation policies are conceivable. Different protocol modules which implement such policies can be plugged into MADIS, thus enabling the MADIS system administrator to suitably choose and exchange the consistency protocol at will.

One of our target applications was that used by medium-size enterprises with geographically distributed business units. Each enterprise's database is supposed to embody a common information repository to the entire company, while taking into account that each work unit may have a particular access pattern of its own: each one has write access to particular "regions" of the database, while only reading the information written or updated by other units.

This kind of scenarios typically requires high availability of data, which usually is achieved by replicating the entire database in each network node. The replication protocols traditionally deployed in such scenarios use *optimistic consistency control*, in order to avoid distributed deadlocks. Due to its optimistic policy, such protocols prevent any locking of objects whenever they are locally accessed. Thus, for maintaining consistency of replicated data, some kind of "versioning" (or "timestamping") in the database objects becomes necessary. At commit time, versions are compared, and inconsistent transactions are aborted. Committing transactions must then propagate their changes to the rest of nodes.When the propagation is completed *within* the commit phase, it is known as *eager update propagation*.

Now, due to the *locality* of its access patterns, our target environment turned out to be suitable for *lazy update propagation protocols*. In contrast to the eager ones, these protocols do not complete the propagation during the commit. Thus, the changes performed by a locally committed transaction can not be completely propagated to the rest of nodes, where other transactions might access out-of-date information, leading also to their abortion.

Computable Parameters. As the database is fully replicated, the number of stored objects, say N, is essentially the same for each node.

For each node $NODE_k$ ($k = 1..K$, for K nodes in the system), it is possible to compute a number of variables:

- nw_k The mean of objects written per write-transaction committed in the system at $NODE_k$.
- $wtps_k$ The number of write-transactions committed per second at $NODE_k$.

2.2   Abortion Rate Analysis

To understand the abortion problem, we proceed to analytically determine the reasons by which a transaction is aborted. To this end, we use statistical techniques to formalize the behaviour of optimistic lazy protocols. Thus, the abortion probability for a transaction S is $PA(S) = 1 - (PC_{conc}(S) \cdot PC_{outd}(S))$ where:

- $PC_{conc}(S)$ is the probability that the transaction concludes without concurrency conflicts.
- $PC_{outd}(S)$ is the probability that the transaction concludes without accessing to outdated objects.

For predicting the behaviour of our algorithms, particularly their abortion rate, it is useful to focus attention on the value of $PC_{outd}(S)$. This probability can be computed in terms of the probability of a transaction to conclude with conflicts produced by the access to outdated objects, $PA_{outd}(S)$.

Our results indicated that each access in a transaction can lead to its abortion with probability

$$PA_{outd}(o_i) = 1 - \left(1 - \tfrac{1}{N}\right)^{\frac{\sum_k nw_k}{K} \times \sum_k wtps_k \times \delta(o_i)} \tag{1}$$

where $\delta(o_i)$ is the local time for which the object o_i has not been updated in the executing node.

This expression, computable with only a few parameters, permits to compute the probability for an object access to cause the abortion of the transaction by an out-of-date access. A transaction commits when none of its object accesses causes its abortion: $PC_{outd}(S) = PC_{outd}(o_1) \times ... \times PC_{outd}(o_{napt})$ This is equivalent to:

$$PC_{outd}(S) = \left(1 - \tfrac{1}{N}\right)^{nwwt \times wtps \times (\delta(o_1) + \delta(o_2) + ... + \delta(o_{napt}))} \tag{2}$$

Only nw_k and $wtps_k$ must be collected in the system nodes for obtaining the expression ($nwwt = \tfrac{1}{K}\sum_k nw_k$ and $wtps = \sum_k wtps_k$). In addition, $\delta(o_i)$ can be locally maintained as metadata, similar to version numbers or timestamps.

The results, although not amazing, serve to understand the main relevance of the different parameters in the problem: N, $nwwt$, $wtps$, and $\delta(o_i)$. We observed that $\delta(o_i)$ is the unique parameter depending on the protocol, since the rest of parameters are inherent to the system. Thus, theoretical analysis guided us to design a lazy propagation algorithm reducing $\delta(o_i)$ to improve the abortion rate.

2.3   Preliminary Validation of the Model

We have validated the algorithm presented above by implementing a simulation of the system. In this simulation, we have implemented nodes that concurrently serve transactions, accessing different objects of a distributed database. We have also modeled the concurrency control and a basic lazy update propagation protocol.

Assumptions. For a preliminary validation of the expression, we performed an implementation of a simulation [8, 9, 10] following a number of assumptions compatible with the ones taken for the model computation. We implemented an optimistic lazy protocol in the simulation. The following load parameter values were set:

- The system has 4 nodes, each holding a full replica of the database, containing the experimental amount of 20 objects, since a small database maximises the probability of access conflicts.
- For each object, a local replica held its value and the version corresponding to its last modification.
- Three kinds of transactions have been considered, with a probability of 0.2, 0.4 and 0.4 to occur, respectively:
  - "Type 0" transactions, that read three objects.
  - "Type 1" transactions, that read three objects, and then write all of them.
  - "Type 2" transactions, that read six objects, and then write three of them.
- The model supports the locality of accesses by means of the probability for each accessed object to be managed by its processing node. For type-0 transactions, locality is set to 1/4. For type-1 and type-2 transactions, locality is set to 3/4.
- The simulation time has been set to discard the simulation stabilisation time. This allowed to scale up to 60,000 transactions.

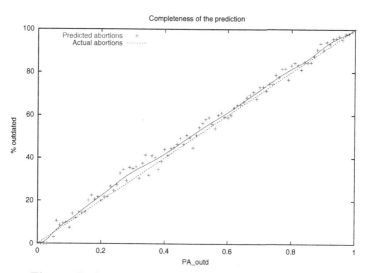

Fig. 1. Evolution of the inaccuracy for different P[update]

Accuracy of the Prediction. In the simulation, we computed the value for the expression at each object access for each started transaction. With this information, a histogram was elaborated holding the computed probability for an object to be out-of-date. For each object, we also built a parallel histogram holding the actual number of objects with an out-of-date value. Thus, the histogram contained 100 cells, each one representing a discrete value of the expression for $PA_{outd}(o_i)$, and containing the number of objects with an out-of-date value. At the end of each experiment, the values of the cells were divided by the total number of accesses performed in the simulation, providing the actual ratio of stale accesses for each expression value.

Figure 1 shows the evolution of the correlation between the values of the expression and the actual abortion rate experimentally obtained.

The optimum line is also shown, corresponding to the diagonal. The more accurate the prediction is, the closer the curves are. The studied prediction differed from the ideal line with a lower bound pattern. As can be seen, it is quite close to the ideal.

3   Design of the Improved Algorithm

The expression obtained statistically evidenced that the clue to improve the abortion rate of lazy update protocols consisted in the reduction of the outdate time of the local replicas of each object (i.e. $\delta(o_i)$). Consequently, the next step consisted in determining the improvement achievable by the reduction of that outdate time.

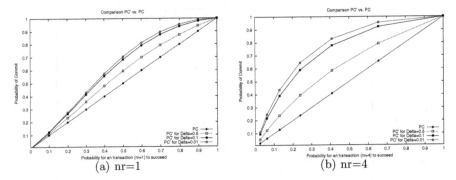

(a) nr=1   (b) nr=4

Fig. 2. Evolution of the improvement varying Δ

3.1   Theoretical Boundary of an Improvement

This step, based on the computation of the serial analysis of the basic expression for $PA(o_i)$, yielded an expression describing, in terms of a single variable Δ, the increase of the success probability for each object accessed by a transaction:

$$\frac{PC'}{PC} = PC^{PC \times (\Delta - 1)}, \text{ where } \Delta = \frac{d'_T}{\delta} \tag{3}$$

From this expression we obtained that the improvement of the probability for an object to be accessed in an adequate way (i.e. not a stale access), is determined by $\frac{PC'}{PC}$, and that it benefits from the decrease of the value of Δ, which determines the existing relation between d'_T (the duration of the transactions on the modified protocol) and δ (the outdate time on the original protocol). This study also brought out the straightfoward relation between d'_T and P_{UPD} (i.e. the probability for an object access to cause an update).

The described expression was used to determine a number of *curves of improvement*. These curves were used to graphically represent the achievable increase of the probability of commit for different types of transactions.

For example, for the most simple transaction, performing a single read access, we established as a parameter the probability for a requested object to be previously updated (i.e. P_{UPD}), and then studied the achieved improvement for different values of Δ (and, consequently, different computational overheads).

Figure 2(a) shows the commit probability for a session accessing **only one object**. It shows how the commit probability can be improved, when the update-time is decreased to one half, up to 120% of the original commit chance. When the update-time is decreased by a tenth, the improvement reaches 140%. Lower values of Δ provide marginal improvements, at higher computational costs.

When more than just one object is accessed in a transaction (figure 2(b)), the results showed higher differences between the commit promises, due to the factorisation of such probabilities. These results pointed to the convenience to apply techniques based on the reduction of the outdate time, in scenarios with parameters as described above.

3.2   The Improved Algorithm

In a *lazy update propagation protocol*, the outdate time of the object replicas held by a particular node depends on the time the object is locally accessed. Objects are updated when a local transaction accesses them in write mode, and the transaction is finally committed. Another situation producing the update of an object arises when a transaction aborts at commit time due to a stale access over this particular object.

To reduce the abortion rate, it becomes necessary to decrease the mean outdate time (represented in the expressions by δ). We observed that this can be achieved by either a *push* (i.e., initiated by an update-propagator replica) or a *pull* model (i.e., initiated by a reader replica, which perhaps has an outdated state). This can be done periodically or on request (i.e., when the object is updated in the push model, or when the object is read in the pull model).

Periodical push execution has the disadvantage of requiring a huge amount of memory, because it needs to manage the $\delta(o_i)$ for each object not totally propagated. On the other hand, periodical pull execution needs to periodically perform a query in order to retrieve a list of objects suitable to be updated, using the metadata (δ).

In contrast, we observed that the implementation of *on request* actions at each node required little memory usage. Moreover, additional metadata (i.e. $\delta(o_i)$) may be used, introducing only a marginal overhead.

The main disadvantage of the *push model* is that it may introduce unneeded propagations, in case there are no explicit requests to which the propagation responds. As a result, the performance of the system may degrade. On the other hand, the *pull model* may require a lot of interaction with the different nodes in the system. However, this disadvantage is not dramatical in systems with high locality of accesses. Consequently, we designed an algorithm based on the pull model, to reduce the outdate time of the replicated objects.

Its basic principle consists in using the computed theoretical expression for estimating the likelihood of an object to be locally updated before being accessed by a session. This estimation, performed with a certain degree of accuracy, depending on the "freshness" of the values of nw_k and $wtps_k$ the node has, was used as an oracle in our algorithm. The precise use of the expression and an adequate mechanism for the propagation of these parameters has been presented in [6].

Algorithm Outline. The COLU (Cautious Optimistic Lazy Update) consistency protocol multicasts object updates to the asynchronous nodes, once the transaction completes its commit phase. Consistency conflicts among transactions are resolved with an optimistic approach, using object versions and checking them during the commit phase. Thus, object accesses are allowed along the transaction execution without any locking.

As seen, the main inconvenience of this Lazy Update Propagation is the increase of the abortion rate. The COLU protocol makes use of the expression for the probability of an object to cause the abortion of a transaction, to predict the convenience for a transaction to ensure that an asynchronously updated object has a recent version in the local database.

In order to apply these results, a threshold of $PA(o_i)$ (i.e., the abort probability of an access to o_i due to a stale access) needs to be established, for considering the object as "convenient to be updated". An adequate value for this threshold is supposed to minimise the number of abortions caused by accesses to outdated objects, keeping low the number of updates for the system. Thus, when a transaction requests an object access, $PA(o_i)$ is computed and compared with the threshold. As a result, the algorithm obtains an updated version for objects predicted to be stale.

The implementation of this principle introduces a new request in the protocol. Now, the active node for a transaction will send update request messages to the owners of the stale accessed objects, in order to get their updated versions. Such update requests are sent along with executing the transaction, in order to ensure that the objects accessed by the transaction are up-to-date, at least to a certain degree.

Minimising the number of updates (obtained with higher thresholds) increases the number of transactions executed in the system per second, because that will decrease the resources used by update propagation. On the other hand, this minimisation causes an increase in the number of aborted transactions, because the number of outdated objects will also be increased. The increase of the abortion rate can also degrade the productivity of the system, because the time spent for transactions that finally abort is futile.

3.3   Experimental Validation

The implementation of the algorithm allowed us to validate it empirically. We scheduled a test plan, in order to validate the simulations performed, as well as the predicted improvement for the abortion rates.

Our results (figure 3(a)) compared the number of objects predicted to be outdated with the number of objects actually outdated. The prediction is an upper bound –in global terms– of the probability for an object to be stale. In the figure, the diagonal shows the behaviour of a perfect predictor, where the same number of predictions should terminate with an abortion. The points shown in the figure are slightly below, though close to this ideal line, evidencing the pessimistic behaviour of this prediction.

When comparing figure 3(b) with figure 1 obtained by simulation, the former shows a more diffuse layout of the measurements with respect to the diagonal than the simulated results. Nevertheless, these differences are small enough to sustain the validity of our conclusions.

We also measured the improvement of our real implementation. A set of tests were performed, specifying for each one a different threshold used in the algorithm. When the value of $PA(o_i)$ exceeds the established threshold, the object is considered to be stale, and the update is requested before such object is accessed. The higher the threshold is, the less requests are performed, and the lower the overhead. In contrast, higher values for the threshold produce higher

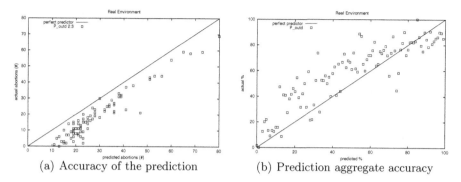

(a) Accuracy of the prediction   (b) Prediction aggregate accuracy

Fig. 3. Accuracy of the prediction for an autoadaptive threshold

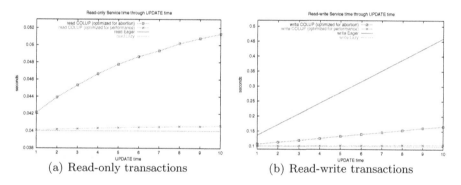

(a) Read-only transactions   (b) Read-write transactions

Fig. 4. Evolution of the service time in the optimum for different K_{LUR}

abortion rates, degrading also the performance of the system, because the use of computation resources of an aborted transaction finally becomes futile.

Figure 4 shows the performance (service time) obtained in the optimum configuration of the algorithm, for different network costs, represented by K_{LUR} (when $K_{LUR} = 2$, the networking cost of each update request will cost twice the cost of a database object recovery).

Optimising the algorithm to minimise the abortion rate, the protocol yields performances comparable to the eager ones, while the optimisation of the performance yields results similar to the obtained with a lazy approach.

Regarding the abortion rate, the results (figure 5) show that the abortion rates obtained by the algorithm were close to the lazy ones, when it was optimised for improving the performance. In contrast, the optimisation of the abortion rate produced results similar to those provided by eager update protocols. In summary, an adequate establishment of the threshold entailed low abortion rates, at reasonable computational costs.

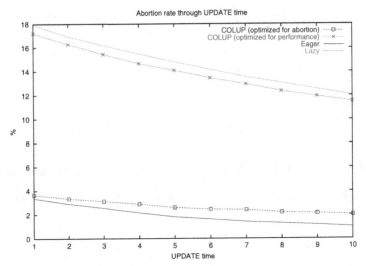

Fig. 5. Evolution of the abortion rate in the optimum for different K_{LUR}

4   Optimising the Implementation Using Formal Techniques

We encountered the establishment of the optimal threshold key for the adequate functionality of our algorithm. For this reason, we designed a number of modifications of the algorithm to automate the establishment of the threshold, and some simplifications that provide the same results requiring only part of the original parameters.

4.1   Dynamic Tuning

When the commit phase is completed (either with an abortion or with a commit), the algorithm compares, for each accessed object, the predictions performed with the termination of the transactions. The collected annotations are summarised, and the threshold is modified:

$$T_{i+1} = T_i \times \frac{K_{hist} + Q(N_{vain}, N_{fail})}{(K_{hist} + 1)} \tag{4}$$

being

$$Q(N_{vain}, N_{fail}) = \begin{cases} K_{inc} & \text{, if } N_{vain} > N_{fail} \\ 1.00 & \text{, if } N_{vain} = N_{fail} \\ 1 - K_{inc} & \text{, if } N_{vain} < N_{fail} \end{cases}$$

The expression $Q(N_{vain}, N_{fail})$ gives values below, equal, or above 1, in order to decrease, keep, or increase the value of T_{i+1}. The constant K_{hist} depends

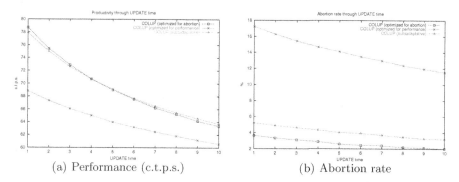

(a) Performance (c.t.p.s.)   (b) Abortion rate

Fig. 6. Comparison for different K_{LUR} of the optimum with adaptive threshold

on the variability of the system (mainly K_{LUR}). To provide faster adaptability, K_{hist} should take lower values. The constant K_{inc} (always $K_{inc} > 1$) depends on the variability of the transactions, taking lower values for systems with homogeneous transactions. Vain update requests (N_{vain}) increase the threshold, while unpredicted abortions (N_{fail}) cause a threshold decrease.

The obtained results (figure 6) validated the quality of this approach, showing the capability of the algorithm for performing optimally, and also for reducing the abortion rate.

4.2   Simplification of the Algorithm

The applied principle to adjust the adequate threshold considered a threshold (always contained in $[0..1]$) to be compared with the expression for $PA(o_i)$. Further experiments showed us that the adjustment of such threshold could be simplified. In other words, the expression of $PA(o_i)$ is used as a sorting function of each object access. Then, the threshold is established to determine, within this arrangement, the limits of "good" and "bad" occurrences.

Theoretically, any other sorting function, equivalent to the original one, should provide the same arrangement of the accesses, and an analogous algorithm could be designed to specify the corresponding threshold within the new arrangement.

The Simplified Dynamic Tuning. Observing the expression for $PA(o_i)$, and with some simple computations, it is easy to see that the expression follows a similar continuity pattern as the expression $\delta(o_i)$, due to the fact that N, $nwwt$ and $wtps$ depend on the environment, and can be introduced in the algorithm by the threshold adjustment.

Thus, the simplification consists in the replacement of the computation of $PA(o_i)$ by $\delta(o_i)$. In addition, the new threshold is not a value for a maximal probability ($\in [0..1]$), but it is now a maximal value for the $\delta(o_i)$.

Consequently, the algorithm only requires the use of $\delta(o_i)$, and no other parameter is required to be collected or transmitted. Finally, the autoadaptive threshold adjustment was also simplified. The results of such modification were identical to the ones obtained from the basic autoadaptive algorithm, with the benefits of a lower computational cost.

Improving the Granularity. Another benefit derived from the simplification of the expression consisted of incrementing the granularity of the solution. Now, the value of the threshold could be applied for each particular object, rather than for the entire system.

Thus, the final version of the algorithm makes use of a general threshold adjustment for those objects that carry only a small amount of historical information (or even nothing). In addition, objects frequently accessed can be managed with particular information, thus producing more accurate predictions.

However, this approach needs that the system manages a higher amount of metadata. In fact, for each object, the local time for each local update has to be stored (it is needed to calculate $\delta(o_i)$ in each access), plus its latest threshold, and the number of observations for it (used to choose between the general threshold and the particular one).

At the cost of this increase on disk usage (the metadata can be also stored in the database), and being it possible to introduce marginal overheads in terms of metadata recovery (the $\delta(o_i)$ metadata must be collected and calculated in any case), the system showed to offer a better response in heterogeneous environments, where the database objects are not accessed with the same access pattern.

5   Related Work

Current work in consistency protocols for replicated databases can be found using either eager [11, 12, 13, 14] and lazy protocols [15, 16, 17]. Each one has its pros and cons, as described in [2]. Eager protocols usually hamper the update performance and increase transaction response times but, on the positive side, they can yield serializable execution of multiple transactions without requiring too much effort. On the other hand, lazy protocols may allow a transaction to read outdated versions of objects, which may increase the abortion rate but usually improves transaction response times.

Pessimistic consistency control for distributed databases [18] is based on the principle of "locks", preventing concurrent transactions to access the same object in an inadequate mode, thus minimising the number of aborted transactions, but at the cost of a degrading performance, due to the suspension produced by the locks and the complexity of distributed locking.

On the other hand, the traditional approach for optimistic consistency control [19] has its main advantage in the reduction of the blocking time of the transactions, using "versions" (or "timestamps" [20]) as the basis for its implementation. Its main disadvantage consists in the increase of the abortion rate.

Lazy update protocols [15, 16, 17] presented a new approach for update propagation, in contrast to the traditionally used "eager replication". Lazy update protocols take advantage of the fact that an object can be written several times for different transactions before another transaction tries to read it.

6   Conclusions

Lazy update protocols have not been widely exploited due to their excessive abortion rate in scenarios with high probability of access conflicts. Nevertheless, such protocols can provide important improvements in the performance of a distributed system, when the abortion rate can be kept low and the access patterns have a sufficient degree of locality.

We have presented the development of a new approach for update propagation protocols, based on a statistical study of the abortion rate (the main disadvantage of lazy protocols), in order to obtain an expression for the probability for an accessed object to be out of date ($PA_{outd}(o_i)$).

An autoadaptive technique for dynamically tuning the designed algorithm was also analyzed. The results showed that such algorithm improves the probability for an object to be up-to-date, thus reducing the abortion rate of lazy update protocols with a minimal cost in terms of performance.

Finally, the algorithm was simplified, making use of a simple continuity analysis for obtaining a reduced expression to be computed at a minimal cost, and with the most possible independence of parameters external to the processing node. The algorithm was finally improved in terms of the solution's granularity, resulting in a good approach for managing heterogeneous replication scenarios.

References

[1] Rahm, E.: Empirical performance evaluation of concurrency and coherency control protocols for database sharing systems. ACM Trans. on Database Sys. **18** (1993) 333–377   248
[2] Gray, J., Helland, P., O'Neil, P., Shasha, D.: The dangers of replication and a solution. In: Proc. of the 1996 ACM SIGMOD International Conference on Management of Data, Canada (1996) 173–182   248, 259
[3] Instituto Tecnológico de Informática: MADIS web site. Accessible in URL: *http://www.iti.es/madis* (2004)   248
[4] Muñoz, F., Irún, L., Galdámez, P., Bernabéu, J., Bataller, J., Bañuls, M. C.: Globdata: A platform for supporting multiple consistency modes. Information Systems and Databases (ISDB'02) (2002) 244–249   248
[5] Irún, L., Muñoz, F., Decker, H., Bernabéu-Aubán, J. M.: Copla: A platform for eager and lazy replication in networked databases. In: 5th Int. Conf. Enterprise Information Systems (ICEIS'03). Volume 1. (2003) 273–278   248
[6] Irún-Briz, L., Muñoz-Escoí, F. D., Bernabéu-Aubán, J. M.: An improved optimistic and fault-tolerant replication protocol. In: Proceedings of 3rd. Workshop on Databases in Networked Information Systems. Lecture Notes in Comp. Sci., Springer-Verlag (2003) 188–200   248, 254

[7] Irún-Briz, L., Muñoz-Escoí, F.D., Bernabéu-Aubán, J.M.: Using standard database resources to support distributed consistency protocols. Technical Report TR-2004-LI04, Instituto Tecnológico de Informática (2004) 249

[8] Chandy, K.M., Misra, J.: Distributed simulation: A case study in design and verification of distributed programs. IEEE Transactions on Software Engineering **SE-5** (1979) 440–452 251

[9] Bagrodia, R.L., Chandy, K.M., Misra, J.: A message-based approach to discrete-event simulation. IEEE Transactions on Software Engineering **SE-13** (1987) 251

[10] Bagrodia, R.L.: An integrated approach to the design and performance evaluation of distributed systems. In: Proceedings of the First International Conference on Systems Integration, IEEE Computer Society (1990) 251

[11] Agrawal, D., Alonso, G., El Abbadi, A., Stanoi, I.: Exploiting atomic broadcast in replicated databases. Lecture Notes in Computer Science **1300** (1997) 496–503 259

[12] Wiesmann, M., Schiper, A., Pedone, F., Kemme, B., Alonso, G.: Database replication techniques: A three parameter classification. In: Proc. of the 19th IEEE Symposium on Reliable Distributed Systems (SRDS'00). (2000) 206–217 259

[13] Jimenez-Peris, R., Patiño-Martinez, M., Alonso, G., Kemme, B.: How to Select a Replication Protocol According to Scalability, Availability, and Communication Overhead. In: 20th IEEE Int. Conf. on Reliable Distributed Systems (SRDS'01), New Orleans, Louisiana, IEEE CS Press (2001) 24–33 259

[14] Rodrigues, L., Miranda, H., Almeida, R., Martins, J., Vicente, P.: Strong replication in the GlobData middleware. In: Proc. of Workshop on Dependable Middleware-Based Systems (in DSN 2002), Washington D.C., USA (2002) G96–G104 259

[15] Chundi, P., Rosenkrantz, D.J., Ravi, S.S.: Deferred updates and data placement in distributed databases. In: Proceedings of the 12th International Conference on Data Engineering, IEEE Computer Society (1996) 469–476 259, 260

[16] Breitbart, Y., Korth, H.F.: Replication and consistency: being lazy helps sometimes. In: Proceedings of the sixteenth ACM SIGACT-SIGMOD-SIGART symposium on Principles of Database Systems, ACM Press (1997) 173–184 259, 260

[17] Holliday, J., Agrawal, D., Abbadi, A.E.: Database replication: If you must be lazy, be consistent. In: Proceedings of 18th Symposium on Reliable Distributed Systems SRDS'99, IEEE Computer Society Press (1999) 304–305 259, 260

[18] Bernstein, P.A., Shipman, D.W., Rothnie, J.B.: Concurrency control in a system for distributed databases (SDD-1). ACM Transactions on Database Systems **5** (1980) 18–51 259

[19] Kung, H.T., Robinson, J.T.: On optimistic methods for concurrency control. ACM Transactions on Database Systems **6** (1981) 213–226 259

[20] Bernstein, P.A., Hadzilacos, V., Goodman, N.: Concurrency Control and Recovery in Database Systems. Addison Wesley, Reading, MA, USA (1987) 259

PEPA Nets in Practice:
Modelling a Decentralised Peer-to-Peer Emergency Medical Application

Stephen Gilmore, Valentin Haenel, Jane Hillston, and Leïla Kloul

Laboratory for Foundations of Computer Science
The University of Edinburgh, Scotland

Abstract. We apply the PEPA nets modelling language to modelling a peer-to-peer medical informatics application, the FieldCare PDA-based medical records system developed by SINTEF Telecom and Informatics, Norway. Medical data on accident victims is entered by medics on handheld devices at the crash site and propagated wirelessly from peer to peer in order to improve information flow and reduce the potential for data loss. The benefits of such a system include improved reliability in patient care and the ability for hospitals to prepare better for incoming trauma patients. The effectiveness and usefulness of the system in practice depends upon both reliability and performance issues. We analyse the functioning of the application through a high-level model expressed in the PEPA nets modelling language, a coloured stochastic Petri net in which the tokens are terms of Hillston's Performance Evaluation Process Algebra (PEPA). We use the PRISM probabilistic model checker to solve the model and evaluate probabilistically quantified formulae which quantify the responsiveness of the system.

1   Introduction

Public medical emergencies occur when trains are derailed or when aeroplanes or other multi-passenger vehicles crash. Doctors and paramedics are dispatched to the crash site in order to assess the severity of injuries, dispense medication and provide best-effort treatment for the victims in situ. Typically the majority of the most seriously-injured patients are transported by medical ambulance to a hospital for further treatment. With them is sent a transcript of the treatment administered at the crash site together with the assessment of the attending physician of the severity of the injuries. The record of medicines dispensed is a vital piece of documentation, preventing potentially injurious overdosing with another drug. Similarly the assessment of the on-site physician contains very important data, facilitating speedy prioritisation of the incoming patients.

At present this documentation is most often sent as paper records or cards which are attached to the patient's clothing. The intention is that when the patient reaches hospital they, and their records, can be transferred into the care of another doctor. In practice the process of documenting treatment in

M. Núñez et al. (Eds.): FORTE 2004 Workshops, LNCS 3236, pp. 262–277, 2004.

this way does not always work well. Records and cards can be lost or damaged or unreadable and the only copy of important medical data is compromised. This usually leads to a predictably poor outcome—overdosing a patient with an already-administered drug, or incorrectly prioritising patients when determining treatment order and thereby lessening the chances of survival of a badly-injured patient.

Medical informatics researchers are working to replace these systems with technologically superior ones. One such effort is the *FieldCare* project, initiated by SINTEF Telecom and Informatics, Norway [1]. The intention of this project is to equip emergency rescue medics in Norway with handheld PDAs on which is recorded the relevant patient information. This information is then replicated from PDA to PDA in peer-to-peer fashion in order to improve the robustness of the information storage. The functioning principle of the system is that all data should be replicated to every potential medical site. Patient care is often handed on from one doctor to another rapidly and poor information flow can be a cause of errors. The propagation of information through the system allows hospital staff to make appropriate preparations in advance of the arrival of patients at hospitals.

The timely operation of a mobile computing system such as this is a significant concern. In this paper we present a model of the FieldCare system implemented as a PEPA net [2], and present an analysis of the system based on this model. PEPA nets are ideally suited to represent a system in which the components of the system find themselves working in a changing context due to mobility. Our analysis is based on the PRISM stochastic model checking tool [3] which allows us to express desirable features of the model in Continuous Stochastic Logic (CSL) [4], a logical specification language which incorporates time- and probability-bounded operators.

The remainder of the paper is organised as follows. In the following section we give a description of the PEPA nets formalism, and its tool support. This includes an explanation of how a PEPA net model can be used as input to the PRISM model checker. In Section 3 we describe the FieldCare system in more detail and present the PEPA net representation of it. The analysis of this system, is given in Section 4, together with a brief overview of the CSL stochastic logic which we use to express desirable properties of the model. Finally, in Section 5, we discuss our conclusions.

2   PEPA Nets

In this section we provide a brief overview of PEPA nets and the PEPA stochastic process algebra. A fuller description, together with supporting theory and proofs is available in [2] and [5]. The purpose of this summary is to provide enough information about the modelling language to make the present paper self-contained.

The tokens of a PEPA net are terms of the PEPA stochastic process algebra which define the behaviour of components via the activities they undertake and the interactions between them. One example of a PEPA component would be a *File* object which can be opened for reading or writing, have data read (or written) and closed. Such an object would understand the methods *openRead()*, *openWrite()*, *read()*, *write()* and *close()*. A PEPA model shows the order in which such methods can be invoked.

$$File \stackrel{def}{=} (openRead, r_O).InStream + (openWrite, r_O).OutStream$$

$$InStream \stackrel{def}{=} (read, r_r).InStream + (close, r_c).File$$

$$OutStream \stackrel{def}{=} (write, r_w).OutStream + (close, r_c).File$$

Every activity in the model incurs an execution cost which is quantified by an estimate of the (exponentially-distributed) rate at which it can occur (r_O, r_r, r_w, r_c).

Such a description documents a high-level protocol for using *File* objects, from which it is possible to derive properties such as "it is not possible to write to a closed file" and "read and write operations cannot be interleaved: the file must be closed and re-opened first".

A PEPA net is made up of PEPA *contexts*, one at each place in the net. A context consists of a number of *static* components (possibly zero) and a number of *cells* (at least one). Like a memory location in an imperative program, a cell is a storage area to be filled by a datum of a particular type. In particular in a PEPA net, a cell is a storage area dedicated to storing a PEPA component, such as the *File* object described above. The components which fill cells can circulate as the tokens of the net. In contrast, the static components cannot move. A typical place might be the following:

$$File[\_] \underset{L}{\bowtie} FileReader$$

where the *cooperation set L* in this case is $\mathcal{A}(File)$, the *complete action type set* of the component, (*openRead*, *openWrite*, ...). This place has a *File*-type cell and a static component, *FileReader*, which can process the file when it arrives. When components cooperate in this way it will usually be the case that one is the active participant (which determines the rate at which the activity is performed) and the other is the passive participant (who is delayed until the activity completes, and cannot hurry its completion). The PEPA notation to denote the passive participant in a cooperation is to use the distinguished symbol $\top$ in place of their rate variable. Thus (a, r) and $(a, \top)$ can cooperate over a to produce a *shared activity* (a, r). The case where two active participants cooperate is defined in [5].

A PEPA net differentiates between two types of change of state. We refer to these as *firings* of the net and *transitions* of PEPA components. Each are special cases of PEPA activities. Transitions of PEPA components will typically be used to model small-scale (or *local*) changes of state as components undertake activities. Firings of the net will typically be used to model macro-step (or *global*) changes of state such as context switches, breakdowns and repairs, one thread yielding to another, or a mobile software agent moving from one network host

$$N ::= D^+ M \qquad \text{(net)}$$
$$M ::= (M_{\mathbf{P}}, \ldots) \qquad \text{(marking)}$$
$$M_{\mathbf{P}} ::= \mathbf{P}[C, \ldots] \qquad \text{(place marking)}$$

$$D ::= I \stackrel{def}{=} S \qquad \text{(component defn)}$$
$$\mid\ \mathbf{P}[C] \stackrel{def}{=} P[C] \qquad \text{(place defn)}$$
$$\mid\ \mathbf{P}[C, \ldots] \stackrel{def}{=} P[C] \bowtie_L P \qquad \text{(place defn)}$$

$$P ::= P \bowtie_L P \quad \text{(cooperation)}$$
$$\mid\ P/L \qquad \text{(hiding)}$$
$$\mid\ P[C] \qquad \text{(cell)}$$
$$\mid\ I \qquad \text{(identifier)}$$

$$C ::= \text{`\_'} \qquad \text{(empty)}$$
$$\mid\ S \qquad \text{(full)}$$

$$S ::= (\alpha, r).S \qquad \text{(prefix)}$$
$$\mid\ S + S \qquad \text{(choice)}$$
$$\mid\ I \qquad \text{(identifier)}$$

Fig. 1. The syntax of PEPA nets

to another. The set of all firings is denoted by $\mathcal{A}_f$. The set of all transitions is denoted by $\mathcal{A}_t$. We distinguish firings syntactically by printing their names in boldface.

Continuing our example, we introduce an instant message as a type of transmissible file.

$$InstantMessage \stackrel{def}{=} (\mathbf{transmit}, r_t).File$$

Part of a definition of a PEPA net which models the passage of instant messages is shown below. An instant message *IM* can be moved from the input place on the left to the output place on the right by the **transmit** firing. In doing so it changes state to evolve to a *File* derivative, which can be read by the *FileReader*.

The syntax of PEPA nets is given in Figure 1.

Definition 1 (PEPA net) *A PEPA net $\mathcal{N}$ is a tuple $\mathcal{N} = (\mathcal{P}, \mathcal{T}, I, O, \ell, \pi, \mathcal{C}, D, M_0)$ such that*

- *$\mathcal{P}$ is a finite set of places and $\mathcal{T}$ is a finite set of net transitions;*
- *$I : \mathcal{T} \to \mathcal{P}$ is the input function and $O : \mathcal{T} \to \mathcal{P}$ is the output function;*
- *$\ell : \mathcal{T} \to (\mathcal{A}_f, \mathbb{R}^+ \cup \{\top\})$ is the labelling function, which assigns a PEPA activity to each transition. The rate determines the negative exponential distribution governing the delay associated with the transition;*
- *$\pi : \mathcal{A}_f \to \mathbb{N}$ is the priority function which assigns priorities (represented by natural numbers) to firing action types;*
- *$\mathcal{C} : \mathcal{P} \to P$ is the place definition function which assigns a PEPA context, containing at least one cell, to each place;*
- *D is the set of token component definitions;*
- *M_0 is the initial marking of the net.*

The structured operational semantics, given in [2], gives a precise definition of the possible evolution of a PEPA net, and shows how a Continuous-Time Markov Chain (CTMC) can be derived, treating each marking as a distinct state.

The firing rule for PEPA nets is a natural extension of the classical firing rule. A transition may fire if there is an input token corresponding to each input arc which can perform a firing activity of the appropriate type. However in addition we require that there is a vacant cell of the correct type corresponding to each output arc of the transition (see [6] for details).

2.1 Tool Support for PEPA Nets

We see the provision of tool support for modelling languages as being analogous to providing tools for programming languages. A software development kit used by a software engineer typically provides a range of tools (compilers, debuggers, profilers, perhaps even model checkers) which perform various types of analysis or conversion on the program. Similarly a model development kit used by a performance engineer contains steady-state and transient solvers, passage-time analysers, model-checkers and other tools which implement a range of analyses for models in the modelling language used.

PEPA nets are directly supported by the PEPA Workbench for PEPA nets, ML Edition [2]. This extends the PEPA Workbench [7] to implement the semantics of the PEPA nets language directly.

Since there already exists comprehensive tool support for PEPA [7, 8, 3, 9] we have recently developed a compiler for PEPA nets which carries out a translation from a PEPA net to a PEPA model [6]. This has the effect of removing the locations within the model and encoding them implicitly within state and activity names. The benefit of this approach is that it allows us to exploit existing tools for PEPA, such as the PRISM probabilistic model checker [3].

In order to define and analyse a model, PRISM requires two input files: a *description of the system* under investigation expressed in a language of reactive modules and a *set of properties* to be checked against it. To integrate PEPA, we built a compiler which compiles PEPA into the reactive modules language. Additionally, PRISM was extended to support PEPA's combinators (parallel and hiding). The PRISM implementation is based on the CUDD [10] binary decision diagram (BDD) library which provides multi-terminal BDD data structures and algorithms. In PRISM, analysis of CTMCs is performed through model checking specifications in the probabilistic temporal logic CSL (see Section 4).

3   The FieldCare System and Its PEPA Net Model

3.1 Description

As previously explained, the FieldCare system has been developed in [1] to address the need of medical teams dealing with accidents to share the information about the status of individual patients. The medical teams include the staff providing first help at the accident scene, the coordination staff at the scene, the ambulance staff and dispatchers in central control rooms, and the local hospitals' staff preparing for the arrival of the casualties. The team members record the information about the patients using hand-held and other computers linked together in a wireless network. The network and team will be very dynamic with members joining and leaving at very short notice.

The particular concern of the authors was to investigate how to achieve reliable data replication between the nodes in a network where some users are very mobile, the radio links may suffer intermittent failures and the connection topology between nodes may vary as team members move around, including moving out of range of a base station. To quote [1], "The goal is that all data, about all patients, should be stored on all nodes.". All nodes have the same status: there is no central server. Fortunately, the lifetime of the database is rather short and the volume of data entered by each user will not be great. Because PDAs are diskless, supporting record-based storage, the entire database will have to be stored in main memory in each PDA. The PDAs are not multifunction; they are specialised only to supporting the FieldCare application. There is one such PDA for each team.

The Reliable Data Replication Approach: Basic Idea. The approach developed consists of replicating everything to everyone. The objective is that all data about all patients should be stored on all nodes. Thus, data entered on one node must be replicated to all nodes including those that are added to the network afterwards. To achieve that each node has a copy of the database and maintains its own transaction table.

The database is assumed to have a very simple data model where each record consists of patient identification number, time stamp, name of the team, and details of the medical observation. All transactions in the database have an identifier which is unique throughout the network. The identifier is generated on the node at which the transaction is originated. Only INSERT operations are allowed on the database; DELETE and MODIFY are not allowed. Furthermore, full database transaction consistency is not necessary; temporary inconsistency between the local copies of the database during data replication is acceptable [1].

The transaction table is unique to the node. It contains one row for each transaction entered in the local copy of the database and shows, for each current neighbour of the node, which transactions it is known to have. To achieve this a column is created and initialised to *false* for each new neighbouring node. Two additional columns are used, one for the unique transaction identifier and one for the transaction sequence number. The identifier is assigned to the transaction by the node where it is originated and the sequence number is local to each node. This corresponds to the position in which the transaction has been entered in the table. Table 1 shows an example.

Transactions Available Protocol. When a new transaction is generated in a node, an identifier is assigned and it is inserted in the local database. A new row is added to the transaction table and the columns corresponding to all current

Transaction name	Sequence no.	Neighbour 1	...	Neighbour n
$(n, 1)$	1	*true*	...	*false*
$(n, 2)$	2	*true*	...	*true*
$(m, 1)$	3	*false*	...	*true*
$\vdots$	$\vdots$	$\vdots$	...	$\vdots$

Table 1. Transaction table

neighbouring nodes are initialised to *false* for this new row. The node sends a *Transaction offer* message to each of its neighbours, to which it expects to receive a *Please send* answer. The node then sends the new transaction using a *Data update* command. When the neighbouring node receives the new patient record, it sends an *I've got it* message. In the original node this triggers a change in the corresponding column value to *true*.

Frequent communication failures are anticipated and because of this expectation there are sporadic updates between neighbouring nodes. Thus each node checks periodically if its current neighbours have all the transactions reported in its own transaction table. The node sends a *Transaction offer* message to those neighbours whose corresponding column for the transaction offered is still set to *false*. The contacted node may respond either with an *I've got it* message because it already has the transaction in its local database or a *Please send* message. In the latter case it receives a *Data update* command to which it answers with an *I've got it* message. Both nodes have then to set the column of the neighbour to *true*.

Moreover, when a node establishes a new node communication after changing its position in the network, both nodes send each other a *"Pleased to meet you"* message and add a new column for each other in their respective transaction table. These nodes have then to offer each other all the transactions in their table using the exchanges of messages described above.

The periodic check allows the network to provide a solution to the problem of possible losses, like the loss of an aknowledgement message *I've got it*.

3.2   The PEPA Net Model

Consider two geographical areas, AREA 1 and AREA 2. The former being, for example, the area where an accident took a place and the latter the location of the hospital. Moreover, consider three medical teams A, B and C moving from one area to the other. The PEPA net model corresponding to this situation is described in Figure 2.

The PEPA net model consists of three places, namely *AREA_1*, *AREA_2* and *OUT*. Place *OUT* is used to model the area where a team is out of range of the base station of either AREA 1 or AREA 2. To model the behaviour of

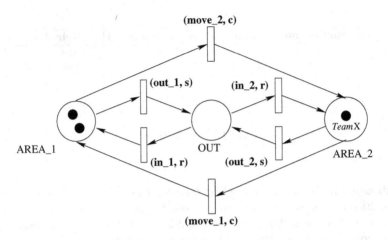

Fig. 2. The PEPA net Model

the different teams, we use components *Team*X where X stands for A, B or C. Moreover a static component *Neighbour* is associated with each place of the PEPA net network. This component allows us to keep track of the local copies of the database which have already been updated and the ones which still have to be updated.

Component *Team*X. This component models the behaviour of a node X representing a medical team in the wireless network. Initially a node may generate a transaction, receive a transaction offer or a *"Pleased to meet you"* message from another node Y. These are modelled using activities *generate_trans*, *trans_offer$_{YX}$* and *pleased$_{YX}$* respectively. The two latter activities have an unspecified rate ($\top$) as they are initiated by another node (component). Furthermore a node may move from one area to another, behaviour that is captured by the firing activity **move_i** where i is the area number where it moves to.

Once a new transaction is generated and inserted (*insert_trans*) into the local transaction table of the node, it is offered, with activity *trans_offer*, and then sent (with activity *please_send*) to all immediate neighbours of the node, that is all the nodes in the same area (place). Activity *end_neighbours_X* allows us to know when all neighbours of node X have been updated with the new transaction. This activity has an unspecified rate as it is controlled by component *Neighbour* presented later.

The periodic check for changes which is done by a node is modelled using the activity *periodic_check*. During this phase of the protocol, the node checks its transaction table using the *check_table* activity and offers a transaction (*trans_offer*) to all its neighbours whose corresponding column has `false` as value.

When a node X moves to a new area it has to establish communication with all nodes already in the area. This is modelled by the activity $pleased_{XY}$. As for the periodic check, the node has then to check its transaction table and to offer the transactions with a `false` value in its line to the corresponding immediate neighbours. Note that in this case the node has to offer all the transactions in its table to all its new immediate neighbours. Indeed when a node moves from one area to a new one, its transaction table does not keep track of its previous neighbours.

When a node is within an area, it may become out of range of the base station of the area. This is captured in the model by the firing activity **out_i** where $i(= 1, 2)$ is the node's current area.

$$TeamX \stackrel{def}{=} (generate\_trans, r).TeamX_1 + \sum_{Y \neq X}(pleased_{YX}, \top).TeamX_0$$
$$+ (periodic\_check, t_1).TeamX_0 + \sum_{Y \neq X}(trans\_offer_{YX}, \top).TeamX_6$$
$$+ (\textbf{move\_1, c}).TeamX_M + (\textbf{move\_2, c}).TeamX_M$$

$$TeamX_M \stackrel{def}{=} \sum_{Y \neq X}(pleased_{XY}, w).TeamX_M + (end\_neighbours\_X, \top).TeamX_0$$
$$+ (\textbf{out\_1, s}).TeamX_{M\,out1} + (\textbf{out\_2, s}).TeamX_{M\,out2}$$
$$TeamX_0 \stackrel{def}{=} (check\_table, c_2).TeamX_2 + \sum_{Y \neq X}(trans\_offer_{YX}, \top).TeamX_{6a}$$
$$+ (\textbf{out\_1, s}).TeamX_{0\,out1} + (\textbf{out\_2, s}).TeamX_{0\,out2}$$

$$TeamX_1 \stackrel{def}{=} (insert\_trans, r_1).TeamX_2$$

$$TeamX_2 \stackrel{def}{=} \sum_{Y \neq X}(trans\_offer_{XY}, r_2).TeamX_3 + (end\_neighbours\_X, \top).TeamX$$
$$+ (\textbf{out\_1, s}).TeamX_{2\,out1} + (\textbf{out\_2, s}).TeamX_{2\,out2}$$
$$TeamX_3 \stackrel{def}{=} \sum_{Y \neq X}(please\_send_{YX}, \top).TeamX_4 + \sum_{Y \neq X}(I've\_got\_it_{YX}, \top).TeamX_5$$
$$+ (\textbf{out\_1, s}).TeamX_{3\,out1} + (\textbf{out\_2, s}).TeamX_{3\,out2}$$

$$TeamX_4 \stackrel{def}{=} \sum_{Y \neq X}(database\_update_{XY}, r_3).TeamX_3 + (\textbf{out\_1, s}).TeamX_{4\,out1}$$
$$+ (\textbf{out\_2, s}).TeamX_{4\,out2}$$
$$TeamX_5 \stackrel{def}{=} (set\_true\_receiver, r_4).TeamX_2$$

$$TeamX_6 \stackrel{def}{=} \sum_{Y \neq X}(please\_send_{XY}, r_6).TeamX_7 + \sum_{Y \neq X}(I've\_got\_it_{XY}, r_5).TeamX$$
$$+ (\textbf{out\_1, s}).TeamX_{6\,out1} + (\textbf{out\_2, s}).TeamX_{6\,out2}$$
$$TeamX_7 \stackrel{def}{=} \sum_{Y \neq X}(database\_update_{YX}, \top).TeamX_8 + (\textbf{out\_1, s}).TeamX_{7\,out1}$$
$$+ (\textbf{out\_2, s}).TeamX_{7\,out2}$$
$$TeamX_8 \stackrel{def}{=} (set\_true\_sender, r_7).TeamX$$

$$TeamX_{6a} \stackrel{def}{=} \sum_{Y \neq X}(please\_send_{XY}, r_6).TeamX_{7a} + \sum_{Y \neq X}(I've\_got\_it_{XY}, r_5).TeamX_{8a}$$
$$+ (\textbf{out\_1, s}).TeamX_{a6\,out1} + (\textbf{out\_2, s}).TeamX_{a6\,out2}$$
$$TeamX_{7a} \stackrel{def}{=} \sum_{Y \neq X}(database\_update_{YX}, \top).TeamX_{8a} + (\textbf{out\_1, s}).TeamX_{a7\,out1}$$
$$+ (\textbf{out\_2, s}).TeamX_{a7\,out2}$$
$$TeamX_{8a} \stackrel{def}{=} (set\_true\_sender, r_7).TeamX_0$$

In component *TeamX* the derivatives $TeamX_{k_{outi}}$ are defined as follows

$$TeamX_{k_{outi}} \stackrel{def}{=} (\mathbf{in\_i}, \mathbf{r}).TeamX_k$$

indicating that for a node which has moved out of range, when it returns it does so in the same state. Firing activity **in_i** models the case where the node becomes reachable again. That is, it is no longer out of range.

Component *Neighbour*. Component *Neighbour* allows us to keep track of the nodes which received a transaction offer and the ones which have not. Similarly it allows us to identify the current node(s) of an area with which a newly arriving node has established communication. The complete behaviour of the component when there are three nodes or teams A, B and C, in the network is as follows:

$$
\begin{aligned}
Neighbour \stackrel{def}{=} \; & (trans\_offer_{AB}, \top).Next_{AC} + (trans\_offer_{AC}, \top).Next_{AB} \\
& + (trans\_offer_{BA}, \top).Next_{BA} + (trans\_offer_{BC}, \top).Next_{BC} \\
& + (trans\_offer_{CA}, \top).Next_{CB} + (trans\_offer_{CB}, \top).Next_{CA} \\
& + (pleased_{AB}, \top).Next_{AC} + (pleased_{AC}, \top).Next_{AB} \\
& + (pleased_{BA}, \top).Next_{BC} + (pleased_{BC}, \top).Next_{BC} \\
& + (pleased_{CA}, \top).Next_{CB} + (pleased_{CB}, \top).Next_{CA} \\
& + \sum_{x=A,B,C}(end\_neighbours\_X, \rho).Neighbour
\end{aligned}
$$

$$
\begin{aligned}
Next_{AB} \stackrel{def}{=} \; & (trans\_offer_{AB}, \top).Next + (pleased_{AB}, \top).Neighbour \\
& + (end\_neighbours\_A, \rho).Neighbour
\end{aligned}
$$

$$
\begin{aligned}
Next_{AC} \stackrel{def}{=} \; & (trans\_offer_{AC}, \top).Next + (pleased_{AC}, \top).Neighbour \\
& + (end\_neighbours\_A, \rho).Neighbour
\end{aligned}
$$

$$
\begin{aligned}
Next_{BA} \stackrel{def}{=} \; & (trans\_offer_{BA}, \top).Next + (pleased_{BA}, \top).Neighbour \\
& + (end\_neighbours\_B, \rho).Neighbour
\end{aligned}
$$

$$
\begin{aligned}
Next_{BC} \stackrel{def}{=} \; & (trans\_offer_{BC}, \top).Next + (pleased_{BC}, \top).Neighbour \\
& + (end\_neighbours\_B, \rho).Neighbour
\end{aligned}
$$

$$
\begin{aligned}
Next_{CA} \stackrel{def}{=} \; & (trans\_offer_{CA}, \top).Next + (pleased_{CA}, \top).Neighbour \\
& + (end\_neighbours\_C, \rho).Neighbour
\end{aligned}
$$

$$
\begin{aligned}
Next_{CB} \stackrel{def}{=} \; & (trans\_offer_{CB}, \top).Next + (pleased_{CB}, \top).Neighbour \\
& + (end\_neighbours\_C, \rho).Neighbour
\end{aligned}
$$

$$
Next \stackrel{def}{=} \sum_{x=A,B,C}(end\_neighbours\_X, \rho).Neighbour
$$

The *Neighbour* component does not have a physical counterpart in the system but can be regarded as representing the knowledge embodied in the wireless LAN, for purposes such as broadcast messaging.

The Initial Marking. The initial marking of the system we consider is the one corresponding to Figure 2.

$$\left(\begin{array}{l} Neighbour \bowtie_{\mathcal{L}} ((\mathit{TeamA}[\mathit{TeamA}] \bowtie_{\mathcal{K}} \mathit{TeamB}[\mathit{TeamB}]) \bowtie_{\mathcal{K}'} \mathit{TeamC}[\_]), \\ Neighbour \bowtie_{\mathcal{L}} ((\mathit{TeamA}[\_] \bowtie_{\mathcal{K}} \mathit{TeamB}[\_]) \bowtie_{\mathcal{K}'} \mathit{TeamC}[\mathit{TeamC}]), \\ \qquad \mathit{TeamA}[\_] \bowtie_{\emptyset} \mathit{TeamB}[\_] \bowtie_{\emptyset} \mathit{TeamC}[\_] \end{array} \right)$$

The cooperation sets $\mathcal{K}$, $\mathcal{K}'$ and $\mathcal{L}$ are defined as follows:

$\mathcal{K} = \{trans\_offer_{AB}, trans\_offer_{BA}, please\_send_{AB}, database\_update_{AB},$
$\qquad I've\_got\_it_{AB}\}$
$\mathcal{K}' = \{trans\_offer_{AC}, trans\_offer_{BC}, trans\_offer_{CB}, trans\_offer_{CA}, please\_send_{AC},$
$\qquad I've\_got\_it_{AC}, database\_update_{AC}, database\_update_{BC}, please\_send_{BC},$
$\qquad I've\_got\_it_{BC}\}$
$\mathcal{L} = \{trans\_offer_{AB}, trans\_offer_{AC}, trans\_offer_{BA}, trans\_offer_{BC}, trans\_offer_{CA},$
$\qquad trans\_offer_{CB}, end\_neighbours\_A, end\_neighbours\_B, end\_neighbours\_C,$
$\qquad pleased_{AB}, pleased_{AC}, pleased_{BA}, pleased_{BC}, pleased_{CA}, pleased_{CB}\}$

4   Model Analysis

The PRISM model checker supports the analysis of probabilistic and stochastic systems by allowing a modeller to check a logical property against a model. Several logics and several types of model are supported. Recently the CSL logic (Continuous Stochastic Logic) [4] has gained some acceptance as a suitable vehicle for expressing performance and performability measures which can be model checked on a CTMC. A CSL formula expresses an assertion about the performance measures of a model which can then be checked to see whether it is true or not. The syntax of CSL is:

$$\phi ::= \mathit{true} \mid \mathit{false} \mid a \mid \phi \wedge \phi \mid \phi \vee \phi \mid \neg\phi \mid \mathcal{P}_{\bowtie p}[\psi] \mid \mathcal{S}_{\bowtie p}[\phi]$$
$$\psi ::= X\phi \mid \phi \, U^I \, \phi \mid \phi \, U \, \phi$$

where a is an atomic proposition, $\bowtie \in \{<, \leq, >, \geq\}$ is a relational parameter, $p \in [0, 1]$ is a probability, and I is an interval of $\mathbb{R}$. An action-based version of CSL has been defined [11] but is not supported by PRISM.

Paths of interest through the states of the model are characterised by the *path formulae* specified by $\mathcal{P}$. Path formulae either refer to the next state (using the X operator), or record that one proposition is always satisfied until another is achieved (the until-formulae use the U-operator). Performance information is encoded into the CSL formulae via the time-bounded until operator (U^I) and the steady-state operator, $\mathcal{S}$.

It is sometimes convenient to introduce some *derived operators* in order to help with the expression of a CSL formula. These operators do not add to the expressive power of the logic, they simply help to make the statements of some formulae more compact. One such operator is *implication* ($\Rightarrow$) which can be

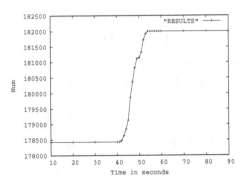

Fig. 3. Plot of satisfying states for the FieldCare model with $p = 0.9$

defined in the usual way, $\phi_1 \Rightarrow \phi_2 \equiv \neg\phi_1 \vee \phi_2$. Another useful operator is *time-bounded eventually* ($\Diamond^I$, where I is an interval of time) which is defined thus: $\Diamond^I \phi \equiv true\ \mathrm{U}^I\ \phi$. This operator is frequently used with intervals of the form $[0, t]$ to capture formally the concept of "*within t time units*".

These derived operators are used in our present case study in the following way. We wish to capture the situation where information sent by one of the participants in the protocol is received by another within a suitable time frame. In a framework with only one sender and one receiver we can characterise the *sending* and *receiving* events by two atomic propositions, **s** and **r**. Then the property which we are interested in can be expressed in CSL as follows.

$$\Phi \equiv \mathbf{s} \Rightarrow \mathcal{P}_{\geq p}[\Diamond^{[0,\ t]}\mathbf{r}]$$

This is a typical CSL formula, combining time, probability and a path through the system evolution. The above formula characterises all states for which either a send event does not occur or it does occur and then a receive event occurs within time t with probability at least p.

Hence, the CSL model-checking problem which we want to check is that $\mathrm{Sat}(\Phi) = S$, where S is the complete state-space of the model.

4.1   Probabilistic Model Checking

In model-checking our CSL formula against our model of the FieldCare system we investigated the formula Φ when p held the value 0.9. We found that the critical time-frame where Φ returns significant information is for t between 40 and 54 seconds. For values of t less than 40 the formula is true in just those states where a send event does not occur (178432 of the 182002 states of the model are in this subspace). For values of t greater than 54 the formula is true even if a send event occurs because with probability at least 0.9 the information will be received within 54 seconds (all of the 182002 states of the model are in this subspace). Figure 3 presents these results.

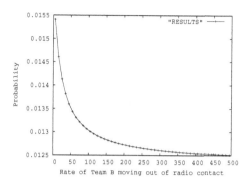

Fig. 4. Plot showing the probability of successfully updating the database decreasing as the rate of movement of teams increases

By presenting the number of satisfying states instead of simply a single truth value PRISM guides the modeller through experimentation with the model in order to select subsequent formulae to verify. If the present formula is true in nearly all of the states in the model then the next values for the probabilistic or time bounds might be close to the present ones. If the formula is satisfied in only a small number of states the next values chosen might be further away.

In studying the growth of the satisfying states in the model we see that the curve is not totally smooth. At around 50 seconds there is a small kink in the curve as a slightly larger than usual subset of the state space moves into the satisfying set for the formula. Shortly after the growth of this set slows. Variations such as this are readily explained as being caused by variability in the connectivity of components in the model.

4.2   Performance Analysis

In addition to model-checking the above formulae we undertook a classical performance analysis of the model. We used the sparse matrix engine of the PRISM tool with its implementation of the Jacobi over-relaxation numerical routine to solve the CTMC representation of the model for its stationary probability distribution. This is an efficient procedure, taking (approximately) 400 seconds to compute on a Pentium IV processor running at 1.8GHz with 256MB of physical RAM.

We then focussed on the probability of being in a distinguished subset of the state space, determined formally from our high-level PEPA net model. Figure 4 shows the impact of the increase in rate of movement of team *TeamB* from one area to another on the database update probability of *TeamA*. As the speed of movement increases, the probability P_{BA} of updating the database of *TeamA* decreases. This is the most typical case where one of the teams is more often required to move than the other one.

5   Conclusions

In this paper we have applied the PEPA nets modelling language to the analysis of a model of a real-world application, the FieldCare medical emergency system being developed by SINTEF Telecom and Informatics, Norway. This application will be used in a safety-critical setting and therefore deserves considered analysis and investigation before it is deployed in earnest.

The analysis which we applied to the system is undertaken by making a high-level model, abstracting away much unnecessary detail in order to focus more clearly on the salient aspects of the problem. Building performance models of realistic real-world systems is an activity which requires careful attention to detail in order to model correctly the intended behaviour of the system. Proceeding with care during this part of the modelling process is a wise investment of effort. If the initial performance model contains errors then all of the computational expense incurred in solving the model and all of the intellectual effort invested in the analysis and interpretation of the results obtained would at best be wasted. In general interpreting a model with errors could lead to making flawed decisions based on erroneous conclusions made from erroneous results. This can lead to perhaps classifying systems as being effectively reliable when a high-level model without these flaws would have demonstrated that they are not. For this reason we consider it important to work with structured, high-level modelling languages which directly support the concepts and idioms of the application domain, such as mobility of users and devices.

Using a suitable high-level modelling language, the PEPA nets notation, our analysis focussed on correctly capturing the behaviour of this dynamically-varying system in use and probing the timely behaviour of its key function: propagating critical data to all neighbours in a peer-to-peer application using a simple and robust protocol. Using the PRISM probabilistic model checker as our analysis tool we were able to ascertain how delays on the receiving of propagated medical information would impact on the system in use.

Other analysis tools for PEPA provide complementary analysis capabilities to those which are provided by PRISM. The Imperial PEPA Compiler (IPC) [9] uses the DNAmaca tool [12] to compute passage-time quantiles for passages through the model delimited by a set of starting states and a set of terminating states. This could be used to investigate other measures over the behaviour of the system including quantifying averages and extremes in response times. One of the reasons to model with a well-supported formal language such as PEPA is that a range of analysis options are available.

Many concerns and questions remain about peer-to-peer emergency medial systems such as FieldCare. Our analysis has said nothing about other very important aspects of the application such as resistance to malicious attack by hostile users of other mobile devices in the area. Similarly other analyses would be appropriate. The application is to be implemented using Java technology operating on hand-held devices under far from ideal conditions of use. We have thrown no light on whether or not the implementation technology can withstand this challenge. Aspects such as these remain to be considered carefully by the designers and developers of the system before the system is deployed in earnest in a life-critical situation.

Acknowledgements

The authors are supported by the Design Environments for Global ApplicationS project (DEGAS) IST-2001-32072 funded by the Future and Emerging Technologies Proactive Initiative on Global Computing. The PEPA to PRISM compiler was developed in collaboration with Gethin Norman and Dave Parker of The University of Birmingham. The authors wish to thank Paolo Ballarini for many helpful suggestions on CSL. Leïla Kloul is on leave from PRISM, Université de Versailles, Versailles, France.

References

[1] J. Gorman, S. Walderhaug, and H. Kvålen. Reliable data replication in a wireless medical emergency network. In *Proceedings of the 22nd International Conference on Computer Safety, Reliability and Security (SAFECOMP'03)*, number 2788 in LNCS, pages 207–220, Edinburgh, Scotland, September 2003. Springer-Verlag. 263, 266, 267

[2] S. Gilmore, J. Hillston, M. Ribaudo, and L. Kloul. PEPA nets: A structured performance modelling formalism. *Performance Evaluation*, 54(2):79–104, October 2003. 263, 266

[3] M. Kwiatkowska, G. Norman, and D. Parker. Probabilistic symbolic model checking with PRISM: A hybrid approach. In J.-P. Katoen and P. Stevens, editors, *Proc. 8th International Conference on Tools and Algorithms for the Construction and Analysis of Systems (TACAS'02)*, volume 2280 of *LNCS*, pages 52–66. Springer, April 2002. 263, 266

[4] A. Aziz, K. Sanwal, V. Singhal, and R. Brayton. Verifying continuous time Markov chains. In *Computer-Aided Verification*, volume 1102 of *LNCS*, pages 169–276. Springer-Verlag, 1996. 263, 272

[5] J. Hillston. *A Compositional Approach to Performance Modelling*. Cambridge University Press, 1996. 263, 264

[6] S. Gilmore, J. Hillston, L. Kloul, and M. Ribaudo. Software performance modelling using PEPA nets. In *Proceedings of the Fourth International Workshop on Software and Performance*, pages 13–24, Redwood Shores, California, USA, January 2004. ACM Press. 266

[7] S. Gilmore and J. Hillston. The PEPA Workbench: A Tool to Support a Process Algebra-based Approach to Performance Modelling. In *Proceedings of the Seventh International Conference on Modelling Techniques and Tools for Computer Performance Evaluation*, number 794 in Lecture Notes in Computer Science, pages 353–368, Vienna, May 1994. Springer-Verlag. 266

[8] G. Clark and W. H. Sanders. Implementing a stochastic process algebra within the Möbius modeling framework. In L. de Alfaro and S. Gilmore, editors, *Proceedings of the first joint PAPM-PROBMIV Workshop*, volume 2165 of *Lecture Notes in Computer Science*, pages 200–215, Aachen, Germany, September 2001. Springer-Verlag. 266

[9] J.T. Bradley, N.J. Dingle, S.T. Gilmore, and W.J. Knottenbelt. Derivation of passage-time densities in PEPA models using IPC: The Imperial PEPA Compiler. In G Kotsis, editor, *Proceedings of the 11th IEEE/ACM International Symposium on Modeling, Analysis and Simulation of Computer and Telecommunications Systems*, pages 344–351, University of Central Florida, October 2003. IEEE Computer Society Press. 266, 275

[10] F. Somenzi. *CUDD: CU Decision Diagram Package*. Department of Electrical and Computer Engineering, University of Colorado at Boulder, February 2001. 266

[11] R.D. Nicola and F.W. Vaandrager. Action versus state based logics for transition systems. In *Proceedings* Ecole de Printemps *on Semantics of Concurrency*, volume 469 of *Lecture Notes in Computer Science*, pages 407–419. Springer Verlag, 1990. 272

[12] W.J. Knottenbelt. Generalised Markovian analysis of timed transition systems. Master's thesis, University of Cape Town, 1996. 275

Integrating System Performance Engineering into MASCOT Methodology through Discrete-Event Simulation

Pere P. Sancho, Carlos Juiz, and Ramon Puigjaner

Universitat de les Illes Balears, Dpt. de Ciències Matemàtiques i Informàtica
Escola Politècnica Superior, Ctra. de Valldemossa, km. 7.5, 07071 Palma, Spain
{cjuiz,putxi}@uib.es
Phone: +34-971-172975, 173288 Fax: +34-971-173003

Abstract. Software design methodologies are incorporating non functional features on design system descriptions. MASCOT which has been a traditional design methodology for European defence companies has no performance extension. In this paper we present a set of performance annotations to the MASCOT methodology, called MASCOTime. These annotations are extending the MDL (MASCOT Description Language) design components transparently. Thus, in order to evaluate the performance of the annotated software designs, a discrete-event simulator prototype is also introduced. The prototype has been implemented with Java objects which are isomorphic to the MASCOTime components. Several examples of MASCOTime models and simulation results are also shown.

1 Introduction

Soft real-time systems differ from traditional software systems in that they have a dual notion of logical correctness. Logical correctness of a real-time system is based on both the correctness of the output and timeliness. That is, in addition to producing the correct output, soft real-time systems must produce it in a timely manner [2], [4].

One of the most usual approaches to software engineering is based on the concept of a system as a set of interacting components. In order to characterize the interaction between the components is also necessary to express a protocol representing the timing constraints on the interaction and to its support by an explicit interconnection in the future implemented system [2]. On the other hand, a software design defines how a software system is structured into components and also defines the interfaces among them.

MASCOT (Modular Approach to Software Construction Operation and Test) is a design and implementation method for real-time software development and brings together a co-ordinated set of techniques for dealing with the design, construction (system building), operation (run-time execution) and testing software, as its acronym wants to depict [21].

At the heart of MASCOT there is a particular form of software structure supported by complementary diagrammatic and textual notations. These notations

M. Núñez et al. (Eds.): FORTE 2004 Workshops, LNCS 3236, pp. 278–292, 2004.
© Springer-Verlag Berlin Heidelberg 2004

give visibility to the design as it emerges during development, and implementation takes place via special construction tools that operate directly on the design data. MADGE (Mascot Design Generator) is one of these tools [7]. Design visibility greatly eases the task of development management, and the constructional approach ensures conformity of implementation to design, and allows traceability of performance back to design.

The functional model allows a system to be described in terms of independently functional units interacting through defined transfers of information. Here is introduced the notion of protocol component which is used to annotate the interaction between processes with a MASCOT representation [22].

Unfortunately, MASCOT does not provide any kind of performance constraint annotation on its functional components that could estimate, running a performance evaluation tool, whether the system being designed will meet or not the performance requirements.

In this paper, we present MASCOTime as the main contribution to the integration of performance engineering practices into a traditional system engineering methodology through performance constraint annotations. MASCOTime interferes minimally with the functional description on original MDL (MASCOT Description Language). In this way, system/software engineers do not perceive any change in the functional description of the future system.

However, once the system design method has been augmented with performance annotations, the information provided for the explicit system design is not evaluated itself. It is necessary either to build a performance tool to directly compute or estimate the performance of the model that MASCOTime generates or to transform the augmented model to other formalism before its indirect evaluation. Since a model could be as complex as the system designer wants, flexibility on evaluation must be achievable. Therefore, we also present a prototype of discrete-event simulator for MASCOTime designs. The implementation of the simulator has been developed using objects that represent directly the MASCOTime (and also original MASCOT) components. Thus, the simulated components that build a system and the objects that the simulator manages are isomorphic. Due to the restrictions that would be imposed to the functional (and performance) model to apply analytical or numerical algorithms, we decide to avoid transforming the MASCOTime model to a traditional formal model for performance evaluation [8]. The discrete-event simulator uses a direct translation between the MASCOTime components and their isomorphic Java objects.

In the following section, direct related works are reminded. In section 3 we are going to review the MASCOT design methodology. Section 4 is focused in the MASCOT Description Language (MDL) as textual description of MASCOT designs. In section 5, we propose MASCOTime as performance engineering extension of MDL blocks. Therefore, in section 6 a discrete-event simulator prototype for MASCOTime designs is overviewed and finally the conclusions and future work are given in Section 7.

2   Related Work

A set of well-known notations exists for each of the description of system, e.g. UML, without augmented information for the performance constraints. Despite the fact that early drafts of UML 2.0 try to fill this gap and also the huge amount of interesting recent software performance engineering proposals for current version of UML, for example in [5], [15], [20], major European defence companies, e.g. MBDA [17], do not use of UML as main system design methodology. Its utilization is only restricted to B2B applications or B2C applications. Thus, the soft real-time systems that MBDA produces are modeled with a software design method called MASCOT [3]. Several works have transformed the MAS-COT components into queueing networks to solve analytically their performance behavior [10], [11], [12] but no tool has been developed from this research. On the other hand, a new software performance engineering technique for MAS-COT was proposed in [19] although but it was relying on a three-stepped meta-model transformation whose result was not very useful. In [18] an early design of a queueing network solver/simulator for MASCOT diagrams was depicted. However, its implementation was revealed unpractical due to the inapplicability of analytical or approximated algorithms and also because of the indirect resolution of the models. Since the system modeling has to be flexible, we decided to build a discrete-event simulator.

3   MASCOT

The origins of MASCOT (Modular Approach to Software Construction Operation and Test) go back to the early seventies, and in particular, to the work carried out at that time by Hugo Simpson and Ken Jackson at the Royal Radar Establishment (RRE) belonging to the U.K. Ministry of Defence. The spur for the creation of MASCOT came from the problems they had experienced in the software development for a large multi-computer real-time system. In other words, a large amount of code to be written for many computers operating in parallel and interacting in real time and with a large number of people engaged simultaneously on the development task that usually produced technical and management problems.

The MASCOT approach to software development, as stated in [9], contains the following features:

- It defines a formal method of expressing the software structure of a real-time system, which is independent of both computer configuration, and programming language.
- It imposes a disciplined approach to design, which yields a highly modular structure, ensuring a close correspondence between design functional elements and constructional elements for system integration.
- It supports a program-acceptance strategy based on the verification of single modules, as larger collections of functionally related modules.

- It provides a small easily implemented executive for the dynamic control of program execution at run time.
- It can be applied to all software lifecycle stages from design onwards.
- It can form the basis for a standard system of software procurement and management.

At the heart of the method there is a particular form of software structure supported by complementary diagrammatic and textual notations. These notations give visibility to the architecture design as it emerges during development, and implementation takes place via special construction tools that operate directly on the design data. Design visibility greatly eases the task of development management, and the constructional approach ensures conformity of implementation to design, and allows traceability of real-time performance back to design. MADGE is one of these construction tools that produces MASCOT designs and automatically generates Ada code. Thus, MADGE and other tools may be used to consider different software/hardware architectures on design but unfortunately they cannot be evaluated.

The future of no method can be predicted with certainty. Nevertheless, one interesting feature to be added would be the performance evaluation of the design elements in early stages of the system design by incorporating the time requirements and constraints. This article is concerned with an extension to the MASCOT method that makes performance evaluation of the designs easier.

3.1   MASCOT Components

The building blocks of MASCOT are namely, activities, intercommunication data areas (IDAs) and servers. There are also complex components, made from modules of the simple ones, known as subsystems. Networks of activities, IDAs, servers and subsystems build system designs in MASCOT methodology.

Activities. Activities are the basic process elements in the system design. They are the unique active components on the MASCOT method. Every activity may be viewed as an implementation thread. Different activities could be executed in parallel but the individual tasks that they perform are sequential. Activities describe the overall process of the system that is being designed. Activities are connected asynchronously through IDAs.

Intercommunication Data Areas (IDAs). The IDAs are components to interchange data among system tasks. Instead of communicating directly each other, tasks use buffer memories asynchronously. IDAs could be structured in any way but there are two specialized components: channels and pools.

Channels provide unidirectional transmission of message data among activities through a buffer. Reading is a destructive operation but writing is not destructive. The operations are served in FIFO manner and the capacity of the channel is the most important performance feature of this component.

Pools are data containers. Reading is not destructive (although it could be concurrent) but writing is a destructive operation on pools.

Generic IDAs are those which do not belong to the channel and pool families. They could include other IDAs and activities to perform their communication.

Routes are the newer elements in the MASCOT methodology. They are special cases of channels and pools. A taxonomy of these elements is provided in [13]. Typical components falling into this category are signals, constants, rendez-vous, etc.

Servers. Servers are connecting the I/O of the system with the external environment. They are receiving or sending data to be processed in the system belonging to the outside.

Ports, Windows and Paths. Every component in MASCOT must be interconnected composing a functional network via paths. A port is a set of operations requested by a component. A window is a set of operations offered by a component. Paths give equivalence among operations among windows and ports.

4 MDL

MASCOT provides a textual notation for components and interconnections known as MDL (MASCOT Description Language). An example of a MDL file is shown in next lines.

```
SYSTEM TMS;
    USES TMS_RADAR, TMS_INTERFACE, TMS_CORE_SUBSYSTEM, TMS_CLOCK;
    SERVER INTERFACE : TMS_INTERFACE;
    SERVER RADAR : TMS_RADAR;
    SUBSYSTEM S_CLOCK : TMS_CLOCK;
    SUBSYSTEM CORE : TMS_CORE_SUBSYSTEM ( P1 = RADAR.W1,
                                          P4 = INTERFACE.W2,
                                          P3 = INTERFACE.W1,
                                          P2 = S_CLOCK.W1 );
END.
```

Every MASCOT model is either a system or a subsystem. Therefore, the MDL system description is a tree structure. This code describes the TMS system that comprises four subsystems: the radar, the interface, the core and the clock. These subsystems are stored in different files by MADGE. The visibility of the TMS system is performed by the set of its components. For example, the core subsystem has four ports (P1, P2, P3 and P4) that are connected to several windows of the other three subsystems. Figure 1 shows the corresponding MASCOT diagrammatic description of the TMS system.

On the other hand, each subsystem could be composed by other subsystems, channels, pools, routes, servers and activities. The following code describes the clock subsystem which uses a signal and performs an interruption through an activity.

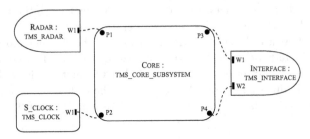

Fig. 1. The MASCOT diagrammatic description of the TMS system

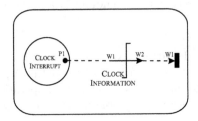

Fig. 2. MASCOT diagrams corresponding to the clock subsystem

```
SUBSYSTEM TMS_CLOCK;
   PROVIDES W1 : GET;
   USES CLOCK_INTERRUPT, SIGNAL;
   ACTIVITY A_CLOCK_INTERRUPT : CLOCK_INTERRUPT
                   ( P1 = CLOCK_INFORMATION.W1 );
   ROUTE CLOCK_INFORMATION : SIGNAL;
   W1 = CLOCK_INFORMATION.W2;
END.
```

Figure 2 shows the corresponding MASCOT diagrams of the clock subsystem. Those kind of modular components are capable to describe the whole system with textual or diagrammatic descriptions.

5 MASCOTime

MASCOTime is a prototype of discrete-event simulator for MASCOT designs that shows the difference on performance among architecture candidates in early stages of software/system construction.

In no way can MASCOTime be regarded as a handle-cranking technique, guaranteed to produce, painlessly, the solutions of complex problems. Success is achieved by using a modular decomposition of MASCOT approach which is relevant to management, design, construction and execution, and which allows problems that contain complexity, to be partitioned into smaller pieces. Design is essentially a creative process requiring the application of skill and experience. MADGE provides the process with visibility and code generation, which gives control over it, and MASCOTime provides the performance evaluation of such designs.

The software/system architecture modeled with MASCOT is based on data flow concepts. The simplicity of its design methodology has several advantages, e.g. allowing the distribution of system functionality to be represented. This textual/diagrammatic representation provides the means for controlling functional interactions and their propagation among the components. However, there is no control in one important non-functional feature of the system that is being modeled: the performance of the software components or even the performance of the overall system. MASCOTime is an extension to MASCOT that provides enough performance information to evaluate the performance of the MASCOT related models. MASCOTime design style mainly describes the service time and the capabilities of the functional components and analyzes them. Therefore, performance annotations for the components have been added to MASCOT in a friendly manner, which allows derivation of a simulation model of the system's architecture.

In order to minimize the training on MASCOTime issues, the extension has been developed avoiding an intermediate interfacing between the design with performance annotations and the simulator. Thus, MASCOTime components and simulator objects are isomorphic. Moreover, the actions applicable on the components are similar to the actions to perform over the Java objects.

5.1   MDL and MASCOTime

Since MDL provides the textual notation of the MASCOT method, MASCOTime extends the notation to incorporate performance information. The way that the extensions are annotated minimizes the perturbation of the functional model created with MDL. Thus, MASCOTime code is enclosed between {* and *} to be distinguished from the traditional MDL comments (written between { and }). Therefore, the MDL model remains intact even though MASCOTime extends the file source. The following code corresponds to the extended version of the clock subsystem example including MASCOTime annotations. Notice that the MDL code is identical to the previous one, but some information has been added as MDL comments (between { and }).

```
SUBSYSTEM TMS_CLOCK;
   PROVIDES W1 : GET;
   USES CLOCK_INTERRUPT, SIGNAL;
   ACTIVITY A_CLOCK_INTERRUPT : CLOCK_INTERRUPT(P1=CLOCK_INFORMATION.W1);
   ROUTE CLOCK_INFORMATION : SIGNAL;
   W1 = CLOCK_INFORMATION.W2;

{*
   BEGIN MASCOTIME
   [ MASCOTime Code...]
   END MASCOTIME
*}
END.
```

The first sentence of a MASCOTime block is always a BEGIN MASCOTime and the last END MASCOTime to enhance the visibility of the code.

MASCOTime Components. Due to the limited extension of the paper we are only going to show some representative examples of the components that MASCOTime uses:

▶ *Channel:* The essential performance constraints of a channel must be its capacity and the mean time (and distribution) to read or write into the buffer. An example of code may be the one beside this paragraph.

```
BEGIN MASCOTIME
    DEFINE INFORMATION_RADAR : CHANNEL
        CAPACITY(4);
        TREAD(EXP(2.5));
        TWRITE(EXP(3.0));
    END DEFINE
END MASCOTIME
```

The channel `Information_Radar` is defined in a block containing its capacity of 4 elements, the mean time to read a position (2.5 units of time, exponentially distributed) and the mean time to write a position in the channel (3.0 units of time, exponentially distributed).

▶ *Pools:* As in channels, the mean times to read or write a pool are necessary to consider the performance of the component however the limit of simultaneous writers may also be of interest. In next lines an example of MASCOTime pool is provided.

```
BEGIN
MASCOTIME
    DEFINE POSITION_ANTENNA : POOL
        TWRITE(HEXP(2.0,0.3));
        TREAD(HEXP(1.0,0.5));
        SYMWRITERS(3);
    END DEFINE
END MASCOTIME
```

The pool `position_antenna` may hold up to three simultaneous writers with their respective mean time to read equal to 1.0 units of time (hypoexponentially distributed, quadratic coefficient of variation equals to 0.5). When an exclusive writer access the pool needs 2.0 units of time to write (also hypoexponentially distributed, quadratic coefficient of variation of 0.3).

▶ *Other Routes:* The example corresponds to a signal element, a buffer with destructive writing. The capacity of the buffer is two positions, and the mean time to read and the mean time to write are different amounts with different statistical distributions.

```
BEGIN MASCOTIME
    DEFINE CLOCK_TICKS : SIGNAL
        CAPACITY(2);
        TREAD(HEXP(1.0,0.5));
        TWRITE(NORM(3.0,1.0));
    END DEFINE
END MASCOTIME
```

The signal `clock_ticks` is defined in a block containing its capacity of 2 elements, the mean time to read a position (1 unit of time, hypoexponentially distributed) and the mean time to write a position in the buffer is 3.0 units of time, in normal distribution with 1.0 of variation.

▶ *Activity:* Since the activities are the processing core of the systems, the sequences of their attached actions imply processing delays that is necessary to compute. However, the order of the actions in these sequences is not functionally trivial.

This example shows that pool3 is read after pool1 and before a processing time of 10.0 units of time (constant). Similarly occurs for channels, but the operations have different parameters.

```
BEGIN MASCOTIME
  DEFINE activitat_1 : ACTIVITY
    BEGIN SEQUENCE
      CRONO ON;
      READ(pool1);
      READ(pool3);
      WAIT(CST(10.0));
      WRITE(channel1);
      READ(channel2);
      WAIT(EXP(20.0));
      WRITE(pool2);
      CRONO OFF;
    END SEQUENCE
  END DEFINE
END MASCOTIME
```

MASCOTime also provides time markers (CRONO ON and OFF) to retrieve the response time of processing sequences.

▶ *Generic IDAs:* MASCOTime provides the modular composition of existing elements to generate a new one, a generic IDA could be an interesting example.

```
BEGIN MASCOTIME
  DEFINE ida_01 : GENERIC IDA
    WINDOWS(2);
    DEFINE set_0 : CHANNEL         [<-- CONTINUED]
      CAPACITY(20);                  DEFINE motor01 : IDA MOTOR ida01
      TREAD(CST(1.0));                 TRIGGER(WRITE,0,Bern(15));
      TWRITE(CST(1.0));              BEGIN SEQUENCE
    END DEFINE;                        FLUSH(set_0);
    DEFINE set_1 : SIGNAL             WRITE(pool1);
      TREAD(EXP(1.0));                WRITE(set_1);
      TWRITE(CST(2.0));             END SEQUENCE
    END DEFINE;                    END DEFINE
    ATTACH(WRITE,0,set_0);       END MASCOTIME
    ATTACH(READ,1,set_1);
  END DEFINE
  [CONTINUED -->]
```

This code provides a buffer structure for input characters coming from a keyboard. Each character enters through the window and stored into the channel (set(0)). Once every 15 writing of characters, on average, the motor of the IDA triggers a sequence of actions: first, the flushes the channel, second writes the characters into the extern pool1 and finally writes in the intern signal to release the window for reading next characters. Figure 3 shows the MASCOT description of this generic IDA, where sequence of operations and processing delays are missing and must be provided by MASCOTime in textual notation.

There are other interesting MASCOTime building blocks as passive and active servers, IDA motors and other routes that are not here included due to the extension of the this text.

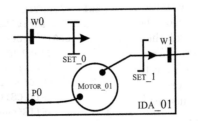

Fig. 3. Generic IDA described with MASCOT diagrams

6   MASCOTime Simulator

Since MASCOTime has no utility without a performance evaluation tool, a discrete-event simulator prototype has been developed for this purpose. This simulator provides enough information to detect the performance behavior of the MASCOT models of future system implementations. The interest of our prototype relies on the data structure chosen for the simulator construction. The objects that the program manages during simulation are isomorphic to the MASCOTime components. Since the system modeling has to be flexible, we decided not to provide an analytical evaluation tool. Thus, it makes no sense to translate MASCOTime data structure into traditional performance formalisms. In this way, software engineers would feel more comfortable using this performance tool. The new prototype of simulator also includes the integration facilities between MASCOTime descriptions and the simulation objects.

6.1   General Features

The discrete-event simulator core of MASCOTime prototype is basically constituted by an asynchronous event processor using a data heap, implemented through Java language. Other features of the simulator are:

- Two operational modes: transient and stationary.
- In transient mode, the simulator selects a small number of samples. Sampling may be stored and represented into a graphical tool to determine the border of both operational modes, if exist. The main parameters to submit a simulation model in transient mode are the amount of sampling and the softener window required [14].
- In stationary mode, the results of the simulation are in confidence intervals. A log file is providing to review the simulation execution. The main parameters to submit a simulation model in stationary mode are the simulation time and the options to avoid the transient time and to resume logging execution.
- The simulation libraries are organized into classes depending on their functionality and their privacy.
- Uniform [0,1] pseudorandom number generator [16], with period 630.360.016.

– Main statistical distributions available are: Constant, Exponential, Normal, Lognormal, Hypo/Hyper-exponential, Weibull, Uniform [0,1], Uniform [a,b], Gamma, Erlang, Pareto, Bernoulli among others [1].
– Chronometer option to compute latency times in any sequence of execution on MASCOTime objects.
– Library of Java objects that are isomorphic to the corresponding MASCO-Time components.

6.2   A Simple Example

MASCOT diagram and code generators, e.g. MADGE, allow software engineers to build system models in MDL and also to obtain Ada skeletons from design. Once the MASCOT code is provided by such tools, software engineers may add the MASCOTime extensions in comments blocks. In this way the original functional model remains intact. Then, an automatic interpreter imports the annotated MASCOT design and translates it to Java code. This Java code is a discrete-event simulator that evaluates the model depending on the parameters submitted. The resulting workflow doesn't require software engineers to know the details of the implementation of the simulator or even to have some knowledge about performance modeling with classical formalisms. In order to illustrate the performance engineering workflow with our proposal, a simple system was designed with MADGE: a radar system has been represented with MASCOT components in figure 4. Five radars send messages to the core of the system through a communications channel. Once the information arrives to a dispatcher it is shown in the display interface and then stored into the disk subsystem. Following the figure 4, the MASCOT MDL code and part of the extended MASCOTime block are shown for the radar system. In particular, the definition of the three channels involved in the system design: the radar_data channel, the disk channel and the buffer channel.

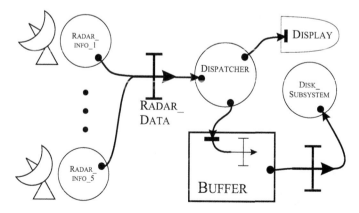

Fig. 4. A simple example of MASCOT diagrams

```
SYSTEM RADAR_STATION;
    USES RADAR_INFO, CHANNEL, DISPLAY, DISPATCHER, DISK, BUFFER;

    IDA IDA_BUFFER : BUFFER ( P1 = DISK_PET.W1 );
    SERVER S_DISPLAY : DISPLAY;
    ACTIVITY A_DISK : DISK ( P1 = DISK_PET.W2 );
    ACTIVITY A_DISPATCHER : DISPATCHER ( P3 = IDA_BUFFER.W1,
                                         P2 = S_DISPLAY.W1,
                                         P1 = RADAR_DATA.W2 );
    ACTIVITY RADAR_INFO5 : RADAR_INFO ( P1 = RADAR_DATA.W1 );
    [...]
    ROUTE DISK_PET : CHANNEL;
    ROUTE RADAR_DATA : CHANNEL;

    {*
    BEGIN MASCOTIME
       DEFINE DISK_PET : CHANNEL
          CAPACITY(20);
          TREAD(CST(2.0));
          TWRITE(CST(0.5));
       END DEFINE;
       DEFINE RADAR_DATA : CHANNEL
          CAPACITY(20);
          TREAD(CST(0.1));
          TWRITE(CST(0.1));
       END DEFINE;
       [...]
       DEFINE IDA_BUFFER : GENERIC IDA
            WINDOWS(1);
            DEFINE SET_0 : CHANNEL
               CAPACITY(5);
               TREAD(CST(0.3));
               TWRITE(CST(0.3));
            END DEFINE;
            ATTACH(WRITE,0, SET_0);
       END DEFINE;
       DEFINE MOTOR_1 : MOTOR IDA IDA_BUFFER
            TRIGGER(WRITE, 0, CLOCK(5));
            BEGIN SEQUENCE
               FLUSH(SET_0);
               WAIT(CST(2.0));
               WRITE(DISK_PET);
               STOP;
            END SEQUENCE;
       END DEFINE;
    END MASCOTIME
    *}
END.
```

Table 1. Simulation results for `radar_data`

Measurements	
Mean arrival time	10.020 ± 0.0238
Mean departure time	10.020 ± 0.0148
Mean number of messages	1.525
% full	7.628 %
Mean number of blocked messages for reading	0.131
Mean number of blocked messages for writing	1.162E-5

With this code we are ready to perform a simulation of the system. First we make the simulator work in a special mode to make it determine the end of the transient warm up. Then we make the simulator perform a simulation of the system discarding the initial transient data. The table below shows the results:

7   Conclusions and Future Work

This paper has depicted the integration of the performance engineering techniques into the software engineering arena through an isomorphic description of the performance behaviour and a discrete-event simulator prototype. The approximation chosen minimizes the interference in the software design methodology by means of performance constraints annotations. In particular, MASCOT design methodology, which has been used for twenty years in European Defence companies, has been extended to MASCOTime, our proposed annotated version for this traditional methodology. Even though several tools have been built to generate automatically system designs from MASCOT diagrams, none of these facilities has been extended to incorporate performance information of such system designs. Particularly, MADGE tool generates Ada code and textual MDL notation from a graphical user interface representing the components that software engineers are using to build the software models of future systems. These components are basically activities, intercommunication data areas (IDAs) and servers. All MASCOT components are functionally connected through windows, ports and paths. Thus, MASCOTime takes advantage of the functional skeleton of the system model to add performance constraints on every component of the design. In order to minimize the interference of software engineering tasks, all the MASCOTime extensions are code comments in MDL. Since the goal of performance engineering is to evaluate the system model, a discrete-event simulator for MASCOTime has been prototyped. Although simulation is only an approximation, it is more flexible than using analytical/numerical solvers which would be very restricted for their application to complex software designs. Therefore, there is no necessity to transform the MASCOTime structure to a traditional formalism and then evaluate the transformed model. Our proposal consists on building the simulator with objects that are isomorphic to the MASCOT components. Thus, the discrete-event simulator has been implemented in Java code that provides other advantages as portability. An interpreter of the MASCO-Time extension has been also built to map design models to simulation objects. Some examples of MASCOTime code and the execution of the discrete-event simulation have also been shown. The prototype that has been implemented must be tested by final users in order to verify its real applicability. In order to get the industrial validation of the prototype, it is going to be informally tested by MBDA, formerly known as Matra British Aerospace. This prototype should be extended in order to increment the approach alternatives to solve analytically some simple components by decomposition-aggregation and then the whole system through hybrid techniques. Depending on the user validation, we may integrate MASCOTime in MADGE tool including the GUI interfacing.

References

[1] Allen, A. O.: *Probability, Statistics and Queueing Theory with Computer Science Applications*. Academic Press, second edition, 1990. 288

[2] Allworth, S. T.; Zobel, R. N.: *Introduction to Real-time Software Design*. Macmillan Education, 1987. 278

[3] Bate, G.: *Mascot 3 an Informal Introductory Tutorial*. Software Engineering Journal, May 1986, 95-102. 280

[4] Cooling, J. E.: *Real-Time Software Systems. An Introduction to Structured and Object-oriented Design*. International Thomson Computer Press (1997). 278

[5] Gilmore, S.; Hillston, J.; Kloul, L.; Ribaudo, M.: *Software Performance Modeling using PEPA Nets*. In Proceedings of WOSP 2004, ACM press, pp.13-23 , 2004. 280

[6] Gomaa, H.: *Software Design Methods for Concurrent and Real-time Systems*. The SEI Series in Software Engineering, N. Habermann (ed.), Addison-Wesley, Reading, Massachusetts (1993).

[7] Harding, M. D.: MASCOT DESIGN GENERATOR (MADGE) v.6.0. Release Notification, n. 5096, issue 11, November 1998. 279

[8] Harrison, P. G., Patel, N. M.: *Performance Modelling of Communication Networks and Computer Architectures*. International Computer Science Series, A. D. McGettrick (ed.), Addison-Wesley, Wokingham, England (1993). 279

[9] Joint IECCA and MUF Committee. *The Official Handbook of MASCOT*, 1987. 280

[10] Juiz, C., Puigjaner, R., Perros, H. G.: *Performance Analysis of Multi-Class Data Transfer Elements in Soft Real-Time Systems using Semaphore Queues*. System Performance Evaluation: Methodologies and Applications, E. Gelenbe (ed.), pp. 275-289, CRC Press, Boca Ratón, Florida (2000). 280

[11] Juiz, C.; Puigjaner, R.: *Performance modelling of pools in soft real-time design architectures*. Simulation Practice and Theory, 9 (3,5):215-240, 2002. 280

[12] Juiz, C.; Puigjaner, R.; Jackson, K.: *Performance evaluation of channels for large real-time software systems*. In Proceedings of ECBS'98, pp. 69-76. IEEE Computer Society, 1998. 280

[13] Juiz, C.; Puigjaner, R.; Jackson, K. : *Performance Modelling of Interaction Protocols in Soft Real-Time Design Architectures: Performance Engineering*, LNCS 2047, pp.300-316, 2001. 282

[14] Law, A. M.; Kelton, D. W.: *Simulation Modelling and Analysis*. McGraw-Hill Higher Education, third edition, 2000. 287

[15] Lopez-Grao, J.P.; Merseguer, J.; Campos, J.: *From UML Activity Diagrams To Stochastic Petri Nets: Application To Software Performance Engineering*. In Proceedings of WOSP 2004, ACM press, pp 25-36. , 2004. 280

[16] Marse, K.; Roberts, S.D.: *Implementing a Portable Fortran Uniform (0, 1) Generator*. Simulation, 41:135-139, October 1983. 287

[17] MBDA web site: http://www.mbda.net/. 280

[18] Munar, O.; Juiz, C.: *Adapting MASCOT to software performance engineering using object-oriented simulation*. In ASTC, pp. 281-288. Proceedings of IEEE Computer Society, 2003. 280

[19] Savino, N.; Anciano, J.L.; Juiz, C.: *Unified System Builder through Interacting Blocks (USBIB) for Soft Real-time Systems*. In Proceedings of WOSP 2002, ACM Press, pp. 83-90, 2002. 280

[20] Wu, X.; Woodside, M.: *Performance Modeling from Software Components*. In Proceedings of WOSP 2004, ACM Press, pp. 290-301 , 2004. 280

[21] Simpson, H.R.: *The Mascot method*, Software Engineering Journal, pp. 103-120, May 1986. 278

[22] Simpson, H.R.: *Protocols for Process Interaction. 1, 2, 3.* Matra BAe Dynamics, 2000. 279

Symbolic Performance and Dependability Evaluation with the Tool CASPA

Matthias Kuntz[1], Markus Siegle[1], and Edith Werner[2]

[1] University of the Federal Armed Forces Munich, Department of Computer Science
{kuntz,siegle}@informatik.unibw-muenchen.de
[2] Georg-August-Universität Göttingen, Institut für Informatik
ewerner@informatik.uni-goettingen.de

Abstract. This paper describes the tool CASPA, a new performance evaluation tool which is based on a Markovian stochastic process algebra. CASPA uses multi-terminal binary decision diagrams (MTBDD) to represent the labelled continuous time Markov chain (CTMC) underlying a given process algebraic specification. All phases of modelling, from model construction to numerical analysis and measure computation, are based entirely on this symbolic data structure. We present several case studies which demonstrate the superiority of CASPA over sparse-matrix-based process algebra tools. Furthermore, CASPA is compared to other symbolic modelling tools.

1 Introduction

Symbolic data structures, such as binary decision diagrams (BDD) [3] and variants thereof, have proven to be suitable for the efficient generation and compact representation of very large state spaces and transition systems. In [13] it has been shown that in the context of compositional model specification formalisms such as process algebra, the size of the symbolic representation can be kept within linear bounds, even if the underlying state space grows exponentially. The key to such compact representation is the exploitation of the compositional structure of a given specification [14, 7, 24]. It is also known that in addition to functional analysis, performance analysis and the verification of performability properties can also be carried out on such symbolic representations [17, 24].

In this paper, we describe the new tool CASPA which offers a Markovian stochastic process algebra for model specification. CASPA generates a symbolic representation of the underlying labelled CTMC, which is based on multi-terminal BDDs (MTBDD), directly from the high-level model, without generating transition systems as an intermediate representation. In addition to specifying the model, the CASPA modelling language allows the user to specify different types of performance and dependability measures of interest. Numerical analysis and computation of measures are also carried out directly on the symbolic representation of the transition rate matrix of the underlying CTMC. To our

M. Núñez et al. (Eds.): FORTE 2004 Workshops, LNCS 3236, pp. 293–307, 2004.
© Springer-Verlag Berlin Heidelberg 2004

knowledge, CASPA is the first stochastic process algebra tool whose implementation relies completely on symbolic data structures.

1.1 Related Work

Among other tools which are based on symbolic data structures are the model analyser SMART [4] and the probabilistic model checker PRISM [20, 21]. While SMART relies on multi-valued decision diagrams and matrix diagrams, PRISM – like CASPA – is based on multi-terminal binary decision diagrams. In Sec. 4, we compare CASPA to PRISM, mainly with respect to compactness of representation and effects of state space ordering. We also performed experiments with SMART, whose state space generation component seems to be even faster. However, we deliberately do not compare the numerical analysis component of SMART to that of CASPA, since this would basically boil down to a comparison of the algorithms of SMART and PRISM, which is not our focus here. In Sec. 4.1 we also compare CASPA to the work presented in [8], which is based on multi-valued decision diagrams and matrix diagrams. With respect to symbolic tools for stochastic process algebra, we also mention the work [11], where a PEPA specification (derived as an intermediate language from a UML specification) is used as input for PRISM.

1.2 Organisation of the Paper

The paper is organised as follows: In section 2 we introduce CASPA's specification language and give an overview of its architecture. Section 3 explains how the specification is translated to MTBDDs. In section 4 we demonstrate the usefulness of our approach by means of several case studies, which includes a comparison with other tools. Section 5 summarises our results and concludes with an outlook on future work.

2 Specification Language and Tool Architecture

In this section we briefly explain how a system and its measures of interest can be described in CASPA. We discuss an example specification and give some details on the tool's architecture and implementation.

2.1 System Specification

CASPA's specification language is derived from the stochastic process algebra TIPP [15, 12]. It provides operators for prefixing, choice, enabling, disabling, parallel composition and hiding. Infinite (i.e. cyclic) behaviour is specified by means of defining equations. All actions are associated with an exponential delay, which is specified by a rate parameter. The technique used for symbolic model representation (cf. Sec. 3) works only for finite state spaces. Therefore the grammar of the input language is such that recursion over static operators

```
(1)     /* Rate and constant definitions */
(2)     rate xi = 0.5;
(3)     rate gamma = 5;
(4)     rate mu = 0.3;
(5)     int max = 3;
(6)     /* System specification */
(7)     System     := (P(0) |[]| P(0)) |[b]| (hide a in Q(10))
(8)     Q(m [10])  := [m > 0] -> (a,xi); Q(m-1)
(9)                   [m = 0] -> (b,mu); Q(10)
(10)    P (n [max]) := [*] -> (b,gamma); P(n) + (c,gamma); stop
(11)                   [n > 0] -> (d,n*mu); P (n-1)
(12)                   [n < max] -> (a,0.3); P (n+1)
(13)    /* Measure specification */
(14)    statemeasure XXX (P{1}(n > 0) & !P{2}(n = max)) | Q(m = 4)
(15)    meanvalue YYY P{2}(n)
(16)    throughputmeasure ZZZ a
```

Fig. 1. Example CASPA specification

(i.e. parallel composition and hiding) is not allowed, which ensures that the underlying state space is finite.

The specification language allows the specification of parameterised processes, i.e. processes which carry one or more integer parameters. This feature is very useful for describing the behaviour of queueing, counting, or generally indexed processes. Within a parameterised process, the enabling of actions may be conditioned on the current value of the process parameters. In CASPA it is possible to define both rate and parameter constants. Parameters are always integer numbers, whereas rates are real numbers.

2.2   Example

We now discuss a small example (see Fig. 1). This specification has no special meaning, its only purpose is to introduce the language elements of CASPA. In lines (2) to (4) we find the definition of specific rate values, in line (5) a global parameter constant is defined. Lines (7) to (12) contain the system specification. Line (7) shows both possibilities to define parallel processes: The two P(0) processes are composed in parallel without interaction, i.e. all their actions are performed independently of each other. In contrast, Q(10) is composed in parallel with the two former processes in a synchronised way, i.e. action b must be performed by one of the P-processes and the Q-process at the same time. The synchronisation semantics is the same as for TIPP [15, 12]. In line (7) we also find the hiding operator: Action a in process Q is hidden from the environment and replaced by the special silent action tau. In line (8) we see an example of guarded choice: Action a can be performed if the value of parameter m is greater than zero. In line (10) we see a guarded choice whose test consists of *, which means the branch can be taken regardless of the actual parameter value. In lines (8) and (10) the maximum value of the respective parameters is given: For process P we chose a global constant max, for process Q the maximum value 10 is given explicitly. As for every process parameter such a maximum value has to be defined, the finiteness of the underlying state space is guaranteed. In

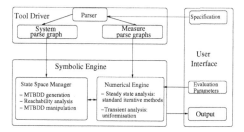

Fig. 2. Tool architecture

line (10) a choice between (b,gamma); P(n) and (c,gamma); stop is given. As all actions have exponential delay the choice of which action is actually taken corresponds to a race condition (as for stochastic Petri nets). In line (11) we see that rates can be arithmetic expressions, which makes it possible to define rates that are dependent on actual parameter values, similar to marking dependent rates in stochastic Petri nets. Finally, in lines (14) to (16) we find examples of measure specifications. We see that state measures can contain Boolean expressions with the usual connectives conjunction (&), disjunction (|) and negation (!). The clause (P{1}(n > 0) & !P{2}(n = max)) characterises states in which parameter n of process P{1} is greater than zero, and parameter n of process P{2} is smaller than the maximum value, where P{i} expresses that we are interested in the i-th of the two P processes. A mean value will return the expected value of the specified process parameter (in line (15) it will be the mean value of parameter n of process P{2}), and a throughput measure will compute the throughput of the given action (in line (16) this is action a).

2.3   Tool Architecture

CASPA is written entirely in C. The lexical analyser was realised using the tool flex, the parser was written in bison. The symbolic engine was implemented using the BDD-library CUDD [25] and the hybrid numerical solution methods developed by Dave Parker [22] within the context of the tool PRISM. The tool architecture consists of three major parts [26], as shown in Fig. 2.

User Interface. Up to now, CASPA has only a textual user interface. A typical call of the tool consists of indicating the file name that contains the system and measure specification, the analysis method, parameters for the numerical analysis and information about the verbosity level. An example call looks as follows:

```
caspa -v 1 -r -T -a TRANSIENT 100 ftcs.cas
```

The textual user interface is also used to present the results of the tool, i.e. number of states, information about the size of the symbolic representation, computation times, results of numerical analysis, etc. Additionally, CASPA can generate output that makes it possible to visualise the state space using the tool davinci [6], or for any graphical tool that can handle the .dot [1] format.

Tool Driver. From the command line the specification file is passed to the tool driver. It parses the system and the measure specification, translates them into their parse graphs and passes the results to the state space manager.

State Space Manager. The state space manager generates (from the parse graphs of the system and measure specification) the MTBDD representation of the labelled CTMC, resp. of the measures. It can perform reachability analysis, and manipulates the MTBDD data structure to allow for efficient numerical analysis (cf. section 3).

Numerical Engine. The numerical engine computes the vector of state probabilities. Several well-known numerical algorithms for both steady-state and transient analysis are implemented. The algorithms and their implementations are taken from PRISM, for their detailed description see [22]. The user can set the parameters of the algorithms, such as accuracy or maximum number of iterations.

3   Markov Chain Generation, Representation and Numerical Analysis

In this section, the approach of CASPA for directly mapping the process terms to MTBDDs is presented. Note that a CTMC is never constructed explicitly, only its symbolic encoding. A more detailed exposition of this translation can be found in [18]. We also briefly describe how the specified measures are related to the Markov chain representation and how the measures are computed.

3.1   Basis for Symbolic Representations

In this subsection we briefly introduce the basics of symbolic state space representation. An exhaustive account of this can be found in [24].

Multi-terminal Binary Decision Diagrams. MTBDDs [10] (also called algebraic decision diagrams (ADDs) [2]) are an extension of binary decision diagrams (BDDs) [3] for the canonical graph-based representation of functions of type $I\!B^n \mapsto I\!R$. We consider ordered reduced MTBDDs where on every path from the root to a terminal vertex the variable labelling of the non-terminal vertices obeys a fixed ordering.

Representation of CTMC. MTBDDs can be employed to compactly represent labelled CTMCs. Let $s \xrightarrow{a,\lambda} t$ be a transition of a labelled CTMC, where s is the source state, a is the action label, λ is the rate and t the target state of the transition, then this transition is encoded by a bit string, $a_1, ..., a_{n_L}, s_1, t_1, ...s_{n_S}, t_{n_S}$ where

- $a_1, ..., a_{n_L}$ encode the action label a
- $s_1, ..., s_{n_S}$ encode the source state s and
- $t_1, ..., t_{n_S}$ encode the target state t

In the MTBDD, there is a Boolean variable for each of these $n_L + 2 \cdot n_S$ bits, and the rate λ will be stored in a terminal vertex. One of the main issues in obtaining a compact MTBDD representation is the choice of an appropriate variable ordering. A commonly accepted heuristics is an interleaved ordering for the variables encoding source resp. target states, i.e. the ordering of the MTBDD will be: $a_1 \prec a_2 \prec ... \prec a_{n_L} \prec s_1 \prec t_1 \prec s_2 \prec t_2 ... \prec s_{n_S} \prec t_{n_S}$. This ordering, together with a proper treatment of the parallel composition operator, ensures the compactness of the resulting MTBDD [13, 24]

Translating the CASPA-Specification to MTBDDs. The basic procedure is as described in [18]. Here we only discuss the translation of parameterised processes, i.e. we describe our approach of how to represent parameterised processes symbolically. The parse graph structure describes the transitions depending on the parameter values, thereby also describing the possible changes of the parameter values. In CASPA the definition of the transitions is separated from the change of parameters. Let X be a parameterised process, then there is in X's parse graph exactly one node, called $PARAM$ node, which describes the possible transitions. The condition list of a guarded choice is stored in this node. Furthermore, the parse graph may contain several nodes that store the possible changes of the parameter values, called $PARAMDEF$ nodes. In order to generate from this information the actual MTBDD representation of a parameterised process, it is necessary that the generation algorithm keeps track of the current parameter value, which information is taken from the $PARAMDEF$ nodes. The $PARAM$ node serves to determine which transitions are possible in view of the current parameter values. For every satisfied condition, the successor process is determined, and the overall representation of a parameterised process is then a choice over all possible successor processes.

3.2 Data Structures for Measure Representation

For state measures and mean values the main task is to identify the states, resp. their binary encodings, that are relevant for the measure. As many states may contribute to a particular measure, we employ BDDs for a compact representation of the state sets.

```
(1)  /* Rate and constant definitions */
(2)  ...
(3)  /* System specification */
(4)  Process      :=  Queue(0)
(5)  Queue(n [3]) :=  [n >= 1] -> (serve,mu); Queue(n-1)
(6)                   [n < 3] -> (arrival,lambda); Queue(n+1)
(7)                   [*] -> (fail,gamma); Repair
(8)  Repair       :=  (repair,rho); Queue(0)
(9)  /* Measure specification */
(10) statemeasure Queuenotfull Queue(n < 3)
(11) meanvalue Fill Queue(n)
(12) throughputmeasure Service serve
```

Fig. 3. Example specification

State Measures. For a given state measure, we first generate its parse graph. Since the state measure is related to one or several process names, each node of the system's parse graph that contains a process which is referenced in the state measure will get a pointer to the respective node in the measure's parse graph. On generation of the MTBDD for the system, the encoding of each process that contains such a pointer is written to the correspondig measure's sub-BDD. After the complete generation of the system's MTBDD representation, the measure's overall BDD is generated by applying the Boolean operators in the measure's parse graph.

Mean Values. For mean values we have to generate for each possible parameter value a BDD that encodes the states in which the parameter has exactly that value. Since processes can have several parameters (and since processes are composed in parallel with other processes), there may be many states in which the parameter of interest has the same value (whereas the values of the remaining parameters, or the states of the other processes, may change). After the generation of the system's MTBDD representation, the measure BDDs are added up, thereby weighing each BDD with the associated parameter value. The result is an MTBDD in which every state encoding is related to its respective parameter value.

Throughput Measures. Throughput measures are not related to specific processes. Therefore no extra BDD for them needs to be generated. The system's MTBDD representation is restricted to the action label whose throughput is to be determined, and the target states are abstracted away. The result is then an MTBDD consisting of the states in which the relevant action is enabled, weighed with the respective transition rates.

3.3   Example

We will clarify the concepts of generating an MTBDD representation for parameterised processes and relating encodings and measures by means of the

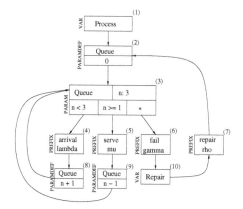

Fig. 4. Parse graph for the specification in Fig. 3

example shown in Fig. 3. The parse graph of the specification can be found in Fig. 4. In the $PARAMDEF$ node (2) the parameter value is initialised to zero. In the $PARAM$ node (3), when it is visited for the first time, the conditions of the first and the third field are fulfilled, therefore we can generate the MTBDD for their respective successor nodes. To generate the successor node we use the information about the actual parameter value and the change of parameter values of the $PARAMDEF$ nodes. In the initial case the successor processes are (arrival,lambda);Queue(1) and (fail,gamma);Repair. For Queue(1) and Repair we then compute again the successor processes, and so on. For Queue(1) all three conditions are fulfilled and we have three successor processes, namely (arrival,lambda);Queue(2), (serve,mu);Queue(0) and (fail,gamma);Repair. For the latter two, the successor nodes are already known, whereas for Queue(2) the successor processes still have to be computed. The overall MTBDD representation is obtained as a choice between the MTBDD representations of all successor processes which were found.

For the state measure Queuenotfull of Fig. 3 the states for Queue(0), Queue(1) and Queue(2) are relevant. Therefore, on generation of the respective MTBDDs the encodings of these states are copied to the measure BDD. For the mean value measure Fill an MTBDD is constructed where the encoding of each reachable state leads to the corresponding value of parameter n. Assuming that states are encoded as shown in Fig. 5 (left), the resulting MTBDD for this mean value measure looks as shown in Fig. 5 (right).

3.4 Numerical Analysis and Computation of Measures

Our experience shows that MTBDDs are a suitable data structure for the compact and efficient storing of extremely large state spaces [24]. However, it is known that purely MTBDD-based numerical analysis is very slow [9]. In [22], it was shown that it is possible to combine the advantages of sparse data structures (efficient matrix-vector multiplication) with those of MTBDDs (compact model

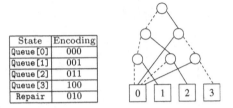

State	Encoding
Queue[0]	000
Queue[1]	001
Queue[2]	011
Queue[3]	100
Repair	010

Fig. 5. State encoding (left) and MTBDD for measure `Fill` (right)

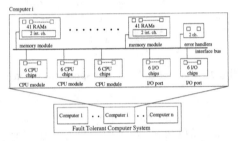

Fig. 6. Configuration of a single computer for the fault-tolerant multi computer system according to [23]

representation), leading to so-called hybrid offset-labelled MTBDDs. These data structures and the associated numerical algorithms were implemented in the stochastic model checker PRISM [20, 21]. Several case studies using PRISM proved the efficiency of the data structures and algorithms, therefore we decided to adopt this approach for CASPA.

In PRISM, and therefore also in CASPA, numerical algorithms for both steady-state and transient analysis are implemented. For steady-state analysis Power, Jacobi, Pseudo-Gauss-Seidel and their overrelaxed versions can be used. For transient analysis uniformisation is employed.

4   Case Studies

In this section we show the applicability of CASPA by means of several case studies: All results were computed on an Intel Pentium IV 3 GHz CPU with 1024 MB RAM, running SuSe 9.0 Linux.

4.1   Fault Tolerant Multi Computer System

This example is based on a case study described originally in [23] and used again in [8]. Due to the different modelling formalisms (stochastic activity networks versus stochastic process algebra), some re-modelling effort was required. The original model consists of n computers each of which has the following components:

- 3 memory modules, of which 2 must be operational
- 3 CPU units, of which 2 must be operational
- 2 I/O ports, of which 1 must be operational
- 2 error-handling chips, which are not redundant.

Each CPU and I/O-port consists of 6 non-redundant chips. Each memory module possesses 41 RAM chips, of which at most 2 may fail, and 2 interface chips that all must be operational. A computer fails, if one of its components fails. The overall system is operational if at least one computer is operational. A diagramatic overview can be found in Fig. 6.

Results. The measure we are interested in is the survival probability of the system. All results were computed using uniformisation with relative precision 10^{-6}. The computation times, including model construction, numerical analysis and measure computation, range from less than one second for the smallest configuration (889 reachable states) to about 30 sec for the largest configuration (750,000 reachable states). In Fig. 7 we see the survival probability for different system configurations: C1 is the configuration of the original system (i.e. consisting of two computers with three memory modules each) which has about 750,000 reachable states. C2 consists of two computers with only one memory module each, and has 2152 reachable states. C3, which is identical to C2 but possesses no redundant I/0 port, has only 889 reachable states. Finally C4 has the same configuration as C2, but consists of 3 computers instead of 2, having 120,000 reachable states. The survival probability, dependent on the mission time, is shown in Fig. 7.

Our results are not directly comparable to the ones reported in [8] (where multi-valued decision diagrams and matrix diagrams are employed as the underlying data structures): Firstly, we consider slightly different system configurations, and secondly, we do not exploit lumpability (which is due to replicated components). However, it is interesting that [8] reports a computation time of 15.5 sec per iteration for a 463,000 state model, while we measured only 0.12 sec per iteration for the 750,000 state model (the machine speeds are almost identical, and ours has only one third of the memory).

4.2 Kanban System

For this case study we computed steady-state probabilities for the well-known Kanban example (originally described in [5]). We model a Kanban system with four cells, a single type of Kanban cards, and the possibility that some workpiece may need to be reworked. The performance measures we compute are the average number of cards in each cell and the throughput of parts with and without rework for each cell.

Results. In Fig. 8 (left) we see the average fill of cells 1 to 4, depending on the number of cards N. Note, that due to the symmetric nature of the model, the

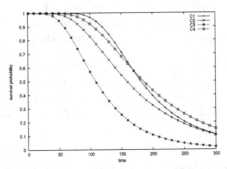

Fig. 7. Survival probability of fault-tolerant multi computer system

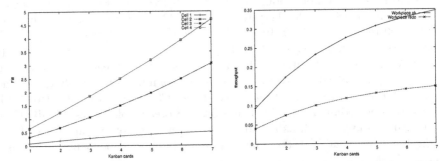

Fig. 8. Left: Average fill of cells 1 to 4. Right: Throughput of workpieces for cell 1

fill of cell 2 and 3 is identical, therefore the two curves are superposed. Fig. 8 (right) shows the throughput measures for cell 1 dependent on the number of cards.

Details about state space size, MTBDD size and time needed for computing the measures can be found in Table 1 (top). The analysis method used here was Pseudo-Gauss-Seidel (which was the most efficient one), with relative precision 10^{-6}.

As a comparison, TIPPtool [12] takes more than 4 hours just to generate the state space of the Kanban model with $N = 4$ (on the same machine), not including numerical analysis and measure computation. This huge difference can be explained by the fact that TIPPtool needs to traverse all transitions of the underlying labelled Markov chain explicitly in a sequential fashion, while CASPA performs a symbolic product space construction followed by a symbolic reachability analysis (where the latter works on sets of states and not on individual states).

We now compare the experimental results obtained with CASPA to those obtained with PRISM, which are shown in Table 1 (bottom). We observe, that the number of MTBDD nodes (column "final") is not the same for both tools:

Table 1. Results for Kanban system

N	Reach. States	MTBDD Nodes peak	final	MTBDD Generation[a]	Iterations	Num. Analysis[b]
CASPA:						
3	58,400	5,739	2,241	0.04 sec.	213	1.63 sec.
4	454,475	14,055	3,990	0.15 sec.	319	20.39 sec.
5	2,546,432	25,514	5,392	0.42 sec.	492	184.44 sec.
6	11,261,376	47,395	8,086	0.94 sec.	625	1191.46 sec.
7	41,644,800	76,230	10,389	1.59 sec.	950	21h
8	133,865,325	116,785	13,998	3.02 sec.	-	-
9	384,392,800	168,694	17,762	4.87 sec.	-	-
10	1,005,927,208	248,461	23,231	8.37 sec.	-	-
11	2,435,541,472	323,115	27,411	12.90 sec.	-	-
12	5,519,907,575	414,719	32,324	17.22 sec.	-	-
PRISM :						
3	58,400	?	2,474	0.12 sec.	230	2.36 sec.
4	454,475	?	4,900	0.49 sec.	370	25.11 sec.
5	2,546,432	?	6,308	1.02 sec.	528	177.60 sec.
6	11,261,376	?	7,876	1.8 sec.	891	1140.48 sec.
7	41,644,800	?	9,521	3.11 sec.	-	-
8	133,865,325	?	14,702	6.10 sec.	-	-
9	384,392,800	?	17,196	8.62 sec.	-	-
10	1,005,927,208	?	19,877	12.43 sec.	-	-
11	2,435,541,472	?	22,666	17.79 sec.	-	-
12	5,519,907,575	?	25,710	24.20 sec.	-	-

[a] including reachability analysis

[b] including measure computation (in the case of CASPA)

While CASPA constructs smaller MTBDDs for small values of N, the converse is the case for larger values of N. We attribute this phenomenon partly to the different state space ordering as caused by the state space generation algorithms of the two tools, and partly to the fact that CASPA's symbolic representation includes the encoding of the action labels which is not the case for PRISM. In the case of CASPA, the peak number of MTBDD nodes during the construction process (column "peak") is much higher than the final number of nodes, but it is still extremely small compared to the size of the state space. Since PRISM does not give peak numbers, the corresponding positions are marked with a "?". State space construction (column "MTBDD Generation") is faster in CASPA, but this is not really significant since state space construction is not the bottleneck. The number of iterations performed is always smaller in CASPA, which again seems to be due to the state space ordering (we emphasize at this point, that finding the optimal state space ordering is an NP-complete problem, therefore one can only resort to heuristics as described e.g. in [13]). A comparison of the total times for numerical analysis is not of interest for two reasons: Firstly, CASPA-times include measure computation while PRISM-times do not. Secondly, the numerical engine of CASPA is taken from PRISM, so the implementations are practically identical.

Table 2. Results for Polling system

N	Reach. States	MTBDD Nodes		MTBDD Generation[a]	Iterations	Num. Analysis[b]
		peak	final			
CASPA:						
10	15,360	3,748	1,193	0.01 sec.	185	0.29 sec.
15	737,280	9,417	2,370	0.05 sec.	150	13.02 sec.
20	31,457,280	19,311	4,556	0.17 sec.	161	741.27 sec.
PRISM:						
10	15,360	?	931	0.02 sec.	74	0.29 sec.
15	737,280	?	1,942	0.05 sec.	97	8.27 sec.
20	31,457,280	?	3,346	0.15 sec.	112	663.65 sec.

[a] including reachability analysis
[b] including measure computation (in the case of CASPA)

4.3   Polling System

As a third case study we consider a polling system, consisting of a server and N stations which are served in a cyclic fashion. This system was originally described in [16] and has since been frequently used as a standard benchmark. The results are shown in Table 2 (where the numerical method was again Pseudo-Gauss-Seidel). We observe that the MTBDDs generated by CASPA are up to 36% larger than the ones generated by PRISM, and that CASPA always needs more iterations. However, quite surprisingly, the time per iteration is always smaller in the case of CASPA.

5   Conclusions

In this paper we have presented CASPA, a stochastic process algebra tool which realises a completely symbolic approach from model construction to the computation of performance and dependability measures. CASPA implements an MTBDD-based state space generation scheme and allows the computation of transient and steady-state measures on the basis of well-established numerical algorithms.

We carried out systematic tests on many case studies: In addition to the ones given here, several queueing models, a mainframe system with software failures and a wireless communication network were analysed using CASPA. The results for all case studies are very positive, both state space generation and numerical analysis have shown to be highly efficient. CASPA is clearly superior to sparse-matrix based tools such as TIPPtool, and it compares well to other symbolic tools such as PRISM.

We are currently working on extending CASPA with a symbolic stochastic model checking engine. We plan to support the powerful action-based logic sPDL [19] which enables the user to define complex performance and dependability requirements in a formal and concise way.

Last but not least, in order to further increase its usability, in the future CASPA shall be equipped with a graphical user interface.

Acknowledgement

The authors would like to cordially thank Dave Parker for making the numerical solution code of PRISM available to the scientific community.

References

[1] AT&T. Drawing graphs with dot http://www.research.att.com. 297
[2] R. I. Bahar, E. A. Frohm, C. M. Gaona, G. D. Hachtel, E. Macii, A. Pardo, and F. Somenzi. Algebraic Decision Diagrams and their Applications. *Formal Methods in System Design*, 10(2/3):171–206, April/May 1997. 297
[3] R. E. Bryant. Graph-based Algorithms for Boolean Function Manipulation. *IEEE Transactions on Computers*, C-35(8):677–691, August 1986. 293, 297
[4] G. Ciardo, R. L. Jones, A. S. Miner, and R. Siminiceanu. SMART: Stochastic Model Analyzer for Reliability and Timing. In *Tools of Aachen 2001 Int. Multi-conference on Measurement, Modelling and Evaluation of Computer Communication Systems*, pages 29–34, 2001. 294
[5] G. Ciardo and M. Tilgner. On the use of Kronecker operators for the solution of generalized stochastic Petri nets. Technical Report 96-35, ICASE, 1996. 302
[6] daVinci V2.1. http://www.informatik.uni-bremen.de/davinci/. 297
[7] L. de Alfaro, M. Kwiatkowska, G. Norman, D. Parker, and R. Segala. Symbolic Model Checking for Probabilistic Processes using MTBDDs and the Kronecker Representation. In *TACAS'2000*, pages 395–410. Springer LNCS 1785, 2000. 293
[8] S. Derisavi, P. Kemper, and W. H. Sanders. Symbolic State-Space Exploration and Numerical Analysis of State-Sharing Composed Models. In *Fourth Int. Conf. on the Numerical Solution of Markov Chains*, pages 167–18167–189, 2003. 294, 301, 302
[9] E. Frank. Codierung und numerische Analyse von Transitionssystemen unter Verwendung von MTBDDs. Student's thesis, Universität Erlangen–Nürnberg, IMMD VII, 1999 (in German). 300
[10] M. Fujita, P. McGeer, and J. C.-Y. Yang. Multi-terminal Binary Decision Diagrams: An efficient data structure for matrix representation. *Formal Methods in System Design*, 10(2/3):149–169, April/May 1997. 297
[11] S. Gilmore and L. Kloul. A unified tool for performance modelling and prediction. In *Proc. 22nd Int. Conf. on Computer Safety, Reliability and Security (SAFECOMP 2003)*, pages 179–192, 2003. LNCS 2788. 294
[12] H. Hermanns, U. Herzog, U. Klehmet, V. Mertsiotakis, and M. Siegle. Compositional performance modelling with the TIPPtool. *Performance Evaluation*, 39(1-4):5–35, January 2000. 294, 295, 303
[13] H. Hermanns, M. Kwiatkowska, G. Norman, D. Parker, and M. Siegle. On the use of MTBDDs for performability analysis and verification of stochastic systems. *Journal of Logic and Algebraic Programming*, 56(1-2):23–67, 2003. 293, 298, 304
[14] H. Hermanns, J. Meyer-Kayser, and M. Siegle. Multi Terminal Binary Decision Diagrams to Represent and Analyse Continuous Time Markov Chains. In *3rd Int. Workshop on the Numerical Solution of Markov Chains*, pages 188–207. Prensas Universitarias de Zaragoza, 1999. 293
[15] H. Hermanns and M. Rettelbach. Syntax, Semantics, Equivalences, and Axioms for MTIPP. In *Proc. of PAPM'94*, pages 71–88. Arbeitsberichte des IMMD 27 (4), Universität Erlangen-Nürnberg, 1994. 294, 295

[16] O. C. Ibe and K. S. Trivedi. Stochastic Petri Net Models of Polling Systems. *IEEE Journal on Selected Areas in Communications*, 8(9):1649–1657, December 1990. 305

[17] J.-P. Katoen, M. Kwiatkowska, G. Norman, and D. Parker. Faster and Symbolic CTMC Model Checking. In *PAPM-PROBMIV'01*, pages 23–38. Springer, LNCS 2165, 2001. 293

[18] M. Kuntz and M. Siegle. Deriving symbolic representations from stochastic process algebras. In *Process Algebra and Probabilistic Methods, Proc. PAPM-PROBMIV'02*, pages 188–206. Springer, LNCS 2399, 2002. 297, 298

[19] M. Kuntz and M. Siegle. A stochastic extension of the logic PDL. In *Sixth Int. Workshop on Performability Modeling of Computer and Communication Systems (PMCCS6)*, pages 58–61, Monticello, Illinois, 2003. 305

[20] M. Kwiatkowska, G. Norman, and D. Parker. PRISM: Probabilistic Symbolic Model Checker. In *MMB-PNPM-PAPM-PROBMIV Tool Proceedings*, pages 7–12. Univ. Dortmund, Informatik IV, Bericht 760/2001, 2001. 294, 301

[21] M. Kwiatkowska, G. Norman, and D. Parker. Probabilistic Symbolic Model Checking with PRISM: A Hybrid Approach. In *TACAS'2002*, pages 52–66. Springer LNCS 2280, April 2002. 294, 301

[22] D. Parker. *Implementation of symbolic model checking for probabilistic systems.* PhD thesis, School of Computer Science, Faculty of Science, University of Birmingham, 2002. 296, 297, 300

[23] W. H. Sanders and L. M. Malhis. Dependability evaluation using composed SAN-based reward models. *Journal of Parallel and Distributed Computing*, 15(3):238–254, 1992. 301

[24] M. Siegle. *Behaviour analysis of communication systems: Compositional modelling, compact representation and analysis of performability properties.* Shaker Verlag, Aachen, 2002. 293, 297, 298, 300

[25] F. Somenzi. CUDD: Colorado University Decision Diagram Package, Release 2.3.1. User's Manual and Programmer's Manual, February 2001. 296

[26] E. Werner. Leistungsbewertung mit Multi-Terminalen Binären Entscheidungsdiagrammen. Master's thesis, Universität Erlangen–Nürnberg, Informatik 7, 2003 (in German). 296

Modeling and Testing Agent Systems Based on Statecharts⋆

Heui-Seok Seo[1], Tadashi Araragi[2], and Yong Rae Kwon[1]

[1] Department of Electrical Engineering and Computer Science
Korea Advanced Institute of Science and Technology (KAIST), Korea
{hsseo,kwon}@salmosa.kaist.ac.kr
[2] Agent Open Laboratory, NTT Communication Science Laboratories
Nippon Telegraph and Telephone Corporation, Japan
araragi@cslab.kecl.ntt.co.jp

Abstract. This paper presents a testing method for an agent system against its specification described with Statecharts. Here, an agent system means an implementation of an agent application. Its testing method generates test sequences from the specification and checks whether the agent system behaves in accordance with the specification by executing the test sequences. For specification-based testing, we have extended Statecharts in order to describe the behavior of an agent system according to the concept of Agent UML. Then, we propose an approach to generating test sequences from the extended Statecharts. Our approach makes effective use of partial order methods for considering representative sequences of equivalent classes divided from all possible sequences. Therefore, we can efficiently manage a large number of possible sequences caused by the agents' autonomy. As a result, we can reduce the number of test sequences and the number of executions to be tested.

1 Introduction

Verification of the agent systems to be used on the Internet is a critical issue because independently developed agent systems make use of each other, and bugs in a single agent system may affect a number of other systems. Moreover, one of the characteristics of agent systems is the autonomy of agents, which allows an agent to execute its behavior based on its own decisions. This autonomy is considered to consist of nondeterministic choices in its behavior, and agent systems have a large number of possible execution sequences. That is, agent systems are concurrent programs with nondeterministic nature. Therefore, applying a testing method to concurrent systems is one of the predominant approaches to verifying agent systems. Its main issue is how to effectively cover the large number of possible sequences [1][2].

In previous agent modeling frameworks like Agent UML [3][4], behaviors of agent systems have been described with message sequence charts. However,

---

⋆ This work is supported in part by Nippon Telegraph and Telephone Corporation (NTT).

M. Núñez et al. (Eds.): FORTE 2004 Workshops, LNCS 3236, pp. 308–321, 2004.

message sequence charts describe a subset of all possible behaviors, so a detailed and elaborate specification is required for testing agent systems accurately. Statecharts may be a viable candidate since Statecharts allow us to describe all possible behaviors [5][6]. However, Statecharts are still inadequate for describing agents' behaviors based on autonomy.

In this paper, we propose an approach to generating test sequences for testing agent systems based on a Statechart specification. First, we extend Statecharts to allow flexible description of agents' behaviors. Then, we present a method to generate test sequences from the extended Statecharts. The testing method uses a reduced reachability analysis based on partial order methods in order to effectively deal with the large number of all possible sequences. It constructs a reduced reachability graph from which the representative sequences of equivalent classes can be generated as substantial test sequences. Then, each equivalent class can be separately generated from such a representative sequence.

The rest of this paper is organized as follows. In Section 2, we briefly describe related works. Section 3 presents our method to extend Statecharts so that they are adequate for describing agent systems. In Section 4, we explain the process of generating test sequences from the extended Statecharts. In Section 5, we conclude the paper and mention directions for future work.

2   Related Works

2.1   Specification of Agent Systems

In recent years, there has been much research on development methodology for agent systems. For example, Tropos [7], INGENIAS [8] and GAIA [9] have proposed methods for agent-oriented software engineering. As with conventional software development, they use systematic processes to develop agent systems, and the processes cover requirements, designs and implementations. However, these development processes are based not on concrete agents but on abstract and logical *roles* of agents, and thus testing an implemented agent system is out of the scope of such work. In the design phase of the above agent-oriented methodologies, an extended sequence diagram is used as a visual description. The extended sequence diagram is defined In the agent UML [3][4]. It deals with roles as basic elements and describe interactions between roles. Moreover, they support extended interactions for concurrent threads: *inclusive or*, *exclusive or* and *and*. However, sequence diagrams are scenario-based descriptions, and they present abstract behaviors of systems.

2.2   Specification-Based Testing of Concurrent Programs

A common approach to generating test sequences by managing concurrency is *the flattening method* [10][11]. From a given specification, it constructs a reachability graph to present all interleavings of concurrent events and generates all possible sequences as test sequences from the reachability graph. However, the critical limitation of this approach is the explosion problems of states and sequences, since a reachability graph presents all possible behaviors of concurrent systems. Moreover, having many test sequences by interleavings requires high costs of test execution. These limitations become more critical in agent systems because they have a huge number of possible execution sequences.

The reduced reachability analysis in [2] and constraints-based testing in [1] are two approaches to alleviating the explosion problems in test sequence generation. In the *reduced reachability analysis*, representative sequences are generated as test sequences by constructing a reduced reachability graph that presents one of all possible interleavings of concurrent events. However, it does not consider other sequences equivalent to each representative sequences. *Constraints-based testing* uses the sequencing constraints that a concurrent program must satisfy in all of its states. Test sequences are generated by covering sequencing constraints. However, it is difficult to acquire sequencing constraints from a specification since they are general properties of a concurrent program.

3   Extending Statecharts for Agent Systems

3.1   Description of Agent Systems with Conventional Statecharts

Statecharts [5][6] is a visual and behavioral specification languages that are suitable for modeling reactive systems. Statecharts is defined as an extension to the FSM with features such as concurrency and broadcast communications. In Statecharts, state transitions triggered by events describes the dynamic behaviors, and those extended features facilitate the description. In this section, we describe agent systems using conventional Statecharts and then discuss on the necessity of extending the Statecharts to make them effective for agent systems.

Agent systems are of course concurrent systems that work through many message exchanges among autonomously behaving agents. We should take this characteristics into consideration in describing agent systems. First, concurrent agents can be directly described with concurrent *AND components* in Statecharts. Next, a large number of interactions among concurrent agents can be described by using *broadcast communication*.

The definition of broadcast communication is briefly phrased as follows: for the transition t with the label (e_{ex}/e_{in}), the external event e_{ex} triggers t and the internal event e_{in} occurs. Then, e_{in} is broadcasted to the entire system, and transitions with the label including (e_{in}) are also triggered in the current state [6]. However, the interactions in an agent system are generally represented by messages. Moreover, an agent system has many decision points established not only by its environments but also by its autonomy, and messages are generated as the results of the decisions. Therefore, we manage the decision point DP as an external event and express its resultant message msg as an internal event. In result, the label of the sending point becomes the form (DP/msg), and the label of the receiving point becomes the form (msg).

Figure 1 shows the marketplace example specified with the conventional Statecharts. Two concurrent agents, *Buyer* and *Shop*, are presented and each agent

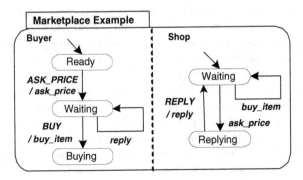

Fig. 1. Example of the Statecharts specification for a marketplace system

reacts to events that express decision points or messages: for understandability, capitalized words indicate decision points and lower-case words indicate messages. To explain interactions between agents, consider the configuration [*Ready, Waiting*], which is one of the system's global states. When *ASK_PRICE* is decided in the configuration, the transition (*ASK_PRICE/ask_price*) is triggered in *Buyer*, and then *ask_price* occurs and it is broadcast to the entire system. In this situation, the transition (*ask_price*) is also triggered in *Shop*. In result, the configuration changes from [*Ready, Waiting*] to [*Waiting, Replying*] as the result of interactions by *ASK_PRICE*.

3.2   Extended Features for Agent Systems

Although conventional Statecharts can represent both concurrency and communication, they are insufficient for describing agent systems due to the systems' characteristics. For example, the agent system in Figure 1 consists of a single buyer and a single shop, but an actual agent system consists of multiple buyers and shops that have similar behaviors. Although the generic charts in the conventional Statecharts reduce duplicated presentation, they cannot present the autonomy of agents and diverse interactions between agents. Therefore, as with other agent-oriented methodologies, we extend Statecharts by focusing on the roles of agents and the various interactions. Moreover, we extend certain states in Statecharts so that they can memorize interacting agents. In this paper, we assume that one agent has only one role and is implemented with one thread.

Role-Based Description. Roles are the logical components of agent systems. Agent systems actually consist of diverse concrete agents, but some agents among them can have the same behavior, that is, the same role. In the design phase, it is not necessary to describe all duplicated agents, and in fact such description is also impossible because we cannot determine the number of concrete agents for one role in advance. Therefore, we extend an AND component into a role-based component as follows:

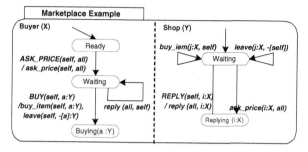

Fig. 2. A marketplace system specified with extended Statecharts

- *Role_Name (Agent_Set)*
  - *Role_Name* : name of agent role
  - *Agent_Set* : the set that contains *id* of all concrete agents of the role

From each role, concrete agents belonging to it are instantiated by giving *id* of such a agent to the parameter in *Role_Name*. For example, *Buyer(X)* is one basic component and one role in Figure 2. If $X = \{1, 2\}$, concrete agents with that role are *Buyer(1)* and *Buyer(2)*, and they show the same behavior such that a buyer asks an item's price to all shops and buys the item from a shop.

Various Event Types. In an agent system, agents can have diverse interactions with different relationships between the role of sender and the role of receiver. Even if concrete agents have the same role, only some agents belonging to it can be related to a given specific interaction. That is, each interaction is related to *one*, *some* or *all* concrete agents with the same role. For example, when a shop replies to the specific buyer asking the item's price, the shop has no relation with the other buyers. To describe this variety of interactions between role-based components, we define new event types and some reserved keywords for communication.

- *Event(Senders, Receivers)*
  - *Sender* : *id*s of specific sending agents
  - *Receiver* : *id*s of specific receiving agents

- Reserved Keywords for *Sender* and *Receiver*
  - **self** : one specific agent (the *id* of itself)
  - -[*agent*] : all agents except *agent*
  - **all**: all agents

The fundamental form of events is *event(a:X, b:Y)*. This means that a concrete agent *Role_X(a)* sends *event* to a concrete agent *Role_Y(b)*. However, reserved keywords or variables can be used instead of concrete agents, since the specification is role-based description. In Figure 2, let $X=\{1, 2\}$ and $Y=\{1, 2\}$. Then, *ask_price(self, all)* in *Buyer(1)* implies that *Buyer(1)* sends *ask_price(1,all)*

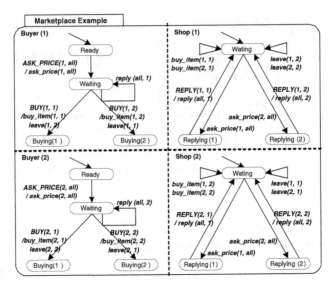

Fig. 3. Specification for marketplace example with actual parameters: this specification follows the semantics of conventional Statecharts

to all shops. *REPLY(self, i:X)* in *Shop(2)* implies that *Shop(1)* sends *REPLY(2,1)* and *REPLY(2,2)* to *Buyer(1)* and *Buyer(2)* respectively. On the other hands, -[agent] is used as follows. Let *Role(Z)* be a role and *Z*={1, 2, 3}. Then, for *Role(2)*, *event(i:X,-[self])* expresses both *event(i:X, 1)* and *event(i:X, 3)*.

Agent Memory in States. Because agent systems have a property that agents can be dynamically created and eliminated, the participant agents in communications should often memorize the information about other participants. For example, a shop should reply only to a specific buyer asking a price. Therefore, we extend states with the agent's *id*: *State(id)*. For example, *REPLY(self, i:X)* in *Shop(Y)* is the reply to *ask_price(i:X, all)*, and *'i:X'* is here set to the same agent as *Buyer(i)* through the state *Replying(i:X)*.

3.3 Comparison of Modeling Agent Systems

For comparison of extended Statecharts and conventional Statecharts, let's consider the specification of the marketplace system described with conventional Statecharts: the specification in Figure 3 shows the same behaviors as the specification in Figure 2 under the restriction, $X = \{1,2\}$ and $Y = \{1, 2\}$.

We have introduced three extended features for agent systems and the characteristics of them are to remove overlapped description in a specification. Three extended features, respectively, fold an overlapped concrete agents, events, and states with parameters. For example, *Shop(1)* and *Shop(2)* in Figure 3 are folded into *Shop(X)* in Figure 2. Thus, *ASK_PRICE(1, all)* in *Shop(1)* and

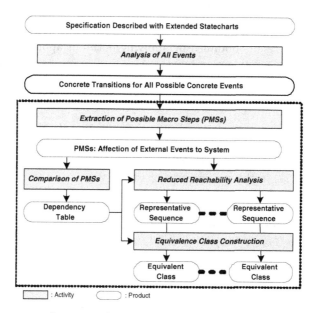

Fig. 4. The process for generating test sequences:we have developed a tool for the bounded area

ASK_PRICE(2,all) in *Shop(2))* are folded into *ASK_PRICE(self, all)* in *Shop(X)*. The concrete states, *Buying(1)* and *Buying(2)*, are folded into *Buying(a:Y)*. As a result, the specification in Figure 3 can be simplified with the specification in Figure 2. From the simplicity of the description, we can conclude that our extended features make it efficient to describe an agent system.

Furthermore, the parameterized description in the extended Statecharts covers the diverse compositions of concrete agents. While we should set the number of concrete agents in conventional Statecharts, the parameterized specification is irrelevant to the number of concrete agents. The concrete agents can be flexibly instantiated from the parameterized description. Therefore, the extended Statecharts are suitable for describing the flexible behaviors caused by the autonomy of agents and the dynamic properties of an agent system.

4   Test Sequence Generation

Figure 4 summarizes our approach to generating test sequences from extended Statecharts. First, it obtains concrete transitions from a parameterized specification. Second, it extracts possible macro steps (PMSs) to present affections of external events to a system and analyzes event dependency by comparing PMSs. Then, it derives a reduced reachability graph from which representative sequences are generated. Finally, it generates equivalent classes from representative sequences separately. Each equivalent class is used as a test controller to control test execution of a program. Refer to [12] for details on how to generate an equivalent class and how to control test execution. Accordingly, Sections 4.1 through 4.3 describe the activities of the process in more detail. Section 4.4 gives a comparison of results obtained by applying both our approach and flattening methods to the marketplace system.

4.1 Event Analysis

Since our approach statically analyzes a specification described with extended Statecharts, we should set the *ids* of concrete agents for obtaining concrete transitions from the specification. Here, we consider two buyers ($X=\{1, 2\}$) and two shops ($Y=\{1, 2\}$) in the specification of Figure 2.

Then, we obtain concrete transitions, which consist of concrete events and concrete states, by interpreting the semantics of the extended features. First, the role-based components are unfolded with concrete agents such as *Buyer(1)*, *Buyer(2)*, *Shop(1)* and *Shop(2)*. Second, concrete events in each concrete agent are acquired by setting **self** to its *id* and instantiating the variable for agent *id* exhaustively. Finally, each state with the agent memory is unfolded with the relevant instantiations of an agent. For example, the following transitions are concrete transitions in *Buyer(1)* to be obtained from transitions in *Buyer(X)*.

- *Buyer(1)*: Transitions = ⟨*source state, event, target state, {internal events}*⟩
    - ⟨ Ready, ASK_PRICE(1,**all**), Waiting, {ask_price(1,**all**)} ⟩
    - ⟨ Waiting, replay(**all**,1), Waiting, { } ⟩
    - ⟨ Waiting, BUY(1,1), Buying(1), {buy_item(1,1), leave(1,2)} ⟩
    - ⟨ Waiting, BUY(1,2), Buying(2), {buy_item(1,2), leave(1,1)} ⟩

The set of the above concrete transitions is equal to the set of transitions in *Shop(1)* of Figure 3. In this way, we can obtain all concrete transitions from the specification described with extended Statecharts.

4.2 PMS Extraction and Event Dependency

For presenting how each external event affects a system, we define a possible macro step (PMS) as a global transition between configurations affected by not only a given external event but also the internal events caused by the external event. Therefore, we introduce the *don't care* state to denoted as '*' in configurations. The *don't care* states indicate agents unaffected by an external event and they can be replaced by any specific states in the agents.

The process of extracting PMSs from concrete transitions finds a global transition for only an external event and then refines the configurations of the global transition with the internal events. The refinement uses the following two rules.

- if transitions for internal events exist in different concrete agents, they refine configurations *together* and one resultant PMS is extracted.
- if transitions for internal events exist in the same concurrent agent, they refine configurations *separately* and several resultant PMSs are extracted.

Possible Macro Steps

PMS	Source Configur..	External Event	Target Configuration
P0	[R,*,W,W]	ASK(1.a)	[W,*,R1,R1]
P1	[W,*,W,W]	BUY(1.1)	[B(1),*,W,W]
P2	[W,*,W,W]	BUY(1.2)	[B(2),*,W,W]
P3	[*,R,W,W]	ASK(2.a)	[*,W,R2,R2]
P4	[*,W,W,W]	BUY(2.1)	[*,B(1),W,W]
P5	[*,W,W,W]	BUY(2.2)	[*,B(2),W,W]
P6	[W,*,R2,*]	REPLY(1.1)	[W,*,W,*]
P7	[*,W,R2,*]	REPLY(1.2)	[*,W,W,*]
P8	[W,*,*,R1]	REPLY(2.1)	[W,*,*,W]
P9	[*,W,*,R2]	REPLY(2.2)	[*,W,*,W]

Dependency Table

	P0	P1	P2	P3	P4	P5	P6	P7	P8	P9
	1	1	1	1	1	1	1	1	1	1
	1	1	1	1	0	0	1	1	1	1
	1	1	1	1	0	0	1	1	1	1
	1	1	1	1	1	1	1	1	1	1
	1	0	0	1	1	1	1	1	1	1
	1	0	0	1	1	1	1	1	1	0
	1	1	1	1	1	1	1	1	0	0
	1	1	1	1	1	1	1	1	0	0
	1	1	1	1	1	1	0	0	1	1
	1	1	1	1	1	1	0	0	1	1

(A) Possible Macro Steps   *(B) Dependency Table*

Fig. 5. For external events of the marketplace, (A) PMSs and (B) event dependency

The first rule indicates that an external event affects several agents simultaneously. The second rule indicates that an external event affects only an agent but the agent shows different behaviors according to its current state. A PMS for an external event is extracted by applying the composition of those rules to all internal events caused by the external event.

In the marketplace example, the configuration consists of the states of four agents: [state of *Buyer(1)*, state of *Buyer(2)*, state of *Shop(1)*, state of *Shop(2)*]. Figure 5(A) shows all PMSs extracted from the marketplace system: each state name is abbreviated to its head character. To clarify the process of extractions, let's consider the event *ASK_PRICE(1,all)*. Due to its direct effect, the source and target configurations of its PMS become [R,*,*,*] and [W,*,*,*] respectively. But the event also invokes *ask_price(1,all)* and both *Shop(1)* and *Shop(2)* react to *ask_price (1,all)*. The event simultaneously changes the configurations from [*,*,W,W] to [*,*,R(1),R(1)]. In result, the overall source and target configurations of the PMS are refined to be [R,*,W,W] and [W,*,R(1),R(1)]. From the PMS, we know that *ASK_PRICE(a,all)* does not affect *Buyer(2)*.

Next, we generate a dependency table that presents the event dependency detected by comparing PMSs. In a concurrent program, the event dependency is formally defined as follows[13]:

– Let E be a set of events and $D \subseteq E \times E$ be a binary, reflexive and symmetric relation. Then, D is a *dependency relation* iff all pairs of independent events $((e_1, e_2) \notin D)$ satisfy the following properties for all global states $s \in S$.
  • if e_1 is executable in s and $(s \xrightarrow{e1} s')$, then e_2 is executable in s if and only if e_2 is executable in s'.
  • if e_1 and e_2 are executable in s, there is a unique state s'' such that $s \xRightarrow{w1} s''$ and $s \xRightarrow{w2} s''$: $w1 = \langle e_1, e_2 \rangle$ and $w2 = \langle e_2, e_1 \rangle$.

In this definition, $(s \xrightarrow{e} s')$ denotes that the global state changes from s to s' by executing an event e, and $(s \xRightarrow{w} s'')$ denotes that the global state changes by executing a sequence $w = \langle e_1, e_2, .., e_i \rangle$. By the definition, the order of independent events does not affect the global states reached by executions, so two sequences obtained from each other by permuting adjacent independent events are *equivalent*. However, it is impractical to directly check the event dependency by using the definition, since it only describes the properties of dependent events. In order to directly obtain event dependency from PMSs, we newly introduce checkable syntactic conditions for event dependency.

- Let E be a set of events and $D \subseteq E \times E$ be a binary, reflexive, and symmetric relation. D is a *dependency relation* iff all pairs of independent events $((e_1, e_2) \notin D)$ satisfy one of following conditions for all agents.
    - either e_1 or e_2 has a *don't care* state for an agent, that is, e_1 and e_2 do not affect the same agent.
    - the state in an agent is the same state if both e_1 and e_2 affect the agent.

These syntactic conditions do not contradict the properties of the previous definition. We show this with simple examples. The two PMSs $\langle$ [S1,S3], e_1, [S2,S3] $\rangle$ and $\langle$ [*,S3], e_2, [*,S3] $\rangle$ satisfy both conditions. In [S1,S3], both e_1 and e_2 are executable. Also, e_1 is executable in [S1,S3] after executing e_2 and vice-versa. After executing both events, the configurations become [S2,S3]. Therefore, e_1 and e_2 satisfy the properties in the previous definition. However, if the event pairs do not satisfy the syntactic conditions they cannot satisfy the properties in the previous definition. Therefore, we can directly find the event dependency by comparing their configurations.

Figure 5(B) shows the dependency table generated by comparing all pairs of events: p_i is a PMS in Figure 5(A), '0' and '1' respectively denotes the independency and the interdependency. For example, p_1:*BUY(1,1)* and p_4:*BUY(2,1)* are independent because they satisfy the first condition for *Buyer(1)* and *Buyer(2)* and the second condition for *Shop(1)* and *Shop(2)*.

4.3   Reduced Reachability Analysis

The reduced reachability analysis constructs a reduced reachability graph with PMSs using event dependency and generates representative sequences of equivalent classes. This reduced reachability analysis is a form of partial order methods. The partial order method is one of the verification approaches used to alleviate the state-explosion problem. Its basic idea is that exploring all interleavings is not necessary for verifying some properties because the orders of independent events are irrelevant to the results or the state that is reached [13].

A reachability graph presents all possible changes of configurations by external events, and a reduced reachability graph is a subgraph of such a reachability graph. The reduced reachability graph does not present the changes of configurations by interleavings except for only one interleaving for independent events. For example, let e_1 and e_2 be independent events, that is, $(s_0 \xrightarrow{e1} s_1 \xrightarrow{e2} s_3)$ and $(s_0 \xrightarrow{e2} s_2 \xrightarrow{e1} s_3)$. While a reachability graph shows both changes, a reduced reachability graph shows either change, and so either s_1 or s_2 is removed.

Therefore, the reduced reachability graph is constructed by presenting precedences of dependent events and only an interleaving of independent events. If e_1

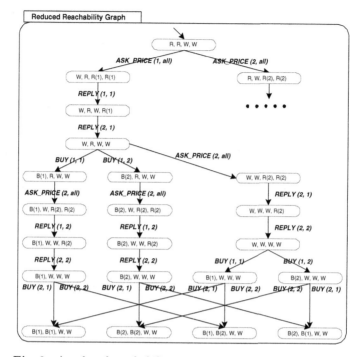

Fig. 6. A reduced reachability graph for the marketplace system

and e_2 are independent, the graph presents only e_1 from s_0 to s_1 and then presents e_2 from s_1 to s_3. If e_1 and e_2 are interdependent, their orders are precedences of them and so the graph presents both events from s_0. From an initial configuration, the algorithm of graph construction is organized as follows:

1 For each configuration s,
    1.1 Take an enabled PMS p whose source configuration includes s. $P = \{p\}$.
    1.2 For all PMSs p in P,
        A if p is enabled in s, add all PMSs p' to P such that p' and p are interdependent and their source configuration can be intersected.
        B if p is disabled in s, add all PMSs p'' to P such that p'' and p are interdependent and that the target configuration of p'' and the source configuration of p can be intersected.
    1.3 Repeat step 1.2 until no more PMSs can be added. Then present all enabled PMSs in P to s in the graph.
2 Repeat the above process for new configurations.

This algorithm is the adapted version of the partial order method in [13] for PMSs. The changed parts are step A and step B that respectively correspond to "in conflict" and "preceding" in the partial order method.

By applying the algorithm to the PMSs of Figure 5(A), the reduced reachability graph of the marketplace system is constructed as shown in Figure 6; it

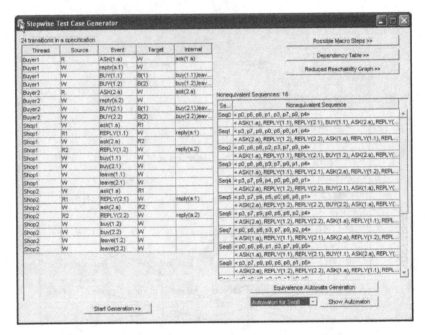

Fig. 7. A snapshot of representative sequences generated from the marketplace system

omits the behaviors to start with *ASK_PRICE(2, all)*. In the graph, we restrict each path does not contain any external event twice and we also note that configurations including the same states are distinguished from each other by a set of events that are executed for reaching the configuration.

In the graph, the configuration [W,W,W,W] shows good examples for the algorithm. Four events, *BUY(1,1)*, *BUY(1,2)*, *BUY(2,1)* and *BUY(2,2)*, are enabled in the configuration, and *BUY(2,2)* and *BUY(2,1)* are independent of *BUY(1,1)* and *BUY(1,2)*. Therefore, the algorithm adds *BUY(1,1)* and *BUY(1,2)* to the configuration and *BUY(2,1)* and *BUY(2,2)* are added in each following configuration. As a result, the sub-sequence ⟨*BUY(1,1), BUY(2,2)*⟩ represents two equivalent sequences ⟨*BUY(1,1), BUY(2,2)*⟩ and ⟨*BUY(2,2), BUY(1,1)*⟩.

4.4   Comparison of Testing Agent Systems

In contrast to flattening methods which uses a complete reachability graph, our approach uses a reduced reachability graph. While the complete graph for the same part shown in Figure 6 includes 27 nodes and 38 edges, the reduced graph contains 21 nodes and 24 edges. Furthermore, our approach obtains 8 representative sequences of equivalent classes from the reduced graph, out of 48 possible sequences. For the entire marketplace system, 16 representative sequences in Figure 7 are generated while there are 96 possible sequences.

Furthermore, the number of test sequences affects costs and efforts in test execution. To verify the behaviors of equivalent classes, flattening methods require

Table 1. Number of equivalent sequences in equivalent classes to test sequences: test sequences are numbered from the leftmost sequence in Figure 7

Test Sequences	Number of Sequences in An Equivalent Class
TS_1	4 Equivalent Sequences
TS_2	4 Equivalent Sequences
TS_3	4 Equivalent Sequences
TS_4	4 Equivalent Sequences
TS_5	8 Equivalent Sequences
TS_6	8 Equivalent Sequences
TS_7	8 Equivalent Sequences
TS_8	8 Equivalent Sequences

48 test executions in the worst case, because they do not consider equivalence relations among test sequences. However, our approach requires only 8 test executions with representative sequences of equivalent classes.

Although our approach generates a smaller number of test sequences than flattening methods, Equivalent classes can be separately generated from representative sequences and they cover all possible sequences [12]. Table 1 presents the number of equivalent sequences for each test sequence: test sequences are numbered from the leftmost sequence in Figure 7. For example, let's consider TS_6: ⟨*ASK_PRICE(1,all), REPLY(1,1), REPLY(2,1), ASK_PRICE(2,all), REPLY(1,2), REPLY(2,2), BUY(1,1), BUY(2,2)*⟩. This sequence has the following pairs of independent events: (*REPLY(1,1), REPLY(2,1)*), (*REPLY(1,2), REPLY(2,2)*) and (*BUY(1,1), BUY(2,2)*). By permuting these independent events, the test sequence has 8 equivalent sequences, including itself, in its equivalent class. In result, all of 48 possible sequences are divided into 8 equivalent classes, so our approach does not omit any sequence in testing the agent system.

5   Conclusions and Future Works

In this paper, we proposed an approach to specification-based testing of an agent system. First, we presented the modeling method for agent systems. For an elaborate description, we extended not sequence diagrams but Statecharts. The extended Statecharts introduce extended features for agent systems, such as *role-based description, various event types* and *agent memory* in states. Because the features consider the autonomy and dynamic properties of agent systems, our modeling approach is suitable for describing flexible behaviors of agent systems.

Then, we proposed an approach to generating test sequences from the extended Statecharts. Because of the autonomy and concurrency in agent systems, conventional analysis methods have limitations such as the large number of test sequences. However, our approach is based on the notion of the partial order method and it generates only representative sequences for equivalent classes. Thus, it efficiently manages possible sequences in a specification and overcomes high costs of not only test sequence generation but also test execution.

Our future work is to extend our analysis method to a dynamic version. In the current approach, we generate a given number of agents and analyze them statically. However, in actual agent systems, agents can be created and eliminated dynamically. Therefore, to test such systems we have to deal with this dynamic behavior effectively. One possible approach is to extend the partial order method so that it is applicable to an unbounded number of homogeneous agents. By developing such an extended method, we believe we can successfully obtain finitely represented control information for dynamic systems.

References

[1] Carver R. H., Tai K. C.: Use of Sequencing Constraints for Specification-based Testing of Concurrent Programs. IEEE Transaction on Software Engineering. **24(6)** (1998) 471–490 308, 310

[2] Tai K. C., Karacali B.: On Godefroid's State-less Search Technique for Testing Concurrent Programs. Proceedings of the 5th International Symposium on Autonomous Decentralized Systems. (2001) 77–84 308, 310

[3] FIPA Interaction Protocol Library Specification. "http://www.fipa.org/specs/fipa00025/XC00025E.html". (2001) 308, 309

[4] Odell J., Parunak H. V. D., Bauer B.: Extending UML for Agents. Proceedings of the Agent-Oriented Information Systems Workshop at 17th National Conference in Artificial Intelligence. (2000) 3–17 308, 309

[5] Harel D.: Statecharts: A Visual Formalism for Complex System. Science of Computer Programming. **8** (1987) 231–274 309, 310

[6] Harel D., Naamad A.: The STATEMATE Semantics of Statecharts. ACM Transaction on Software Engineering and Methodology. **5(4)** (1996) 293–333 309, 310

[7] Mylopoulos J., Kolp M., Castro J.: UML for Agent-Oriented Software Development: The Tropos Proposal. Proceedings of the 4th International Conference on the Unfied Modeling Language (UML 2001). (2001) 309

[8] Gomez Sanz J., Fuentes R.: Agent Oriented Software Engineering with INGENIAS. Proceedings of the 4th Iberoamerican Workshop on Multi-Agent Systems (Iberagent 2002). (2002) 309

[9] Wooldridge M., Jennings N. R., Kinny D.: The Gaia Methodology for Agent-Oriented Analysis and Design. Journal of Autonomous Agents and Multi-Agent Systems. **3(3)** (2000) 285–312 309

[10] Hong H. S., Kim Y. G., Cha S. D., Bae D. H., Ural H.: A Test Sequence Selection Method for Statecharts. Software Testing, verification and Reliability. **10(4)** (2000) 203–227 309

[11] Tsai B. Y., Stobart S., Parrington N., Mitchell I.: An Automatic Test Case Generator Derived from State-based Testing. Proceedings of Asia-Pacific Software Engineering Conference (APSEC98), (1998) 270–277 309

[12] Seo H.-S., Chung I. S. Kim B. M. Kwon Y. R.: A Design Implementation of Automata-based Testing Environment for Java Multi-thread Programs. Proceedings of Asia-Pacific Software Engineering Conference (APSEC01). (2001) 221–228 314, 320

[13] Godefroid P.: Partial-Order Methods for the Verification of Concurrent Systems - An Approach to the State-Explosion Problem. Lecture Notes in Computer Science(LNCS-1032), Springer. (1996) 316, 317, 318

Testing of Autonomous Agents Described as Utility State Machines*

Manuel Núñez, Ismael Rodríguez, and Fernando Rubio

Dept. Sistemas Informáticos y Programación, Universidad Complutense de Madrid
E-28040 Madrid, Spain
{mn,isrodrig,fernando}@sip.ucm.es

Abstract. We introduce a methodology to test autonomous agents described by means of utility state machines. In contrast with the classical approach for testing state machines, we will use other utility state machines as test. In fact, the machine playing the role of the test will be in charge of guiding the IUT so that it performs the operations (i.e. exchanges of resources) indicated by the specification.

1 Introduction

E-commerce technologies introduce several advantages in usual human economic interaction. For instance, they allow vendors to sell products without temporal or storage restrictions and they provide customers with powerful mechanisms to compare prices. In particular, *autonomous commerce agents* are one of the most interesting and challenging technologies in e-commerce (see e.g. [3, 4, 14, 8, 5]). They are autonomous entities that perform, on behalf of their respective users, some of the activities required in economic processes. For instance, autonomous commerce agents may search for interesting products, advise their users about interesting offers, negotiate with other agents, or even perform transactions autonomously. Besides, e-commerce platforms and multi-agent e-commerce systems use to be heterogeneous distributed systems where different components perform complex interactions. Actually, guaranteeing a correct behavior is specially hard in this kind of systems. However, reliability is a must for the success of e-commerce systems: Since they directly affect the patrimony of the users, their social implantation dramatically depends on whether users can trust them.

Taking as objective the validation of e-commerce systems, several works have been proposed to study the correctness of *commerce communication protocols* [10, 1]. Communication protocols are a key aspect in the validation of any e-commerce system, since any economic environment takes as first premise that any message sent by an economic party arrives correctly at the receiver. Only in this case commercial negotiation can be successfully performed. However, let us note that techniques for validating commerce communication protocols are

---

* Research supported by the MCyT project *MASTER* (TIC2003-07848-C02-01), the Junta de Castilla-La Mancha project *DISMEF* (PAC-03-001) and the Marie Curie RTN *TAROT* (MCRTN 505121).

M. Núñez et al. (Eds.): FORTE 2004 Workshops, LNCS 3236, pp. 322–336, 2004.
© Springer-Verlag Berlin Heidelberg 2004

not different to those used to check any kind of communication protocol, as they mainly focus on analyzing low-level details that are common to any distributed system. Nevertheless, e-commerce systems have enough intrinsic peculiarities to suggest the development of new specific validation techniques for this domain. Let us note that e-commerce systems are economic environments where entities compete for resources. Hence, a suitable conceptualization of the high-level details of such systems consists in representing and studying the *economic* behavior of the entities appearing in them.

In this paper we will provide a testing methodology to validate the high-level behavior of autonomous commerce agents in e-commerce systems. The aim of the testing mechanism will be to check whether the economic behavior of an implemented agent conforms to its corresponding specification. The high-level specification of an agent, concerning its economic behavior, can be defined as *"get what the user said he wants and when he wants it"*. We will consider that the specific preferences of the users will conform a *specification*. Therefore, we will need a proper formalism to represent this kind of specifications, that we will call *utility state machines* (see [12, 13]).

In our testing methodology we will stimulate the implementation under test (that is, the IUT is the implementation of an agent) according to a given test case/suite. Since we are interested in high-level behavior, it would not be coherent to stimulate the IUT by sending a sequence of actions that conforms to a given communication protocol. Thus, in contrast with usual testing approaches, the part of the behavior to be tested will not be *which* actions the agent performs but the *result* of these actions, that is, whether the results of the actions conform to the specific user expectations. In other words, we will test whether the *tested agent* is able to gain some profit according to the user preferences. So, our primary goal is not to test whether an agent behaves according to a given communication protocol since, as we said before, there already exist other formalisms to perform this task. On the contrary, as we are interested in abstracting low-level issues, the only suitable way to perform the stimulus will be by giving the tests the form of another autonomous commerce agent, so that they interact with the IUT in the same way as a real system would do.

In terms of related work there are innumerable papers on e-commerce in general or on topics as e-commerce systems/architectures and agent-mediated e-commerce. This number strongly decreases when considering formal approaches. In this case we may mention [6, 7] where, taking as basis the language PAMR [9], process algebras to specify e-barter systems were introduced. Regarding testing and validation techniques for e-commerce we may mention [11, 2] where specific case studies are considered. In fact, as far as we know, our paper represents the first generic framework to formally specify and test e-commerce systems.

The rest of the paper is structured as follows. In Section 2 we briefly review the formalism that allows us to specify autonomous commerce agents. In Section 3 we present our testing methodology. The main highlight of this approach is that in order to test the behavior of an agent we use a suitable agent as test. Finally, in Section 4 we present our conclusions and some lines for future work.

2   Utility State Machines

In this section we briefly review the notion of *utility state machine*. A more detailed presentation of this formalism can be found in the companion paper [13]. We use these machines to describe agents representing users. The preferences of the user in a given moment will be given by its *utility function*. Utility functions associate a value (a utility measure) with each possible combination of resources a user could own.

Definition 1. *We consider* $\mathbb{R}_+ = \{x \in \mathbb{R} \mid x \geq 0\}$. *We will usually denote vectors in* $\mathbb{R}^n$ *(for* $n \geq 2$*) by* $\bar{x}, \bar{y}, \ldots$ *We consider that* $\bar{0}$ *denotes the tuple having all the components equal to zero. Given* $\bar{x} \in \mathbb{R}^n$, x_i *denotes its* i-th *component. We extend some usual arithmetic operations to vectors. Let* $\bar{x}, \bar{y} \in \mathbb{R}^m$. *We define* $\bar{x} + \bar{y} = (x_1 + y_1, \ldots, x_n + y_n)$ *and* $\bar{x} \cdot \bar{y} = (x_1 \cdot y_1, \ldots, x_n \cdot y_n)$. *We write* $\bar{x} \leq \bar{y}$ *if for any* $1 \leq i \leq n$ *we have* $x_i \leq y_i$.

Let us suppose that there exist n *different kinds of resources. A utility function is any function* $f : \mathbb{R}_+^n \longrightarrow \mathbb{R}_+$. □

In order to specify agents we use *utility state machines* [12, 13]. This formalism is indeed an adaption and extension to our purposes of the classical notion of *extended finite state machines* (**EFSM**). In particular, we have to take into account *time* as a factor that influences the preferences of users. Besides, time will affect agents in the sense that any negative transaction will imply a deadline for the agent to retrieve the benefits of it. In addition, time will appear as part of the freedom that specifications give to implementations: It does not matter whether an agent immediately performs a transaction as long as its decision is useful to improve the utility in the long term.

Definition 2. *We say that the tuple* $M = (S, s_{in}, V, U, at, mi, T)$ *is a utility state machine, in short* **USM**, *where we consider that*

- S *is a set of states.*
- $s_{in} \in S$ *is the initial state of* M.
- $V = (t, x_1, \ldots, x_n)$ *is a tuple of variables, where* t *represents the time elapsed since the machine entered the current state and* $x_1, \ldots, x_n$ *represent the resources that are available to be traded in the e-commerce environment.*
- $U : S \longrightarrow (\mathbb{R}_+^{n+1} \longrightarrow \mathbb{R}_+)$ *is a function associating a utility function with each state in* M.
- *at is the amortization time. It denotes the maximal time* M *may stay without retrieving the profit of the negative transactions that were performed in the past.*
- *mi is the maximal investment. It denotes the maximal amount of negative profit the machine should afford.*
- T *is the set of transitions. Each transition is a tuple* (s, Q, Z, s'), *where* $s, s' \in S$ *are the initial and final state of the transition, and* $Q : \mathbb{R}_+^{n+1} \longrightarrow Bool$ *is a predicate on the set of variables, and* $Z : \mathbb{R}_+^n \longrightarrow \mathbb{R}_+^n$ *is a transformation over the current variables. We require that for any state* s *there*

do not exist two different transitions $t_1, t_2 \in T$, *with* $t_1 = (s, Q_1, Z_1, s'_1)$ *and* $t_2 = (s, Q_2, Z_2, s'_2)$, *and a tuple* $\bar{r}$ *such that both* $Q_1(\bar{r})$ *and* $Q_2(\bar{r})$ *hold.* □

It is worth to point out that the set of transitions T does not include the complete set of transitions the specification will allow real agents to perform. Some additional transitions must be considered: *transactions* and *passing of time*. The former will be used to denote the transactions agents will be allowed to perform. Given a USM M, both transaction and time consumption transitions may be *implicitly* inferred from the definition of M. We will give the formal representation in the forthcoming Definition 5. Next we introduce the notion of *configuration*, that is, the data denoting the current situation of a USM. A configuration consists of the current state, the current values of the variables, and the *pending accounting* of the machine.

Definition 3. *Let* $M = (S, s_{in}, V, U, at, mi, T)$ *be a* USM. *A configuration of* M *is a tuple* $(s, \bar{r}, l)$ *where*

- $s \in S$ *is the current state in* M,
- $\bar{r} = (u, r_1, \ldots, r_n) \in \mathbb{R}_+^{n+1}$ *is the current value of* V, *and*
- $l = [(p_1, e_1), \ldots, (p_m, e_m)]$ *is a list of pairs (profit,time) representing the list of pending accounts.* □

For each pair $(p, e) \in l$ we have that p represents a (positive or negative) *profit* and e represents the *expiration date* of p, that is, the time in which a profit greater than or equal to $-p$ must be retrieved, if p is negative, or the time in which p will be considered a *clear* profit if no negative profit is registered before.

Next we present some auxiliary definitions. Intuitive explanations of these notions can be found in [13].

Definition 4. *Let* $M = (S, s_{in}, V, U, at, mi, T)$ *be a* USM *and* $c = (s, \bar{r}, l)$ *be a configuration of* M, *with* $\bar{r} = (u, r_1, \ldots, r_n)$ *and* $l = [(p_1, e_1), \ldots, (p_m, e_m)]$. *The maximal waiting time for* M *in the configuration* c, *denoted by* MaxWait(M, c), *is defined as* $\min\{e_1, \min\{u' \mid \exists (s, Q, Z, s'') \in T : u' \geq u \wedge Q(u', r_1, \ldots, r_n)\}\}$

If e_1 *is actually the minimal value and* $p_1 > 0$ *then we say that* M *performs a clear profit, which is indicated by setting true the auxiliary condition* ClearProfit(M, c). *On the contrary, if* e_1 *is the minimal value and* $p_1 < 0$ *then we say that* M *fails its economic objective, which is indicated by setting true the auxiliary condition* TargetFailed(M, c).

The update of the list of pending accounts l *with the new profit* a, *denoted by* Update(l, a), *is defined as:*

$$
\text{Update}(l, a) = \begin{cases} [(a, at + u)] & \text{if } l = [\,] \\ l +\!\!+[(a, at + u)] & \text{if } l = (p_1, e_1) : l' \wedge \frac{p_1}{a} \geq 0 \\ (p_1 + a, e_1) : l' & \text{if } l = (p_1, e_1) : l' \wedge \frac{p_1}{a} < 0 \wedge \frac{p_1 + a}{p_1} \geq 0 \\ \text{Update}(l', p_1 + a) & \text{if } l = (p_1, e_1) : l' \wedge \frac{p_1}{a} < 0 \wedge \frac{p_1 + a}{p_1} < 0 \end{cases}
$$

Finally, the accumulated profit of a list of pending accounts l, denoted by `Accumulated`(l), *is defined as*

$$\texttt{Accumulated}(l) = \begin{cases} 0 & \text{if } l = [\,] \\ p + \texttt{Accumulated}(l') & \text{if } l = (p,e) : l' \end{cases} \qquad \square$$

Let us note that profits in any (non-empty) list of pending accounts are either all positive or all negative. We have used a functional programming notation to define lists: $[\,]$ denotes an empty list, $l ++ l'$ denotes the concatenation of the lists l and l', and $x : l$ denotes the inclusion, as first element, of x into the list l.

Given a USM M, an *evolution* of M represents a configuration that the USM can take from a previous configuration. We will consider four types of evolutions: *changing the state, passing of time, passing of time with failure,* and *performing a transaction.*

Definition 5. *Let* $M = (S, s_{in}, V, U, at, mi, T)$ *be a* USM *and* $c = (s, \overline{r}, l)$ *be a configuration of* M, *with* $\overline{r} = (u, r_1, \ldots, r_n)$ *and* $l = [(p_1, e_1), \ldots, (p_m, e_m)]$. *An evolution of* M *from* c *is a tuple* $(c, c', tc)_K$ *where* $c' = (s', \overline{r'}, l')$, $K \in \{\alpha, \beta, \beta', \gamma\}$ *and* $tc \in \mathbb{R}_+$ *are defined according to the following options:*

(1) *(Changing the state) If there exists* $(s, Q, Z, s'') \in T$ *such that* $Q(\overline{r})$ *holds then* $K = \alpha$, $tc = 0$, $s' = s''$, *and* $\overline{r'} = (0, r'_1, \ldots, r'_n)$, *where* $(r'_1, \ldots, r'_n) = Z(r_1, \ldots, r_n)$ *and* $l' = [(p_1, e_1 - u), \ldots, (p_m, e_m - u)]$.
(2) *(Passing of time) If the condition of* (1) *does not hold then for any* $tr \in \mathbb{R}_+$ *such that* $0 < tr \leq \texttt{MaxWait}(M, c) - u$, *we have* $tc = tr$, $s' = s$, $\overline{r'} = (u + tr, r_1, \ldots, r_n)$, *and* l' *is defined as follows:*

$$l' = \begin{cases} [(p_2, e_2), \ldots, (p_m, e_m)] & \text{if } \texttt{ClearProfit}(M,c) \vee \texttt{TargetFailed}(M,c) \\ l & \text{otherwise} \end{cases}$$

In addition, $K = \beta'$ *if* `TargetFailed`(M, c) *and* $K = \beta$ *otherwise.*
(3) *(Transaction)*
If the condition of (1) *does not hold then for any* $\overline{r''} = (u, r''_1, \ldots, r''_n) \geq \overline{0}$ *such that* $U(s)(\overline{r''}) - U(s)(\overline{r}) + \texttt{Accumulated}(l) > -mi$, *we have* $K = \gamma$, $tc = 0$, $s' = s$, $\overline{r'} = \overline{r''}$, *and* $l' = \texttt{Update}(l, U(s)(\overline{r'}) - U(s)(\overline{r}))$.

We denote by `Evolutions`(M, c) *the set of evolutions of* M *from* c.
A trace of M *from* c *is a list of evolutions* l *with either* $l = [\,]$ *or* $l = e : l'$, *where* $e = (c, c', v)_K \in \texttt{Evolutions}(M, c)$ *and* l' *is a trace of* M *from* c'. *We denote by* `Traces`(M, c) *the set of traces of* M *from* c. $\qquad \square$

First, if one of the guards associated with a transition between states holds then the state changes, the time counter of the state is reset to 0 and the expiration dates of the pending accounts are shifted to fit the new counter. The second clause reflects the situation where the machine let the time pass an amount of time less than or equal to the maximal waiting time. Besides, if the elapsed time corresponds to the one when a positive or negative previous profit expires, then either this profit is considered *clear* or a *failure* is produced, respectively, being such profit eliminated from the list. Finally, if a machine performs a transaction then we require that it does not give resources that it does not own and that the accumulated losses stay below the maximal threshold. Let us note that the second and third types of transition can be performed only if the corresponding USM cannot change its state.

In the next definition we identify the traces that are free of failures.

Definition 6. *Let M be a USM and c be a configuration of M. Let us suppose $c_1 = c$ and let $\sigma = [(c_1, c_2, t_1)_{K_1}, \ldots, (c_{n-1}, c_n, t_{n-1})_{K_{n-1}}] \in \textit{Traces}(M, c)$ be a trace of M from c. We say that σ is a valid trace of M from c if there does not exist $1 \leq i \leq n-1$ such that $K_i = \beta'$. We define the set of valid traces of M from c by $\textit{ValidTraces}(M, c)$.*   □

Next we extend the previous framework so that *systems*, made of USMs interacting among them, can be defined. Intuitively, systems will be defined just as tuples of USMs, while the configuration of a system will be given by the tuple of configurations of each USM.

Definition 7. *Let have $M_i = (S_i, s_{in\ i}, V, U_i, at_i, mi_i, T_i)$. We say that the tuple $S = (M_1, \ldots, M_m)$ is a system of USMs. For any $1 \leq i \leq m$, let c_i be the configuration of M_i. We say that $c = (c_1, \ldots, c_m)$ is the configuration of S.*   □

The transitions of a system will not be the simple addition of the transitions of each USM within the system, as some of the actions a USM can perform will require *synchronization* with those performed by other USMs. This will be the case of passing of time and transactions. In fact, the only actions that do not require a synchronization are the ones associated with changing the state of a USM. In contrast with transactions and passing of time, changing the state is not a *voluntary* action. In other words, if the condition for a USM to change its state holds then that USM must change its state. In the meanwhile, transactions and passing of time transitions will be forbidden.

In the following definition we identify the set of evolutions a system can perform from a given configuration. In order to make explicit the *failure* of any of the USMs in the system, we distinguish again passing of time transitions producing a failure. In this case, we will explicitly indicate the set of USMs producing a failure. Hence, the label β_A denotes a passing of time transition in which the USMs included in A produced a failure. So, a failures-free passing of time transition is denoted by $\beta_\emptyset$.

Definition 8. *Let $S = (M_1, \ldots, M_m)$ be a system and $c = (c_1, \ldots, c_m)$ be a configuration such that we have $M_i = (S_i, s_{in\ i}, V, U_i, at_i, mi_i, T_i)$ and $c_i = (s_i, \overline{r_i}, l_i)$ for any $1 \leq i \leq m$. An evolution of S from c is a tuple $(c, c', tc)_K$ where $c' = (c'_1, \ldots, c'_m)$, with $c'_i = (s'_i, \overline{r'_i}, l'_i)$, $K \in \{\alpha, \gamma\} \cup \{\beta_A \mid A \subseteq \{1, \ldots, m\}\}$, and $tc \in \mathbb{R}_+$ are defined according to the following options:*

(1) (Changing the state) If there exists $(c_i, c''_i, 0)_\alpha \in \textit{Evolutions}(M_i, c_i)$ then $K = \alpha$, $tc = 0$, and for any $1 \leq j \leq m$ we have $c'_j = c_j$ if $i \neq j$, while $c'_i = c''_i$.

(2) *(Passing of time)* If the condition of (1) does not hold and there exits tr such that for any $1 \leq i \leq m$ there exists $(c_i, c_i'', tr)_\delta \in \text{Evolutions}(M_i, c_i)$ with $\delta \in \{\beta, \beta'\}$, then $tc = tr$, $c_i' = c_i''$ for any $1 \leq i \leq m$, and $K = \beta_A$ where the set A is defined as $A = \{i \mid (c_i, c_i'', tr)_{\beta'} \in \text{Evolutions}(M_i, c_i)\}$.

(3) *(Transaction)* If the condition of (1) does not hold and there exist two indexes j and k, with $j \neq k$, such that for $l \in \{j, k\}$ we have $(c_l, c_l'', 0)_\gamma \in \text{Evolutions}(M_l, c_l)$ and $c_l'' = (s_i'', \overline{r_i''}, l_i'')$, with $\overline{r_j} + \overline{r_k} = \overline{r_j''} + \overline{r_k''}$, then $K = \gamma$, $tc = 0$, $c_j' = c_j''$, $c_k' = c_k''$, and for any $1 \leq i \leq m$, with $i \neq j, k$, we have $c_i' = c_i$.

We denote by $\text{Evolutions}(S, c)$ the set of evolutions of S from c.

A trace of S from c is a list of evolutions l where either $l = [\,]$ or $l = e : l'$, being $e = (c, c', v)_K \in \text{Evolutions}(S, c)$ and l' a trace of S from c'. We denote by $\text{Traces}(S, c)$ the set of traces of S from c . □

If a USM can change its state then the corresponding transition is performed while any other USM remains unmodified (first clause). If no USM can modify its state then passing of time and transaction transitions are enabled. In the first case, the system can let the time pass provided that all the USMs belonging to the system can. In the second case we require that trading USMs can (individually) perform the exchange and that goods are not created/destroyed as a result of the exchange. Let us note that only bilateral transactions are considered since any multilateral exchange can be expressed by means of the concatenation of some bilateral transactions.

Similarly to the reasoning that we did for single agents, we can identify the valid traces of systems. In this case, we are interested in identifying the traces such that a specific USM belonging to the system produces no failure.

Definition 9. *Let $S = (M_1, \ldots, M_m)$ be a system and c be a configuration of S. Let us suppose $c_1 = c$ and let $\sigma = [(c_1, c_2, t_1)_{K_1}, \ldots, (c_{n-1}, c_n, t_{n-1})_{K_{n-1}}] \in \text{Traces}(S, c)$ be a trace of S from c. σ is a valid trace of S from c for the USM M_i if there does not exist $1 \leq j \leq n - 1$ such that $K_j = \beta_A$ with $i \in A$. We denote the set of valid traces of S from c for M_i by $\text{ValidTraces}(S, c, M_i)$.* □

3   Testing Autonomous Commerce Agents

In this section we describe how to *interact* with an IUT so that the observed behavior is as helpful as possible to infer conclusions about its validity with respect to a specification. We will create *artificial* environments to stimulate the IUT according to a foreseen plan. These environments will be the *tests* in our testing process. As we said in the introduction, tests will be defined in the same way we define specifications. Thus, the definition of tests will focus only on the high-level economic behavior. Besides, the actions available for tests will be the same as those for specifications. Let us remark that if tests included low-level details that made *explicit* their way to interact with the implementation then the test would check details that the specification actually does not define.

As it is usually the case in formal approaches to testing, the design of tests will be guided by the specification. The main aim of a test will be to check whether the IUT exchanges items as the specification says. It is worth to point out that the behaviors of the specification producing a *failure* (that is, a β' transition) will not be considered as valid in the implementation, since they should be avoided. Each test will focus on testing a given state (or set of states). So, the first objective of a test will be to *conduct* the IUT to the desired state of the specification. Then, the test will behave according to a given economic behavior. Thus, we will check whether the joint evolution of the test and the IUT conforms to the (failure free) behavior we would have in the specification of a system containing both agents.

Conducting the IUT to a desired state consists in taking it through states *equivalent* to those of the specification until that state is reached. In other words, the test has to *induce* the IUT to fulfill the guards governing the transitions between states. The test will be able to do so by *exchanging* resources with the IUT so that the guards are fulfilled. In order to perform this task, the utility functions of the test must be designed so that they favor the correct flow of resources, that is, the test must *get happier* by giving resources to the IUT in such a way that the IUT fulfills its guards. Nevertheless, endowing the test with the suitable utility functions is not enough to guarantee that the test and the IUT will *always* evolve together until the corresponding guards are fulfilled. This is so because the specification leaves a free room for the IUT to *non-deterministically* perform transactions. Thus, the joint evolution of the IUT and the test could lead the IUT to own different baskets of resources to those expected. Since deviating from the foreseen path of the test is not incorrect in general, tests will be designed so that they provide diagnosis results even when the desired path is not followed by the IUT.

In order to define a test, the first decision consists in fixing the set of states it will be intended to guide the IUT through.

Definition 10. *Let $M = (S, s_{in}, V, U, at, mi, T)$ be a USM. A path of states in M is a list $[s_1, \ldots, s_m]$ where $s_1 = s_{in}$ and for each $1 \leq i \leq m - 1$ we have that there exists $(s_i, Q, Z, s_{i+1}) \in T$.* □

The availability of a part of a path to be performed will be strongly influenced by the exchanges performed in previous states of the path. The key to understand and predict the evolution of resources at a given state is that a USM is forced to perform exchanges so that, in the long term, utility never worsens. Therefore, if a guard between states is only fulfilled in configurations where the utility is less than the current utility then the USM will never be able to perform the corresponding transition. The following definition checks whether it will be *possible* for a USM to evolve across a given path. Prior to formally define this concept we introduce some auxiliary notation. We give a simple notion to identify the list of states ranged in a trace as well as both the baskets of resources which made possible each transition and the baskets obtained after each transition. These baskets give us a possible way to deal with resources so that the test can guide the IUT through the path. In the following definition we also introduce notation to access some elements within a list of tuples. Given a list l we have that $l.i$ denotes a list formed by the ith element of each tuple appearing in l. Besides, l_i denotes the ith element of the list. For example, if we consider $l = [(1,2,3),(3,4,1),(5,2,7),(8,1,6),(6,5,4)]$ then $l.2 = [2,4,2,1,5]$ and $l_3 = (5,2,7)$. Moreover, we can combine both functions. For instance, $(l.2)_4 = 1$.

Definition 11. *Let M be a USM, c be a configuration of M, and $\sigma \in Traces(M,c)$ be a trace of M from c. The list of state transitions through σ, denoted by $StateTran(\sigma)$, is defined as*

$$StateTran(\sigma) = \begin{cases} [\,] & \text{if } \sigma = [\,] \\ (s,\overline{r},\overline{r'}) : StateTran(\sigma') & \text{if } \sigma = ((s,\overline{v},l),(s',\overline{v'},l'),0)_\alpha : \sigma' \\ StateTran(\sigma') & \text{if } \sigma = e_K : \sigma' \land K \neq \alpha \end{cases}$$

where $\overline{r} = (r_1,\ldots,r_n)$ and $\overline{r'} = (r'_1,\ldots,r'_n)$, with $\overline{v} = (t,r_1,\ldots,r_n)$ and $\overline{v'} = (t',r'_1,\ldots,r'_n)$.

Let l be a list of n-tuples. For any $i \in \mathbb{N}$, with $i \geq 1$, such that l has at least i elements we denote by l_i the i-th element of l. For any $1 \leq i \leq n$ we define the list $l.i$ as

$$l.i = \begin{cases} [\,] & \text{if } l = [\,] \\ x_i : (l'.i) & \text{if } l = (x_1,\ldots,x_i,\ldots,x_n) : l' \end{cases}$$

We say that the path $\eta = [s_1,\ldots,s_m]$ in M is possible from c if there exists a trace $\sigma = [(c_1,c_2,t_1)_{K_1},\ldots,(c_{n-1},c_n,t_{n-1})_{K_{n-1}}] \in ValidTraces(M,c)$ such that $\eta = StateTran(\sigma).1 ++ [st_n]$, where $c_n = (st_n,\overline{r_n},l_n)$. In this case we say that $StateTran(\sigma).2$ is a possible use of resources to perform η and that σ is a possible trace to perform η. □

Once we have identified a possible use of resources to perform a given path, we can define a test that gives to the IUT the resources it needs to perform the next transition of the path at every state. Basically, the test will be initially provided with the resources needed to lead the IUT to the final state. These can be computed by using the notion of *possible use of resources* introduced in the previous definition. Besides, the test will be built in such a way that each state in the path will have a respective state in the test. In each of these states, the utility function of the test will induce that the test does not care about giving to the IUT as much resources as it needs so that it may pass to the next state. In order to do so, the utility function of the test will return the same utility regardless of the amount of items it owns, provided that it keeps the needed *reserve* of resources. This reserve of resources consists of the resources the test will give to the IUT in future states to continue guiding it towards the final state of the path. The only exception will be the case when some of the resources of the IUT must be *removed* in order to fulfill the transition guard. In order to *steal* the appropriate resources from the IUT, so that it fulfills the guard, the test will reward these items with its utility function. In the following definition we describe how to create the utility function of the test so that it promotes an exchange between the resources the test wants to remove from the IUT and those it wants to give to it. In this case, $\overline{v}$ plays the role of the former and $\overline{w}$ plays the role of the latter. Let us note that each kind of resources will have to be either given or removed, but not both.

Definition 12. *Let* $\overline{v}, \overline{w} \in \mathbb{R}_+^n$ *such that* $\overline{v} \cdot \overline{w} = \overline{0}$. *Let* $\rho, \varrho \in \mathbb{R}_+$ *be such that* $\rho > \varrho$. *If* $\overline{v} \neq \overline{0}$ *then the function denoting preference of* $\overline{v}$ *over* $\overline{w}$, *denoted by* $\Psi_{\overline{v},\overline{w}}$, *is defined, for any* $\overline{x} \in \mathbb{R}_+^n$, *as*

$$\Psi_{\overline{v},\overline{w}}(\overline{x}) = \rho \cdot \Phi\left(\sum_{1 \leq i \leq n} \Phi(x_i, v_i), \, |\, \{v_i \mid v_i > 0\}\,|\, \right) +$$
$$\varrho \cdot \Phi\left(\sum_{1 \leq i \leq n} \Phi(x_i, w_i), \, |\, \{w_i \mid w_i > 0\}\,|\, \right)$$

where $\Phi(a, b)$ *is equal to* $\frac{a}{b}$ *if* $b \neq 0$ *and equal to* 0 *if* $b = 0$. *If* $\overline{v} = \overline{0}$ *we simply consider that* $\Psi_{\overline{v},\overline{w}}(\overline{x}) = 0$. □

Lemma 1. *Let* $\overline{v}, \overline{w} \in \mathbb{R}_+^n$ *such that* $\overline{v} \neq \overline{0}$ *and* $\overline{v} \cdot \overline{w} = \overline{0}$. *We have that* $\Psi_{\overline{v},\overline{w}}(\overline{v}) > \Psi_{\overline{v},\overline{w}}(\overline{w})$.

Proof. Let us compute $\Psi_{\overline{v},\overline{w}}(\overline{v})$. First, we have $\sum_{1 \leq i \leq n} \Phi(v_i, v_i) = |\{v_i \mid v_i > 0\}|$. This is so because the addition in the left hand side adds 1 for each $v_i > 0$. Hence, $\Phi(\sum_{1 \leq i \leq n} \Phi(v_i, v_i), \, |\{v_i \mid v_i > 0\}|\,) = 1$, and so we have that the first additive factor in the expression $\Psi_{\overline{v},\overline{w}}(\overline{v})$ is ρ. Besides, since for any $1 \leq i \leq n$ it holds $v_i = 0$ or $w_i = 0$, we have that $\Phi(v_i, w_i) = 0$, for any $1 \leq i \leq n$. Thus, it is fulfilled $\sum_{1 \leq i \leq n} \Phi(v_i, w_i) = 0$. Then, the second additive factor in expression $\Psi_{\overline{v},\overline{w}}(\overline{v})$ is 0, so we obtain $\Psi_{\overline{v},\overline{w}}(\overline{v}) = \rho$. By using similar arguments we obtain $\Psi_{\overline{v},\overline{w}}(\overline{w}) = \varrho$ and since $\rho > \varrho$ we conclude $\Psi_{\overline{v},\overline{w}}(\overline{v}) > \Psi_{\overline{v},\overline{w}}(\overline{w})$. □

Let us remark that by using the function $\Psi_{\overline{v},\overline{w}}$ as a component of the test we will favor that the test and the IUT exchange resources so that the appropriate transition guards of the IUT hold. This is so because both agents will get happier by exchanging the exact resources we want them to exchange. In particular, if $\Psi_{\overline{v},\overline{w}}$ is *adequately* inserted in the test so that $\overline{v}$ represents the resources the test must take from the IUT and $\overline{w}$ represents those it will give to the IUT, then the exchange we want to perform would improve the utility of the test, since its utility function will return a higher value with $\overline{v}$ than with $\overline{w}$. Besides, if the exchange of $\overline{v}$ by $\overline{w}$ is represented in a *possible use of resources* of the specification then the specification will fulfill its guard to change its state by performing that exchange. Since a possible use of resources takes into account only those exchanges where the USM does not lose utility, the utility function of the specification will accept such a exchange. Similarly, any IUT conforming to the specification will do so.

We are now ready to define the test that will lead the IUT through a given path. As we said before, each state in the test will represent the corresponding state of the specification in the path. Besides, in order to properly track the IUT, we need the test to change its state exactly when the specification is supposed to do it. Therefore, the guards of the transitions of the tests will hold exactly when the corresponding guard of the specification does. As we know the total amount of resources in the system, the test can trivially compute the resources the IUT has by subtracting its own resources from the total amount and accounting the resources introduced or removed from the market in previous transitions. Thus, the guards of the test can be easily defined in terms of its own resources. The next definition provides a mechanism for creating a test to guide the IUT through a given path. In this definition, $\widehat{U}$ and $\widehat{r}$ denote, respectively, the utility function and the resources the test will apply in its last state.

Definition 13. *Let* $M = (S, s_{in}, V, U, at, mi, T)$ *be a USM and let* $c = (s_{in}, \overline{r_{in}}, [\,])$ *be a configuration of* M. *Let* $\eta = [s_1, \ldots, s_m]$ *be a possible path of* M *from* c *and let* $\sigma \in ValidTraces(M, c)$ *be such that* σ *is a possible trace to perform* η. *A test leading* M *through* η *and applying* $\widehat{U}$ *and* $\widehat{r}$ *is a USM* $T = (S', s'_{in}, V, U', at, mi, T')$ *where*

- $S' = \{s'_1, \ldots, s'_m\}$, *where* $s'_1, \ldots, s'_m$ *are fresh states.*
- $s'_{in} = s'_1$.
- $U'(s'_m) = \widehat{U}$ *and for any* $1 \le i \le m - 1$ *we have*

$$U'(s'_i)(t, \overline{x}) = \begin{cases} \Psi_{Steal_i, Give_i}(\overline{x} - Reserve_i) & \text{if } \overline{x} \ge Reserve_i \\ 0 & \text{otherwise} \end{cases}$$

where

$$Reserve_i = \widehat{r} + \sum_{i < j \le m} \Omega((StateTran(\sigma).2)_j - (StateTran(\sigma).3)_{j-1})$$
$$Steal_i = \Omega((StateTran(\sigma).3)_{i-1} - (StateTran(\sigma).2)_i)$$
$$Give_i = \Omega((StateTran(\sigma).2)_i - (StateTran(\sigma).3)_{i-1})$$

where Ω *returns the original tuple but substituting negative numbers by* 0 *and we assume that* $(StateTran(\sigma).3)_0 = \overline{r_{in}}$.
- $T' = \{(s'_1, Q'_1, id, s'_2), \ldots, (s'_{m-1}, Q'_{m-1}, id, s'_m)\}$ *is such that for any* $1 \le i \le m$ *we have* $Q'_i(t, \overline{r}) = Q_i(t, (\overline{r_{in}} + Reserve_0 - \overline{r}))$, *where id is the identity function,* Q_i *is such that* $(s_i, Q_i, Z_i, s_{i+1}) \in T$ *and* $Q_i(t', (StateTran(\sigma).2)_i) = True$ *for some* t' *and* Z_i, *with* $Z_i((StateTran(\sigma).2)_i) = (StateTran(\sigma).3)_i$, *and* $Modif_i = \sum_{1 \le j < i}(StateTran(\sigma).3)_j - (StateTran(\sigma).2)_j$

The initial configuration of T *is given by* $c' = (s'_{in}, (0, Reserve_0), [\,])$.   □

Let us comment the previous definition. Every state in the path η has a corresponding state in the test. Let us remark that if η contains cycles then each occurrence of the same state in η will be represented by a different state in the test. The utility function of each state in the test will promote that the resources the test wants to give to the IUT (that is, $Give_i$) are less valued than those it wants to take from the IUT (that is, $Steal_i$). Since, by construction, the preferences reflected in the specification are opposite to those of the test, the exchange will be possible if the IUT conforms to the specification. Besides, the utility function of the test will take care of keeping the needed resources for future states in the path (given by Reserve_i). This is done by setting the utility to null if these resources are not owned. The values of Give_i, Steal_i, and Reserve_i are calculated by analyzing σ, that is the possible trace we choose to execute the path η. By comparing the available resources when arriving at the current state and when leaving it (denoted by $(\text{StateTran}(\sigma).3)_{i-1}$ and $(\text{StateTran}(\sigma).2)_i$, respectively), we calculate the resources the IUT must get/lose in each state to advance along the path η. The transitions of the tests will be activated exactly when the specification would do it. Thus, the guards of the test (Q_i') are defined in terms of the guards of the specification (Q_i). Let us remark that the expression $\overline{r_{in}} + \text{Reserve}_0 + \text{Modif}_i - \overline{r}$ allows the test to determine the resources the specification owns, assuming that the test owns the basket $\overline{r}$. The reason is that $\overline{r_{in}} + \text{Reserve}_0$ is equal to the total amount of resources existing initially in the system, while Modif_i denotes the subsequent variation of this amount due to the resources introduced/removed by the specification in the next transitions by its functions Z_i. The value Modif_i is computed by comparing the tuples of resources before and after each modification of the state (denoted by $(\text{StateTran}(\sigma).2)_j$ and $(\text{StateTran}(\sigma).3)_j$, respectively). Let us note that the test does not modify the total amount of resources since its functions of transformation of resources are always given by the identity function.

Once a test is defined, we can apply it to the IUT to detect faults. We will be able to detect faults by comparing the *ideal* observable behavior of a system consisting of the specification and the test with the *real* observable behavior of the real system consisting of both agents. In order to perform these observations we have to fix the kind of actions we will be able to observe. First of all, we will suppose that the initial amount of resources of the tested agent is known. Second, we will suppose that each agent in the system provides us a mechanism to observe its basket of resources at any time. This requirement will be basic to trace the economic behavior of the system. Let us note that if we can access the baskets of resources of the agents then we can detect the performed transactions just by checking whether the baskets change.[1] Besides, another event we can detect is the passing of time. Nevertheless, as we assume that the tested agents are black boxes, we will not be able to check whether an agent changes its state. Summarizing, the visible events will be the transactions of our agents and the elapsed time. The following definition formalizes the kind of traces we will be able to observe from a system of agents.

Definition 14. *An observable trace of a system is a list* $[e_1, \ldots, e_m]$ *where for any* $1 \leq i \leq m$ *we have that either* $e_i = (t, \beta)$, *with* $t \in \mathbb{R}_+$, *or* $e_i = (\overline{x}, (a_1, a_2), \gamma)$, *with* $\overline{x} \in \mathbb{R}_+^n$. $\qquad \square$

In the previous definition (t, β) represents the passing of t units of time while $(\overline{x}, (a_1, a_2), \gamma)$ represents a transaction between the agents M_{a_1} and M_{a_2}. In this last case the difference between the new and the old baskets of resources is equal

---

[1] Alternatively, we could suppose that the performed transactions are the only information we can observe. In this case it is also trivial to infer the baskets of resources of the agents at any time.

to $\overline{x}$ in the case of the agent M_{a_1} and equal to $-\overline{x}$ in the case of the agent M_{a_2}. In order to avoid unneeded redundancies we assume $a_1 < a_2$. Let us note that we have not included a special label to denote a *failed* passing of time because the observation of a system does not explicitly provide such information. In order to detect a fault in one of the agents included in a system (in this case, the IUT) we will need to check whether the observed behavior matches a possible behavior of the specification of the system in which such an agent produces no failure. This can be done by checking whether the observed trace belongs to the set of valid traces of the specification *for that agent*, that is, those for which that agent does not fail.[2] However, we must take into account that the traces of the specification include information about the *internal* behavior of the system. Thus, we must first identify the set of *visible* traces of the specification. Intuitively, a trace becomes visible after removing all the events related to the modification of the states and by joining all the consecutive passing of time transitions together into a single one. In the following definition, we identify the set of observable traces of a system. We will require that the behavior of *one* of the USMs included in the system is free of failures. The reason is that our aim is to identify the observable traces of a system consisting of a specification and a test where the behavior of the specification is correct. By comparing them with the traces of the system consisting of the IUT and the test we will be able to detect failures in the IUT.

Definition 15. *Let $S = (M_1, \ldots, M_m)$ be a system, let $1 \le i \le m$, and let $\sigma \in \text{ValidTraces}(S, c, M_i)$. The observable trace of the trace valid for M_i σ, denoted by $\text{OTr}(\sigma, M_i)$, is defined as $\text{OTr'}(\sigma, M_i, 0)$, where*

$$
\text{OTr'}(\sigma, M_i, t) =
\begin{cases}
[(t, \beta)] & \text{if } \sigma = [\,] \\
\text{OTr'}(l', M_i, t) & \text{if } \sigma = (c', c'', 0)_\alpha : l' \\
\text{OTr'}(l', M_i, t + t') & \text{if } \sigma = (c', c'', t')_{\beta_A} : l' \wedge \\
& \quad i \notin A \\
(t, \beta) : (\overline{x}, (a_1, a_2), \gamma) : \text{OTr'}(l', M_i, 0) & \text{if } \sigma = (d', d'', 0)_\gamma : l'
\end{cases}
$$

where

$$d' = ((s_1', \overline{r_1'}, l_1'), \ldots, (s_{a_1}', \overline{r_{a_1}'}, l_{a_1}'), \ldots, (s_{a_2}', \overline{r_{a_2}'}, l_{a_2}'), \ldots, (s_m', \overline{r_m'}, l_m'))$$
$$d'' = ((s_1', \overline{r_1''}, l_1'), \ldots, (s_{a_1}', \overline{r_{a_1}''}, l_{a_1}''), \ldots, (s_{a_2}', \overline{r_{a_2}''}, l_{a_2}''), \ldots, (s_m', \overline{r_m''}, l_m'))$$

and $\overline{x} = \overline{r_{a_1}''} - \overline{r_{a_1}'}$.

Let $S = (M_1, \ldots, M_m)$ be a system and c a configuration of S. We define the set of observable traces of S from c for a valid M_i, denoted by $\text{ObsTraces}(S, c, M_i)$, as $\{\sigma' \mid \exists \sigma \in \text{ValidTraces}(S, c, M_i) : \sigma' = \text{OTr}(\sigma, M_i)\}$. □

Now that we can compute the observable traces of a system specification, we can detect whether the observable behavior of a IUT represents a faulty behavior.

---

[2] Let us remark that we only require that the behavior of the IUT is free of faults, as a fault of the test does not mean the incorrectness of the IUT.

A trace observed in the composition of the IUT and the test represents a *fault* if it does not belong to the set of observable traces of the system consisting of the (non-failing) specification and the test.

Definition 16. *Let $S = (Spec, Test)$ be a system where $Test$ is a test to guide the specification $Spec$ through a given path η. Let σ'' be an observable trace of a real system RS consisting of an IUT and the test $Test$. Let c denote the initial configuration of S. We say that σ'' represents a fault of the IUT with respect to $Spec$ if $\sigma'' \notin ObsTraces(S, c, Spec)$.* □

4   Conclusions and Future Work

In this paper we have presented a framework to test agents whose underlying model is given by a utility state machine. The main highlight of our *active* testing approach is that tests, in contrast with the usual situation, are also given by agents. This paper together with [13] firmly sets the basis for a formal model to deal with autonomous commerce agents. However, we consider that further work on this topic should follow to complement and extend the existing framework. First, other notions of testing should be explored. In particular, we are working with a more *passive* approach where an agent is simply observed. Second, we think that in order to asses the usefulness of our framework it is necessary to deal with other agent-based e-commerce systems (as we have done with Kasbah).

References

[1] K. Adi, M. Debbabi, and M. Mejri. A new logic for electronic commerce protocols. *Theoretical Computer Science*, 291(3):223–283, 2003. 322

[2] A. Cavalli and S. Maag. Automated test scenarios generation for an e-barter system. In *19th ACM Symposium on Applied Computing, SAC'04*, pages 795–799. ACM Press, 2004. 323

[3] A. Chavez and P. Maes. Kasbah: An agent marketplace for buying and selling goods. In *PAAM'96*, pages 75–90, 1996. 322

[4] R. Guttman, A. Moukas, and P. Maes. Agent-mediated electronic commerce: A survey. *The Knowledge Engineering Review*, 13(2):147–159, 1998. 322

[5] M. He, N. R. Jennings, and H. Leung. On agent-mediated electronic commerce. *IEEE Trans. on Knowledge and Data Engineering*, 15(4):985–1003, 2003. 322

[6] N. López, M. Núñez, I. Rodríguez, and F. Rubio. A formal framework for e-barter based on microeconomic theory and process algebras. In *Innovative Internet Computer Systems, LNCS 2346*, pages 217–228. Springer, 2002. 323

[7] N. López, M. Núñez, I. Rodríguez, and F. Rubio. A multi-agent system for e-barter including transaction and shipping costs. In *18th ACM Symposium on Applied Computing, SAC'03*, pages 587–594. ACM Press, 2003. 323

[8] M. Ma. Agents in e-commerce. *Communications of the ACM*, 42(3):79–80, 1999. 322

[9] M. Núñez and I. Rodríguez. PAMR: A process algebra for the management of resources in concurrent systems. In *FORTE 2001*, pages 169–185. Kluwer Academic Publishers, 2001. 323

[10] J. A. Padget and R. J. Bradford. A pi-calculus model of a spanish fish market - preliminary report. In *AMET'98, LNCS 1571*, pages 166–188. Springer, 1998. 322

[11] R. L. Probert, Y. Chen, M. Cappa, P. Sims, and B. Gahaziadeh. Formal verification and validation for e-commerce: Theory and best practices. *Journal of Information and Software Technology*, 45(11):763–777, 2003. 323

[12] I. Rodríguez. Formal specification of autonomous commerce agents. In *19th ACM Symposium on Applied Computing, SAC'04*, pages 774–778. ACM Press, 2004. 323, 324

[13] I. Rodríguez, M. Núñez, and F. Rubio. Specification of autonomous agents in e-commerce systems. In *Workshop on Theory Building and Formal Methods in Electronic/Mobile Commerce (TheFormEMC), LNCS 3236*. Springer, 2004. 323, 324, 325, 335

[14] T. Sandholm. Agents in electronic commerce: Component technologies for automated negotiation and coalition formation. In *CIA'98, LNCS 1435*, pages 113–134. Springer, 1998. 322

Generation of Integration Tests
for Self-Testing Components*

Leonardo Mariani, Mauro Pezzè, and David Willmor

Dipartimento di Informatica, Sistemistica e Comunicazione
Universita degli Studi di Milano Bicocca
Via Bicocca degli Arcimboldi, 8, I-20126 - Milano, Italy
{mariani,pezze,willmor}@disco.unimib.it

Abstract. Internet software tightly integrates classic computation with communication software. Heterogeneity and complexity can be tackled with a component-based approach, where components are developed by application experts and integrated by domain experts. Component-based systems cannot be tested with classic approaches but present new problems. Current techniques for integration testing are based upon the component developer providing test specifications or suites with their components. However, components are often being used in ways not envisioned by their developers, thus the packaged test specifications and suites cannot be relied upon. Often this results in conditions being placed upon a components use, however, what is required is a method for allowing test suites to be adapted for new situations. In this paper, we propose an approach for implementing self-testing components, which allow integration test specifications and suites to be developed by observing both the behavior of the component and of the entire system.

1   Introduction

Software for the Internet often presents a strong integration of computation, data and communication aspects. Classic software products are often deployed and tested independently from communication services that are accessed as external libraries. In many Internet applications, such as e-commerce software, communication aspects cannot be easily separated from traditional software, but must be tightly integrated in the product. Such integration of heterogeneous aspects results in new development and testing challenges.

A popular approach for addressing complexity and heterogeneity relies on the use of components and component-based design methodologies. Components enhance reuse and can facilitate the sound integration of heterogeneous services. Components can be developed by different teams with specific expertise and abilities: communication experts may focus on communication services, while software and integration experts may focus on traditional data and computational aspects.

---

* This work has been partially funded by a grant from the SegraVis Research Training Network – www.segravis.org.

M. Núñez et al. (Eds.): FORTE 2004 Workshops, LNCS 3236, pp. 337–350, 2004.

The independent development of reusable components and the adoption of component-based methodologies introduce new verification challenges that derive from the absence of knowledge about the final system when developing components, and about the components' internals when developing the target application. Good components are widely re-used, and component designers cannot anticipate all possible uses at development time. System designers should be able to reuse components without knowing all internals to benefit from component developers' expertise. Test designers must be able to test single components independently from the applications, and component-based systems without accessing the internals of their components.

The scientific community is investigating various solutions to these new verification challenges: providing components with an associated specification [1], deploying together the component with its test suite [2], or developing components with testing facilities [3].

The approaches investigated so far work under specific hypotheses on both components and their integration, and thus inevitably restrict the use of components and may fail when the verification hypotheses are violated. In this paper, we propose a novel approach that tries to overcome these limitations by moving testing from development to deployment time. The proposed approach is based on self-testing components, a method successfully exploited in hardware design: components are augmented with self-testing capabilities that can be exploited when the components are reused in a novel system. However, self-testing features are targeted at testing for chip malfunctions and the assumption is made for hardware components that the functionality of the component is sound. Self-testing components can self-verify their behavior in the new context and thus in principle can be reused without any a-priori limitation.

We propose a framework that generates self-testing features from components' test and execution. When testing and using components in traditional settings, we capture components' executions, and distill Invariants that model the components' behavior as experienced during execution. These Invariants provide the information for generating test cases that can be automatically executed when components are reused in new systems. Thus new systems can be tested without restricting components' reuse or requiring specific knowledge about components.

Section 2 presents the basic idea underlying self-testing components. Section 3 describes how we derive the Invariants that we use for generating test suites associated to components. Section 4 presents the different techniques that we developed for filtering test cases for self-testing. Section 5 discusses the problems of executing self-tests. Section 6 highlights the advantages of the new approach presented in this paper comparing it with related work. Finally, Section 7 outlines on-going and future work seeded by the technique proposed in this paper.

2   Self-Testing Components

Components are usually produced by different software vendors and are then assembled by component deployers, to build the final system. Component developers know neither the context of the components execution nor the ways in which they will be used. Moreover, component developers implement components under implicit assumptions regarding the behavior of other components that may be violated in certain environments.

Component integrators have limited knowledge of the reused components, since components are often deployed either without or with incomplete specifications and the source code is seldom provided. Integration testing becomes difficult, and does not always provide a sufficient level of confidence in the final system. Many major failures confirm the difficulties in achieving an acceptable level of confidence even in critical scenarios, for example the Mars Climate Observer [4], the Mars Polar Lander [5] or the Arianne 5 [6] problems.

In hardware testing, some of these problems have been addressed by developing Built-In Self-Test (BIST) features. "BIST is a Design-for-Testability technique in which testing (test generation and test application) is accomplished through built-in hardware features" [7]. BIST features are automatically derived from the design, and system integrators do not have to care about component testing since it is automatically performed by BIST features. The same idea can be extended to software components by producing *self-testing components*, i.e., components which automatically test their integration in a larger system.

Self-testing software components differ from BIST hardware both for: the time of test execution, and the type of tests that are performed. In the case of testing hardware components, test cases are executed regularly to check for faults that may arise due to chip problems, while tests for software components are executed *only once at deployment time* since software components do not change during their lifetime (unless they are replaced with newer versions). Moreover, since hardware can degrade its performance or stop working correctly, BIST embedded features refer mainly to unit testing, whilst, in the case of software components, it is more important to consider *integration tests* since unit testing is performed during development.

There are several ways to implement self-testing components: by embedding specifications [8], by adding testing functionalities into the component [3], and by associating test suites to components [9]. This work suggests various approaches and provide encouraging preliminary results. Our work enhances the previous solutions proposing a novel approach for generating test cases to create self-testing components.

The successful execution of all test cases associated with a component C newly integrated in a system assures that C integrates correctly into the system, i.e., the interactions from C to the system are correct. The successful execution of all test cases associated with components that interact with C assures that the system integrates well with C, i.e., all interactions from the system to C are correct. Insights regarding the execution of test cases are provided in Section 5. Self-testing components present several advantages:

- System integrators who operate with classic components need to design integration test strategies without knowing details of each single component; while with self-testing components integration tests are obtained automatically.
- Self-testing components do not require the generation of test cases for each new system.
- Self-tests can be automatically re-executed for testing the correctness of modifications without additional effort.
- Self-testing components can be augmented with oracles derived from executions in previous systems, thus reducing the need for additional scaffolding.

Test suites associated with self-testing components can be derived in different ways:

- The test suite can be *manually provided by the component developer* [10]. In this case the test suite is generated by using the experience and intuition of the component developer without using any explicit criterion. This brute force approach takes advantage of the ability of the developer, but rarely meets the requirements of soundness and completeness.
- The test suite can be *generated from (formal) specifications* [11]. In this case a specification of the software component is provided from which the test suite is generated. Whilst this method produces test suites which are highly effective it is reliant upon the existence of an accurate and complete specification.
- The test suite can be *generated from component executions* [12]. In this case the test suite is obtained by observing previous executions, selecting meaningful ones, and then storing them in a repository. This case is dependent upon the component being used completely during observation. Therefore the longer the component is observed the more likely it is for coverage to be obtained.

Our approach to creating self-testing components is based upon an amalgamation and extension of the second and third methods. A specification, in the form of *derived/inferred* properties, is generated from either source code or observed executions. This specification can then be used to *filter* observed executions to be used as test cases. Our proposed method has the following benefits over the previous methods: the technique (1) can be used on binary components, e.g., when a third party component is purchased, (2) is very practical, thus it requires little effort by either the component developer or the component assembler, and (3) is for the large part automatic.

Our approach is based on three main phases:

Generating Invariants: in this phase, we generate both proper and likely Invariants. Proper Invariants are generated from statically analyzing the source code, and describe properties of interactions of the component with the systems it is used in. Likely Invariants are automatically generated by monitoring the component behavior when integrated in running systems, and describe both interactions and exchanged values between the component and the embedding systems. Invariants provide the information required during the test generation phase to discriminate relevant behaviors that are selected as interesting test cases.

Recording Behaviors: in this phase, we record behaviors during normal executions of systems that embed the target component, to gain information that can later be used for generating test cases.

Generating Test Suites: in this phase, we generate test suites by sampling the set of collected behaviors according to the recorded Invariants.

The main contribution of this paper is first in assembling previously exploited technology to derive Invariants and record behaviors and then in proposing a set of criteria to sample the space of behaviors for selecting test suites.

3   BCT Framework

The BCT Framework [13] is a suite of tools that we use to monitor and dynamically verify components. BCT dynamically extracts information regarding components' behaviors as Invariants and records actual behaviors. We will show in the next sections how to use this information to generate test cases.

Invariant Generation

The information extracted during component monitoring consists of a specification of components interactions in the form of Interaction and I/O Invariants. Interaction Invariants describe the protocol that the monitored component uses to communicate with the other components. I/O Invariants describe what information is passed between components.

Interaction Invariants represent the pattern of interactions of each service of a component with other components. These Invariants are captured at run-time as a finite state machine which can then be expressed as a regular expression. For instance, the Interaction Invariant associated to a service `viewCart` of a `Cart` component for webshop applications can be:

$$(\texttt{Catalog.getItemDetail(ImageUtility.loadImage } |\epsilon))*$$

and indicates that visualization of the content of the `Cart` causes from 0 to n interactions with the `Catalog` component for retrieving detailed information about items. For each item in the cart, an additional interaction with the `ImageUtility` component may be required if a picture of the item is provided.

Regular expressions consist of elements of the alphabet, and operators. The alphabet represents interactions with other components. In the context of Interaction Invariants two operators are used. | is the union operator which specifies that either the left or right symbol can be matched, and ∗ is the Kleene operator which specifies that the previous symbol can be matched 0 or more times. In the example $a * (b|c)$ the alphabet consists of $\{a, b, c\}$ while the operators $\{*, |\}$ are used.

We derive Interaction Invariants both statically and dynamically. We statically generate Interaction Invariants by building a reduced control-flow graph where nodes represent services requests. A regular expression can then be inferred from this graph. We dynamically generate Interaction Invariants by monitoring the components interactions with the system, further details can be found in [13, 14]. Static generation produces Interaction Invariants which represent all possible interactions of a components. This is in contrast to dynamic generation which produces Invariants representing only the observed behaviors of a component.

I/O Invariants represent properties over parameters of the components interaction with the system. For example, an Invariant $qt > 0$ associated to the interaction of a service `addItem` of a component `Cart` by a service `buyItem` of a component `Purchase` indicates that variable qt (item quantity) is always positive when the service is invoked in that context.

We derive I/O Invariants dynamically by monitoring the execution of a component. Thus, I/O Invariants are Invariants over observed executions, that represent "likely" Invariants for the target component. Further information regarding how state data is extracted from complex objects can be found in [13, 14].

Recording Observed Behaviors

The BCT Framework has the facility to record observed behaviors of a component. An observed behavior consists of some form of stimulus to the component as well as its effect in the form of an interaction trace (the sequence of interactions triggered by the stimulus) and I/O values. These observed behaviors can be stored allowing them to be used as test cases for integration testing. However, indiscriminately storing these behaviors will soon produce large test suites that are of no practical use. Therefore, it is necessary to define filtering criteria for distinguishing which behaviors are meaningful or more specifically those likely to expose integration faults. These filtering criteria are presented in Section 4.

4   Test Case Selection

The monitoring of a component records a set of observed behaviors which can be used as possible tests. We produce test suites by extracting a subset of this set according to suitable *filtering criteria*. These filtering criteria utilize the generated Invariants as a specification of the components behavior. Our filtering criteria differ from classic testing methodologies in that we do not intend to test the components compliance to the Invariants, instead we use them as a means of identifying meaningful test cases. In this context we refer to a "meaningful test case" as one likely to expose integration faults.

In this section we propose a number of filtering criteria based upon the generated Interaction and I/O Invariants. These filtering criteria can be further categorized as those based upon post-execution filtering and those performed during the process of generating the Invariants.

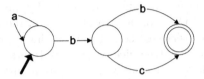

Fig. 1. The finite state machine that is equivalent to the regular expression $a^*b(b|c)$. The node with the string incoming edge represents the initial state, while the node with the double border represents the final state

Filtering criteria based on Interaction Invariants can be defined for Invariants expressed as either regular expressions or the corresponding finite state machines.

Three entities can be considered in a regular expression: the alphabet, the operators, and possible subexpressions. We therefore propose three filtering criteria based upon each entity:

Alphabet Coverage: A test suite TS satisfies the Alphabet Coverage criterion if for each symbol a in the alphabet, there is at least a test case TC in TS that contains a.

For example, the test suite $\{abc\}$ satisfies the alphabet coverage for the regular expression $a^*b(b|c)$.

Executing a test suite that satisfies alphabet coverage results in exercising all services accessed by the component-under-test at least once.

Operator Coverage: A test suite TS satisfies the Operator Coverage criterion if

- for each union operator | occurring in the regular expression, TS includes at least one test case TC_a that contains the first operand and one test case TC_b that contains the second operand.
- for each Kleen operator $*$ occurring in the regular expression, TS includes at least one test case TC_a that corresponds to no iterations of the operand, one test case TC_b that corresponds to exactly one iteration of the operand, and one test case TC_c that corresponds to more than one iteration of the operand.

For example, the test suite $\{bb, abc, aabb\}$ satisfies the Operator Coverage criterion for the regular expression $a^*b(b|c)$.

Expression Coverage: A test suite TS satisfies the Expression Coverage criterion if for each choice of operators that results in a sentence S up to consecutive iterations of the Kleen operators, it contains at least one test case TC corresponding to S.

For example, the test suite $\{bb, bc, abb, abc, aabb, aabc\}$ satisfies the expression coverage criterion for $a^*b(b|c)$.

Execution of a test suite that covers expressions result in the component executing each possible combination of behaviors.

Three entities can be considered in a finite state machine (FSM): nodes, edges and paths. We therefore propose three filtering criteria based upon each entity:

Node Coverage: A test suite *TS* satisfies the Node Coverage criterion if for each node n of the FSM there is at least one test case *TC* that traverses n. For example, the test suite $\{bb\}$ satisfies the Node Coverage criterion for the FSM in Figure 1.

Execution of a test suite that satisfies the node coverage criterion corresponds to covering all states of the component-under-test where a decision about the next interaction can take place.

Edge Coverage: A test suite *TS* satisfies the Edge Coverage criterion if for each edge e of the FSM there is at least one test case *TC* that traverses e. For example, the test suite $\{abb, abc\}$ satisfies the Edge Coverage criterion for the FSM in Figure 1.

Execution of a test suite that satisfies the edge coverage criterion results in requesting the execution of all services accessed by the component-under-test at least once in each different situation.

Path Coverage: A test suite *TS* satisfies the Path Coverage criterion if for each path p of the FSM there is at least one test case *TC* that traverses p. Cycles are covered according to the boundary interior criterion that limits path coverage to each different path contained within the cycle at least once [15]. For example, the test suite $\{bb, bc, abb, abc\}$ satisfies the Path Coverage criterion for the FSM in Figure 1.

Execution of a test suite that covers all paths results in the component executing all possible "linear indepedent" combinations of behaviors at least once.

I/O Invariants describe properties over possible values of the parameters of a component's service. We can therefore refer to the properties specified by I/O invariants to derive a new filtering criterion. White and Cohen proposed a test case selection criterion based on mathematical properties over variables [16]. Test cases selected by the White and Cohen criterion include stimuli that are both feasible and infeasible according to the specification. We propose a criterion that applies White and Cohen criterion to our set of I/O Invariants. We restrict the criterion to feasible stimuli only, since it is not possible to observe infeasible stimuli at run-time. The obtained filtering criterion is:

Domain Value Coverage: A test suite *TS* satisfies the Domain Coverage criterion if for each I/O Invariant it contains at least one test case corresponding to both boundary and normal values as shown in Table 1

All filtering criteria defined so far are applicable to a set of observed behavios that derive from previously recorded executions. We identify them as *post-execution* criteria.

Recording a large set of executions may be space consuming. Therefore, we define additional criteria that can be used at run time, thus reducing the set of executions to be recorded. We identify this new set of criteria as *run-time* criteria.

We propose the following set of *run-time* criteria:

Table 1. Filtering criteria for I/O Invariants. x, y and z are variable names or sequences; a, b and c are constants; fn is any language specific function; and $-$ shows that no test cases are necessary to cover the Invariant

Invariants over any variable		Invariants over three numeric variables	
Invariant	**Test Case Spec**	**Invariant**	**Test Case Spec**
$x = a$	-	$z = ax + by + c$	-
$x = uninit$	-	$y = ax + bz + c$	-
$x \in \{a, b, c\}$	$x = a,\ x = b,\ x = c$	$x = ay + bz + c$	-
		$z = fn(x, y)$	-
Invariants over a single numeric variable		**Invariants over a single sequence variable**	
Invariant	**Test Case Spec**	**Invariant**	**Test Case Spec**
$a \leq x \leq b$	$x = a,\ x = a + 1,$ $a + 1 < x < b - 1,$ $x = b - 1,\ x = b$	Min and Max values	-
		nondecreasing	-
$x \neq 0$	$x < -1,\ x = -1,\ x = 1,\ x > 1$	nonincreasing	-
$x \equiv a(mod\ b)$	-	equal	-
$x \not\equiv a(mod\ b)$	$x < a - 1(mod\ b),$ $x = a - 1(mod\ b),$ $x = a + 1(mod\ b),$ $x > a + 1(mod\ b)$	inv. over all elem.	-
		Invariants over two sequence variables	
Invariants over two numeric variables		**Invariant**	**Test Case Spec**
Invariant	**Test Case Spec**	$y = ax + b$	-
$y = ax + b$	-	$x < y,\ x \leq y,$ $x > y,\ x \geq y,$ $x \neq y$	test specs for the single element applied to all elements
$x < y$	$y = x + 1,\ y > x + 1$		
$x \leq y$	$y = x,\ y = x + 1,\ y > x + 1$		
$x > y$	$x = y + 1,\ x > y + 1$	$x = y$	-
$x \geq y$	$x = y,\ x = y + 1,\ x > y + 1$	x subsequence of y, or vice versa	subsequence at the beginning, middle, and end
$x = y$	-		
$x \neq y$	$y = x + 1,\ x = y + 1,\ x < y,$ $y > x$	x is the reverse of y	-
$x = fn(y)$	-	**Invariants over a sequence and a num. var.**	
any inv. over $x + y$	triple tests with $x = 0,\ y = 0,\ x, y \neq 0$	**Invariant**	**Test Case Spec**
		$i \in s$	i at the beginning, middle, and end of s

Interaction Invariant Modification: the test suite is built incrementally by adding all observed behaviors whose execution causes an Interaction Invariant to be modified.

Interaction Invariant Modification with Observed Frequencies: this criterion extends the previous one by adding special cases corresponding to the Kleene operators. We add an observed behavior to the test suite if the behavior corresponds to a number of iterations of the operand of a Kleen subexpression not yet experienced.

I/O Invariant Modification: we incrementally add observed behaviors whose execution results in the modification of an I/O Invariant. This criterion is based upon the work of McCamant and Ernst [17].

Subsumption Relationship

The filtering criteria we have proposed do not produce test suites that are mutually exclusive. In that certain criteria expand upon the coverage provided by others. We can therefore classify filtering criteria into a subsumption hierarchy. We define subsumption as:

A filtering criterion C_1 *subsumes* a filtering criterion C_2 if every test suite that satisfies C_1 also satisfies C_2.

Figure 2 summarizes the relationships among the filtering criteria presented in this paper. The reasoning behind these relations is as follows:

- The subsumption relationship between Alphabet Coverage, Operator Coverage and Expression Coverage is quite obvious. As is the relationship between Node Coverage, Edge Coverage and Path Coverage.
- Edge Coverage subsumes Alphabet Coverage as each edge in the FSM corresponds to different symbols. Thus covering all edges implies that all symbols are covered.
- Operator Coverage subsumes Edge Coverage as operators are represented as edges. Thus covering all operators implies that all edges are covered.
- Expression Coverage subsumes Path and Operator Coverage as it considers all possible combinations of behaviors.
- Interaction Invariant Modification subsumes Edge Coverage due to the way in which Invariant modification is defined in [13]. In this definition a new edge is added if a new behavior is observed. Thus covering all modifications implies all edges are covered.
- Finally, Interaction Invariant Modification with Observed Frequencies is a clear extension of Interaction Invariant Modification.

5   Executing the Test Suite

Integration testing focuses upon how components interact within the embedding system. Two forms of interactions can be observed: how a component uses the system, and how the system uses a component. Integration faults can occur in either or both situations. The first form of interaction can be tested by executing a test suite covering the Interaction and I/O Invariants of the component over the accessed services. The second form of interaction can be tested by executing test suites of all components that interact with the component.

Components can be both stateless and stateful. Stateless components can be tested by simply invoking services over the tested component and checking the

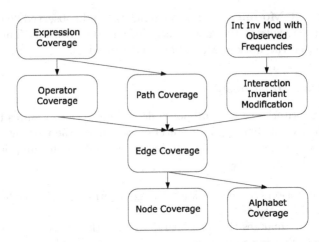

Fig. 2. Subsumption relationship over the proposed filtering criteria

result. Stateful components could be directly executed but since our test cases are extracted from observed behaviors of the component they are only valid when the system is in that state. Therefore, if actual state is different from the state at test case extraction time, the test case may not necessarily be compatible. Moreover, even if the state of the component has remained, the state of the system with which it interacts may have changed. Furthermore, if a test case was to fail, the tester does not know if it was caused by an integration error or a state error.

One possible solution to distinguishing the type of errors is to prevent test cases from being executed if the current state is not applicable. This can be accomplished by packaging test cases with conditions that specify what state the component and system must be in. Whilst this approach prevents state errors from occurring it risks test cases not being executed negating the confidence in the test suite.

The solution that we envision is to design the components for testability, by adding an interface that would facilitate the storing and resumption of state. In this way, it is possible to store the state of components involved in an execution and to resume them when necessary. Combining the existence of a repository of resumable states and query interfaces leads to the production of an effective framework for managing stateful components.

The framework can be implemented with limited efforts on top of existing middleware that supports component persistency. In fact, some middleware already provides features for storing and resuming the status of components as well as functionalities for querying the storage of status, for instance see the EJB framework [18] and the EJB-Object Query Language [18].

6   Related Work

The basic problems of testing component-based systems are summarized by Vitharana [19] . Vithrana highlights how even though individual components are tested in isolation, it is very difficult to rely upon this, and complex integration testing is necessary to ensure the reliability of the system.

Binder [20] introduces the concept of building testability directly into the objects of an object-oriented system during their development. This is achieved by a combination of approaches including formalized design and testing strategies and embedded test specifications. However, whilst this method is possible when the entire system is being developed within a single group, in component-based systems, it would require all of these approaches being standardized and adhered to by a number of different developers.

Both Bertolino and Polini [2] and Martins *et al* [1] discuss different methods for making components self-testable. Their methods differ in that Bertolino and Polini package test cases with their components, whilst Martins *et al* require the user to generate the test cases. However, in both cases the test cases are generated from a developer defined test specification that is packaged with the component. We assume that components may be deployed in ways not previously envisioned by the developer. Therefore, pre-defined test specifications may no longer be valid. We address this situation by constructing test suites based upon the observed behaviors of the running system.

Liu and Richardson [9] introduce the concept of using software components with retrospectors. Retrospectors record the testing and execution history of a component. This information can then be made available to the software testers for the construction of their test plan. Liu and Richardson retrospectors do not take into account automatic generation and execution of test cases since test case generation is entirely delegated to the system integrator. Moreover, the problem of dealing with state is not addressed. On the contrary, our self-testing components are deployed with test suites in a framework enabling their automatic execution, thus the system integrator does not have to generate the test cases.

7   Conclusions and Future Work

Component-Based software engineering is a promising approach for developing complex heterogeneous software systems that integrate classic computation and communication aspects. Testing component-based systems presents new problems with respect to classic software systems, since components are developed with limited knowledge about their use, and system developers have limited information about the internals of the reused components.

In this paper, we propose a new approach for automatically developing self-testing components. The proposed approach augments classic components with self-testing features by automatically extracting information from components when they are used as part of running systems. Automatically generated self-testing features support automatic execution of integration testing at deployment time. In this paper, we focus on the problem of automatically generating test cases from behavior Invariants of components.

We are currently developing a prototype for experimenting with self-testing components. Through this experimental work we aim to be able to evaluate the filtering criteria, specifically with reference to the fault revealing capability and the size of the test suite.

Regarding the use of filtering criteria to create test suites, we do not expect to find a single ideal criterion. As with many situations within software engineering the choice of filtering criteria largely depends upon the intentions of the component developer or system integrator. For example, a developer constructing a component for an embedded system (where resources are limited) may prefer a test suite of minimal size whilst still covering all common integration errors. This is in contrast to a developer of a safety critical component who may prefer a test suite which covers all possible interactions and where test suite size is less important. We aim to evaluate each filtering criteria, highlighting their strengths and weaknesses, both generally and related to specific applications scenarios, e.g., enterprise components versus embedded components. We expect that this work will allow a developer to select the most appropriate filtering criteria for their specific application.

References

[1] Martins, E., Toyota, C., Yanagawa, R.: Constructing self-testable software components. In: Proceedings of the 2001 International Conference on Dependable Systems and Networks (DSN '01), Washington - Brussels - Tokyo, IEEE (2001) 151–160 338, 348

[2] Bertolino, A., Polini, A.: A framework for component deployment testing. In: Proceedings of the 25th International Conference on Software Engineering, IEEE Computer Society (2003) 221–231 338, 348

[3] Edwards, S. H.: A framework for practical, automated black-box testing of component-based software. Journal of Software Testing, Verification and Reliability 11 (2001) 338, 339

[4] Oberg, J.: Why the mars probe went off course. IEEE Spectrum 36 (1999) 34–39 339

[5] Jet Propulsion Laboratory: Report on the loss of the mars polar lander and deep space 2 missions. Technical Report JPL D-18709, California Institute of Technology (2000) 339

[6] Weyuker, E.: Testing component-based software: A cautionary tale. IEEE Internet Computing 15 (1998) 54–59 339

[7] Agrawal, V., Kime, C., Saluja, K.: A tutorial on built-in self-test. I. principles. IEEE Design & Test of Computers 10 (1993) 73–82 339

[8] Binder, R.: Design for testability in object-oriented systems. Communications of the ACM 37 (1994) 87–101 339

[9] Liu, C., Richardson, D.: Software components with retrospectors. In: Proceedings of the International Workshop on the Role of Software Architecture in Testing and Analysis (ROSATEA). (1998) 63–68 339, 348

[10] Beizer, B.: Software Testing Techniques. 2nd edn. Van Nostrand Reinhold Computer (1982) 340

[11] Ramachandran, M.: Testing reusable software components from object specification. SIGSOFT Softw. Eng. Notes **28** (2003) 18 340
[12] Leon, D., Podgurski, A., White, L. J.: Multivariate visualization in observation-based testing. In: Proceedings of the 22nd International Conference on Software Engineering, ACM Press (2000) 116–125 340
[13] Mariani, L., Pezzè, M.: A technique for verifying component-based software. In: International Workshop on Test and Analysis of Component Based Systems, Electronic Notes in Theoretical Computer Science (ENTCS) (2004) 16–28 341, 342, 346
[14] Mariani, L.: Capturing and synthesizing the behavior of component-based systems. Technical Report LTA:2004:01, Università di Milano Bicocca (2003) 342
[15] Howden, W.: Methodology for the generation of program test data. IEEE Transaction Computer (1975) 344
[16] White, L., Cohen, E. J.: A domain strategy for computer program testing. IEEE Transactions on Software Engineering **6** (1980) 247–257 344
[17] McCamant, S., Ernst, M. D.: Predicting problems caused by component upgrades. In: proceedings of the 9th European Software Engineering Conference and the 10th International Symposium on Foundations of Software Engineering, ACM Press (2003) 287–296 346
[18] Microsystems, S.: Enterprise Javabeans^{TM} Specification. Final Release Version 2.1, Sun Microsystems (2003) 347
[19] Vitharana, P.: Risks and challenges of component-based software development. Commun. ACM **46** (2003) 67–72 348
[20] Binder, R. V.: Design for testability in object-oriented systems. Communications of the ACM **37** (1994) 87–101 348

Model-Checking Plus Testing: From Software Architecture Analysis to Code Testing

A. Bucchiarone[1], H. Muccini[2], P. Pelliccione[2], and P. Pierini[1]

[1] Siemens C.N.X. S.p.A., R. & D.
Strada Statale 17, L'Aquila, Italy
antonio.bucchiarone@siemens.it
pierluigi.pierini@siemens.com
[2] Dipartimento di Informatica, Università dell'Aquila
Via Vetoio 1, 67100 L'Aquila, Italy
{muccini,pellicci}@di.univaq.it

Abstract. Software Model-Checking and Testing are some of the most used techniques to analyze software systems and identify hidden faults. While software model-checking allows for an *exhaustive* and *automatic* analysis of the system expressed through a model, software testing is based on a clever selection of "relevant" test cases, which may be manually or automatically run over the system.

In this paper we analyze how those two analysis techniques may be integrated in a specific context, where a Software Architecture (SA) specification of the system is available, model-checking techniques are used to validate the SA model conformance with respect to selected properties, while testing techniques are used to validate the implementation conformance to the SA model.

The results of this research are applied to an SDH Telecommunication system architecture designed by Siemens CNX.

1 Introduction

Testing and model-checking are between the most important techniques applied in practice to detect and fix software faults.

Software Model-Checking [7] *analyzes concurrent systems behavior with respect to selected properties* by specifying the system through abstract modelling languages. Model-checking algorithms offer an *exhaustive* and *automatic* approach to *completely* analyze the system. When errors are found, counterexamples are provided. The main limitations model-checking suffers are that it may only verify systems expressed through state-based machines, it is more limited than theorem proving, and it suffers of the *state explosion* problem. Moreover, model-checking may be difficult to be applied, since it usually requires skills on formal specification languages.

Software Testing, instead, refers to the dynamic verification of a system's behavior based on the observation of a selected set of controlled executions, or

M. Núñez et al. (Eds.): FORTE 2004 Workshops, LNCS 3236, pp. 351–365, 2004.

test cases [3]. Testing involves several demanding tasks. However, the problem that has received the highest attention in the literature is, by far, test-case selection: in brief, how to identify a suite of test cases (i.e., a finite set of test cases) that is effective in demonstrating that the software behaves as intended, or, otherwise, in evidencing the existing malfunctions. Clearly, a good test suite is the crucial starting point to a successful testing session.

Comparing model-checking with testing analysis techniques, we may identify the following differences: i) while model-checking offers an *exhaustive* check of the system, testing is based on a clever selection of "relevant" test cases; ii) while model-checking is a completely automated process, testing is usually left to the tester experience; iii) while model-checking requires skills on formal methods, testing may not; finally, iv) while model-checking (usually) helps to find bugs in high-level system designs, testing (in its traditional form) identifies bugs in implementation level code.

Considering the strong complementarity between those two worlds, we believe an integration between model-checking and testing may provide an useful tool to test modern complex software systems.

In this paper we analyze how those two analysis techniques may be integrated in a specific context, where a Software Architecture (SA) [24, 11] specification of the system is available, some properties the SA has to respect are identified and the SA specification has been implemented. Model-checking techniques are used to validate the SA model conformance with respect to selected properties, while testing techniques are used to validate the implementation conformance to the SA model. In the context of this research, the model checker validates the SA conformance to functional properties, while the testing approach provides confidence on the implementation fulfillment to its (architectural) specification (i.e., the so called "conformance testing").

The *advantages* we expect are manifold: we apply the model-checking technique to higher-lever (architectural) specifications, thus governing the state-explosion problem, while applying testing to the final implementation. We check and test the architecture and the system implementation with respect to architectural (functional) properties. Moreover, the test case selection phase is driven by the architectural model. In Siemens CNX systems this approach allows to unify some design steps: in fact, differently from current practices, test cases may be derived from an architectural model, which has been previously checked to be compliant to a set of functional requirements thus ensuring a continuous process from the design step to the integration testing phase.

In proving the validity of this idea, we use the model-checker SPIN in conjunction with the CHARMY framework [6], and apply this approach to a Siemens CNX application.

The following Section 2 motivates our research work by describing some existent related work. Section 3 describes our proposal, by outlining how model-checking is currently used to validate properties on an architectural model and how current testing methodologies allow to test the source code conformance with respect to architectural decisions. The approach is applied to a Siemens

CNX telecommunication application in Section 4, by providing preliminary results. Section 5 draws some considerations while Section 6 concludes the paper and outlines future work directions. A list of abbreviations is provided at the end of the paper.

2 Motivations and Approach Outline

Many work have been developed in using model-checking to generate test cases [1, 12, 5, 22, 14]. The key idea that connects these two validation techniques is to generate, by using model checker features, counter-examples successively used to derive test cases.

The generation of counter-examples is obtained identifying (from the requirements) the properties that the system must satisfy. Actually, to obtain test cases the focus must be put on negative requirements, thus the model checker can generate counter-examples automatically turned into executable tests. Typically, the properties negation is obtained by using the *mutation* technique [10] where a mutation is a small syntactic change in the state machine or in the property. A mutant model is obtained by a single mutation operator on the original model. The rationale is to generate test cases for the critical parts of the system.

Unfortunately, the automatic test generation process (by applying model-checking) is not mature in the software industry, for several reasons:

P1 : due to models complexity, the model checker techniques become inapplicable, thus not allowing to identify test cases;

P2 : even on little examples, the number of generated test cases causes the intractability;

P3 : as underlined also by [12] one of the drawback is on assuming the existence of the properties as part of the problem specification.

In this paper we propose a solution which covers problems P1 and P2 by *combining model-checking and testing at different abstractions level*. Problem P3 is also taken into account when using the proposed model-checking approach.

As graphically shown in Figure 1, we use model-checking (MC) techniques in order to validate the architectural model conformance with respect to identified functional properties, and a testing approach which selects test cases driven by the architectural models and the model checking results. The combination of SA-level model-checking and SA-based code testing allows to *guarantee that the architecture correctly reflects important requirements and the code conforms to the software architecture specification*.

This approach produces two benefits: by using an *incremental process* which allows to specify the architecture, model-check it and refine critical sub-parts, we are able to punctually identify details of subsystems identified as critical, working always with smaller models. Together with the fact that model checking is applied to an high-level model (the SA), we reduce the complexity of the model to be analyzed, thus limiting the state explosion problem (i.e., P1). We

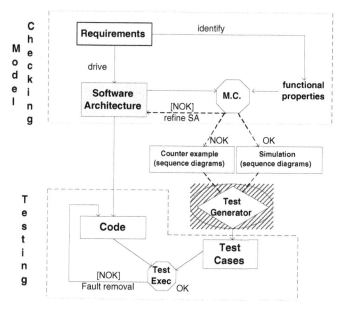

Fig. 1. Approach outline

gain then precision in selecting test-cases maintaining tractable models in terms of dimension and verification time.

3   Our Proposal

The approach we are proposing is composed by two correlated activities: validating SA specifications with respect to functional properties through model-checking, and using such models and results to drive an SA-based code testing approach. In the following sections we describe both activities (in Section 3.1 and 3.2) and how to move from the one to the other.

3.1   Validating Architectural Specifications: The CHARMY Approach

In recent years, the study of Software Architecture (SA) [13, 11] has emerged as an autonomous discipline enabling the design and analysis of complex distributed systems through suitable abstractions. SAs support the formal modeling of a system, through components and connectors, allowing for both a *topological* (static) description and a *behavioral* (dynamic) one.

There is not a unique way to specify an SA, and one of the most challenging tasks is on analyzing functional and non functional properties on the selected architecture [19, 11]. Naturally, a good architecture is the one which satisfies at best the system requirements, acting as a bridge between the requirements (the planned architecture must satisfy) and the implementation code (which has to reflect architectural properties), as advocated in [13].

CHARMY is a framework that, since from the earlier stage of the software development process, aims at *assisting the software architect in designing software architecture and in validating them against expected properties.*

We start specifying an initial, prototypal and even incomplete SA which may identify few (main) components and a set of high-level properties. From this specification we obtain an initial model that can be validated with respect to significant high-level behaviors. This first validation step allows us to gain confidence on the global architectural design and choices, and to identify portions of the SA that might need further and deeper investigation. In fact, when an inconsistency is identified (by producing a counter example), the SA specification may be refined by focussing on relevant system portions. The process is iterated until any critical sub-part is deeply analyzed.

To some extent, our approach is similar to extracting test cases. In eliciting test cases a tester focusses on the critical parts of the system in order to verify his intuitions. In the same way we elicit the properties that represent potentially critical flows and check them on the system model by using model checking techniques.

State machines and scenarios are the source notations for specifying software architectures and behavioral properties they should satisfy, respectively.

CHARMY analyzes these models in order to automatically generate two different outputs, successively used for model-checking purposes. Figure 2 graphically summarizes how the framework works:

- In Step 1, component state machines are automatically translated into a Promela formal prototype. The translation algorithm makes also use of extra information (embedded in the state machine specification) in order to identify which kind of communication is required. SPIN standard checks over Promela may be performed [16];
- In Step 2, scenario specifications (in the form of extended Sequence Diagrams) are automatically translated into Büchi Automata [4]. Such automata describe properties should/should not be verified;
- Finally, in Step 3 the model checker SPIN evaluates the properties validity with respect to the Promela code. If unwanted behaviors are identified, an error is reported.

CHARMY is tool supported and offers a graphical user interface to draw state diagrams and scenarios, a plugin which allows to input existing diagram in the XMI format, and a translation engine to automatically derive Promela code and Büchi Automaton. For more information on the CHARMY project, please refer to [6].

3.2   Software Architecture-Based Code Testing

Having a software architecture validated whit respect to functional requirements is not enough. In fact, when the architectural information is used to drive the

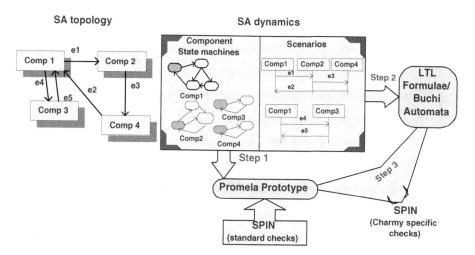

Fig. 2. The CHARMY Framework

source code realization, we need to validate the implementation conformance to the architecture.

SA-based testing is a particular instantiation of specification-based testing, devoted to check that the Implementation Under Test (IUT) fulfills the (architectural) specifications [23, 2]. The abstraction provided by a SA allows testing to take place early and at a higher-level. The SA-based testing activity allows the detection of structural and behavioral problems before they are coded into the implementation. Various approaches have been proposed on testing driven by the architectural specification, as analyzed in [20].

The approach we propose spans the whole spectrum from test derivation down to test execution. Our approach is based on the specification of SA dynamics, which is used to identify useful schemes of interactions between system components, and to select test classes corresponding to relevant architectural behaviors. The goal is to provide a test manager with a systematic method to extract suitable test classes for the higher levels of testing and to refine them into concrete tests at the code level.

In this paper we instantiate/adapt the general SA-based testing framework proposed in [20] (graphically sketched in Figure 3, steps 0-4) to be integrated with model checking techniques. In particular, we here provide guidelines on how the integration happens. Both Figures 1 and 3 will help understanding the idea:

- Step A: the SA is specified through the topology and state diagrams produced in Section 3.1 following the CHARMY approach;
- Step B: when in CHARMY subsystems, considered critical, are identified for further analysis, we intentionally restrict our visibility of the system behaviors by removing "not interesting" behaviors from the original system. To some extent, this approach is similar to extracting test cases. In eliciting test cases a tester focusses on the critical parts of the system in order to verify

his intuitions. In the same way, we elicit the properties that represent potential flows and check them on the system model by using model checking techniques.

- Step C: when model-checking is run, we may have two different results: the system property of interest is not verified (NOK label in Figure 1), thus counter-examples are found, or it is verified (OK label in Figure 1). In traditional approaches where model-checking is used to identify test cases, counter-examples are generated (by producing properties negation) and automatically turned into tests. In our context, even when a property (i.e., a scenario) is verified on the architectural model (i.e., the Promela model), it may be still of interest as a test case. In fact, since we span from SA checking to code testing, both OK and NOK results are of interest. When a NOK happens, it may depend on two different reasons: the architectural model does not conform to the property (thus we refine the architectural model in order to make it compliant to the functional property (Figure 1)) or we checked the negation of a formula (i.e., NOK means that the property is verified, similarly to what happens in the mutation technique). In some cases, we may still use the counter-example to test if the code conforms to the SA. When an OK result is found, we may simulate the system in order to produce more detailed scenarios which satisfy the property. In fact, we need to remember that the property we wish to verify may be very high-level, by missing many details. Through the simulation process, we may identify more detailed scenarios which very the high-level property on the architectural (Promela) model. A Test Generator Engine (TGE)(Figure 1) may be used to select only a (relevant) portion of the generated scenarios. The most simple algorithm for a TGE may select just a scenario for each OK property and the NOK scenarios. More precise algorithms may be identified;
- Step D: following the current Siemens CNX practices, such detailed scenarios (called test specifications) may be used to manually or automatically derive executable tests.

4   Proposal Application to a Siemens Telecommunication System

In this section we apply the approach just described to a real system developed in Siemens CNX. We initially outline the *Siemens' design process*, thus we describe the *standard telecommunication functional model* in Siemens, as a way to formally describe the SA of telecommunication systems. We thus select, among the set of relevant architecture components we apply the proposed approach, the *Engineering Order Wire (EOW) application*, as an example to show some initial results (in Section 4.1).

In currently applied practices in Siemens CNX, SA and tests design are two parallel activities starting from the system requirements specification. Then two different teams analyse system requirements and divergencies are possible causing errors caught late during the test execution phase. A strong review process

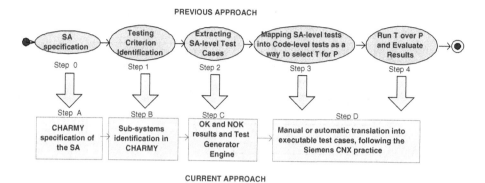

Fig. 3. Steps 0-4: General Testing Framework. Steps A-D: Model-Checking plus Testing

(time consuming) is adopted to align all the design phases, eliminating the most part of such type of errors. The application of the MC techniques to validate SA provides a set of simulation results that can be used as a base to define tests. Defining tests in this way unify some design steps. In particular, deriving test traces from MC formal verification of system architecture compliance to the requirements, guarantees consistency of the whole project and, virtually, eliminates the need of the review process.

The standard telecommunication functional model in Siemens is the Synchronous Digital Hierarchy (SDH), a well defined standard by ETSI and ITU-T. Following the standards, a "Functional Model" (for an SDH system) describes the way an equipment accepts, processes and forwards information contained in the transmission signal, defining the internal processes, the internal and external interfaces, the supervision and the performance criteria and relevant recovery actions

The functional model is built around two specific concepts: "network layering", with a client/server relationship between adjacent layers, and the "atomic functions", to specify the behaviour of each layer.

A *network layer* is a set of processing and supervision functions described by atomic functions, related to a specific set of transmitted information. Each layer faces to a couple of adjacent layers: a server layer, which provides transport services to the current layer, and a client layer which uses the transport services the current layer provides. Figure 4.a shows some different layers.

Each layer is a group of *atomic functions* (as shown in Figure 4.b). Three basic atomic functions are defined: connection, termination and adaptation functions. They are combined on the basis of combination rules. In addition, application functions (performing specific tasks) should reside at the top of a specific layer as shown for the EOW function in Figure 4.

A *network element* (NE), i.e. a node in the SDH network, is a combination of network layers, thus composed by many atomic functions distributed in different

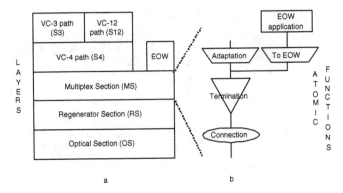

Fig. 4. SDH Layers and Atomic Functions

layers and relevant application functions. Many NE may be interconnected and each atomic function (in a specific layer in a NE) is directly related in a peer-to-peer connection to an identical function, in the same layer but in a different NE. In other words, a direct "virtual network connection" between the two relevant mate functions is created by the transport services.

EOW is an application on top of a specific SDH layer. The EOW application supports a telephone link between multiple NEs by using dedicated voice link channels defined on the SDH frame. An *EOW node* is represented by the EOW application implemented by a SDH NE. An *EOW network* is an overlay network over the SDH network (using the previously mentioned voice link channel). The EOW network is a switch circuit interconnecting several EOW nodes.

An EOW network defines a *Conference*. An EOW node may participate on an EOW conference by being connected to an EOW network by means of EOW ports. An operator (sometime called subscriber) interfaces the EOW functionalities by means of a handset device. The EOW procedures allow an operator to: i) make a call dialling a selective number, ii) receive a call, iii) enter a conference (with the special number-sign key) when a call is already in progress, and iv) exit the conference (cleanly terminate a call).

4.1 Properties Verification with CHARMY and Test Specification Selection: Initial Results

Given the EOW application and the SDH telecommunication functional model, we initially identified some of the functional properties the EOW application should conform to, and in parallel, we defined an architectural model.

Based on the EOW specification, we identified four functional requirements the system has to satisfy:

– Requirement 1 and 2: when an operator *makes a call* dialling a selective number, the target operator must *receive the call*.

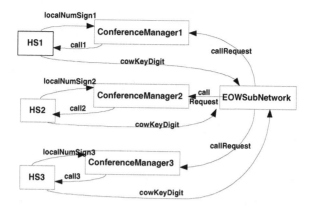

Fig. 5. EOW Software Architecture

- Requirement 3: it must be possible to *enter a busy conference* (with the special number-sign key) when a call is already in progress.
- Requirement 4: It must be always possible to *exit to the conference* (cleanly terminate a call).

We also abstracted away many details of an SDH network and EOW application, and produced an architectural model where each network element is abstracted into a couple of architectural components (the `ConferenceManager` (CM) and the `Handset` (HS) components) while a connector is used to simulate the network connections (the `EOWSubNetwork`). A network model, composed by several network elements, is then abstracted as a set of component instances which may communicate through a connector.

The CM interfaces the EOW network, through ports, by sensing embedded signalling to capture incoming calls and taking into account the conference status (free: when no subscribers are in conference; busy: when calls are in progress). The HS component interfaces and manages the external physical device used by the subscriber. It senses for hook status and key digit pressed and evolves through different internal states to cleanly manage the outgoing and incoming call sequences and signalling taking in care the speech channel connection to the conference. In the following, we take into consideration an EOW network, virtualized by means of a connector component (the `EOWSubNetwork`), with three node instances. Figure 5 shows the EOW architectural configuration of interest. We opted for a configuration with three node instances since this is the minimum configuration required to validate any of the system properties.

Given the architectural specification in Figure 5, the four requirements/ properties to be proven have been formalized in the form of CHARMY scenarios. The notation used in Figure 6 is the CHARMY notation for modeling scenarios where messages are typed with prefix *e:* or *r:*. Notation details may be found in [17].

- Requirement 1 and 2: if the HS1 component dials the number to call the HS2 component (*eowKeyDigit*), then component `EOWSubNetwork` must send a *callRequest* message to the `ConferenceManager2` component that must send *call2* to the HS2 component.

- Requirement 3: if the HS3 component makes an *offHook* then it must send the *localNumSign3* to the `ConferenceManager3` to enter the conference.
- Requirement 4: if HS1, HS2 and HS3 components terminate the call in progress, they must send the *localNumSign* and perform the internal operation *onHook*.

By using the CHARMY tool, the three scenarios have been automatically translated into Büchi Automata while the architectural state machine model has been translated into Promela code. SPIN has been run and no errors have been detected. This initial analysis (realizing the top part of Figure 1) gives us the assurance that the identified architectural model correctly reflects the three expected behaviors.

In the following of this section, we describe how test specifications may be extracted (thus implementing the mid portion of Figure 1) through simulation.

We thus simulate the Promela prototype obtained from the CHARMY tool, through the use of the SPIN interactive simulation feature. This feature allows to simulate the Promela model, starting from the model initial state, and selecting a branch at each nondeterministic step. We thus started simulating the Promela prototype by reproducing the properties scenarios previously presented. Through interactive simulation, we are able to get a more detailed description of each scenario, with possible sub-scenarios.

Applying the interactive simulation on the EOW model, driven by the first property (Requirements 1 and 2 in Figure 6), we obtained the following test specifications:

```
Config1 ->

[onHook1,
offHook1 -> onHook1] ->

offHook1 ->

[ _ ,
(cbusy==true) -> onHook1 -> offHook1,
(cbusy==false) -> timeout1 -> onHook1 -> offHook1] ->

(cbusy==false) -> eowKeyDigit(..,..) -> callRequest2 ->

*[Config2 -> offHook2 -> onHook2 -> offHook2 -> (cbusy==false),
Config2 -> offHook2 -> onHook2 -> offHook2 -> (cbusy==true),
Config2 -> offHook2 -> onHook2, Config2 -> onHook2 -> offHook2 ->
(cbusy==false), Config2 -> onHook2 -> offHook2 -> (cbusy==true),
Config2 -> offHook2]  ->

call2.
```

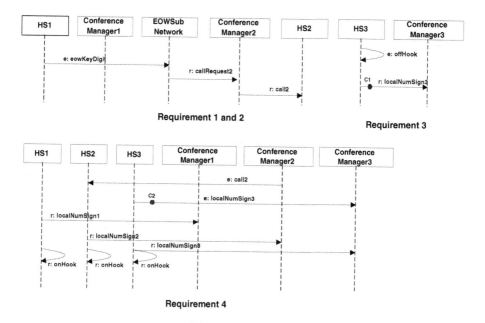

Fig. 6. Properties

This textual description specifies many detailed scenarios (i.e., test specifications) where "a -> b" means a followed by b, "[a,b]" means a XOR b, "[_,b]" means *null* xor b, and "*a" means that a may happen everytime between the first and the last operation. Naturally, such test specifications are oriented to test no more than the property of interest, hiding any other (irrelevant) interleaving, and making the test specification more precise and concise.

Following Figure 1, a Test Generation engine (to be implemented) will identify a relevant subset of those test specs which will be converted in test cases by the Test Identification and Execution group in Siemens CNX and run on the EOW application. This activity will be analyzed in future work.

In order to produce other relevant test cases, some refinements have been developed to improve the model, taking into account additional functional and non functional requirements like, DTMF embedded signalling, different calling type, EOW port configurations and so on. Such refinements are currently used to analyze the quality and advantages of the CHARMY iterative specification and analysis process, and more mature results will be reported in future work.

5   Some Considerations

Differently from other approaches, we shown how model-checking and testing may be combined to span from requirements to SAs and finally to code. In our approach, since model-checking is used only to validate the architectural specification while test cases are executed over the final implementation, the idea on how to identify test cases is different. While previous approach use model-checking counter-examples to derive test cases, we may use both verified and not verified scenarios.

The *main advantages* our approach exhibits are listed in the following:

- by applying model-checking at the architectural level, we reduce the modeling complexity and the state explosion problem;
- by using CHARMY we may provide an easy to use, practical, approach to model-checking, hiding the modeling complexity;
- the iterative model-checking approach proposed in Section 3.1 allows to identify the most important properties to be validated, to refine the architectural model and finally to identify critical sub-systems and focus on them;
- through interactive simulation we may identify traces of interest for testing the whole system or just a relevant subsystem. This guarantees a bigger synergy among model-checking and testing application. Since models are small enough, interactive simulation is possible;
- the most important advantage, with respect to how testing has been previously done in Siemens CNX, is that test specifications are identified from the architectural model (instead of directly from requirements) thus creating a bigger synergy between software architects and testers, and eliminating the problem of keeping SA specification and Test specification aligned when requirements change.

The proposed approach also suffers *some limitations*: currently, the Test Generator engine shown in Figure 1 is not yet implemented. This means that the simulated traces need to be manually selected, while it could be automated. The generation of executable tests starting from the test specifications in Siemens CNX is a non automated activity. We started cooperating with the Test Identification group in Siemens CNX in order to make rigorous the translation among test specifications and executable tests. Naturally, even if the iterative model-checking approach at the architectural level reduces the state explosion problem, we still need to carefully handle models dimension and complexity.

Some techniques have been proposed in order to create a model of the implemented system (e.g., [9]) and apply model-checking on it. Our perspective is different from those work. We use model-checking to analyze functional properties at an high-level of abstraction, thus reducing the model complexity.

6   Conclusions and Future Work

An architectural specification represents the first, high-level, step in the design of a software system. In this paper we have shown how such specification may be incrementally built, how it may be checked for consistency with respect to some selected functional requirements and how it may be used to select some high-level functional tests which may be successively refined in order to produce test cases.

The approach here presented is partially tool supported even if the generation of test cases from test specifications needs to be better investigated and supported in future work.

In future work we will improve the test specification identification, by improving and automating as much as possible the Test Generator Engines as well as the simulation process. We will also investigate an automated way to produce test cases from test specifications. We are also interested in investigating the use of Rational Quality Architect - Real Time (RQA-RT) to validate an architectural specification and to generate test specifications.

List of Abbreviations

SA [Software Architecture], MC [Model-Checking], IUT [Implementation Under Test], TGE [Test Generator Engine], EOW [Engineering Order Wire], SDH [Synchronous Digital Hierarchy], NE [Network Element], RQA-RT [Rational Quality Architect-Real Time], HS [Handset], CM [Conference Manager]

References

[1] Ammann, P., Black, P.: Abstracting formal specifications to generate software tests via model checking. In *Proceedings of the 18th Digital Avionics Systems Conference (DASC99)*, volume 2, page 10.A.6. IEEE, October 1999. 353

[2] Bertolino, A., Inverardi, P.: Architecture-based software testing. In *Proc. ISAW96*, October 1996. 356

[3] Bertolino, A.: Software Testing, In SWEBOK: Guide to the Software Engineering Body of Knowledge,IEEE. 352

[4] Buchi, R.: On a decision method in restricted second order arithmetic. In *Proc. of the International Congress of Logic, Methodology and Philosophy of Science*, pages pp 1–11. Standford University Press, 1960. 355

[5] Callahan, J., Schneider, F., Easterbrook, S.: Automated software testing using modelchecking. In *Proceedings 1996 SPIN Workshop*, Aug. 1996. 353

[6] Charmy Project. Charmy web site. http://www.di.univaq.it/charmy, March 2004. 352, 355

[7] Clarke, E. M., Grumberg, O., Peled, D. A.: Model Checking. The *MIT Press*, Cambridge, second edition, year 2000. 351

[8] Compare, D., Inverardi, P., Pelliccione, P., Sebastiani, A.: Integrating model-checking architectural analysis and validation in a real software life-cycle. In *the 12th International Formal Methods Europe Symposium (FME 2003)*, number 2805 in LNCS, pages 114–132, Pisa, 2003.

[9] Corbett, J. C., Dwyer, M. B., Hatcliff, J., Laubach, S., Păsăreanu, C. S., Robby, Zheng, H.: Bandera: extracting finite-state models from java source code. In *International Conference on Software Engineering*, pages 439–448, 2000. 363

[10] DeMillo, R. A., Lipton, R. J., Sayward, F. G.: Hints on test data selection: Help for the practicing programmer. In *IEEE Comp, 11(4):34-41*, 1978. 353

[11] *Formal Methods for Software Architectures*. Tutorial book on Software Architectures and formal methods. In SFM-03:SA Lectures, Eds. M. Bernardo and P. Inverardi, LNCS 2804., 2003. 352, 354

[12] Gargantini, A., Heitmeyer, C. L.: Using model checking to generate tests from requirements specifications. In *ESEC / SIGSOFT FSE*, pages 146–162, 1999. 353

[13] Garlan., D.: Software Architecture. *Encyclopedia of Software Engineering*, John Wiley & Sons, Inc. 2001. 354, 355

[14] Heimdahl, M. P., Rayadurgam, S., Visser, W., Devaraj, G., Gao, J.: Auto-generating test sequences using model checkers: A case study. In *FATES 2003*. 353

[15] Holzmann, J. G.: The logic of bugs. *In Proc. Foundations of Software Engineering (SIGSOFT 2002/FSE-10)*, 2002.

[16] Holzmann, G. J.: *The SPIN Model Checker: Primer and Reference Manual*. Addison-Wesley, September 2003. 355

[17] Inverardi, P., Muccini, H., Pelliccione, P.: Charmy: A framework for model based consistency checking. TR., Dept. of Comp. Science, Univ. of L'Aquila, May 2004. 360

[18] Peterson, I.: Fatal Defect: Chasing Killer Computer Bugs. Random House Publisher, 1995.

[19] Muccini, H.: Software Architecture for Testing, Coordination Models and Views Model Checking. PhD thesis, University of L'Aquila, year 2002. On-line at: <http://www.HenryMuccini.com/publications.htm>. 354

[20] Muccini, H., Bertolino, A., Inverardi, P.: Using Software Architecture for Code Testing. In IEEE Transactions on Software Engineering. Vol. 30, Issue N. 3, March 2004, pp. 160-171. 356

[21] Pnueli, A.: The temporal logic of programs. In *In Proc. 18th IEEE Symposium on Foundation of Computer Science*, pages pp. 46–57, 1977.

[22] Rayadurgam, S., Heimdahl, M. P. E.: Coverage based test-case generation using model checkers. In *In 8th Annual IEEE International Conference and Workshop on the Engineering of Computer Based Systems (ECBS)*, Apr. 2001. 353

[23] Richardson, D. J., Wolf, A. L.: Software testing at the architectural level. *ISAW-2* in Joint Proc. of the *ACM SIGSOFT '96* Workshops, pp. 68-71, 1996. 356

[24] Shaw, M., Garlan, D.: Software Architecture: Perspectives on an Emerging Discipline. Prentice-Hall, 1996. 352

A Meta-model for TTCN-3

Ina Schieferdecker[1,2] and George Din[1]

[1] Fraunhofer FOKUS
{schieferdecker,din}@fokus.fraunhofer.de
http://www.fokus.fraunhofer.de/tip
[2] Technical University Berlin, Faculty IV
Chair on Design and Testing of Telecommunication Systems

Abstract. The Testing and Test Control Notation TTCN-3 is a test specification and implementation language that has been defined classically in form of a formal syntax and a semiformal semantics. UML, MOF and MDA has shown that on contrary meta-model based language definitions impose new ways of defining language semantics as a separation of syntax and semantic concept space, of integrating languages via a common meta-model base and of generating and deriving models from other models via model transformers. This paper defines a meta-model for TTCN-3, such that TTCN-3 can take advantage of meta-model based approaches - in particular for integrating test but also system development techniques. It also discusses the realization of the TTCN-3 meta-model and its use for meta-model based tools.

1 Introduction

Model-based development is known in testing since years and used for test generation from models, test validation against models and test coverage analysis. Recently, it has gained a lot in the context of UML. However, with the ability to define tests graphically via the graphical format of TTCN-3 [9] or the UML 2.0 testing profile [4], the need for further integration of test techniques and tools with system development techniques and tools as well as the need for (graphical) model exchange become apparent. Even more gains from other advances in model-based development can be expected. Along the Model Driven Architecture initiative of OMG [15], where system artefacts are developed on different levels of abstraction such as platform independent models (PIM) and platform specific models (PSM), the same concepts and ideas apply to test artefacts. There are platform independent tests (PIT) taking into account test aspects for the general business logic and platform specific tests (PST) taking into account test aspects for platform and technology dependent characteristics of the system under test. Furthermore, PIT and PST (skeletons) can be developed with the help of model transformers from PIMs and PSMs, such that they can reuse information provided in the system models.

This paper considers the first steps towards such an MDA-based test approach: the development of a meta-model for the Testing and Test Control Notation TTCN-3. The main language architecture of TTCN-3 is based on a common

M. Núñez et al. (Eds.): FORTE 2004 Workshops, LNCS 3236, pp. 366–379, 2004.

concept space being specific for the testing domain (in particular for black-and grey-box testing of reactive systems), on the basis of which test specifications can be denoted, developed, visualized and documented by different presentation formats. TTCN-3 supports three different presentation formats: the textual core language [7], the tabular presentation format [8] and the graphical one [9]. Further presentation formats can be defined.

However, TTCN-3 did not take the approach of separating the testing concept space from the presentation formats: it combined the definition of the concept space with the definition of the textual core language. This complicates not only the maintenance of TTCN-3 but also the construction of tools and the exchange of models. For example, the exchange of graphical and tabular TTCN-3 specifications is left open, or, the TTCN-3 semantics definition is mixed with the syntactic definition of the core language.

A solution to these problems is provided by OMG's Meta-Object Facility (MOF): a MOF model can be used as a (structural) definition of a modelling language. It supports mechanisms that determine how a model defined in that modelling language can be serialized into an XML document and represented, inspected, and managed via a CORBA, a Java API, or alike APIs. For a complete language definition, a MOF model has to be enhanced with language syntax (i.e. the presentation formats of TTCN-3 [7, 8, 9]) and a semantics definition (e.g. the operational semantics of TTCN-3 [10]).

Related work to this paper is rather limited as it is the first time that a meta-model is proposed for a test specification language. The work has been inspired by the work on the UML 2.0 Testing Profile [4], which is based on the UML meta-model. A proposal on defining meta-models for ITU languages (and hence including also TTCN) has been presented at SAM 2004 [3], where the emphasis is on deriving meta-models for specification languages from their BNF grammar definitions. In this paper, the meta-model has been developed differently: by considering the semantic concepts of TTCN-3 and identifying the relations between them, the constituting meta-classes and their associations have been identified.

This paper will present a MOF-based TTCN-3 meta-model in Section 2 and discuss its role in the TTCN-3 language architecture for the exchange of models and the construction of tools. A realization and usage of this meta-model in Eclipse will be discussed in Section 3. Section 4 will provide an outlook how to integrate test development with system development.

2   The Development of the TTCN-3 Meta-model

The test meta-model represents the concept space of the Testing and Test Control Notation TTCN-3, which has been developed at ETSI [7, 9] and which has also been standardized at ITU-T. In addition, TTCN-3 served as a basis for the development of the UML 2.0 Testing Profile [4], which has been finalized recently.

The main objectives for the development of a TTCN-3 meta-model were

- The separation of concerns by separating the TTCN-3 concept space and semantics (represented in the TTCN-3 meta-model) from TTCN-3 syntactic aspects (defined in the core language and the presentation formats).
- The ability to define the semantics on concept space level without being affected by syntactic considerations e.g. in the case of syntax changes.
- To ease the exchange of TTCN-3 specifications of any presentation format and not of textual TTCN-3 specifications only.
- To ease the definition of external language mappings to TTCN-3 as such definitions can reuse parts of the conceptual mapping from other languages.
- To integrate TTCN-3 tools into MDA based processes and infrastructures.

2.1   Overview on TTCN-3

Before looking into the details of the TTCN-3 meta-model let us recall some aspects of TTCN-3. TTCN-3 is a language to define test procedures to be used for black-box testing of distributed systems. Stimuli are given to the system under test (SUT); its reactions are observed and compared with the expected ones. On the basis of this comparison, the subsequent test behaviour is determined or the test verdict is assigned. If expected and observed responses differ, then a fault has been discovered which is indicated by a test verdict fail. A successful test is indicated by a test verdict pass.

The core language of TTCN-3 is a textual test specification and implementation language and has been developed to address the needs of testing modern technologies in the telecom and datacom domain. It looks similar to a traditional programming language, but provides test specific concepts. These test specific concepts include e.g. test verdicts, matching mechanisms to compare the reactions of the SUT with an expected range of values, timer handling, distributed test components, ability to specify encoding information, synchronous and asynchronous communication, and monitoring. It has been shown already that test specifiers and engineers find this general-purpose test language, more flexible, user-friendly and easier to use than its predecessors and adopt it as a testing basis for different testing contexts.

TTCN-3 is applicable to various application areas in telecommunication and IT such protocol and service testing (e.g. in fixed and mobile networks and the Internet), system-level testing (e.g. for end-to-end and integration testing), component-level testing (e.g. for Java and C++ objects), platform testing (for CORBA, CORBA components and Web services platforms). It supports different kinds of tests such as functional, interoperability, interworking, robustness, performance, load, scalability, etc. tests.

With TTCN-3 the existing concepts for test specifications have been consolidated. Retaining and improving basic concepts of predecessors of TTCN-and adding new concepts increase the expressive power and applicability of TTCN-3. New concepts are, e.g., a test execution control to describe relations between test cases such as sequences, repetitions and dependencies on test outcomes, dynamic concurrent test configurations and test behaviour in asynchronous and synchronous communication environments. Improved concepts are, e.g., the integration of ASN.1, the module and grouping concepts to improve the test suite structure, and the test component concepts to describe concurrent and dynamic test setups.

A TTCN-3 test specification (also referred to as test suite) is represent by a TTCN-3 module (or a set of TTCN-3 modules). A TTCN-3 module consists of four main parts:

- Type definitions for test data structures,
- Templates definitions for concrete test data,
- Function and test case definitions for test behaviours, and
- Control definitions for the execution of test cases.

2.2   The Meta Object Facility

The meta-model for TTCN-3 has been defined using MOF - the Meta Object Facility by OMG. MOF resulted from requirements along the extensive application of models and modelling techniques within the scope of the development and use of CORBA-based systems. This lead to the definition of a unique and standardized framework for the management, manipulation and exchange of models and their meta-models. The architecture of MOF is based on the traditional four-layer approach to meta-modelling (see Fig. 1):

- Layer L0 - the instances: information (data) that describes a concrete system at a fixed point in time. This layer consists of instances of elements of the L1-layer.
- Layer L1- the model: definition of the structure and behaviour of a system using a well defined set of general concepts. An L1-model consists of L2-layer instances.
- Layer L2 - the meta-model: The definition of the elements and the structure of a concept space (i.e. the modelling language). An L2-layer model consists of instances of the L3-layer.
- Layer L3 - the meta-meta-model: The definition of the elements and the structure for the description of a meta-model.

MOF supports the following concepts for the definition of meta-models:

- Classes: Classes are first-class modelling constructs. Instances of classes (at M1-layer) have identity, state and behaviour. The structural features of classes are attributes, operations and references. Classes can be organized in a specialization/generalization hierarchy.
- Associations: Associations reflect binary relationships between classes. Instances of associations at the M1-layer are links between class instances and do neither have state nor identity. Properties of association ends may be used to specify the name, the multiplicity or the type of the association end. MOF distinguishes between aggregate (composite) and non-aggregate associations.

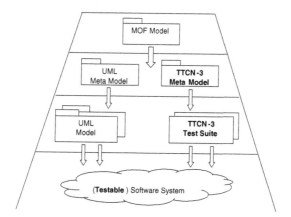

Fig. 1. Model levels of MOF

- Data types: Data types are used to specify types whose values have no identity. Currently MOF comprises of data comparable to CORBA data types
  and IDL interface types.
- Packages: The purpose of packages is to organize (modularize, partition and
  package) meta-models. Packages can be organized by use of generalization,
  nesting, import and clustering.

The MOF specification defines these concepts as well as supporting concepts
in detail. Because there is no explicit notation for MOF, the UML notation has
been deliberately used to visualize selected concepts.

2.3   Details of the TTCN-3 Meta-model

The TTCN-3 test meta-model defines the TTCN-3 concept space with additional support for the different presentation formats. It does not directly reflect
the structure of a TTCN-3 modules but rather the semantical structure of the
TTCN-3 language definition. It is defined as a single package with concept structures for

- Types and expressions,
- Modules and scopes,
- Declarations, and
- Statements and operations.

Because of lack of space only excerpts from the meta-model can be presented.
Please refer to [2] for further reading. The principal building blocks of test specifications in TTCN-3 are modules (see Fig. 2). A module defines a scope and
contains a number of declarations, which can be imports, types, global data
covering module parameters, constants, external constants and templates, and
functions covering external functions, data functions, behavioural functions, altsteps, test cases and control.

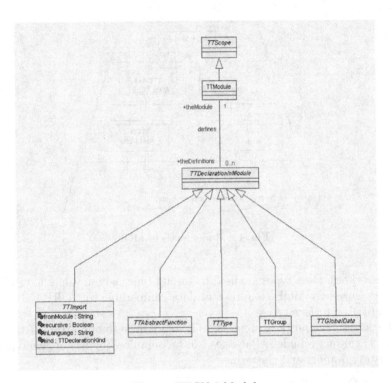

Fig. 2. TTCN-3 Modules

All declarations in TTCN-3 assign an identifier to the declared object and may have a number of with attributes for further characterization of that object (see Fig. 3). As such an object may contain itself a number of other objects, the with attributes may optionally not be applied to some of those.

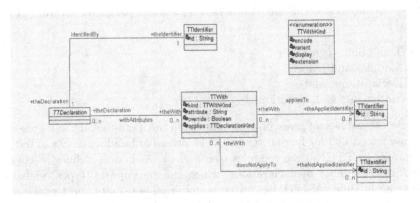

Fig. 3. TTCN-3 Declarations 1

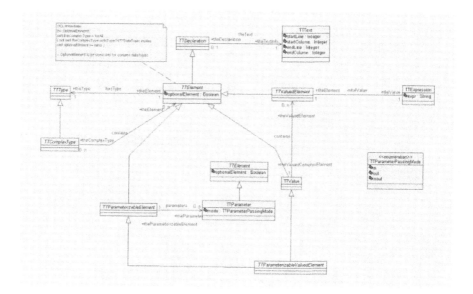

Fig. 4. TTCN-3 Declarations 2

Many declarations in TTCN-3 are typed - we call those declarations ele-ments. Elements can themselves contain elements - in that case the element has a complex type, for example is of a structured type or of a component type. In addition, an element can have an assigned value - such elements are called valued element. Or, an element can be parameterized - then it is called parameterizable element. An element which is both parameterizable and has an assigned value is called parameterizable valued element.

TTCN-3 functions are parameterizable elements with an own scope (Fig. 5). They can be external functions, pure functions, behavioural functions, controls, altsteps, and test cases.

An example for statements is given in the following. Input statements in TTCN-3 cover statements to receive a message, receive a timeout, get a call, get a reply, catch an exception, trigger for a message, check for the top element in the queue, and check for the status of a test component (see Fig. 6). An input statement is always related to a port. The received input as well as the parameters of e.g. an incoming call can be bound to variables. The sender address can be stored as well.

The use of the TTCN-3 meta-model changes the general language architec-ture of TTCN-3 from a core language centred view to a meta-model centred view while keeping the general front-end to the user but adding new support and tool capabilities to TTCN-3 (see Fig. 7).

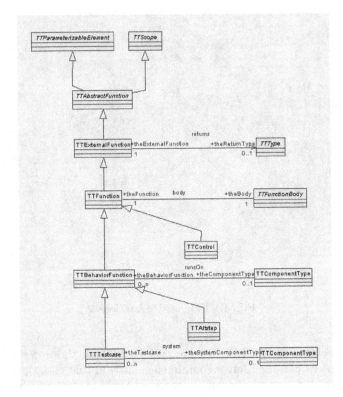

Fig. 5. TTCN-3 Functions

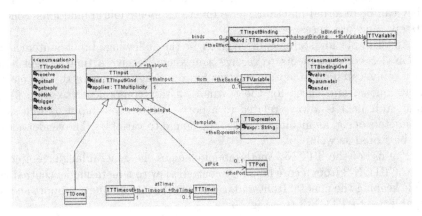

Fig. 6. TTCN-3 Inputs

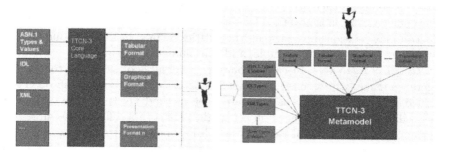

Fig. 7. The change to a meta-model centric TTCN-3 language architecture

3   The Integration of TTCN-3 Tools via the Meta-model

The meta-model for TTCN-3 language was technically realized by using the
Eclipse Modelling Framework provided by Eclipse [14]. This allowed us to integrate not only test development and execution tools but also to integrate the
development of system artefacts with the development of test artefacts (see Section 4).

3.1   The Realization in Eclipse

This subsection addresses the main capabilities of EMF framework (being part
of Eclipe [14]) and discusses the way we used it to implement the TTCN-3 meta-
model. EMF is a Java framework and code generation facility for building tools
and other applications based on meta-models defined in EMF; it helps turning
models rapidly into efficient, correct, and easily customizable Java code. EMF
is itself based on a model called Ecore. At the beginning this was intended to
be an implementation of the MOF [11], but it evolved from there, now being
considered as an efficient Java implementation of a core subset of the MOF API.
The EMF Ecore is the meta-model for all the models handled by the EMF.

We used the Rational Rose tool to define the TTCN-3 meta-model in UML.
The EMF generator can create a corresponding set of Java implementation
classes from such a Rose model. Additional methods and instance variables can
be manually added and still regenerated from the model as needed: they will be
preserved during the regeneration.

EMF consists of two fundamental frameworks: the *core framework* and
EMF.Edit. The core framework provides basic code generation through Java
EmitterTemplates and Java Merge tools and runtime support to create Java
implementation classes for a model. EMF.Edit extends and builds on the core
framework, adding support for the generation of adapter classes that enable
viewing and command-based editing of a model and even a basic working model
editor.

For every class in the meta-model, a Java interface and corresponding implementation class will be generated. Each generated interface contains getter and

setter methods for each attribute and reference of the corresponding model class. The code generation is governed by a couple of mapping rules which coordinates the complex relationships between the entities defined in the meta-model being either one-way, two-way, multiple, and containment references.

One-way references. In case of one-way references objects, the role, i.e. the reference name, will be used to access the target object. Because an object reference is to be handled, the generated get method needs to take care of the possibility that the referenced object might persist in a different resource (document) from the source object. As the EMF persistence framework uses a lazy loading scheme, an object pointer may at some point in time be a proxy for the object instead of the actual referenced object.

Instead of simply returning the object instance variable, the framework method eIsProxy() must be called first, to check if the reference is a proxy, and if it is, then EcoreUtil.resolve() should be called. The resolve() method will attempt to load the target object's document, and consequently the object, using the proxy's URI. If successful, it will return the resolved object. If, however, the document fails to load, it will just return the proxy again.

Two-way references. The two roles of the reference should be used to target two linked objects. The proxy pattern applies also as in the one-way reference case. When setting a two-way reference, one must be aware that the other end of the reference needs to be set as well. This should be done by calling the framework method eInverseAdd().

Multiple references. Multiple references - i.e. any reference where the upper bound is greater than 1 - are manipulated by EMF framework using a collection API, therefore only a get method is generated in the interface.

Containment references. A containment reference indicates that a container-object aggregates, by value, none or more contained-objects. By-value aggregation (containment) associations are particularly important because they identify the parent or owner of a target instance, which implies the physical location of the object. Two very important remarks must be made regarding the way the containment reference affects the generated code. First of all, because a contained object is guaranteed to be in the same resource as its container, proxy resolution will not be needed. Secondly, as an object can only have one container, adding an object to a containment association also means removing the object from any container it's currently in, regardless of the actual association.

Inheritance. Single-inheritance is handled by the EMF generator through the extension of the super interface by the generated interface. Similarly to Java, EMF supports multiple interface inheritance, but each class can only extend one implementation base class. Therefore, in case of a model with multiple inheritance, one needs to identify which of the multiple bases should be used as the implementation base class. The others will then be simply treated as mix-in interfaces, with their implementations generated into the derived implementation class.

Operations. In addition to attributes and references, operations can be added to the model classes. The EMF generator will generate their signature into the interface and an empty method skeleton into the implementation class. EMF does not support any method of specifying the operation behaviours in the model and therefore the methods must be implemented by hand in the generated Java class.

Factories and Packages. In addition to the model interfaces and implementation classes, EMF generates two more interfaces (and implementation classes): a Factory and a Package. The Factory, as its name implies, is used for creating instances of the model classes, while the Package provides some static constants (e.g. the feature constants used by the generated methods) and convenience methods for accessing the meta-data of the model.

3.2   Use of Generated Java Classes

The generated Java classes can be used to instantiate models and model elements, to manipulate them and to store and load models.

Instantiation. Using the generated classes, a client program can create and access instances with simple Java statements.

Reflective API. Every generated model class can also be manipulated using the reflective API defined in interface EObject. The reflective API is slightly less efficient than calling the generated get and set methods, but opens the model for completely generic access. For example, the reflective methods are used by the EMF.Edit framework to implement a full set of generic commands (AddCommand, RemoveCommand, SetCommand) that can be used with any model.

Serialization and deserialization. Serialization is the process of writing the instance data into a standardized, persistent form, a file on the file system. Loading (sometimes referred to as "deserialization") is the process of reading the persistent form of the data to recreate instances of EObject in memory. In EMF, loading can be accomplished either through an explicit call to a load API or it can happen automatically whenever a reference to an EObject that has not yet been loaded is encountered.

The Eclipse based realization of the TTCN-3 meta-model enabled the integration of the TTCN-3 tools into Eclipse. For the user, the TTCN-3 language support is given via Eclipse plugins, which offer editing, compiling and execution functionality from the Eclipse IDE.

4   Outlook: Integration of System and Test Development

An integrated meta-model based system and test development environment can provide information about system and test artefacts on different levels:

These artefacts are all developed by use of modelling tools and are all stored by use of model repositories (see Fig. 8). A MOF based model bus is used to get access to these models and to transport information between models. Model transformers [1, 2, 13] are used to transform models into models, for example PSM models to code models.

	Platform independent	Platform specific
System artefacts System artefacts	PSM: Platform independent system model	PSM: Platform specific system model
Test artefacts Test artefacts	PIT: Platform independent test model	PST: Platform specific test model

Test generation methods can then be realized in form of model transformers. Having multiple separate models for an entire (test) system, the transformation of these models takes place by the definition of how elements of a source model are transformed into elements of a target model. Using MOF as semantic domain, where the model semantics is defined by MOF meta-models, the transformation definition is also specified at the meta-layer. The specific details of the transformation are given in form of Object Constraint Language (OCL [12]) constraints. One example for such a transformation is the transformation of a CORBA based PSM to a PST. For further details please refer to [2]. An IDL module is transformed to a TTCN-3 module (see Fig. 9). Special control structures within an IDL module (such as include and define) are handled beforehand by a pre-processor. The name of the TTCN-3 module is the same as the name of the IDL module. It contains an import statement that imports the original IDL specification. The TTCN-3 module covers all the TTCN-3 declarations that belong to the transformation for that IDL module.

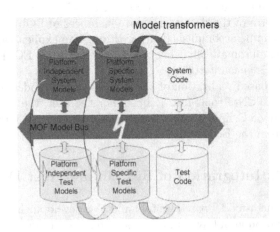

Fig. 8. An integrated system and test development environment

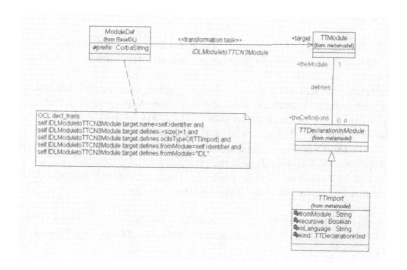

Fig. 9. IDL Modules to TTCN-3 Modules Transformation

5   Summary and Future Work

This paper has discussed the need and aims for a meta-model for TTCN-3. It has described the structure of the meta-model and has shown selected examples of the meta-model definition. Subsequently, the realization of a repository and tool environment based on this TTCN-3 meta-model in Eclipse has been described. Finally, the integration of system development and test development has been discussed in the context of MDA. On the basis of the meta-model, model transformers can be used to derive, generate and transform between PIM, PSM, PIT and PST models.

Our future work will continue in investigating model transformers in particular for platform independent system models to platform independent tests (PIM to PIT) and platform specific system models to platform specific tests (PSM to PST). We do not see much advantage in platform independent tests to platform specific tests (PIT to PST) as the addition of platform specifics is already covered in the transition from PIM to PSM. For the PSM to PST transformer we will consider CORBA based system and base the development on the IDL to TTCN-3 mapping which will give use a TTCN-3 type system and some TTCN-3 structures. In addition, we will add test skeletons for IDL interfaces such as tests on whether the interface exists, whether it provides all defined operations and whether the operations accept correct parameters. Finally, we try to prepare a "ground" for a TTCN-3 meta-model at ETSI as we believe that a TTCN-3 meta-model can ease the language architecture and add to the integration capabilities both between testing methods and tools but also between system development and testing methods and tools.

References

[1] FOKUS, etc: RIVAL T Project: Rapid Engineering, Integration and Validation of Distributed Systems for Telecommunication Applications, Milestone 1: Meta-Models, Dec. 2003. 376

[2] FOKUS, etc: RIVAL T Project: Rapid Engineering, Integration and Validation of Distributed Systems for Telecommunication Applications, Milestone 2: Infrastructure, Transformations and Tools, Febr. 2004. 370, 376, 377

[3] Joachim Fischer, Michael Piefel, and Markus Scheidgen: A Meta-Model for SDL-2000 in the Context of Meta-Modelling ULF, SAM 2004, SDL and MSC Workshop, Ottawa, Canada, June 2004. 367

[4] Object Management Group: UML 2.0 Testing Profile, Final Specification, ptc-2004-04-02, April 2004. www.fokus.fraunhofer.de u2tp. 366, 367

[5] Marius Predescu: Meta-Model Based Test Development in Eclipse, MSc Thesis, Politehnica University of Bucharest, Department of Computer Science, September 2003.

[6] Alexandru Cristian Tudose: Meta-model based test suites development - Graphical test specifications under the Eclipse platform, MSc Thesis, Politehnica University of Bucharest, Department of Computer Science, September 2003.

[7] ETSI ES 201 873 - 1, v2.2.1: The TTCN-3 Core Language, Oct. 2003. 367

[8] ETSI ES 201 873 - 2, v2.2.1: The Tabular Presentation Format of TTCN-3 (TFT), Oct. 2003. 367

[9] ETSI ES 201 873 - 3, v2.2.1: The Graphical Presentation Format of TTCN-3 (GFT), Oct. 2003. 366, 367

[10] ETSI ES 201 873 - 4, v2.2.1: The Graphical Presentation Format of TTCN-3 (GFT), Oct. 2003. 367

[11] Object Management Group: Meta-Object Facility (MOF), version 1.4, http://www.omg.org/technology/documents/formal/mof.htm. 374

[12] Object Management Group: UML 2.0 OCL 2nd revised submission, http://www.omg.org/cgi-bin/doc?ad/2003-01-07. 377

[13] K.Czarnecki, S.Helsen: Classification of Model Transformation Approaches. University of Waterloo, Canada, Technical Report, 2003. 376

[14] Eclipse: Open Source Integrated Development Environment, www.eclipse.org. 374

[15] Grady Booch: MDA: A Motivated Manifesto? Software Development Magazine, August 2004 366

Author Index